THE FIRST

FEDERAL COURT

THE FEDERAL APPELLATE PRIZE COURT

OF THE AMERICAN REVOLUTION

1775–1787

HENRY J. BOURGUIGNON

THE FIRST FEDERAL COURT

Memoirs of the
AMERICAN PHILOSOPHICAL SOCIETY
Held at Philadelphia
For Promoting Useful Knowledge
Volume 122

THE FIRST
FEDERAL COURT

THE FEDERAL APPELLATE PRIZE COURT
OF THE AMERICAN REVOLUTION
1775–1787

HENRY J. BOURGUIGNON

Associate Professor, University of Toledo College of Law

THE AMERICAN PHILOSOPHICAL SOCIETY
Independence Square • Philadelphia
1977

Library of Congress Catalog Card Number 77-79209
International Standard Book Number 0-87169-122-1
US ISSN 0065-9738

TO

THE MEMBERS OF THE JESUIT ORDER

Preface

The first federal court, though little known and seldom discussed after it completed its work in 1787, remained fresh in the memories of some of the leaders who helped create and establish the new federal judiciary under the Constitution. Although its jurisdiction was narrowly restricted to appeals in prize cases from state admiralty courts, it conducted sufficient business and faced enough intractable predicaments, to help judges, lawyers, and merchants appreciate the necessity for a more effective judiciary. This court served as an attenuated link in continuity between the appellate judicial system of the Privy Council and the Lords Commissioners for Prize Appeals of the colonial period and that of the Supreme Court which helped strengthen the bond of the union of states under the Constitution.

During the years I have carried out research on the history of this court, I have become indebted to many persons without whose encouragement, guidance, and assistance this book could hardly have been completed.

I am grateful for the research grants from the Rackham School of Graduate Studies of the University of Michigan, the American Bar Foundation, and the American Philosophical Society.

Many librarians and archivists have eased the labor of research. It is impossible individually to thank these people in so many archives, historical societies, and libraries for making accessible the wealth of material they supervise. I want to thank especially the helpful staffs at the University of Michigan Law Library, the William L. Clements Library, Ann Arbor, the Public Record Office, London, the Jamaica Archives, Spanish Town, and the Law and Manuscript Divisions of the Library of Congress. I also appreciate the permission of the Public Record Office to quote from some of the material deposited there.

I also thank Mrs. Gay Escobar for typing the final manuscript with remarkable accuracy and great patience. I thank my wife, Cheryl, for encouraging and gently prodding me to complete this book and for being an ever appreciative audience for my work.

Though, of course, I assume full responsibility for the final product, this book would certainly not be what it is without the invaluable scholarly comment, criticism, and encouragement from several historians and law professors. I thank the late Professor Paul G. Kauper and Professor William W. Bishop of the University of Michigan Law School, Professor Gordon S. Wood of Brown University, and Professor L. Kinvin Wroth of the University of Maine Law School for their comments on this work when it was first written in dissertation form. They showed me that further research and revision would be worth the effort and they helped me focus on the proper questions for this research. I am grateful also for the constructive comments and encouragement of Mr. Herbert A. Johnson, Editor of the John Marshall papers. I likewise appreciate the helpful suggestions of Mr. D. E. C. Yale of Christ College, Cambridge, which facilitated and made more fruitful my research into the English sources. Finally, there is no way of adequately expressing my gratitude to and admiration of Professor William R. Leslie of the University of Michigan and Professor Joseph H. Smith of Columbia Law School. Their continuing personal interest in this work and exacting standards of scholarship have made me strive for the highest level of scholarly achievement.

I have dedicated this book to the members of the Jesuit Order of which I was for a good number of years a member. Many Jesuits have shown me examples of meticulous pursuit of intellectual goals and have made possible for me unique educational opportunities.

H.J.B.

FREQUENTLY USED ABBREVIATIONS

CHS — Connecticut Historical Society (Hartford).

Clark, *NDAR* — Clark, William B., *et al.* eds., 1964–. *Naval Documents of the American Revolution* (7 v., Washington).

CSL — Connecticut State Library (Hartford).

DAB — Johnson, Allen and Malone, Dumas, eds., 1928–1958. *Dictionary of American Biography* (22 v., New York).

Ford, *JCC* — Ford, Worthington C., ed., 1904–1937. *Journals of the Continental Congress* (34 v., Washington).

HCA — High Court of Admiralty Papers, Public Record Office (London).

HSP — Historical Society of Pennsylvania (Philadelphia).

JA — Jamaica Archives (Spanish Town, Jamaica).

Jenkins, *Microfilm* — Jenkins, William S., ed., 1949. *Records of the States of the United States—A Microfilm Compilation* (Washington).

LC Law — Law Division, Library of Congress (Washington).

LC Mss — Manuscript Division, Library of Congress (Washington).

MA — Massachusetts Archives, State House (Boston).

MHR — Maryland Hall of Records (Annapolis).

MHS — Massachusetts Historical Society (Boston).

MSJC — Massachusetts Supreme Judicial Court, Office of the Clerk (Boston).

NA — National Archives (Washington).

NYHS — New York Historical Society (New York).

NYPL, Mss — Manuscript Division, New York Public Library (New York).

CONTENTS

INTRODUCTION
Roots in the Past

An APPELLATE PRIZE COURT, the focal point of this book, today is an unfamiliar type of institution even for lawyers. The legally authorized capture of enemy ships and cargoes in time of war, the taking of prizes, has not been a practice of recent wars. Prior to the Declaration of Paris of 1856 which abolished privateering, certainly at the time of the American Revolution, when navies were small or non-existent, privateers in quest of prizes carried on much of the naval warfare of all European nations. A privateer is an armed vessel, owned, fitted out, and manned by private parties with a commission from a belligerent government authorizing it to capture the vessels and cargoes of the enemy. The commission, called a letter of marque, impressed upon the privateer's activities a legitimacy in international law without which privateers could be hung as pirates by any nation with ships fast enough to capture them. The letter of marque served as a legal basis for an admiralty court to condemn the captured property, the prize, to the privateers who took it.

These bare definitions of prize, privateer, and letter of marque, however, do not begin to describe the historical context into which was born the first federal court, the American appellate prize court of the Revolutionary War. A brief review of the origins, growth, and partial eclipse of the English admiralty court reveals the ancestors from which the American appellate prize court descended. The story of the development of vice-admiralty courts in America, often amidst controversy, discloses the more immediate parentage of the state prize courts established during the Revolution.

The title "admiral" was not used in England until the beginning of the fourteenth century. The admiral at first was a fleet commander with various administrative and disciplinary functions over seamen and others on board his fleet. For the first half of the fourteenth century he had no judicial authority to hear pleas or administer justice. At various times there were several admirals, of the North or West or South, or of the Cinque Ports, each in charge of a fleet.[1]

---

[1] Reginald G. Marsden, *Select Pleas in the Court of Admiralty* (2 v., London, 1894–

3

Before the birth of the admiralty court, port or marine courts sat in the various seaport towns administering maritime law for merchants and seamen.[2] These seaport courts, even after the admiralty court was established, struggled to retain their ancient rights to maritime jurisdiction especially over wreck and, until the latter half of the sixteenth century, asserted their privileges to be outside the admiralty court's jurisdiction. The franchises of the Cinque Ports, so important to the king because of their location, were especially extensive and were never subjected to the Lord Admiral's jurisdiction. Several statutes expressly provided that the liberties of the Cinque Ports not be interfered with. The king from early times maintained some supervision over these local maritime courts since they often touched sensitive questions that affected foreign affairs.[3]

For half a century English kings were troubled by claims of various nations of piracy and illegal captures perpetrated by English vessels. Edward III had settled some claims of Genoese and Venetian merchants out of his own pocket. Other attempts by common law courts or by arbitrators had failed to silence the complaints.[4]

The court of the admiral began between 1340 and 1357 because of these difficulties of the king in dealing with piracy and spoil claims made by or against foreign sovereigns. Common law courts had failed to redress the grievances expressed in the frequent complaints exchanged by the sovereigns. The chancellor at times had exercised jurisdiction over questions of piracy and the ownership of property captured at sea. Arbitrators had also been relied on to settle these disputes affecting other nations. The admiralty court was, therefore, established in the middle of the fourteenth century largely to demonstrate the existence of England's authority to deal justly and effectively with piracy and other offenses committed at sea.[5]

By the latter half of the fourteenth century cases of piracy,

---

1897) **1**: p. xi; Reginald G. Marsden, "The Vice-Admirals of the Coast," *English Hist. Rev.* **22** (1907): pp. 468–469.

[2] Marsden, *Select Pleas* **1**: pp. xii–xiii.

[3] William S. Holdsworth, *A History of English Law* (12 v., London, 1903–1938) **1**: pp. 531–533; Marsden, "Vice-Admirals," *English Hist. Rev.* **22**: pp. 472–473.

[4] Marsden, *Select Pleas* **1**: pp. xxxv–xxxvi.

[5] *Ibid.*, pp. xiv–xxiii.

royal fish, obstructions on shores or rivers, spoil of wreck, and restitution of captured goods, which previously had been heard by common law courts or by the king's council or by specially appointed arbitrators, were tried before the admiral.[6] In 1361 the patent issued to the admiral, besides the usual grant of disciplinary powers, bestowed maritime jurisdiction with power to appoint a deputy, probably to be judge of the newly erected court. This patent used broad strokes to outline the court's jurisdiction. It gave the admiral

> full power . . . of hearing plaints of all and singular the matters that touch the office of the admiral and of taking cognisance of maritime causes and of doing justice and of correcting and punishing offences and of imprisoning [offenders] and of setting at liberty prisoners who ought to be set at liberty and of doing all other things that appertain to the office of the admiral as they ought to be done of right and according to the maritime law.[7]

In 1357 a prize case was tried by the admiralty court. When the Portuguese owners of the captured property petitioned for the restoration of the property condemned by the court, the king in council refused to interfere with the admiral's sentence.[8] From its inception, therefore, the admiralty court without special authorization determined prize cases. Appeal in this prize case from the admiralty court, as throughout much of its history, lay to the king in council.[9]

The earliest parts of the Black Book of the Admiralty, which became the handbook of admiralty practice, date from this same period. The transfer of jurisdiction from the common law courts to this new tribunal apparently led to this compilation of precedents as a guide to judges and practitioners in the admiralty court. The part of the Black Book dealing with the practice and procedure of the admiralty court dates from the fifteenth century. These documents show that the court's business consisted of shipping and mercantile as well as criminal cases. The Black Book makes it clear that from the first the admiralty court looked for its

---

[6] *Ibid.*, pp. xl–xli.

[7] Quoted in *ibid.*, pp. xlii–xliii.

[8] Reginald G. Marsden, ed., *Documents Relating to Law and Custom of the Sea* (2 v., n.p., 1925–1926) 1: pp. 81–84.

[9] Edward S. Roscoe, *A History of the English Prize Court* (London, 1924), p. 5.

models, not to the English common law, but to foreign civil law procedure.[10]

A petition to Parliament in 1371 complained that various people had been forced to answer charges against them without a common law jury, probably referring to the civil law procedure of the admiral's court.[11] The marine or port courts, long accustomed to determine disputes between merchants, found the admiralty court a threat to their ancient franchises. Common law courts apparently objected to encroachments upon their jurisdiction by the admiralty court. Parliament, therefore, hearing of the great irregularities committed by one judge of the court of the Admiral of the West, passed two statutes to define and restrict the admiral's jurisdiction. The first statute, passed in 1389, simply stated that "the admirals and their deputies shall not meddle from henceforth of anything done within the realm, but only of a thing done upon the sea."[12] Parliament, by the second statute of 1391, tried to draw the line more precisely between common law and admiralty jurisdiction. It provided:

> That of all manner of contracts, pleas, and quarrels, and all other things rising within the bodies of the counties, as well by land as by water, and also of wreck of the sea, the admiral's court shall have no manner of cognizance, power, nor jurisdiction, but all such manner of contracts, pleas, and quarrels, and all other things rising within the bodies of counties, as well by land as by water, as afore, and also wreck of the sea, shall be tried, determined, discussed, and remedied by the laws of the land, and not before nor by the admiral, nor his lieutenant in any wise. Nevertheless, of the death of a man, and of a maihem done in great ships, being and hovering in the mainstream of great rivers, only beneath the bridges of the same rivers nigh to the sea, and in none other places of the same rivers, the admiral shall have cognizance, and also to arrest ships in the

---

[10] Marsden, *Select Pleas* 1: pp. xliii–xliv, liv; Holdsworth, *History* 5: pp. 125–126.

[11] Marsden, *Select Pleas* 1: pp. xlvii. Apparently the admiralty court, in the fourteenth and fifteenth centuries, did on occasion present a case to a jury.

[12] 13 Ric. II, c. 5. The preamble of this Act recited the grievances it was intended to remedy:

"[F]orasmuch as a great and common clamour and complaint hath been oftentimes made before this time, and yet is, for that the admirals and their deputies hold their sessions within divers places of this realm, as well within franchise as without, accroaching to them greater authority than belongeth to their office, in prejudice of our lord the King, and the common law of the realm, and in diminishing of divers franchises, and in destruction and impoverishing of the common people. . . ."

See also, Marsden, *Select Pleas* 1: p. 1.

great flotes for the great voyages of the King and of the realm; saving always to the King all jurisdiction upon the said flotes, during the said voyages only, saving always to the lords, cities, and boroughs their liberties and franchises.[13]

Apparently these statutes were ignored. Thus in 1400 Parliament imposed penalties upon those who sued in the admiral's court in violation of the earlier statutes.[14]

Most of the fifteenth century in England was dominated by foreign and civil war, internal conflicts and dissentions. The business of the admiralty court, both civil (shipping and mercantile) and criminal, expanded during this period of turmoil. Sometime during this century the courts of the Admirals of the North, South, and West ceased to exist. The earliest extant patent of a judge of the admiralty court dates from 1482. It empowered the judge to hear and determine the controversies and business of all things which pertained to the principal court of admiralty.[15]

Piracy flourished during the latter part of the fifteenth century. English, French, Spanish, Portuguese, Genoese, Venetian, Flemish, and German pirates preyed on the shipping of all countries indiscriminately. With the accession of a stronger monarch, Henry VIII, in the next century, the admiralty court was specially commissioned to provide a speedy and informal trial, in accordance with treaties, for all piracy claims. Judgment was to be given according to the merits and no appeal was allowed except to the king in council. During the reign of Henry VIII the records of the admiralty court began.[16]

Henry VIII intended by the patents to his admirals to confer a wider jurisdiction than that defined in the statutes of Richard II. The patent to his natural son, Prince Henry, as admiral granted him power

---

[13] 15 Ric. II, c. 3. The preamble again recited the evils to be cured by the Act: "[A]t the great and grievous complaint of all the commons made to our lord the King in this present parliament, for that the admirals and their deputies to incroach to them divers jurisdictions, franchises, and many other profits pertaining to our lord the King, and to other lords, cities, and boroughs, other than they were wont or ought to have of right, to the great oppression and impoverishment of all the commons of the land, and hindrance and loss of the King's profits, and of many other lords, cities, and boroughs through the realm. . . ."

[14] 2 Hen. IV, c. 11.

[15] Marsden, *Select Pleas* 1: pp. li–lv.

[16] *Ibid.*, p. lvi.

of hearing and terminating plaints of all contracts between the owners [and] proprietors of ships and merchants or [between] any other person whomsoever, and the same owners and proprietors of ships and of all other vessels concerning anything to be done on the sea or beyond sea, [and] of all and singular contracts to be performed beyond sea, or contracted beyond sea, and also in England, and of all other things that concern the office of the admiral.

The other patents for Henry VIII's admirals conferred even broader powers. To remove any doubts arising from the statutes of Richard II, these patents of Henry VIII added a *non obstante* clause, "any statutes, acts, ordinances, or restrictions to the contrary passed, promulgated, ordained, or provided notwithstanding."[17]

The records of the admiralty court during the sixteenth century show the wide-reaching jurisdiction it exercised. The court heard cases of piracy and spoil to determine the legitimacy of the seizure of property. Where foreign parties were involved, the king's council often interfered with directions telling the judge how to deal with a particular case. The court also heard a wide variety of cases involving shipping and commercial matters, such as: contracts made abroad, bills of exchange, commercial agencies abroad, charter parties, insurance, average, freight, non-delivery of or damage to cargo, negligent navigation, and breach of warranty of seaworthiness. Cases involving wreck, salvage, collision, and other maritime torts also appear in these admiralty court records. The criminal jurisdiction of the admiralty court, however, was substantially narrowed and eventually eliminated. The civil law procedure of trial by witnesses had become the model of the admiralty court's criminal procedure. Aware of the fact that this procedure often meant that crimes committed at sea went unpunished, Parliament in 1536 transferred the admiralty court's jurisdiction over treasons, felonies, robberies, murders, and confederacies to commissioners appointed under the Great Seal who were to try the offenses as if committed on land. In 1799 Parliament extended this Act to include all offenses committed on the high seas. The chancellor invariably chose some common law judges as the special commissioners, so the criminal jurisdic-

---

[17] *Ibid.*, pp. lvii–lix.

tion of the admiralty court in practice was transferred to judges of the common law courts. Trial was by jury and counsel were barristers.[18]

Under Henry VIII the creation of the new office of vice-admiral occurred at the same time as the Lord High Admiral's office and court were being enhanced. When the king's son, Henry, Duke of Richmond and Somerset, was made Lord High Admiral at the age of six, several vice-admirals carried out the duties of his office. Vice-admirals were also appointed for various maritime counties. These vice-admirals functioned mainly to collect the droits and perquisites owed to the admiral from wreck, flotsam, derelict property, whales, and a tenth share of all prizes. Vice-admirals were supposed to act as a check on the piratical and wrecking propensities of those living near the coast, but some connived with pirates and joined in spoiling the wrecks. Vice-admirals also had power to arrest vessels, inventory cargoes of ships involved in litigation, examine witnesses, and execute sentences of the court. The vice-admirals of the coast frequently held court through deputies especially during and after the eighteenth century. These courts determined cases of wreck, fisheries, and other local maritime business. At the same time many of the ancient port or marine courts, especially that of the Cinque Ports, continued to function more or less under the control of the High Court. In assessing these various vice-admiralty courts, it is well to remember that throughout the sixteenth and seventeenth centuries the office of admiral was regarded mainly as a source of profit. Apparently by the late seventeenth century, vice-admiralty judges and court offices were commissioned by the High Court of Admiralty.[19] These vice-admiralty courts and the judges' commissions served as prototypes for the American colonial vice-admiralty court system which will be discussed later.

Vice-admirals of the counties continued to function till the middle of the nineteenth century. During the sixteenth century one vice-admiral held office in Ireland; after that several were appointed for the provinces. In the eighteenth century a High Court of Admiralty sat in Dublin apparently with

---

[18] *Ibid.*, pp. lxv–lxxi; 28 Hen. VIII, c. 15; 4, 5 William IV, c. 36; Holdsworth, *History* 1: pp. 550–551.

[19] Marsden, "Vice Admirals," *English Hist. Rev.* **22**: pp. 473–477.

concurrent original jurisdiction with the provincial vice-admiralty courts. After the Act of Union in 1707, several vice-admirals were named for the various regions of Scotland.[20]

Under Elizabeth the business of plunder at sea became a major patriotic fascination and a significant aspect of foreign policy. Most of these private armed vessels, which preyed especially upon Spanish shipping, carried letters of reprisal to shelter them from the charge of piracy. Letters of reprisal, a self-help remedy for merchants injured by foreign parties, were issued by the High Court of Admiralty in time of peace to allow the bearer to seize property belonging to individuals of a certain nation in recompense for alleged injuries suffered by the bearer at the hands of that nation. Reprisals at sea had been made, with or without legal authority, for many centuries. The injured English party had to file a pleading in the High Court, supported by witnesses, seeking a letter of reprisal. The Court would promulgate a decree stating the amount of the losses sustained and licensing the injured party to recoup his losses by force from any property belonging to individuals of the nation causing the alleged injury. But proof of loss in many cases became a legal fiction; letters of reprisal were bought and sold and local admiralty officials traded these commissions in exchange for a share in the venture.[21] Only the thin line of these letters of reprisal, often of dubious validity, distinguished some Elizabethan sea rovers from pirates.

The admiralty court sought to control within some legal bounds the activities of these private adventurers. The promoter of a venture, before obtaining a letter of reprisal, had to provide a bond to assure that his vessel would observe the instructions or rules governing the conduct of the voyage and the disposal of the prizes. The legitimacy of the prizes was adjudicated in the High Court. The admiral was entitled to a tenth of the value of any prize, an interest he jealously

---

[20] *Ibid., English Hist. Rev.* **23** (1908): pp. 736–757.

[21] Kenneth R. Andrews, *Elizabethan Privateering* (Cambridge, 1964), pp. 3–23; Kenneth R. Andrews, ed., *English Privateering Voyages to the West Indies, 1588–1595* (Cambridge, 1959), pp. 2–12, 16–28. The terminology of the seventeenth century had not yet become common. The commissions to recoup private losses were called letters of reprisal, letters of marque and reprisal or letters of marque, indiscriminately. Similarly the term privateer was not used till the seventeenth century. Marsden, *Law of the Sea* **1**: pp. xxvi–xxvii; Andrews, *Elizabethan Privateering*, p. 5.

guarded. Since these captures involved many disputes with foreign parties, the Privy Council took a deep interest in the admiralty court's prize work, often infringing upon the court's judicial functions. The constant political interference undermined the court's prestige. With the vice-admiralty and admiralty officials chiefly concerned to profit from their offices, corruption was widespread.[22]

During the Tudor period, therefore, the admiralty court grew both in its prize work and in its jurisdiction over a wide range of civil maritime disputes. Criminal jurisdiction over treasons, felonies, robberies, murders, and confederacies, committed within the ordinary sphere of the admiralty court's jurisdiction, was transferred by Parliament to a special commission appointed by the chancellor to try the offenses as if they had been committed on land. The prize business was not yet differentiated from the court's civil, commercial business. Not until the Tudor period did the basic principle become established that there must be an adjudication in the admiralty court of all prizes taken in virtue of letters of marque or letters of reprisal. The instructions for reprisal ventures began in Elizabeth's reign and served as patterns for privateering instructions in the seventeenth and eighteenth centuries.[23]

Appeals from the admiralty court lay to the Court of Delegates, the appellate court for cases of civil law, whether ecclesiastical or lay. Although the delegates appointed by the king in the sixteenth century were usually civil lawyers, after 1650 the commissions always included some common lawyers. By the latter half of the seventeenth century, if not earlier, appeals from the admiralty court in prize cases were heard by the Lords Commissioners for Prize Appeals. Review of decrees of the Lords Commissioners by the Court of Delegates was considered legally possible but in fact was extremely rare.[24]

As we have already noted, the civil law's foreign influence on the admiralty court, as on the ecclesiastical court, was

---

[22] Andrews, *Elizabethan Privateering*, pp. 23–31.

[23] Reginald G. Marsden, "Early Prize Jurisdiction and Prize Law in England," *English Hist. Rev.* **24** (1909): pp. 675–697; Roscoe, *Prize Court*, pp. 10–11; Marsden, *Select Pleas* **2**: p. xvii; Holdsworth, *History* **1**: pp. 550–551.

[24] Holdsworth, *History* **1**: p. 547; Marsden, *Select Pleas* **1**: p. lxxix; **2**: pp. lix–lxii; G.I.O. Duncan, *The High Court of Delegates* (Cambridge, 1971), pp. 17–35, 66–71, 79–80.

strong. Doctors of civil law from the Continent taught in England and Englishmen went abroad to take degrees in civil law. In 1511 an unofficial group of professors and practitioners of civil law organized into a professional association which subsequently became Doctors' Common, analogous to the Inns of Courts for the common lawyers except that it never became a teaching body. These civil lawyers, with a degree of doctor of civil law from Oxford or Cambridge, were advocates in admiralty, comparable to barristers at common law. Because a large part of their work was in the ecclesiastical court, the Archbishop of Canterbury regulated admissions to Doctors' Common. Civil lawyers, besides their monopoly in ecclesiastical courts, practiced in the sphere of diplomacy and the court of admiralty and participated in special cases before Star Chamber and Chancery. Their knowledge of the rapidly evolving law of nations and the foreign maritime and commercial law suited them for this practice which was outside the ordinary ken of the common lawyer.[25]

During Elizabeth's reign complaints began to be made that the common law courts were encroaching on the admiralty court's jurisdiction, the first skirmishes in a battle which would leave the admiralty court in the next century badly crippled. Writs of prohibition, ordering the admiralty court to cease its proceedings in a case because it was outside its jurisdiction, were issued by common law courts before James I succeeded Elizabeth and had reached an acute stage before 1606 when Lord Coke was raised to the bench.[26]

The common law courts coveted the admiralty court's jurisdiction over the growing commercial business of England. They, therefore, issued prohibitions especially to prevent the admiralty court from hearing cases of contracts entered into abroad or in English ports. By the legal fiction that these contracts had been made in England, common law courts took jurisdiction, even though the common law and its procedures were ill suited to deal with such cases. The merchant class suffered from these attacks on admiralty jurisdiction. Admiralty process was more speedy and better adapted to deal with cases of merchants and seamen. The admiralty

[25] Holdsworth, *History* **4**: pp. 234–238.
[26] Marsden, *Select Pleas* **2**: pp. xii, xli.

court could issue commissions to examine witnesses abroad, examine the parties themselves, arrest the ship as security or allow seamen to bring a common suit for wages, all beyond the common law's power. The civilians, with their knowledge of the law merchant, understood contracts made abroad far better than common lawyers.[27]

With the accession of James I, the struggle between the common law courts and the admiralty court was subsumed into the larger battle between the king and Parliament as to the source of the sovereign power in the state. The admiralty court, as a prerogative court, owed its authority to the king and sided with the view that ultimately the prerogative was the locus of sovereignty. The common law courts took the view that the law was supreme and that the prerogative was limited by it. Edward Coke, especially after he became chief justice of Common Pleas in 1606, used his enormous knowledge of the common law to lead the forces of those who wanted the king's prerogative limited. Coke's *Fourth Institute* dealt with the jurisdiction of the courts. Here, with considerable straining of early precedents, he articulated a narrow view of admiralty jurisdiction, a view which would carry great weight in the years that followed.[28] With Coke as chief justice prohibitions became frequent, even occasionally in spoil cases. Common law courts anxiously strained to capture for themselves the lucrative commercial business of the admiralty court. The king tried to retaliate in 1609 by ordering the vice-admiralty officers to execute the sentences of the admiralty court and to restore illegally captured goods, notwithstanding any prohibitions.[29]

Efforts at compromise and attempts, during and after the Commonwealth period, to have Parliament settle the jurisdiction of the admiralty court proved futile. By the latter half of the seventeenth century the admiralty court's civil and commercial jurisdiction (called instance jurisdiction to distinguish it from the court's prize jurisdiction) had been restricted to the following: torts committed on the high seas, contracts made on the high seas to be executed there, *in rem* proceedings on bottomry bonds entered into abroad, suits

---

[27] Holdsworth, *History* 1: pp. 553–554.
[28] Sir Edward Coke, *The Fourth Part of the Institutes of the Laws of England* (London, 1797), pp. 134–146; Holdsworth, *History* 5: pp. 423–471.
[29] Marsden, "Prize Law," *English Hist. Rev.* 25: p. 245.

for mariners' wages, salvage, and the enforcement of judgments of a foreign admiralty court. During the eighteenth
century the volume of the court's instance business was
trifling in comparison with its civil and commercial business
in the sixteenth century.[30] After the Restoration the English
common law was supreme; the ordinary courts of law and
equity had captured jurisdiction over most maritime commercial cases.[31]

During the reign of Charles I, about 1625, the prize records of the admiralty court for the first time were distinguished from the court's civil and mercantile cases, the instance cases.[32] Though the instance business of the court
declined during the seventeenth and eighteenth centuries, its
prize work remained intact. In spite of a few prohibitions
issued by common law courts to challenge admiralty jurisdiction in matters of prize, the court's prize jurisdiction was
never seriously contested.[33] After the Restoration the admiralty court held distinct sessions for prize and instance cases.
The Council issued special rules to govern the admiralty
court's prize jurisdiction.[34]

Although there was authority for the admiralty court to
assert inherent jurisdiction over prize cases, at least after
1702 it became the practice for the Lord High Admiral or
the Lords Commissioners of the Admiralty at the outbreak of
each war to issue special commissions to the High Court
authorizing the judge to hear cases of prize.[35] The Prize Act
of 1708 gave parliamentary recognition to the admiralty
court's prize jurisdiction and gave to the captors (whether a
naval vessel or privateer) a statutory right to the whole of the
prize, thereby surrendering any right of the king to a share.
Parliament throughout the eighteenth century re-enacted
this Prize Act in essentially the same form at the start of each
war.[36]

---

[30] Holdsworth, *History* 1: p. 557; Marsden, *Select Pleas* 2: p. lxxix.
[31] Holdsworth, *History* 1: pp. 556–558; 5: pp. 152–154; 12: p. 692.
[32] Marsden, "Prize Law," *English Hist. Rev.* 25: p. 255.
[33] Marsden, *Select Pleas* 2: p. lxxix.
[34] Marsden, *Law of the Sea* 2: pp. 53–57; Holdsworth, *History* 1: p. 564.
[35] Roscoe, *Prize Court*, pp. 44–46.
[36] 6 Anne c. 13 and 37. The later prize acts are: 13 Geo. II, c. 4 (1739); 17 Geo. II,
c. 34 (1744); 29 Geo. II, c. 34 (1756); 32 Geo. II, c. 25 (1759); 19 Geo. III, c. 67
(1778); 33 Geo. III, c. 66 (1793). The fullest discussion of Crown rights and the
Lord High Admiral's rights in prizes is: H.C. Rothery, *Prize Droits* (London, 1915).
Rothery points out that (p. 19):

The owners and crews of privateers before the voyage settled the method of dividing any prizes they might take. By the articles of agreement between the captain and crew, various rules and regulations of conduct aboard were prescribed and the precise share of a prize for each member of the crew was set forth. There was no general rule for determining the proportions to be awarded to each crew member. The prize acts did not interfere with the distribution between the owners and crews but merely ratified whatever contracts the parties agreed to with each other. Besides prize money the crews of privateers, as well as crews of naval vessels, enjoyed two other privileges: gun or head money, and pillage. The crews received a special bonus proportional to the number of men and guns aboard the captured vessel to encourage the privateers to take the greater risk of capturing the enemy's armed vessels rather than the more defenseless merchant vessels. Pillage was the carefully regulated right of the capturing crew to take anything found on or above the gun deck of the prize vessel, except its tackle and furniture. The owners of privateers tried to restrict this right of pillage for fear their crews would deprive them of their share of the prize.[37]

During and after the seventeenth century the ministry sought to maintain some control over the activities of privateers by requiring bonds to be provided before a letter of marque was issued and by publishing instructions for privateers. Though privateers did multiply a nation's sea power in time of war, their unbridled pursuit of plunder and profit through capture could cause serious embarrassment to the home government, besieged with complaints by neutrals of the illegal activities of its privateers. By the end of the seventeenth century the practice of reprisals had fallen into disuse and it became common to issue letters of marque,

---

"The title deeds, so to speak, under which commissioned captors are entitled to claim for their own benefit the whole proceeds of any prizes captured by them during hostilities, are the [Crown's Prize] Proclamation and the Prize Act; and if at the commencement of any war these were not issued, the prizes captured during that war even by commissioned vessels would be condemned as droits of the Crown."

[37] 6 Anne, c. 13 and 37; Richard Pares, Colonial Blockade and Neutral Rights, 1737-1763 (Oxford, 1938), pp. 7-16. An example of the articles of agreement is given in Wyndham Beawes, Lex Mercatoria Rediviva or the Merchant's Directory (London, 1752), pp. 225-227. Marsden, Law of the Sea 2: pp. 299-300 gives the British proclamation confirming and ratifying such agreements.

authorizing privateers to prey upon enemy shipping in time
of war. The privateers' instructions were apparently modeled on the instructions issued earlier to sea rovers with
letters of reprisal.

The English ministry tried to control the high-handed
practices of privateering captains through these instructions,
copies of which were issued to each captain as he received his
commission and provided sureties for his compliance with
the instructions. Instructions in slightly modified form were
issued from time to time during the seventeenth and
eighteenth centuries to fit the circumstances of the various
wars. Five topics of special concern to the government, however, run through all of them. The instructions forbade the
suppression or distortion of evidence, prohibited embezzle-
ment of cargoes, condemned cruelty to the crews of prize
vessels, insisted that prizes be brought before a proper court
for adjudication, and attempted to protect neutral rights. A
reading of one of these privateering instructions brings viv-
idly to mind the whole gamut of tricks, deceits, and fraud
which the government had found from sad experience was
often a consequence of using privateers to carry on naval
warfare.[38]

To put teeth in the instructions, owners and captains of
privateers had to provide adequate sureties whose bond
could be put in suit if the instructions were violated. This
bond at times had turned out to be worthless, so an act of
1759 required the sureties to swear that they were worth
more than the sum for which they bound themselves. The
bond was meant to provide a direct method for an injured
party to recover for any loss or damage he had suffered by
the unlawful capture of his property. The government could
also put the bond in suit to punish the privateer captain for
any glaring misbehavior.[39]

Any parties injured by a British privateer could bring a
civil suit in an admiralty court for damages against the captain, the owners of the privateer, or the sureties. Recovery
against the sureties was limited to the amount of their bonds,
which in most cases should have sufficed if the sureties could

[38] Marsden, *Law of the Sea* **2**: pp. 403–435; Pares, *Colonial Blockade*, pp. 53–64;
Marsden, "Prize Law," *English Hist. Rev.* **26**: pp. 41–53; Holdsworth, *History* **10**: pp.
374–375.

[39] 32 Geo. II, c. 25; Pares, *Colonial Blockade*, pp. 48–53.

be forced to pay that amount. The privateer captain was in theory answerable for the full amount of the damage, but in practice probably could not pay. The owners were liable for damages at least to the extent of the value of their ship which they had entrusted to the command of the offending captain.[40]

This threat of civil suit proved insufficient to stop all injury to neutrals, so during the Seven Years' War the Parliament passed a statute to put a stop to another clear violation of neutral rights. By this act any privateer who demanded a ransom from a neutral before releasing his ship or cargo could be punished as a pirate, that is, with capital punishment. Ransom, often indistinguishable from extortion, had been a short cut of dubious legality to avoid the delays and possible damage awards from prize adjudication in a court. This law attempted to force privateers either to release without ransom any neutral vessels not liable to lawful seizure, or to bring them in for a fair trial before an admiralty court.[41]

Since prize cases could touch important questions of foreign policy, the Privy Council often tried to interfere in specific cases with the admiralty court's exercise of its prize jurisdiction. The Crown did effectively influence prize adjudications by elucidating or modifying substantive prize law through its royal proclamations, orders in council, and treaties.[42]

The procedures for prize adjudication became well defined by the late seventeenth century. The captor generally retained custody of the captured vessel or cargo before condemnation. The Council in 1665 outlined the procedures for a trial in the prize court.[43] Without departing from this basic outline, Parliament, by the various prize acts of the eighteenth century, more fully spelled out the details of prize adjudication. The procedural provisions of the prize acts will be discussed in chapter V.

By the middle of the eighteenth century, therefore, the admiralty court's cases fell into two distinct categories, the

---

[40] Richard Lee, *A Treatise of Captures in War* (London, 1759), pp. 226–232; Marsden, *Law of the Sea* 2: pp. 327–328; Henry Wheaton, *A Digest of the Law of Maritime Captures and Prizes* (New York, 1815), pp. 43–45.

[41] 32 Geo. II, c. 25.

[42] Roscoe, *Prize Court*, pp. 26, 34, 40–43; Holdsworth, *History* 1: pp. 566–567.

[43] Roscoe, *Prize Court*, p. 30; Marsden, *Law of the Sea* 2: p. 56.

court's prize jurisdiction and the court's instance jurisdiction, that remnant of its once flourishing civil and commercial business. In a key case during the American Revolution, Lord Mansfield described more than a century of English prize practice when he stated: "The whole system of litigation and jurisprudence in the prize court, is peculiar to itself: It is no more like the court of Admiralty [instance], than it is to any court in Westminster Hall [common law]."[44] As we shall see in chapters V and VII, the American prize practice did not comprehend this distinction in England between the prize side and the instance side of the admiralty court.

As we have seen, prior to 1628 appeals from the admiralty court lay to the king in chancery, where they were heard by commissioners or delegates appointed for each case. With the increased number of prize cases and with the prize and instance records of the court distinguished, appeals in prize cases after 1628 were heard by a standing commission of the Privy Council. These Lords Commissioners for Prize Appeals could review the sentences and proceedings of the admiralty court in all cases of prize. Civilian advocates, sometimes accompanied by barristers, represented the parties before the members of the Council commissioned to hear prize appeals. At times in the seventeenth and eighteenth centuries only a certain number of Council members were commissioned, but at other times all members of the Council received these commissions.[45]

In 1748 a standing commission was issued which included some of the judges of the common law who were not privy councillors. Doubts were raised as to the legality of this inclusion of non-members of the Council. Parliament settled the dispute by confirming the commission to the common law judges, but provided that no decree issued under the commission would be valid unless a majority of the commissioners were members of the Privy Council.[46] Throughout the rest of the eighteenth century this practice continued so that common law judges were regularly included in the commission for hearing prize appeals.

With members of the Privy Council always in the majority

---

[44] *Lindo* v. *Rodney and Another*, Douglas, 591 at 592; 99 *English Reports*, 385 at 386.
[45] Marsden, "Prize Law," *English Hist. Rev.* **25:** p. 257; Roscoe, *Prize Court*, pp. 87–88.
[46] 22 Geo. II, c. 3; Roscoe, *Prize Court*, pp. 88–89.

of the Lords Commissioners for Prize Appeals, one might suspect that reasons of state would often control their determinations more than purely legal reasons. It seems, however, that during the eighteenth century the leading political members of the Council tried hard to avoid participating in prize appeals so that they could freely deplore and denounce an unpopular decree. The sessions of the Lords Commissioners show that the councillors most often in attendance were minor political figures with an unsatisfied craving for activity to keep themselves occupied. Reasons of state were hardly ignored, but the Lords Commissioners were not merely functioning as English politicians.[47]

The legal principles for prize adjudication applied by the Lords Commissioners and the High Court were not yet clearly formulated. Published reports of prize cases did not appear till the end of the eighteenth century. Treaties, orders in council, and proclamations, of course, influenced prize decrees. During the seventeenth and early eighteenth centuries, however, the writers on the law of nations, especially on the Continent, stated norms and rules for captures made in time of war, based more on philosophical reasoning and historical examples than on legal decisions. The civilians, who practiced before the prize court, must have followed these developments closely. It is significant that at the same time the English prize court was developing into a distinct institution, the continental thinking on the rights of capture of enemy property was in a state of ferment, with clearer ideas developing on the rights of belligerents and neutrals on both sides of the Channel. As we shall see in a subsequent chapter, these continental writers were relied on by American lawyers and judges when considering prize issues.

Hugo Grotius in 1625 published the first edition of his *De Jure Belli ac Pacis* which intensified interest in questions of the law binding on all nations. He stressed the principles of law common to all mankind, the law of human society. In his treatment of the law of war in Book III, he discussed what the law of nations permitted in time of war. He stated a few principles relevant to prize litigation: that destruction or capture of enemy property is permitted; that the rule "enemy ships make enemy goods" was merely a rebuttable

---

[47] Pares, *Colonial Blockade*, pp. 101–108.

presumption; that property rights in a movable object are lost by the original owner when he no longer has probable expectation of regaining it. Many of the legal issues of neutral rights, joint captures, and others which were crucial to judicial determinations in prize cases were not discussed by Grotius fully enough to assist the admiralty court or its bar.[48]

Stimulated largely by the work of Grotius, several philosophical writers on the law of nations made significant contributions to the rapidly expanding literature of international law. Pufendorf, Wolff, and Vattel led this philosophical school. Samuel von Pufendorf's large tome deduced the whole legal theory of rules governing relations between states from his analysis of the law of nature. His treatment of the law of war was limited to one chapter and included several sections on the capture of enemy property.[49] Christian Frederick von Wolff's opaque writings on the law of nations reduced the necessary law of nations to axioms rigorously derived from prior principles. He separated the norms governing the relations between states (the law of nations) from those principles which govern the relations of individuals (natural law). He stressed consent of all nations as the basis of a legal order within the commonwealth of nations. He discussed a few issues which would be directly applicable in prize adjudication.[50] Emmerich de Vattel, on the other hand, expressed his philosophical principles in a clear, relaxed, and readable style. He drew heavily upon historical examples as he developed the law of nations, which he regarded as the law of nature as applied to nations. Since politicians and diplomats could understand his treatise, its influence was enormous. In his humane treatment of war, Vattel studied in much greater detail than his predecessors the issues involved in captures made in time of war.[51]

Cornelius van Bynkershoek stood apart from these philos-

---

[48] Hugo Grotius, *De Jure Belli ac Pacis Libri Tres,* Francis W. Kelsey, tr. (2 v., London, 1925) **2**: pp. 626–629, 663–689, 712–715; Edward Dumbauld, *The Life and Legal Writings of Hugo Grotius* (Norman, Okla., 1969), pp. 57–72.

[49] Samuel Pufendorf, *De Jure Naturae et Gentium, Libri Octo* C.H. Oldfather and W.A. Oldfather, trs. (2 v., London, 1934) **2**: pp. 1310–1315.

[50] Christian Wolff, *Jus Gentium, Methodo Scientifica Pertractatum,* Joseph H. Drake, tr. (2 v., London, 1934) **2**: pp. 424–444, 458–467, 516–517.

[51] Emer de Vattel, *Le Droit des Gens, ou Principes de la Loi Naturelle, appliqués à la Conduite et aux Affaires des Nations et de Souverains,* Charles G. Fenwick, tr. (3 v. Washington, 1916) **2**: pp. 259–260, 268–273, 279–280, 291–295, 307, 313–320.

ophers as the chief exponent of the positivist or historical school of international law. As an advocate and judge, he was thoroughly immersed in the legal decisions and treaties which in practice affected relations between nations. He examined, more concretely and in greater detail, the precise issues raised in cases which dealt with captures and neutral commerce in time of war.[52]

This sketch of the origins and growth of the English admiralty institutions will supply a fuller, more detailed background for studying the American appellate prize court during the Revolution. As we shall see, eighteenth-century Americans were aware of many elements of the history of the English court of admiralty. They knew with greater familiarity, of course, the vice-admiralty courts which had functioned in most of the growing port cities in America. A brief outline of these colonial vice-admiralty courts will suggest the attitudes which colored American thinking when prize courts had to be established on the eve of the Revolution. Since American judicial institutions varied greatly from colony to colony, only a generalized sketch will be attempted here. In chapter V the unique characteristics of some of these vice-admiralty courts will be mentioned.

Prior to the return of the monarchy in England in 1660, the American colonies struggled with the admiralty cases thrust upon them with little system and less guidance from the otherwise preoccupied government at home. Massachusetts found in its Charter implicit authority to hear admiralty cases. The General Court, which functioned as the executive, legislative, and judicial body of the colony, tried a wide variety of admiralty cases, including prize, employing special common law juries. Apparently even the county courts, when established, heard admiralty suits, with little or no knowledge of the maritime law or admiralty practice.[53]

Similarly in Virginia and Maryland, prior to 1660, the admiralty cases, whether instance, prize, or criminal, were brought before the existing common law courts of the colonies. Neither colony felt the need for a separate admiralty

---

[52] Cornelius van Bynkershoek, *Quaestiones Juris Publici, Libri Duo*, Tenney Frank, tr. (2 v., London, 1930), **2**: pp. 32–48, 54–97, 104–119.

[53] Helen J. Crump, *Colonial Admiralty Jurisdiction in the Seventeenth Century* (London, 1931), pp. 37–55.

court presided over by trained civilians and following distinctive admiralty procedures.[54]

In the latter half of the seventeenth century the continuous naval warfare of England highlighted the need for courts in the colonies to deal with cases of prize. Piracy continued to be a problem also calling for vice-admiralty courts. The distinction between privateers and pirates remained tenuous.[55] The Governor of Jamaica about 1660 acted, apparently without special authorization, to issue letters of marque and to determine prize cases with the help of commissioners or his council.

After 1661 some interest was shown in organizing a colonial admiralty system, for James, Duke of York, the king's brother, besides his office as Lord High Admiral of England, received a special patent as Lord Admiral of certain enumerated dominions outside England, including New England, Jamaica, Virginia, Barbados, St. Christopher, Bermuda, and Antigua. The exercise of admiralty jurisdiction in these colonies depended upon a commission from him. The Governor of Jamaica, as vice-admiral, received what was apparently the first patent from James authorizing him to establish a vice-admiralty court. The Jamaica court was used especially for cases of prize and piracy.[56]

In the American colonies, where prize and piracy cases were less frequent, there was no coherent admiralty court system until after 1696. Governors in the royal provinces were made vice-admirals in virtue of their commissions, but they exercised this power without discernible consistency. The commissions apparently bestowed administrative as well as judicial powers, similar to the vice-admirals of the coast in England. It is doubtful, however, whether colonial governors, by virtue of their commissions, exercised judicial powers in any significant way. In the chartered colonies like Massachusetts, the local authorities resorted to various special arbitration committees or courts to hear admiralty cases.[57]

---

[54] *Ibid.*, pp. 56–78.

[55] *Ibid.*, pp. 91, 94; J. Franklin Jameson, ed., *Privateering and Piracy in the Colonial Period* (New York, 1923), pp. xiii–xiv.

[56] Crump, *Colonial Admiralty*, pp. 94–116; Marsden, *Law of the Sea* 2: pp. 41–46, 161–162; Joseph H. Smith, *Appeals to the Privy Council from the American Plantations* (New York, 1950), p. 88.

[57] Crump, *Colonial Admiralty*, pp. 117–164; L. Kinvin Wroth, "The Massachusetts

England, through the acts of trade, had tried to regulate the commercial activity of the colonies to ensure its own and its colonies' self-sufficiency. Of course, the colonies were expected to be satisfied with a position of permanent subordination in the economic evolution of the empire. The customs officers charged with the responsibility of imposing this English administrative system upon the colonies had experienced the difficulty of the task and the depth of colonial opposition. The local courts, as well as the governors, the naval officers, and the inhabitants had shared in undermining effective colonial administration. English officials in America complained to the home government that some local customs officers winked at forged ship papers while others exploited their position to enrich themselves. The response of Parliament was the Navigation Act of 1696 "for Preventing Frauds, and Regulating Abuses in the Plantation Trade."[58]

This Act noted the great abuses committed every day by the cunning of certain ill-disposed persons, causing loss to English trade. It tightened the restrictions on allowing foreign vessels to participate in the colonial trade; no goods could be brought to or from the colonies except in English built and owned ships or in vessels captured and condemned as prizes. The governors had to swear, under pain of dismissal and heavy fine, to uphold the provisions of this Act. Customs officers, entrusted with enforcement of the Act, were entitled to use writs of assistance, equivalent to general search warrants. The proceeds from seizures of goods for violation of the acts of trade would be distributed, one-third to the king, one-third to the governor, and one-third to the person who brought the prosecution. The owners of the seized property had to bear the burden of proof in suits alleging illegal importation or exportation. Colonial laws or customs repugnant to the English acts were declared void. Customs officers could require ship captains to post special bonds which would be forfeited if their ship papers proved to be falsified.[59]

Vice-Admiralty Court," In: George A. Billias, ed., *Law and Authority in Colonial America* (Barre, Mass., 1965), pp. 34–35.

[58] 7 & 8 William III, c. 22; Thomas C. Barrow, *Trade and Empire: The British Customs Service in Colonial America, 1660–1775* (Cambridge, Mass., 1967), pp. 1–3, 37–53.

[59] Barrow, *Trade and Empire*, pp. 53–56.

The 1696 Act contained contradictory provisions granting
jurisdiction to hear suits for violations of the navigation acts.
One section specified that penalties and forfeitures could be
recovered in "any of his Majesty's Courts at Westminster, or
in the Kingdom of Ireland, or in the Court of Admiralty held
in . . . [the] Plantations respectively, where such Offense shall
be committed, at the Pleasure of the Officer or Informer. . . ."
But another clause explicitly required trial by jury, which
would make trials in the vice-admiralty courts impossible.
Perhaps the drafters of the Act had intended that violations
of the acts of trade could be brought in colonial courts of
exchequer, where a jury was proper. In England the Court
of Exchequer had jurisdiction over such cases. But exchequer courts were not established in most of the American
colonies so the contradiction was left unresolved to cause
much grief to the colonial administration for the next sixty
years. The Act was officially interpreted to bestow concurrent jurisdiction on vice-admiralty courts and common law
courts, at the choice of the party bringing suit. Because of the
ambiguity in the Act, American merchants, accused of illegal
trade, could obtain a writ of prohibition from a common law
court to block prosecutions in the vice-admiralty courts and
to ensure trial before a sympathetic local jury. Furthermore,
it was unclear whether vice-admiralty courts were courts of
record, the terminology used in some of the earlier acts.[60]

The Act of 1696 did not create vice-admiralty courts in
America; it assumed they already existed. By 1700 eleven
vice-admiralty courts were functioning in the American and
West Indian colonies, some with jurisdiction reaching to
more than one colony: Virginia, North Carolina and the
Bahamas, Maryland, Massachusetts Bay, New Hampshire,
Rhode Island, New York, East New Jersey and Connecticut,
Pennsylvania, the Lower Counties and West New Jersey, and
South Carolina. Georgia did not have a vice-admiralty court
till much later.

After 1696 some colonial governors occasionally appointed vice-admiralty judges, even though governors generally were no longer commissioned as vice-admirals. After

---

[60] *Ibid.*, pp. 55–59, 62–64, 87–89, 112, 154; Charles M. Andrews, "Vice Admiralty
Courts in the Colonies," In: Dorothy S. Towle, ed., *Records of the Vice-Admiralty Court
of Rhode-Island, 1716–1752* (Washington, 1936), pp. 5–8.

passage of the Act for Preventing Frauds, the practice of
appointment of vice-admiralty judges gradually became
clear: upon warrants from the Lord High Admiral or the
Lords Commissioners of the Admiralty, commissions to the
vice-admiralty judges were issued under seal of the High
Court of Admiralty.[61] These judges held office during pleasure only and the Lords of the Admiralty sometimes dismissed them by appointing a new judge through the usual
warrant procedure.[62] But apparently the governors in the
colonies continued to influence the appointment of vice-
admiralty judges. Judgeships were often political favors to be
bestowed by governors on deserving friends and support-
ers.[63]

During the first sixty years of the eighteenth century, the
jurisdiction of the American vice-admiralty courts covered
three categories of cases, instance (civil or commercial) suits,
prize suits, and actions to enforce the acts of trade.

Instance jurisdiction brought before the vice-admiralty
courts cases of seamen's wages, bottomry bonds, charter parties, contracts for building, furnishing, and freighting ships,
salvage of wrecks, possession or part-ownership of a vessel,
collision, rights to drift whales and fish. In some colonies
many of these same issues could also be heard in common
law courts; in Connecticut all maritime cases apparently were
heard in the county courts. If the vice-admiralty courts exercised somewhat wider jurisdiction than the English High
Court in the eighteenth century, it is perhaps because the
vice-admiralty court's jurisdiction was in some cases not challenged by writs of prohibition as would have happened in
England. The records show that litigants could successfully
bar a vice-admiralty court's exercise of instance jurisdiction
in a particular case by obtaining a writ of prohibition from a
common law court, or even from a governor. No doubt the
vice-admiralty courts provided useful and convenient
forums to protect seamen's rights and to adjudicate the many
disputes which arose in the ever-growing maritime communities of the American port cities.[64]

---

[61] Andrews, "Vice-Admiralty Courts," In: Towle, *Records*, pp. 13–14; Smith, *Appeals*, pp. 89–91; Jameson, *Privateering*, pp. 519–523.

[62] Pares, *Colonial Blockade*, p. 84.

[63] Carl Ubbelohde, *The Vice-Admiralty Courts and the American Revolution* (Chapel Hill, 1960), pp. 7–8.

[64] Andrews, "Vice-Admiralty Courts," In: Towle, *Records*, pp. 24–35, 59–60,

During time of war the vice-admiralty courts also heard prize cases, but a special commission from the Lords Commissioners of the Admiralty was required to empower vice-admiralty courts to hear these cases of capture of enemy ships and cargoes.[65] Whatever doubts existed as to the authority of vice-admiralty courts to hear prize cases were removed by the parliamentary "Act for the Encouragement of Trade to America" of 1708.[66] The Lords of the Admiralty were authorized to issue commissions to colonial governors or other suitable persons, empowering them to issue letters of marque to privateers.[67] The whole value of all lawful prizes belonged to the privateers, to be divided among the owners, commander, and crew as they had previously agreed. Captures by these American privateers could be adjudicated in any of the colonial vice-admiralty courts. Although by the eighteenth century no one challenged the prize jurisdiction of the admiralty court in England, in the colonies the common law courts occasionally issued prohibitions to prevent the vice-admiralty courts from determining prize cases.[68]

In addition to their instance and prize jurisdiction, the vice-admiralty courts also had concurrent jurisdiction with the common law courts of suits for violations of the acts of trade. Violations took many forms: failures to observe the requirements of the acts for entering, clearing, and registering vessels, failures to carry authentic ship papers, trading in ships which were not English owned and built or legally made English by proper condemnation as a prize, sailing without an English master or the required number of English seamen, smuggling or engaging in illicit trade with French, Spanish, or Dutch ports. Vice-admiralty courts also had received jurisdiction over cases alleging violations of the 1722 act which forbade the cutting of white pines suitable for masts.[69] As has already been pointed out, these suits for

---

69–75; Wroth, "Massachusetts Vice-Admiralty," In: Billias, *Law and Authority*, pp. 40–49, 57–58.

[65] Jameson, *Privateering*, pp. xi, 524; Pares, *Colonial Blockade*, pp. 78–79.

[66] 6 Anne, c. 37. This is not to say that individual governors did not still attempt to try cases of capture in virtue of their earlier commissions as vice-admirals, see Jameson, *Privateering*, pp. 318–333.

[67] Jameson, *Privateering*, pp. x, 355–356; Andrews, in "Vice-Admiralty Court," in Towle, *Records*, p. 60, suggests that vice-admiralty judges issued letters of marque.

[68] Pares, *Colonial Blockade*, pp. 79–84.

[69] Andrews, "Vice-Admiralty Courts," In: Towle, *Records*, pp. 42–59.

violations of the acts of trade in England would have been brought in the Court of Exchequer which, unlike admiralty courts, sat with a jury.

Much doubt and difference of opinion existed, in England as well as in America, as to the proper forum to review decrees of the colonial vice-admiralty courts. Prize appeals were carried, without much question, to the Lords Commissioners for Prize Appeals. Instance appeals went to the Privy Council, although some statements suggested that the High Court of Admiralty was the appropriate appellate court. But appeals from vice-admiralty sentences in navigation act cases continued to be taken either to the High Court of Admiralty or to the Privy Council. Up to the time of the Revolution, appellate jurisdiction remained uncertain; English officials gave contradictory advice on whether to bring act of trade appeals to the High Court or to the Privy Council.[70]

The vice-admiralty courts formed a part of the machinery for English administration of the colonies. Through the first six decades of the eighteenth century, the inadequacies of the colonial system were glaring. Major complaints about the vice-admiralty courts reached England, especially concerning their role as one forum to hear suits for violations of the acts of trade. These courts, however, along with the rest of the system, were left unreformed until after the Seven Years' War. While English officials at home ignored the warning signals from America, the colonists continued, by fraud or intimidation, to undermine the operation of the machinery set up to assure enforcement of the navigation acts. From the English point of view, act of trade enforcement constituted the principal *raison d'être* for the vice-admiralty courts.

Englishmen, born to a constitutional system of government based so much on custom and tradition, should have realized that habit is a powerful factor to reckon with. The reports and accounts to English officials from the colonial customs officers in America repeatedly emphasized that the royal administration in the colonies was often circumvented and parliamentary acts received mere lip service. When the home government allowed this situation to continue through much of the eighteenth century, it tolerated the beginnings of dangerous precedents for the future. The longer it took to

---

[70] Smith, *Appeals*, pp. 88–95, 177–193.

correct the abuses, the harder it would be to insist on the
enforcement of the navigation acts. Nevertheless up to the
time of the attempted reforms of colonial administration in
1763 and 1764, salutary neglect remained the policy in England and nonenforcement of the navigation acts continued
to be a frequent occurrence in the American colonies.[71]

The English authorities during these long decades, therefore, had received many reports from the colonial customs
officers of illegal activities by American commercial interests.
The stories of false papers, intimidated government witnesses, biased juries, and secret landings of illegal goods did
not arouse the English officials to action. But during the
Seven Years' War the reports finally convinced the ministry
in England that the American merchants had been trading
with the enemy during the war, as well as during the previous war. This abuse was too great to ignore. The ministry
determined to find some effective means of control for American trade. Such direct trade with England's declared enemies
in time of war appeared not only illegal but traitorous. Anger
led to reform efforts which mere violations of law did not
arouse.[72] Governors and customs officials had for years appealed to England for help in enforcing the navigation acts.
The long, jagged coastline of America made enforcement
hard enough. Even after detection, however, the accused
smuggler might successfully challenge the jurisdiction of the
vice-admiralty courts in order to have his case tried in a
common law court with sympathetic juries and a tradition of
verdicts favorable to local merchants. Government officials
occasionally were sued at common law after losing a case
against a merchant in admiralty. The official could be forced
to pay damages for interfering with the merchant's trade.
Once aroused to act, the ministry found in these reported
abuses ample basis for reform.[73]

Finally the English government saw the need for a tighter,
more effective administration of the navigation acts. The
British people after the Seven Years' War found themselves
burdened with an enormous war debt. This debt, coupled
with disgust in Britain with the reported wartime conduct of
the colonists, prepared the way for reform of the colonial

---

[71] Barrow, *Trade and Empire*, pp. 62–63, 79–95, 104, 116.
[72] *Ibid.*, p. 160.
[73] Ubbelohde, *Vice-Admiralty Courts*, pp. 23–37.

administration. The accession of George III in 1760 brought about fundamental changes in the political establishment in England; between 1762 and 1765 an equilibrium between the Crown and Parliament was achieved. It lasted just long enough to carry out the fateful decision to reform the administration of the colonies.[74]

The first of the efforts to reform the colonial customs administration, the Navy Act of 1763, did not modify the vice-admiralty courts.[75] It did give the Americans an omen of things to come, however, for it implied an intent in London to tighten the reins. The Act, extending to the colonies the Hovering Act of 1718, gave customs officials authority to inspect and seize vessels under fifty tons hovering off the coast without adequate explanation. The Navy Act also provided that naval officers of the men-of-war in American waters could seize and prosecute violators of the acts of trade and divide with the whole crew a share of the profits from the condemnation of the seized vessels and cargoes. As in previous acts, violations were to be tried in any court of admiralty or in any court of record in the colony near the place of the offense. The forty-four naval vessels stationed in American waters, now an extended arm of the customs service, angered merchants by harassing many ships entering or departing, with little discernment of the requirements of the laws they were supposed to be enforcing.[76]

The Revenue or Sugar Act of 1764 started the reform of the vice-admiralty courts, but, of course, the reforms were not directly aimed at the court's instance or prize jurisdiction. This Act sought to improve the revenue of Great Britain to pay for the defense of the colonies.[77] By reducing the duty on non-British molasses from six to three pence a gallon, the English authorities thought they could make smuggling unprofitable and increase the total revenue from the duty. The Act also sought to increase the Crown's income from the duty on foreign sugar, coffee, indigo, wine, textiles, and rum. To

---

[74] Barrow, *Trade and Empire*, pp. 173–174.

[75] 3 Geo. III, c. 22. *See also,* 5 Geo. I, c. 11. The legal ramifications of the Hovering Act, in the context of a significant, well litigated American case, are studied in detail in Herbert A. Johnson and David Syrett, "Some Nice Sharp Quillets of the Customs Law: The *New York* Affair, 1763–1767," *William and Mary Quart.*, 3d ser., 25 (July, 1968): pp. 432–451.

[76] Ubbelohde, *Vice-Admiralty Courts*, pp. 37–40.

[77] 4 Geo. III, c. 15.

strengthen the hand of the customs officials, the Act required the posting of various bonds and the carrying of certain papers by merchants. A severe penalty was imposed for false or altered ship papers and for failure to pay the required duties. In Great Britain, the penalties and forfeitures were to be sued for in the common law courts, but in the American colonies suit could be brought in the common law courts or in the vice-admiralty court where the offense was committed or in a new vice-admiralty court to be established with jurisdiction over all America. Any merchant opposing the condemnation of his seized goods had to provide good security for costs in case he lost his suit and had to bear the burden of proving that he had violated no law in importing or exporting these goods. In order to immunize the customs officials from subsequent damage suits at common law for illegal seizure, the judge who heard the original suit for violations of the acts of trade could certify that there had been probable cause for the seizure. Once the customs officer was shielded with this certificate, even if the owner won the suit for restoration of his goods, the owner could not get costs in that case nor damages for illegal seizure from the official in any later action. Halifax, a city far removed from any American city, was selected as the site of the new vice-admiralty court to have concurrent jurisdiction over all suits for revenue and navigation act violations.[78] In granting vice-admiralty courts jurisdiction over revenue cases, this Act set a precedent.

Americans strongly objected to the jurisdictional provisions of the Sugar Act. Merchants accused of violations faced losing their property merely because they could not defend it in the new court in Halifax; the judge of this Halifax court was to be paid out of the proceeds from the property he condemned which seemed to some to be an inducement for him to condemn the seizures brought before him. The authority of the judges to certify probable cause of seizure destroyed the merchants' common law right to be indemnified for false arrest, and the extension of admiralty jurisdiction deprived Americans of the right to trial by jury which they would have enjoyed had suits for acts of trade or revenue violations been brought in England.[79]

---

[78] Ubbelohde, *Vice-Admiralty Courts*, pp. 50–54.
[79] *Ibid.*, pp. 60–63.

Undeterred by the colonists' objections to the Sugar Act, the ministry in England the next year drafted the Stamp Act and guided it through Parliament.[80] This further attempt to tax Americans imposed a stamp duty on legal papers of every description, pleadings, bonds, licenses, deeds, wills, leases, contracts, as well as on dice, playing cards, newspapers, and almanacs. Unstamped legal papers were inadmissible in court. Severe penalties, even death for forging, altering, or counterfeiting stamps, were imposed for violating the Act. Prosecutions for violation of this revenue act could be brought in any common law court or vice-admiralty court, where the offense had been committed, or in the vice-admiralty court at Halifax, at the election of the party bringing the suit. The Halifax court, besides this concurrent original jurisdiction, was now given appellate jurisdiction over the American vice-admiralty courts in all cases brought under the various acts of trade or revenue, a new threat, in the eyes of Americans, to their constitutional rights.

Americans responded to the Stamp Act, not only with angry pamphlets, heated denunciations, and carefully drafted resolutions, but with riots, threats, and intimidation. Mobs compelled various British officials in America to resign or to decline to enforce the Act. Because British authority had been unable to force compliance, the Stamp Act became a dead letter; commercial business eventually was carried on as usual without the required stamps, while courts acted without the stamps or ceased to function until news of the repeal of the Act reached America. Government in many American cities was effectively in the hands of the Sons of Liberty who had led the opposition to the Stamp Act.[81]

A tactical retreat was called for in England. Parliament, observing that "the continuance of the [Stamp Act] would be attended with many inconveniences, and may be productive of consequences greatly detrimental to the commercial interests," repealed the Act.[82] But at the same time Parliament took note of the various American assemblies which had recently claimed for themselves "the sole and exclusive right of imposing duties and taxes." Parliament, therefore, to re-

---

[80] 5 Geo. III, c. 12.
[81] Edmund S. Morgan and Helen M. Morgan, *The Stamp Act Crisis* (rev. ed., New York, 1963), pp. 99–262.
[82] 6 Geo. III, c. 11.

move all doubts, declared "That the said colonies and plantations in America have been, are, and of right ought to be,
subordinate unto, and dependent upon the imperial crown
and parliament of Great Britain."[83]

With Charles Townshend at the head of the ministry,
Parliament passed three acts in 1766 and 1767 to achieve
effective control of the trade in America and to assure
sufficient revenue to pay for the salaries of British officials
there. It authorized the appointment of a Board of Commissioners of the Customs for America, to sit in America with
full power over the colonial revenue system.[84] It imposed a
schedule of import duties on glass, lead, paper, tea, and
paint.[85] Parliament thought the colonists would accede to
these duties since they clearly were not the internal taxes
against which the Americans had protested in the Stamp Act.
Since the colonists had objected to the remote vice-admiralty
court in Halifax, with its concurrent and appellate jurisdiction, Townshend obtained parliamentary approval for a system of four appellate vice-admiralty courts. The four appellate courts received concurrent original jurisdiction and appellate jurisdiction over the vice-admiralty courts within their
districts. The Boston court had jurisdiction over New Hampshire, Massachusetts, Rhode Island, and Connecticut; the
Philadelphia court over New York, New Jersey, Pennsylvania, Delaware, Maryland, and Virginia; the Charleston
court over North and South Carolina, Georgia, and the two
Floridas; and the Halifax court over Quebec, Newfoundland, and Nova Scotia. Appeals determined by these four
new courts could be further appealed either to the king in
council or to the High Court of Admiralty in England.[86]

Throughout these years of attempted colonial reforms,
Americans, led by the merchants and lawyers, protested
against the use of admiralty courts to try violations of the acts
of trade nearly as much as they proclaimed what they viewed
as a basic constitutional principle: no taxation without representation. Vice-admiralty courts had always borne a burden of distrust and unpopularity. They employed foreign
civil law procedures, not trial with common law juries; they

---

[83] 6 Geo. III, c. 12.
[84] 7 Geo. III, c. 41.
[85] 7 Geo. III, c. 46.
[86] 8 Geo. III, c. 22; Ubbelohde, *Vice-Admiralty Courts*, pp. 129–133.

enforced the unpopular acts of trade which in England would be enforced by common law courts. Owing to a long-standing dispute, some questioned whether vice-admiralty courts were courts of record. With the passage of the Sugar Act, the Stamp Act, and the other administrative reform acts of the 1760's, Americans vigorously protested the expanded use of vice-admiralty courts. They were to be tried by one judge alone, deprived of the benefit of juries, faced with the possibility of a trial or appeal in remote Halifax, forced to bear the burden of proving their innocence, and subjected to admiralty procedures in cases which in England would be heard in common law courts.[87] Of course, these complaints of merchants and politicians touched only the area of expanded jurisdiction of the vice-admiralty courts, the cases tried for violations of the navigation and revenue acts. Prize cases and instance cases were not tried before a jury in England. But these complaints against vice-admiralty courts so colored the thinking of Americans in the 1760's and 1770's that they would soon import a strange and virtually unheard-of procedure into their own prize courts. After 1775 they grafted jury trials upon traditional prize procedures when they established courts to hear cases of capture during the Revolution.

The outraged cries of American commercial interests against the new parliamentary acts today sound exaggerated if not paranoid. But to understand them properly it is necessary to try to recapture the context, the general mental outlook or frame of reference of the men who uttered them. In the first place there had been a long policy of neglect. The forms of commercial behavior, which in 1763 or 1764 could suddenly be the cause of a costly prosecution by customs officials, had for long years been an accepted practice by merchants and often winked at by earlier officials. But perhaps more important, the rhetoric of the leaders of the revolutionary movement should not be written off as mere inflated propaganda. When they spoke with such vehemence

---

[87] Ubbelohde, *Vice-Admiralty Courts*, pp. 38–88, 179–201; David S. Lovejoy, "Rights Imply Equality: The Case Against Admiralty Jurisdiction in America, 1769–1776," *William and Mary Quart.* 3d ser., **16** (October, 1959): pp. 460–482. On the constitutional dimension of the opposition to expanded vice-admiralty court jurisdiction, see Julius Goebel, Jr., *History of the Supreme Court of the United States*, Vol. I, *Antecedents and Beginnings to 1801* (New York, 1971), pp. 83–95.

of the outrage of being deprived of the right of trial by jury
or of being forced to assume the burden of proving their
innocence for violations of the navigation acts, their words fit
into the larger view of what they believed was happening in
England and in America as a result of the new reform acts.
Ultimately, because of their long and thorough reading of
the various opposition Whig writers from seventeenth- and
eighteenth-century England, Americans saw the attempts to
enforce the navigation acts and to collect revenue from the
colonists as part of a deliberate design, a conspiracy of the
English ministers and their underlings to overthrow the
British constitution and to restrict traditional British liberties. These British writers, especially the early eighteenth-
century coffeehouse radicals and opposition politicians,
helped create in their avid American readers a vision of the
political world. Man was considered lustful by nature and
totally untrustworthy when in power; free government was
threatened from all sides, but especially by ministers in office
who sought only to aggrandize their power by the corrupt
use of their influence; corruption in government by the
manipulation and bribery of members of Parliament was
threatening to destroy liberty in England.[88]

This attitude toward government, therefore, inspired by
long and careful reading of the radical Whig writers, stirred
a vehement response in American leaders to the British
attempts to reform the customs service and tax the colonists.
Daniel Dulany, for instance, declared in a widely read pamphlet that the Stamp Act, with its assumed power to tax and
to substitute an "arbitrary Civil Law Court, in the Place of . . .
the Common-Law-Trial by Jury" left Americans without
"even the Shadow of a Privilege." The sacred right of trial by
jury, insisted John Dickinson, had been violated "by the
erection of arbitrary and unconstitutional jurisdictions." The
Constitutional Courant, a radical paper, likened admiralty
courts to the feared and hated "high commission and star
chamber courts" and warned Americans that, since Parliament by the Stamp Act gave these courts "jurisdiction over
matters that have no relation to navigation or sea affairs, they

---

[88] Bernard Bailyn, *The Ideological Origins of the American Revolution* (Cambridge,
Mass., 1967), pp. 33–159, and *The Origins of American Politics* (New York, 1968), pp.
10–58; Gordon S. Wood, *The Creation of the American Republic, 1776–1787* (Chapel
Hill, 1969), pp. 3–45.

may, with equal propriety, have jurisdiction in cases of life and death. This is a real representation of the slavish state we are reduced to by the Stamp Act, if we ever suffer it to take place among us." James Otis declared that admiralty courts "savour more of modern Rome and the Inquisition, than of the common law of England and the constitution of Great-Britain."[89]

In the years leading up to the American Revolution these issues remained calm, or simmered, or boiled, depending much on the effectiveness of customs enforcement. After the Boston Tea Party and the closing of the Port of Boston, open warfare with the mother country was only around the corner. When the American delegates met in 1774 to declare their grievances, they had not forgotten the extension of the "jurisdiction of courts of Admiralty, not only for collecting the said duties, but for the trial of causes merely arising within the body of a county." They listed among their rights as Englishmen: "That the respective colonies are entitled to the common law of England, and more especially to the great and inestimable privilege of being tried by their peers of the vicinage, according to the course of that law." They enumerated several acts which they considered infringements of their rights, including those which "extend the powers of the admiralty courts beyond their ancient limits, deprive the American subject of trial by jury, authorize the judges' certificate to indemnify the prosecutor from damages that he might otherwise be liable to."[90] In July, 1775, the Continental Congress declared the causes of taking up arms, among which were "statutes . . . passed for extending the jurisdiction of courts of Admiralty, and Vice-Admiralty beyond their ancient limits; for depriving us of the accustomed and inestimable privilege of trial by jury, in cases affecting both life and property."[91]

The vice-admiralty courts at the time of the Revolution, therefore, had taken on in the minds of Americans much of the coloring of real or imagined British oppression. The new parliamentary acts expanding admiralty jurisdiction ap-

---

[89] All quoted in Lovejoy, "Rights Imply Equality," *William and Mary Quart.*, 3d ser., **16**: pp. 446–467.

[90] Worthington C. Ford, ed., *Journals of the Continental Congress* (34 v., Washington, 1904–1937) **1**: pp. 64, 69, 71.

[91] *Ibid.* **2**: p. 145.

peared as one more proof of a vast conspiracy to deprive Americans of their treasured rights and liberty.

It is, of course, true that this heated controversy over expanded vice-admiralty jurisdiction and trial without a jury did not directly affect the procedures for trial of prize causes. Juries were basically unheard of in prize courts in England or its colonies. Unheard of, that is, until the Americans in 1775 and 1776 set up their own prize courts for trial of British ships and cargoes captured by American vessels.

PART ONE
Historical Development

PART ONE, in general, focuses on an historical survey of the first federal court from its beginnings in 1775 till it completed its work in 1787. Some analysis of the work of the court must be included, but the main function of these first three chapters is to view the growth of this judicial body from the outside, as a creation of the Continental Congress.

Part Two, on the other hand, looks primarily to the inner workings of this appellate court, the procedures it followed, the law it applied, and the jurisdiction it exercised. Here again the distinction between historical development and legal analysis breaks down. A broader background into historical precedents for this court will be necessary in order to analyze the work of the court. The central chapters of Part Two, therefore, focus on the procedure, substantive law, and jurisdiction of this court. The historical context of these topical categories, however, cannot be severed from the analysis of how the court functioned.

Chapter I narrates how the Continental Congress in November, 1775, at the urging of General George Washington, gave birth to the first federal court. Washington had entreated Congress to provide some mode of adjudicating the captures of vessels and cargoes by the few armed ships he had sent out from Massachusetts to seize British property. Congress merely recommended that the newly created states should each establish some courts to try the legality of the prizes taken by Washington's naval vessels or by the privateers it would commission. The states, each in its own way, followed the recommendation of Congress and set up prize courts, but with diverse restrictions on the right of appeal to Congress. Some disregarded the congressional resolve that all appeals in prize cases should be to the persons Congress would appoint for that purpose.

The second chapter traces the origins of the first federal court, an appellate institution created by Congress to hear all prize appeals from the state courts. It began as a series of legislative committees individually authorized by Congress to hear a particular prize appeal. Soon Congress appointed a standing committee, with legally trained personnel, to serve as an appellate court to determine appeals in cases of capture. Congress itself, however, continued to be directly involved in questions of captures at sea, for it had to formulate the legal norms for these captures and to prepare commissions and instructions to control privateers. Although for a time continuing as a committee made up of members of Congress, the Committee on Appeals soon shed its legislative character and took on the form and procedures of a court.

The third chapter tells the story of the capture and trial of the sloop *Active*. When this case was reviewed and the trial court reversed by the Committee on Appeals, a constitutional crisis developed, for Pennsylvania refused to execute the decree of the congressional Committee. As a result of this confrontation between Congress and Pennsylvania, Congress recognized the inadequacy of the Committee on Appeals and decided to establish the Court of Appeals in Cases of Capture, with judges who were not members of Congress. Judges with high professional qualifications were appointed and they continued to review state prize decrees from 1780 till the work of the Court of Appeals was completed in 1787. Congress, meanwhile, had to devote some of its time to a revision of its prize laws and to various other questions raised by the captures at sea by American vessels. It also tried to legislate a firmer basis for its appellate prize court.

I. The Birth of Prize Jurisdiction

IN THE FALL OF 1773 Lord North's ministry undertook to assist the financially ailing East India Company. The company was permitted to ship its tea directly to America without paying the ordinary duties in England. American tea drinkers, the British authorities reasoned, would be able to pay less for their tea while the company would be financially strengthened. Even smugglers could not supply the Americans with Dutch tea at a lower price. It certainly must have seemed in England to be the very model of a rational measure to inveigle the colonists to pay a tax and save money in the process. In America, however, city after city refused to accept the cargoes of this monopoly-privileged tea and Boston residents expressed their opposition in a gesture of anger and determination which precipitated the final separation of the colonies from the mother country. On December 16 a band of men disguised as Indians boarded the tea vessels and dumped the cargo into Boston harbor.

This destruction of British private property along with the unspoken challenge to British authority could not be ignored. The reaction of the British ministry and Parliament to the Boston Tea Party was quick and, they thought, decisive. Determined to temporize no longer, Parliament early in 1774 passed the intolerable acts which were intended to coerce recalcitrant New England by closing the port of Boston, dominating the local government in Massachusetts, and quartering troops in the city. The spirit of resistance in Boston and other cities was only stiffened. The Massachusetts assembly, encouraged by expressions of sympathy and outrage, invited all the colonies to send delegates to a general American congress to meet in Philadelphia.

When the delegates finally assembled early in September at Carpenter's Hall in Philadelphia, it was clear that they were divided into two main groups, those insisting on efforts at reconciliation with Britain and those determined to resist the forceful assertion of British authority over the colonies.

The latter group soon demonstrated that it controlled the Congress, and after weeks of discussion the delegates agreed to cut off all importation of goods from Britain by December, 1774, and to cease exporting colonial commodities to the British Isles and the West Indies after September 10, 1775. These resolutions to stop all commercial dealings with Britain were to be enforced by the Continental Association, a solemn covenant of the colonies to pursue a rigid policy of no commercial intercourse. The machinery to make this agreement effective was set up in the committees which Congress had instructed the colonies to establish in every town to insure compliance. The First Continental Congress also approved a statement of fundamental rights derived from the laws of nature, the principles of the English constitution as well as from the colonial charters. Among the rights insisted on were the rights to a free and exclusive power of legislation in their own colonial assemblies, the right to trial by jury, the right of assembly and petition, and the right to be free of a standing army in time of peace. Not then willing or able to declare full independence, however, the delegates conceded the right of the British Parliament to regulate external commerce. With this much work accomplished and with a new sense of cohesion among themselves, the delegates departed from Philadelphia before the end of October. Before adjourning they decided that the colonies should select representatives to a second congress to meet the following May unless the grievances that had brought them together should be redressed by that time.[1]

Before the delegates were scheduled to reassemble, however, hostilities broke out in the skirmishes at Lexington and Concord. The king and Parliament made the fateful decision to stop all compromise and use armed force to ensure compliance with parliamentary measures. The most pressing order of business for the Second Continental Congress when the representatives reached Philadelphia was to assure adequate military preparedness. Though many in Congress still sought a compromise solution to the increasingly tense situation, it prepared at the same time for armed resistance by naming George Washington as Commander in Chief and

---

[1] Edmund C. Burnett, *The Continental Congress* (New York, 1941), pp. 33–59; Merrill Jensen, *The Articles of Confederation* (Madison, 1940), pp. 54–73.

promising reinforcements for the thin line of undisciplined troops outside Boston. In July, 1775, Congress debated and passed a series of resolutions urging the colonies to put their militias into a state of readiness. It also resolved: "That each colony, at their own expense, make such provision by armed vessels or otherwise . . . for the protection of their harbours and navigation on their sea coasts, against all unlawful invasions, attacks, and depredations, from [British] cutters and ships of war."[2]

Responding to this congressional recommendation and to their own sense of need, Massachusetts, Rhode Island, Connecticut, Pennsylvania, and South Carolina in September and October, 1775, started taking steps toward building their own naval forces.[3] Washington also saw the wisdom of arming vessels manned with militiamen to capture British ships and their much-needed military cargoes. By September he had several armed vessels at sea.[4] Congress also realized the need to seize supplies for its troops and to cut off any further support sent to the British army. On October 5 it informed Washington that two ships loaded with arms, powder, and other stores were sailing for Quebec without convoy. Urging Washington to obtain armed vessels from Massachusetts to intercept this shipment, it authorized him to encourage and instruct other crews to capture British transports with cargoes of ammunition, clothing, or other military supplies.[5] During October and November Congress took the first steps toward fitting out armed vessels and establishing a tiny navy for the defense of all the colonies.[6]

Early in the conflict Congress had to face the complex questions that can result from building a navy and capturing British ships. It considered what should be done with the crew and passengers of a British transport who were captured when the ship ran aground. It permitted two ships suspected of trading with the British to proceed on their

[2] Ford, *JCC* **2**: p. 189.
[3] William B. Clark, *et al.*, *Naval Documents of the American Revolution* (7 v., Washington, 1964–   ) **1**: pp. 1255–1259; **2**: pp. 26, 48, 97, 99, 117, 122, 126, 154, 180, 189, 203, 228, 236, 270, 272, 285, 299, 330, 378, 382, 394, 425, 480–483, 529, 654, 662, 962.
[4] William B. Clark, *George Washington's Navy* (Baton Rouge, 1960), pp. 3–64.
[5] Ford, *JCC* **3**: pp. 277–278; John Hancock to Nicholas Cooke, 5 October, 1775, Clark, *NDAR* **2**: p. 312.
[6] Ford, *JCC* **3**: pp. 293–294, 311–312, 316; Clark, *NDAR* **2**: pp. 647–652.

voyage but tried to make sure that the cargoes would not fall into British hands.[7] Clearly Congress had begun to appreciate the need for some method of settling maritime disputes.

Meanwhile Washington also was learning that disputes over captured ships can involve questions difficult for a general to settle. He urged Congress immediately to set up some proper courts "for the decision of Property and the legallity [sic] of Seizures: otherwise I may be involved in inextricable difficulties."[8] A few days later he wrote again, enclosing a copy of an act of the Massachusetts legislature that provided for trial of ships captured by the vessels of that state. He noted that the armed ships fitted out at the expense of Congress did not come under the law. Therefore he urged Congress to find some summary mode of proceeding in cases of captures by congressional armed ships.

> Should not a Court be established by Authority of Congress, to take cognizance of the Prizes made by the Continental Vessels? Whatever the mode is which they are pleased to adopt, there is an absolute necessity of its being speedily determined on, for I cannot spare Time from Military Affairs, to give proper attention to these matters.[9]

Congress did act late in November, passing a series of resolves which laid the foundation for all prize appeals. But Washington still insisted on the need for some court which could expeditiously hear and settle prize disputes involving congressional armed ships and get his navy back on the seas, capturing more ships.[10] Congress soon provided for a

---

[7] Ford, *JCC* **3**: pp. 305, 309, 354; New Hampshire Delegates to the Committee of Safety, 26 October, 1775, and Josiah Bartlett to New Hampshire Committee of Safety, 12 November, 1775, Edmund C. Burnett, ed., *Letters of Members of the Continental Congress* (8 v., Washington, 1921–1936) **1**: pp. 241, 255.

[8] Washington to the President of Congress, 8 November, 1775, John C. Fitzpatrick, ed., *The Writings of George Washington from the Original Manuscript Sources, 1745–1799* (39 v., Washington, 1931–1944) **4**: p. 73. See also Washington to John Augustine Washington, 13 October, 1775; Washington to Richard Henry Lee, 8 November, 1775, and Washington to Joseph Reed, 20 November, 1775, *ibid.*, pp. 25–28, 75, 103–107.

[9] Washington to the President of Congress, 11 November, 1775, *ibid.*, pp. 81–82.

[10] Washington to President of Congress, 4 December, 1775, 14 December, 1775, 24 March, 1776, 25 April, 1776, *ibid.*, pp. 142, 160, 425, 515–518; Washington to Richard Henry Lee, 26 December, 1775; Washington to Joseph Reed, 10 February, 1776; and Washington to Major General Artemas Ward, 4 April, 1776 and 18 April 1776, *ibid.*, pp. 186–187, 318–323, 461, 490.

method of trial for captures made by congressional naval vessels by using state maritime courts for trial of these prizes. But the problem of delay in adjudicating prize cases was never adequately solved; the crews had to learn to wait for their shares in the captures.

The resolves of Congress of November 25, 1775, mark the origin of Congress's appellate jurisdiction in prize cases. A committee had been appointed to study the suggestions made by General Washington in his letter of the eighth of November. Congress placed delegates of wide-ranging ability, mostly lawyers, on this committee: George Wythe, Edward Rutledge, John Adams, William Livingston, Benjamin Franklin, James Wilson, and Thomas Johnson.[11] Its report to Congress on the twenty-fifth pointed out that British ships had illegally seized and without charge or trial had rifled American ships that had cleared according to the regulations of Parliament. Furthermore the British navy had orders in the king's name to proceed against seaport towns to destroy fortifications and disable ships fitting out. Under these orders the navy "have already burned and destroyed the flourishing and populous town of Falmouth [now Portland]." Thinking of the ancient right of reprisal, the committee pointed to the determination of the Americans to prevent such destruction and to seek some reparation by fitting out armed vessels. In executing these plans, however, some innocent parties could suffer. Therefore, there must be laws to regulate captures and tribunals competent to determine the legality of prizes taken. Eight resolutions followed authorizing the capture of certain types of ships and cargoes, controlling privateers, recommending that the colonies establish prize courts, providing for appeal from these courts to Congress, and specifying the shares of the prizes to be awarded to the various parties involved in the capture.

The first two resolves authorized the capture and condemnation of all ships of war, frigates, sloops, cutters, and armed vessels which were employed in war against the United Colonies, and of cargoes of military supplies for the British army carried in any transport vessels. The transports themselves, however, were liable to forfeiture only if they belonged to Americans. (By this clause Congress early indi-

---

[11] Ford, *JCC* 3: pp. 357–358.

cated its special animosity for the loyalists. Within several weeks Congress modified this second resolve making all transport vessels carrying troops or military cargo liable to seizure and condemnation.) Following the tradition of the law of capture at sea, the third resolution forbade commanders of vessels from making prize of any ship or cargo until they had obtained a commission from Congress.

In the fourth and fifth provisions, Congress recommended that the colonial assemblies establish courts to decide cases of capture. All trials should be by jury, an unheard of innovation for prize courts, obviously inspired by the decade of complaints against the lack of jury trials in vice-admiralty courts. The court of the colony within which a ship was captured had jurisdiction to try the capture. The courts in any colony, to suit the captor's convenience, could hear cases of capture made at sea. Of course, the captor could not move his prize from one competent jurisdiction to another.

The sixth resolution established the first federal appellate jurisdiction. Congress provided: "That in all cases an appeal shall be allowed to the Congress, or such person or persons as they shall appoint for the trial of appeals." Time limits for appeals to Congress were specified. Appeals must be requested of the lower court within five days after the definitive decree and must be lodged with the secretary of Congress within forty days. Furthermore, the party appealing must give security to prosecute the appeal to effect.

The seventh resolve determined the shares of prizes to go to various parties concerned in the capture. Captures by privateers would be for the use of the owners of the vessel. The owners could make their own arrangements for dividing the prizes with their masters and crews. If the vessel making the capture was fitted out at the expense of one of the colonies, one-third would be for the use of the captors and two-thirds for the use of the colony. (Congress soon dropped this provision and allowed the colonies to decide for themselves the proportion of the prize to be awarded to the master and crews of vessels which the various colonies paid to equip.) If the ship was prepared at the expense of Congress, then a third would go to the captors and the remainder to the use of the United Colonies. But in place of the customary gun money and head money, as an extra incentive to crews of colonial or congressional naval vessels to attack armed ships, the captors of British ships of war would receive one-half its value. In all cases costs of condemnation would be deducted before distribution of the prize money.

The final resolution looked to the recent past and stated that all captures previously made by Congress's naval vessels were justifiable. Washington's determination of these cases and his distribution of the captors' shares were confirmed.[12]

There is little resemblance between this brief, pragmatic series of resolutions of Congress and the British prize acts of the eighteenth century with which many Americans were familiar from their privateering experience or prize practice during the Seven Years' War. The British acts described in elaborate detail the full process of obtaining commissions, giving security, trying cases of capture in the admiralty courts, and executing the sentence of the court. Whereas the British acts allowed the naval vessels to keep the entire proceeds from sale of any lawful prize, the congressional resolutions provided that naval vessels fitted out at the charge of a colony or of Congress would receive only one-third of the value of the prizes taken, the remaining two-thirds going to the colony or to Congress. (Congress eventually modified this provision to make naval service more attractive.) Both the British acts and the congressional resolutions allowed privateers to retain the full proceeds from the sale of legal

---

[12] *Ibid.*, pp. 371–375. The precise wording of the crucially important fourth, fifth, and sixth resolutions read as follows:

"4. That it be and is hereby recommended to the several legislatures in the United Colonies, as soon as possible, to erect courts of Justice, or give jurisdiction to the courts now in being for the purpose of determining concerning the captures to be made as aforesaid, and to provide that all trials in such case be had by a jury under such qualifications, as to the respective legislatures shall seem expedient.

5. That all prosecutions shall be commenced in the court of that colony in which the captures shall be made but if no such court be at that time erected in the said colony, or if the capture be made on open sea, then the prosecution shall be in the court of such colony as the captor may find most convenient, provided that nothing contained in this resolution shall be construed so as to enable the captor to remove his prize from any colony competent to determine concerning the seizure, after he shall have carried the vessel so seized within any harbour of the same.

6. That in all cases an appeal shall be allowed to the Congress, or such person or persons as they shall appoint for the trial of appeals, provided the appeal be demanded within five days after definitive sentence, and such appeal be lodged with the secretary of Congress within forty days afterwards, and provided the party appealing shall give security to prosecute the said appeal to effect, and in case of the death of the secretary during the recess of Congress, then the said appeal to be lodged in Congress within 20 days after the meeting thereof."

See also the modification of the second resolve, 19 December, 1775, *ibid.*, p. 437.

prizes, to be divided according to whatever agreement the owners, masters, and crews settled on. Both likewise insisted that privateering commissions must be obtained from the proper governmental authority. It is significant that as early as November, 1775, Congress reserved to itself the exclusive power to issue commissions for privateers. (The various colonies, as we shall see, did not always feel themselves constrained by what Congress viewed as its exclusive power.) The British prize acts required privateers to give security upon receiving their commission to help insure against illegal captures. Though Congress soon would make such provision, it was not included in the November 25 resolutions. Whereas the British acts went into great detail setting forth the judicial procedures for trial of prizes, the resolves of Congress left these details to the colonies which Congress had urged to establish prize courts. Finally both the British prize acts and the resolves of Congress allowed appeals from the trial court if requested within a specified time after the sentence (fourteen days for the British act and five days for the congressional resolves). Both required that security be given by the party taking an appeal to assure that he prosecuted his appeal to effect.[13]

Congress, therefore, amidst its preoccupation with many pressing and seemingly insoluble problems, at least took a long stride toward guaranteeing adequate judicial determination of the captures which were starting to occur. The wisdom of insisting on the exclusive right to issue commissions (and by implication to regulate privateering), and to hear and determine finally all appeals in cases of capture, would become much clearer as the years of the war passed. This insistence also tells us something of the attitude of many delegates to Congress as early as November, 1775, toward the need for final control by a central authority of questions touching the rights of other nations.

Though in November, 1775, Congress provided by these resolutions for appeals in all prize cases, the first appeal was not requested till July 4, 1776. In the meantime Congress continued to deal with many maritime affairs, including disputes over captured vessels. For example, the captured transport *Nancy* had a cargo of molasses belonging to Chris-

---

[13] 29 Geo. II, c. 34.

topher Leffingwell. He requested Congress to restore his share of the cargo, but Congress referred the case to the court for captures set up in Connecticut.[14] The ship *Blue Mountain Valley* was captured with supplies aboard for the British troops. But the captain and mates claimed part of the cargo as their private ventures. Since New Jersey had appointed no admiralty judge, Congress assumed the role of a court and restored the property to the claimants who were permitted to return to England. Michael Kearney claimed that his boat had been confiscated to make the capture of the *Blue Mountain Valley* and was, in the process, taken by the British. Congress compensated him for the loss.[15]

In April, 1776, an even clearer prize dispute came before Congress. James M'Knight, prize master on the *Sally*, ran it ashore in a storm. (A prize master was the commander placed on board the captured vessel by the captors.) On request from M'Knight Congress asked the committee of inspection of Burlington County, New Jersey, where it ran aground, to sell the *Sally* and to pay one-half the proceeds to M'Knight and retain the other half for the original owners.[16] Congress then received a petition from Peter Simon and Israel Ambrose, Americans, claiming the *Sally* as their property. They said they had been sailing from the West Indies to North Carolina with a valuable cargo when they were taken by a British ship. For want of a more reliable prize master the British put M'Knight on board with orders to take the *Sally* to Cape Fear. M'Knight had been mate on a ship captured the previous day by the British. A gale drove him northward and ran the *Sally* aground. Simon and Ambrose claimed that M'Knight ran it ashore in order to convert it to his own use. Apparently M'Knight had broken open everything of value on the ship, misrepresented the circumstances of the capture to Congress, and falsified the value of the cargo. He had obtained Congress's permission to dispose of the sloop and its cargo. Simon and Ambrose claimed a loss of £3,000.[17] Congress, therefore, set aside its earlier order and decreed

---

[14] Ford, *JCC* **3**: pp. 420, 424; **4**: p. 174; Papers of the Continental Congress (National Archives), Item 78, X, 43.

[15] Ford, *JCC* **4**: pp. 100, 106, 174–175, 227, 266; Burnett, *Letters*, **1**: pp. 336, 357, 382; Journal of New Jersey Provincial Congress, 29 February, 1776, Clark, *NDAR* **4**: pp. 119–120.

[16] Ford, *JCC* **4**: p. 256.

[17] Petition dated 1 May, 1776, PCC, Item 42, VII, 3.

that M'Knight should restore to the owners the money taken from the *Sally* and also the money he received for the sale of the wreck, its tackle and furniture, and of the effects from the sloop.[18]

These three cases show that Congress as early as 1776 was acting in some ways as a judiciary. The final decision of Congress in the case of the *Sally*, for instance, reads more like a judicial decree than an act of a legislature. It is not surprising that legislative and judicial functions were at times blended and blurred together by Congress. Throughout the eighteenth century the American colonial assemblies had on occasion exercised judicial responsibilities.[19] The line dividing the judiciary and the legislature had never been clearly defined in England or in the colonies. Even when Congress began to hear prize appeals a few months later, the line between legislative and judicial functions at first remained blurred.

In the months before the Declaration of Independence, Congress also spent considerable time and energy drawing up regulations for the capture of British ships. On November 28, 1775, just three days after establishing a right of appeals in prize cases, Congress agreed upon a set of rules to regulate the new navy. Along with detailed regulation of recruiting, seamen's life aboard ship, and modes of trial for crimes, the rules included provisions for the treatment of prize ships and for division of money from prizes captured by ships equipped at the expense of Congress.[20]

On December 5 Congress filled a noticeable gap in its resolutions of the twenty-fifth of November. With one eye on the British prize acts, Congress provided for cases of recapture of American ships from the British. The recaptors, whether privateers or naval vessels, would receive a certain percent of the value of the recaptured ship and cargo in lieu of salvage (identical to the percentages allowed to privateers for recaptures in the British prize acts): one-eighth if the ship had been in possession of the British for less than twenty-four hours; one-fifth if the British held it for more than twenty-four hours and less than forty-eight; one-third if more than forty-eight hours and less than ninety-six; one-

---

[18] Ford, *JCC* 4: pp. 374–375, 384.
[19] Wood, *American Republic*, pp. 154–155.
[20] Ford, *JCC* 3: pp. 378–387; see also pp. 395–402.

half if more than ninety-six hours. If a captured American ship had been legally condemned as prize in a British admiralty court, the recaptors had a right to the whole of it.[21] In the British prize acts, as applied in British courts, all British property recaptured, even after condemnation, was to be restored on payment of the proper amount of salvage by the original owners.[22]

In response to Washington's continued urging, Congress debated at some length, with appropriate quotations from the authorities on the law of nations, how to deal with ships taken by Congress's tiny navy. On December 20 it ordered that British vessels captured by congressional naval vessels and taken into Massachusetts should be proceeded against "by the rules of the law of Nations, and libelled in the courts of admiralty erected in said colony."[23] This solved Washington's immediate problem; he no longer had to decide upon the legality of captures made by the ships he had fitted out. This act also illustrates the reception of the law of nations by Congress. In subsequent years the law of nations would play a key role in decisions in the cases of appeals decided by the various committees and the Court of Appeals set up by Congress.[24]

On January 6, 1776 Congress determined how the shares of prizes awarded to naval vessels should be divided between the officers and men.[25] During February and March Congress debated proposals, first introduced by Samuel Chase, recommending that the colonies prepare privateers to cruise against all British property on the high seas.[26] Petitions started coming to Congress seeking permission to fit out privateers to seize all ships of Great Britain, Ireland and other British dominions. Congress was sharply divided over the issue, with some opposed to the measure altogether, others in favor of commissioning letters of reprisal only, but opposed to general privateering against all British shipping,

21 *Ibid.*, p. 407; see also 29 Geo. II, c. 34, § 24.

22 29 Geo. II, c. 34, § 24. See chapter VII below.

23 Ford, *JCC* 3: p. 439; Richard Smith, Diary, 14 December, 1775; and President of Congress to Washington, 22 December, 1775, Burnett, *Letters* 1: pp. 275, 285–286.

24 See chapter VII below.

25 Ford, *JCC* 4: pp. 36–37; Smith, Diary, 6 January, 1776; and Thomas Lynch to Washington, 16 January, 1776, Burnett, *Letters* 1: pp. 300, 314.

26 Smith, Diary, 13 February, 1776, Burnett, *Letters* 1: p. 348.

at least without a declaration of war. Reprisals, under certain circumstances, could be appropriate against British shipping even in time of peace, but privateering, according to the authorities on the law of nations, could only be lawful when properly commissioned by a belligerent government in wartime.[27]

The British government spurred Congress to a decision in favor of general privateering. An act of Parliament of December 22, 1775, had in effect removed the American colonies from the protection of the Crown, prohibited trade with them, established at least on paper a complete naval blockade of America, and authorized the capture and condemnation of American ships and cargoes.[28] Congress learned of this virtual declaration of war in the midst of its debate on the privateering statute. "By the late pirating act, the Colonies are entirely cast out of the kings [sic] protection, in an explicit manner. It behoves [sic] us therefore to take care of ourselves."[29] Once again the American fears and suspicions of a grand scheme to destroy their liberties were confirmed by this act expressing the position of the king and his ministers as well as Parliament.

Such were the thoughts among the delegates to Congress as they continued to debate various ways of defending themselves. Thomas Paine's Common Sense had just come off the press; the congressional delegates in Philadelphia must have been reading and discussing the vigorous arguments Paine used to demolish the deep-seated American respect for the Crown. Their link with the king was a delusion, Paine insisted. Restraint, caution, and awe were misplaced, for the king was as bad, if not worse, than his ministers. Some in Congress thought that any privateering statute should explicitly name the king the author of American miseries and make the property of all British subjects liable to seizure. The final proposals, however, directed ambiguously to Parliament and the "royal authority," were strong enough to suit most.[30] They carried Congress a long step closer to independence.

---

[27] Smith, Diary, 1 and 13 March, 1776, ibid., pp. 371, 386. For a discussion of reprisals and privateering, see introduction, above.

[28] 16 Geo. III, c. 5.

[29] Oliver Wolcott to Lyman, 16 March, 1776, Burnett, Letters 1: p. 397.

[30] Smith, Diary, 18 and 22 March, 1776; and Joseph Hewes to Samuel Johnston, 20 March, 1776, ibid., pp. 398, 401, 404.

The preamble recalled that petitions of the colonies for redress of grievances had been rejected and treated with scorn while the efforts of the colonists to defend themselves against hostile and enslaving acts were declared rebellion. An unjust war against the Americans was already in progress with the British army and navy "wasting, spoiling, and destroying the country, burning houses and defenceless towns." Furthermore, Parliament had recently declared the colonies to be in rebellion and prohibited all trade with Americans, declaring their property liable to capture on the high seas until the Americans would "accept pardons, and submit to despotic rule." Since these acts clearly indicated a scheme to deprive Americans of their liberty, they had a right by the law of nature and the English constitution to provide for their defense and security. They were justified in making reprisals and otherwise injuring British shipping according to the laws and usages of nations.

Congress therefore resolved:

> That the inhabitants of these colonies be permitted to fit out armed vessels to cruize on the enemies of these United Colonies. . . . That all ships and other vessels, their tackle, apparel, and furniture, and all goods, wares, and merchandizes, belonging to any inhabitant or inhabitants of Great Britain, taken on the high seas, or between high and low water mark, by any armed vessel, fitted out by any private person or persons, and to whom commissions shall be granted, and being libelled and prosecuted in any court erected for the trial of maritime affairs, in any of these colonies, shall be deemed and adjudged to be lawful prize.

All British ships and cargoes, therefore, could be seized by American privateers, but ships or cargoes belonging to subjects of British colonies or Ireland were not yet liable to capture. Congress further provided for paying the wages of the crews of prize ships, a humane practice of the customary law of nations. Ships bringing settlers or military supplies to America, however, would not be subject to capture. If a seizure was made by a congressional naval vessel one-third would be awarded to the officers and crew and the remainder to the use of the United Colonies. Altering its earlier provision, Congress declared that where the ship making the capture was fitted out at the expense of one of the colonies, the division would be according to whatever plan the assembly of that colony should agree to. Any ships belonging to British inhabitants or any other ship carrying supplies to the British army would be considered lawful prize even though the captors had no commission, if the property was captured near the shore of any of the colonies by the people of the colony or by detachments from the army. In this case the money from sale of the prize, after deducting costs of trial and condemnation, would be divided among all who had actually engaged in taking the prize. If a militia detachment made the capture, distribution of the prize would be in proportion to the pay of the officers and soldiers. Finally, Congress ordered these resolutions published.[31] Captures of property belonging to inhabitants of Great Britain, therefore, could be made by the naval vessels fitted out at the expense of Congress or of any individual colony, by privateers commissioned by Congress or by non-commissioned inhabitants or militias provided the capture was made near the shore of one of the colonies.

Since general privateering was to be legal, Congress had to produce commissions for the individuals who intended to fit out an armed vessel at their expense and also to draft instructions to try to control the conduct of the privateering commanders, as well as forms for bonds to provide sureties for the privateers. The committee appointed to prepare these various forms looked to the obvious source of examples to guide its work, the British commissions, and instructions for privateers. The commission, which borrowed many phrases from British privateering commissions, provided forms, signed by the president of Congress, with blanks to be filled in by the assemblies or committees of safety of the colonies giving information to identify a particular vessel, its owners and master, and the colony from which it sailed. The commissions authorized the named privateer

> to fit out and set forth . . . in warlike manner, and . . . by force
> of arms, to attack, seize and take the ships and other vessels
> belonging to the inhabitants of Great Britain . . . with their . . .
> ladings, on the high seas, or between high water and low water
> marks, and to bring the same to some convenient ports in the
> said colonies, in order that the courts which are or shall be

---

[31] Ford, *JCC* 4: pp. 229–232.

there appointed to hear and determine causes . . . may proceed, in due form, to condemn the said captures, if they be adjudged lawful prize.[32]

The instructions for privateers drawn up by Congress followed closely in order and phraseology the instructions which the British admiralty issued during the various eighteenth-century wars. The committee which prepared these instructions, besides studying carefully the British models, incorporated the provisions of the recent privateering resolutions of Congress. After describing the vessels liable to capture in terms of the congressional resolutions of March 23, the instructions listed arms, gunpowder, and ammunition as contraband in terms of the corresponding section of the British instructions. Congress, however, added provisions for the British army or navy to the contraband list. To ensure a fair trial of the legality of the capture, the congressional instructions, closely following the British model, insisted that all property taken be brought to some convenient American port for trial. The captors were ordered to bring with the prize several principal members of the crew of the captured vessel as well as all its papers. As in the British instructions, the captors were to take care not to damage or sell the cargo. Furthermore, the instructions threatened the captors with serious punishment for any cruelty to the crew of the prize. Skipping several provisions of the British instructions not relevant to the American situation, the congressional instructions concluded by ordering privateers to inform Congress of their captures and of any intelligence information of British troop or naval movements. As in the British instructions, one-third of the crew of privateers were to be landsmen. Privateers were forbidden to ransom any prisoners and were warned that any violations of these instructions would lead to forfeiture of their commission, liability to suit for breach of the condition of their bond, as well as personal liability of the commander for damages to any party resulting from violations. Congress also drafted a form for the bond for sureties which the commander of the privateer had to provide before he was granted a commis-

---

[32] 2 April, 1776, *ibid.*, pp. 247–248; compare with a British commission in Beawes, *Lex Mercatoria*, pp. 219–220. See also Letter of President of Congress to New Hampshire Assembly, 12 April, 1776, Burnett, *Letters* 1: p. 418.

sion. This bond, generally comparable to the bonds required of British privateers, was intended to help assure compliance with the instructions.[33] The delegates in Congress, therefore, so thoroughly imbued with British values and traditions, could not even plan naval warfare against Britain without looking to British forms and patterns to guide them.

At the beginning of April, 1776, Congress removed most restrictions on trading with the rest of the world, Great Britain and its dominions excepted. With this opening of the American ports to world trade came the corollary, that

all goods, wares, and merchandise, except such as are made prize of, which shall be imported directly or indirectly from Great Britain or Ireland, into any of these United Colonies, contrary to the regulations established by Congress, shall be forfeited and disposed of . . . and shall be liable to prosecution and condemnation in any court erected, or to be erected, for the determination of maritime affairs, in the colony where the seizure shall be made.[34]

This legalized the capture of all British goods imported into the colonies, regardless of whose ships carried them. Trial for violations of this importation restriction was to be in the admiralty courts set up by the colonies, just as under British rule the colonial vice-admiralty courts had jurisdiction over violations of the Acts of Trade and Navigation.

For six months before declaring independence, therefore, Congress had discussed and debated the pros and cons of warring against British shipping. While planning for a defensive war against Great Britain, Congress could not resist the second-nature instinct of consulting British laws and legal forms as models for the resolutions and forms it was preparing. At first Congress made only military supplies liable to capture but soon authorized attack on all British ships and their cargoes, and finally all British goods imported into the colonies were made liable to condemnation. The debates, sprinkled with apt quotes from Vattel and other authorities on the law of nations,[35] brought forth a series of resolutions regulating the capture and condemna-

---

[33] 3 April, 1776, Ford, *JCC* 4: pp. 251–254. Compare with British instructions in Beawes, *Lex Mercatoria*, pp. 221–223 and in Marsden, *Law of the Sea* 2: pp. 403–435; and a British bond in Beawes, *Lex Mercatoria*, pp. 223–224.

[34] Ford, *JCC* 4: pp. 257–259.

[35] Smith, Diary, 14 December, 1775, Burnett, *Letters* 1: p. 275.

tion of British ships. Congress also saw the need for some right of appeal beyond the confines of any of the colonies. It determined that appeals should be allowed in all prize cases to Congress or to the persons appointed by Congress to hear such appeals. As early as November 25, 1775, therefore, Congress, seeing the likelihood of international and inter-colonial disputes, realized the need for some central jurisdiction, some appellate structure to review the prize decisions of courts in the colonies. The years ahead would strongly support the wisdom of this early decision.

During the spring and fall of 1775 Congress received requests from several colonies seeking advice on organizing some form of government since the royal governments had disintegrated once fighting broke out. Congress at first suggested that Massachusetts resume its old colonial Charter of 1691 as the frame of government. By the end of 1775, however, Congress had advised New Hampshire, South Carolina, and Virginia to call a fully representative assembly to form whatever government it thought necessary for the duration of the struggle between Great Britain and the colonies. By the early months of 1776 Americans were vigorously engaged in discussions on the organization and establishment of new governmental structures for their colonies. Continuity with past British institutions characterized the forms of government adopted. In May, 1776, Congress recommended to the colonies that all British authority should be totally suppressed. The people themselves should exercise all the powers of government.[36]

During these months, therefore, the colonies were discussing and some, at least, taking the first steps toward establishing new forms of government. At the same time some were beginning to establish courts to hear cases of captures of British vessels and cargoes. The congressional resolutions of November 25 had recommended that each colony establish some court or courts to hear cases of capture in the first instance. Each colony acted in its own way and at its own pace. Some colonies established only a prize court or added instance jurisdiction later as an afterthought. Elsewhere a full admiralty court, with prize and instance jurisdiction, was set up. Or a colony could continue its long-established vice-

---

[36] Wood, *American Republic*, pp. 130–143.

admiralty court in force with merely a change of name and personnel. One colony set up no new court at all but ordered the common law courts to sit in special admiralty sessions to hear cases of capture. Other colonies, occupied by the British during most of the war years, had little opportunity to establish prize courts. Furthermore, the various colonies felt it proper to impose their own limitations upon the right of appeal to Congress. The courts established reflected local situations and traditions, though with some borrowing of ideas from the British prize acts and from the statutes of other colonies. Although all the fine points of the provisions for these maritime courts are not directly pertinent to this work, some description of their legislative basis is necessary to explain the whole process of appeals to the Continental Congress.

As might be expected, Massachusetts led all the rest in setting up maritime courts. Even before Congress recommended that the colonies establish prize courts, Massachusetts had acted. In July, 1775, Congress had debated and passed a series of resolutions urging the colonies to put the militias into a proper state of defense. These resolves, as we have seen, suggested that each colony arm vessels at its own expense for the protection of its harbors and its navigation against attacks by British war vessels.[37] On November 1, 1775, while Boston was occupied and its harbor blockaded, the Massachusetts assembly passed "An Act for Encouraging the Fixing out of Armed Vessels to Defend the Sea-coast of America, and for Erecting a Court to Try and Condemn All Vessels That Shall Be Found Infesting the Same." The preamble listed the familiar acts of despotism charged to the British ministry and justified the statute as authorized by the Massachusetts charter which gave its council the power, in the absence of the governor, to provide for the colony's self-defense. The resolution of Congress of the previous July, just referred to, was also quoted, to show that each colony should exert itself to defend its sea coasts and also to keep supplies from the enemy.

The Massachusetts assembly, before Congress had authorized any captures, legalized the capture of British ships found making unlawful attacks on the coasts or the naviga-

---

[37] Ford, *JCC* 2: p. 189.

tion of America or ships supplying the British army or fleet. After empowering the council to commission privateers by letters of marque and reprisal, the assembly established prize courts in three districts to try any cases of capture made under this act. No instance jurisdiction was allowed at this time or for several years. Apparently the common law courts took jurisdiction to settle whatever civil maritime suits might be brought. Aware of the widespread criticism of the vice-admiralty courts for not allowing trial by jury, the assembly imposed a jury requirement on its newly created prize courts. Once the jury had determined that the facts charged in the captor's bill were true, the judge was authorized to condemn the ships and cargoes for the use of the captors.[38] Although the authorized jurisdiction of this court could be read to accommodate captures by congressional naval vessels, apparently Washington, then in Cambridge with his small military force, was advised that some special court established by Congress would be required. This prompted him to urge Congress early in November to establish courts to hear prize cases where the captures had been made by vessels fitted out by Congress. His letters, as we have already seen, brought Congress to pass the resolves of November 25, which were probably influenced by the provisions of the Massachusetts act of November 1.

Several weeks after Massachusetts established three prize courts, Congress passed its resolves of November 25 recommending that the colonies establish courts to hear cases of capture of British ships and grant appeals to Congress. Massachusetts reacted to these resolves of Congress in February, 1776, by repealing its own act of the previous November and passing another act to encourage fitting out vessels for defense of the sea coast and for erecting a court to try all captures. By this new law captured ships could be brought into port for trial within any of the American colonies. Again establishing prize courts in three districts, the Massachusetts

---

[38] *Acts and Resolves, Public and Private, of the Province of Massachusetts Bay* (21 v., Boston, 1869–1922) **5:** pp. 436–441. A committee of the Massachusetts assembly had been appointed 9 October, 1775, to prepare this bill, Clark, *NDAR* **2:** pp. 370–371. See also, *ibid.*, pp. 269, 304, 323. The assembly on November 10 authorized condemnations to non-commissioned parties seizing British property near the shore, *ibid.*, p. 966. The assembly in December appointed Nathan Cushing, Timothy Pickering, and James Sullivan as judges of the three prize courts, *ibid.* **3:** p. 274.

assembly now provided for appeals to Congress with the time
limit provisos of the congressional resolutions. The assembly
also enacted substantially the resolves of Congress of December which ordered prizes made by congressional naval
ships to be tried in colonial admiralty courts and which established the share of recaptured ships to be adjudged to the
recaptor.[39]

This compliance with Congress's recommendations, however, lasted only a month in Massachusetts. On March 19,
1776, the assembly had an abrupt change of heart. It repealed its act of February and temporarily authorized the
admiralty court judges to continue to function under the
statute of the first of November. On April 13 the assembly
passed amendments to its November act, completely super-
seding the intervening act of February 14. This new, more
comprehensive act defined the British vessels liable to seizure
and condemnation somewhat more narrowly than Congress
had in its resolves of March 23. The Massachusetts assembly,
obviously viewing itself as the proper authority to draw the
limits for such questions, legalized captures of all vessels
engaged in attacking the American coast or used to supply
the British army or navy, as well as all vessels which had
carried supplies to the British. (Congress in March had authorized the capture of all vessels and cargoes belonging to
any British subject.)[40] The Massachusetts assembly gave the
three maritime court judges leave to hold their courts in
several cities within each of the three districts. The details of
procedures for the trial of prizes were fully set forth.[41] Trials
were still to be by jury. The assembly carefully followed the
congressional resolutions in authorizing the disposition of
prizes taken by naval vessels of any other colony or of Congress, and in providing for the payment of a certain percent
of the value of a vessel as salvage in cases of recapture of
American vessels. But when it came to authorizing appeals,
the assembly sharply restricted the cases which could be
reviewed by Congress. For prizes taken by the naval vessels
prepared at the expense of Congress, and only for such
cases, did the assembly allow appeals to the persons ap-

---

[39] *Acts and Resolves of Massachusetts* 5: pp. 462–468; Ford, *JCC* 3: pp. 407, 439.
[40] Ford, *JCC* 4: p. 230. Perhaps the March resolves of Congress had not yet
reached Massachusetts.
[41] Prize procedures will be analyzed in chapter VI below.

pointed by Congress. In all other cases of capture, appeals were to be taken to the Massachusetts Superior Court of Judicature. Instance jurisdiction was still not granted to these maritime courts.[42]

The Massachusetts assembly in May modified the scope of the prize jurisdiction, authorizing the capture and condemnation of all British-owned ships and cargoes in accordance with the resolves of Congress.[43] Two years later the assembly granted jurisdiction to the maritime courts to hear disputes over mariner's wages, marine salvage, and complaints between joint owners of merchant vessels. Besides granting this carefully defined instance jurisdiction, the assembly allowed juries in prize cases to grant damages against the captors if there had been no probable cause for the seizure.[44] Only in June, 1779, after several controversial cases involving neutral vessels captured by Americans and tried in Massachusetts courts, did the assembly slightly expand the class of cases in which appeals to Congress would be allowed. Thereafter a party could appeal to Congress in any case in which a subject of any friendly nation had filed a claim to the property captured.[45]

Clearly the Massachusetts assembly viewed itself as the source of authority to establish maritime courts, define their jurisdiction, set limits on the authority of privateers to make captures, and grant or refuse appeals to Congress. The assembly did in places employ the norms Congress had set forth in its resolves, but always with an air of independence of Congress. Furthermore, the Massachusetts assembly did not draw any ideas or language from the British prize acts. There is not a trace of the phrases or structure of the British acts in the various prize statutes passed by Massachusetts.[46]

The Rhode Island assembly at its March, 1776, session passed "An Act for Encouraging the fixing out and Authoriz-

---

[42] *Acts and Resolves of Massachusetts* 5: pp. 474–477.

[43] *Ibid.*, pp. 503–504.

[44] *Ibid.*, pp. 806–808. See also Act of 19 February, 1779, authorizing trial in the maritime courts of ships sailing from Massachusetts with a cargo of masts and spars of a specified size, *ibid.*, pp. 930–931.

[45] *Ibid.*, pp. 1077–1078. For the cases involving disputes over the jurisdiction of Congress to hear appeals from Massachusetts martime courts, see chapter VIII below.

[46] For a different analysis of the Massachusetts maritime court acts, see Goebel, *Antecedents*, pp. 160–161.

ing Armed Vessels to Defend the Sea-Coast of America, and
for erecting a Court to try and condemn all Vessels that shall
be found infesting the same." Largely a verbatim copy of the
Massachusetts act of November, 1775, this act set up one
admiralty court to try captures made according to the law.
The governor was empowered to issue privateering commissions; property liable to capture was defined in the same
terms as in the Massachusetts act with a jury required to try
the facts. The assembly made no mention in this act of
instance jurisdiction or of appeals to Congress or to any
other court.[47] At the May, 1776, session the Rhode Island
assembly cited the resolves of Congress of the previous
March as the basis for allowing general privateering against
the ships and cargoes of subjects of Great Britain. Incorporating in the law of the colony these resolves of Congress,
the assembly directed the admiralty judge "to proceed and
govern himself . . . according to the aforesaid Resolves of the
Congress, and the aforesaid Act of the General Assembly of
this Colony, passed in March, 1776."[48] These two statutes
governed the Rhode Island admiralty court till 1780.
Though the assembly did not mention appeals to Congress,
appeals were requested of the judge and granted, apparently
without any challenge, as early as November, 1776.[49] There
is no indication that the right of appeal to Congress ever
became an issue in Rhode Island.

While its court existed, the Rhode Island assembly elected
and each year re-elected John Foster as admiralty judge. He
was essentially a one-man court, occasionally drawing up the
pleadings for litigants and personally endorsing most of the
file papers and writing the greater portion of the minute
books himself. The assembly set his fees and probably felt the
judge showed proper submission to it when he admitted in
1778 that "he considers himself only as the servant of the
General Assembly, and cannot pretend to any authority but
what he receives from them."[50]

[47] *Rhode Island Session Laws* (facsimilies of the originals, 18 v., Providence, n.d.),
March session, 1776, pp. 312–320.

[48] *Ibid.*, May session, 1776, pp. 41–44.

[49] *Kingston Packet (Derby v. Hopkins)*, 18 September, 1777, #6 and *Phoenix (Darrel
v. Peirce)*, 3 September, 1777, #8 and #19, Records of the Court of Appeals in Cases
of Capture (National Archives). Both cases were decided in Rhode Island and
appeals granted in November, 1776. For an explanation of the method of citation of
these cases, see bibliography, below.

[50] John Foster, Rhode Island judge of admiralty, is quoted in Frederick B.

At its second session in July 1780, the Rhode Island assembly passed a comprehensive act establishing an admiralty court. The court received instance jurisdiction for the first time, defined in practically the same terms as in the Massachusetts act of April, 1778. Jury trial was preserved but if no party filed a claim to the prize, the judge could proceed to condemn it by default without impaneling a jury. The judge, in hearing all matters within the jurisdiction of the court, was to determine all cases "according to the Laws of this State, the Resolves of Congress, and the Customs, Usages and Laws of Nations, respecting maritime Affairs." The statute included instructions for filing the libel and claim, for delivering to the judge the ship papers of the prize and for giving notice in the newspapers of the trial of the prize. It also specified the mode of condemnation and sale of lawful prizes. As in the Massachusetts prize acts, if either party should be dissatisfied with the sentence of the court, he could appeal either to the Superior Court of Judicature of the state or to the commissioners appointed by Congress. No limits, however, were placed by this act on the right of appeal to Congress. In case of appeal to Congress the resolutions of November 25 controlled the time limits for appeal and the posting of the bond to prosecute the appeal. Rhode Island, however, added a requirement, similar to a common provision of the British prize acts, that the appellee give a bond to pay the appellant the amount of the sale of the condemned property, plus costs, if the sentence should be reversed on appeal.[51] The Rhode Island assembly did retaliate against other states which restricted the right of appeal to Congress. In 1780 it enacted that no appeal should be allowed to Congress in any case where the appellant was from a state which refused to allow appeals to Congress.[52]

The Connecticut assembly at its May session, 1776 passed "an Act for Establishing Naval Offices in This Colony." Following the recommendation of the Continental Congress, the assembly authorized the five county courts of the colony to try and determine by jury or otherwise all cases of capture and ordered them, when sitting as maritime courts, to follow the civil law, the law of nations, and the resolutions of Con-

---

Wiener, "Notes on the Rhode Island Admiralty, 1727–1790," *Harvard Law Rev.*, **46** (1932): p. 60, and discussed in general, pp. 59–62.

[51] *Rhode Island Session Laws*, July, second session, 1780, pp. 9–14.

[52] *Ibid.*, November session, 1780, pp. 18–19.

gress as the rule of their decisions. No instance jurisdiction was granted; the county courts, however, most likely would have taken jurisdiction over civil maritime disputes if any were brought. Appeals to Congress were allowed, governed by the restrictions and directions of the congressional resolves.[53] This brief act served the needs of Connecticut during the period of the Continental Congress. At the May session, 1778, the lower house tried to repeal the section granting appeals to Congress, but the upper house, made up predominantly of judges of the county and superior courts, rejected this proposal.[54]

The Connecticut government throughout the war made strenuous efforts to stop illegal trade and importation from Long Island which was held by the British. As part of this attack on illicit trade, the assembly granted jurisdiction over these cases to the maritime sessions of the county courts but decreed that no appeals should be allowed from the county courts in cases of ships and cargoes prosecuted under this act.[55]

On July 3, 1776, the assembly of New Hampshire pieced together a prize act made up, with only incidental modifications, of paragraphs taken from the Massachusetts acts of November 1, 1775, April 13, and May 8, 1776. Appeals to Congress were granted, as in Massachusetts, only in cases where the prize was taken by an armed ship fitted out at the expense of the United Colonies.[56] This New Hampshire statute continued in force, with only one significant modification, throughout the years of the war. The limitation on appeals to Congress in this act would greatly complicate the important case of the brigantine Lusanna, which was ap-

[53] Connecticut session laws, May session, 1776, pp. 419–420. *Records of the States of the United States of America—A Microfilm Compilation*, ed. by William S. Jenkins (Washington, 1949).

[54] This bill is in Revolutionary War Collection (Connecticut State Library), 1st ser., X, 237. Journals of the lower or upper houses are not extant for this session. See also, Charles J. Hoadley et. al., eds., *The Public Records of the State of Connecticut* (9 v., Hartford, 1899–1953) **3**: pp. 3–5.

[55] Connecticut session laws, May session, 1780, pp. 553–557 and November session, 1780, p. 563. Connecticut's relations with Long Island will be discussed in chapter VII below.

[56] Albert S. Batchellor et al., eds., *Laws of New Hampshire including Public and Private Acts and Resolves* (10 v., Manchester, 1904–1922) **4**: pp. 25–32. In January, 1776, the assembly had appointed Joshua Bracket as judge of the court of admiralty. Clark, *NDAR* **3**: p. 950.

pealed to Congress from New Hampshire in 1778.[57] In November, 1779, the assembly, under pressure from Congress, relented and, following closely the wording of the act of Massachusetts of the previous June, allowed appeals to Congress "in all maritime causes that shall be tried and determined in this state, wherein any subject or subjects or any foreign nation or state in amity with this & the united states of america [sic] shall in due form of law claim the whole or any part of the vessell [sic] & cargo in dispute." To show its reluctance to grant even this narrow leave to appeal, the assembly limited the time for a party to request an appeal to twenty-four hours.[58] As in Massachusetts, if both parties were residents of any state of the United States, they could not appeal to Congress.

The Pennsylvania assembly led the way among the central colonies in establishing an admiralty court. On March 26, 1776, it passed a series of resolves, based in part on the Massachusetts acts, providing for a court of justice to determine cases of captured vessels. All the procedural details of the court were spelled out. The assembly allowed appeals to Congress according to the congressional resolutions of November 25. It also went along with Congress's recommendation that the trial of prizes be by jury.[59]

In September, 1778, Pennsylvania got around to passing a more detailed act establishing a court of admiralty. The jurisdiction of the court was extended to cover "all manner of controversies, suits and pleas, within the jurisdiction of the admiral and not determinable at common law," with the exception of crimes committed on the high seas. The judge of this admiralty court, with full instance and prize jurisdiction, was to determine the cases according to maritime law and the laws of Pennsylvania. Again the assembly regulated the procedures but in the section on the jury it added that

---

[57] *Lusanna (Doane v. Penhallow)*, 17 September, 1783, #30, RCA. This case will be discussed in chapters VII and VIII below.

[58] Batchellor, *Laws of New Hampshire* **4**: p. 238.

[59] James T. Mitchell and Henry Flanders, eds., *The Statutes at Large of Pennsylvania* (18 v., Harrisburg, 1896–1915) **8**: pp. 519–521. In February, 1776, the Pennsylvania Committee of Safety had provided for the disposition of British vessels taken in the Delaware River, Clark, *NDAR* **3**: p. 1116. On April 5, 1776, the Pennsylvania assembly appointed George Ross as judge of the admiralty, Samuel Hazard, ed., *Pennsylvania, Colonial Records* (16 v., Harrisburg, 1838–1853) **10**: pp. 537–538. Upon the death of Ross in July, 1779, Francis Hopkinson was appointed admiralty judge. *Ibid.* **12**: pp. 49, 50.

"the finding of the said jury shall establish the facts without re-examination or appeal." This refusal to allow appellate review of facts determined by a jury would be the central issue of the most significant case which came before the Committee on Appeals of Congress, that of the sloop *Active*.[60] Furthermore, in granting appeals to Congress, Pennsylvania narrowed the time limits recommended by Congress. Appeals would have to be demanded within three days after definitive sentence and lodged with the secretary of Congress within thirty days. The resolutions of Congress and Pennsylvania's earlier act had allowed five days and forty days respectively as the time limits.

The Pennsylvania assembly in this statute, incorporating a section from the British prize acts,[61] also provided that the decree of the court should not be suspended by reason of an appeal to Congress. If the court's decree was executed pending appeal, however, the appellee must give sufficient security to pay the full value of the ship and cargo to the appellant in case the decree was reversed on appeal. A final section of the Pennsylvania law stated that the supreme court of the state could issue writs of prohibition to stop any proceedings in the admiralty court "in like manner, and to the like effect as by the laws of England the courts of admiralty have been [subjected] to the prohibition of the court of King's Bench."[62]

The Pennsylvania assembly in March, 1780, again reconsidered the jurisdiction of the admiralty court. Basically the new act was intended to provide for the trial of crimes and piracies committed on the high seas by setting up a special court of oyer and terminer. The structure of the admiralty court remained the same except for two significant modifications. This act added the law of nations to the maritime law and the laws of Pennsylvania as the rule for decisions in admiralty.

> [The] judge of the admiralty . . . shall hold a court of admiralty and therein have cognizance of all controversies, suits and pleas of maritime jurisdiction, not cognizable at the common law; offenses and crimes, other than contempts against the said court only excepted, and thereupon shall pass sentence and

---

[60] *Active (Olmsted v. Houston)*, 15 December, 1778, #39, RCA. This case and the issue of judicial review of issues of fact will be discussed in chapter III below.

[61] 29 Geo. II, c. 34 § 9.

[62] Mitchell and Flanders, *Statutes of Pennsylvania* 9: pp. 277–283.

decree according as the maritime law, the law of nations, and the laws of this commonwealth shall require.

The second significant change in the admiralty court undoubtedly grew out of the long, much-debated dispute over the case of the sloop *Active*. The Pennsylvania assembly dropped the requirement that trial of prizes should be by jury. Thereafter prize cases were to be tried "by witnesses according to the course of the civil law." The forced symbiosis of juries and prize procedure thus came to an end in Pennsylvania. Appeals to Congress, therefore, could be granted without any restriction as to the right of review of questions of fact determined by the trial court jury.[63]

The New Jersey Provincial Congress in February, 1776, considered establishing an admiralty court, but after being advised by William Livingston, one of the colony's delegates to the Continental Congress, that it could suffer no harm from deferring a decision, finally put off any action to erect such a court "until some future day."[64] The following October the assembly still did not enact a statute to regulate admiralty jurisdiction but merely gave the governor and council the power to establish an admiralty court and commission its officers.[65] The assembly of New Jersey made no attempt to formulate the structure or procedures of this court from this time till December, 1778. During this period, while military movements and battles were taking place in and near the state, no records exist of cases from New Jersey appealed to Congress until the fall of 1778.

In September and October, 1778, four cases were appealed to Congress,[66] perhaps indicating an increased business of the state admiralty court which prompted the New Jersey assembly to give detailed prescriptions for the admiralty court. The act of December 5, 1778, resembles the Pennsylvania laws. The assembly gave the court jurisdiction

---

[63] *Ibid.* **10:** pp. 97–106.

[64] 2, 15, 23 and 29 February, 1776, Clark, *NDAR* **3:** pp. 1102, 1303; **4:** pp. 54, 119–120.

[65] New Jersey session laws, 1st sitting, 6 October, 1776, pp. 7–8, in Jenkins, *Microfilm*.

[66] *Speedwell (Yandell v. Shaler)*, November, 1778, #29; *John and Sally (Stevens v. Henderson)*, 11 March, 1779, #35; *Lark (Jennings v. Taylor)*, 28 January, 1780, #36; *Lovely Nancy (Ingersol v. Shewell)*, 22 August, 1780, #38, RCA. For the difficulty of convening a court in an area of military operations, see New Jersey session laws, 28 February, 1777, chapter XV, 17, Jenkins, *Microfilm*.

"for the Trial of all, and all Manner of Causes arising on the
high Seas, or any navigable River or Bay, and not within the
Body of any County, nor determinable at Common Law,
Piracies and Felonies committed on the high Seas excepted."
This grant of instance jurisdiction which failed to mention
prize jurisdiction at all (though most of the act provided for
the disposition of prizes) represented a widespread misun-
derstanding of admiralty jurisdiction which had for a long
time existed in the American colonies. Many, as we shall see
in a later chapter, acted as though prize jurisdiction were a
part of ordinary admiralty jurisdiction, governed by the
same rules and procedures. The act specified that the judge's
decrees should conform to civil and maritime law in so far as
they are not controlled by the resolutions of Congress or the
laws of the state. Juries, governed by the rules of the common law courts, were to decide the facts. Appeals to the
persons appointed by Congress were allowed with the time
limits Congress had set forth in its November, 1775, resolves.[67]

Three years later the New Jersey legislature passed an
even more detailed act regulating admiralty jurisdiction. The
court's structure and the right of appeal to Congress remained unchanged. This act, however, did add a section,
verbatim from the Pennsylvania law of March 8, 1780, that
the execution of the decree of the judge in any prize case
from which an appeal was granted would not be suspended
or delayed by reason of the appeal. The parties appealing
had to give sufficient security which could be sued on by the
party successful on appeal. This act also gave the supreme
court of the state authority to issue prohibitions to the proceedings of the court of admiralty. This provision, as the one
in Pennsylvania on which it was modeled, could be read as
authorizing prohibitions in prize cases.

> [A]ll and every the Proceedings of the Court of Admiralty of
> this State shall be liable to the Prohibition of the Supreme
> Court of Judicature, in like Manner and with like Effect as the
> Prohibition of the Court of King's Bench in *England* in like
> Case.[68]

---

[67] New Jersey session laws, 3rd session, 1st sitting, pp. 18–24, Jenkins, *Microfilm.*
For a discussion of the American view of prize jurisdiction as part of admiralty
jurisdiction, see chapter IV below.
[68] New Jersey session laws, 6th assembly, 1st sitting, 18 December, 1781, pp.
13–21, Jenkins, *Microfilm.*

Of course, the Court of King's Bench did not issue prohibitions against proceedings in prize cases, but it is not clear that this limitation of prohibitions to instance cases was understood by the New Jersey assemblymen.

For two colonies, New York and Delaware, no statutory basis for their admiralty courts can be found in the session laws. This is less surprising for New York than for Delaware; the parts of New York adjacent to the sea were under the control of the British during most of the war. The prize cases heard in New York City involved captures of American ships by the British, so, of course, no appeals came to Congress. After British evacuation of New York in 1783, apparently the state admiralty court began to function. Only in 1784 did the New York assembly briefly consider the admiralty court; probably the statute means that the assembly granted appeals in prize cases to Congress.[69] Both New York and Delaware did mention an admiralty court in the constitutions adopted early in the war.[70] The session laws of both states refer to the admiralty court or admiralty judge but never establish such a court or regulate its proceedings.[71] Apparently the courts of the colonial period continued to function much as before with new personnel but the same basic procedure. There are no known court records to prove that the New York admiralty court ever heard a case of capture from the British during the war. It appears that Delaware's admiralty court did function as it had in colonial times. Prize cases were heard, but without any mention of jury trials, so foreign to traditional prize practices. Five cases were appealed from the Delaware admiralty court to Congress.[72]

Among the southern colonies Virginia acted first to establish admiralty jurisdiction. In many ways the Virginia court

[69] Julius Goebel, Jr., ed., *The Law Practice of Alexander Hamilton, Documents and Commentary* (2 v., New York, 1964–1969) **2**: p. 779; New York session laws, eighth session, November, 1784, chapters VI and XI.

[70] Francis N. Thorpe, ed., *The Federal and State Constitutions, Colonial Charters, and Other Organic Laws of the States, Territories and Colonies, Now or Heretofore Forming the United States of America* (7 v., Washington, 1909) **1**: pp. 564–565 (Delaware Constitution, 21 September, 1776), and **5**: pp. 2633–2634 (New York Constitution, 20 April, 1777).

[71] New York session laws, chapter XII, 16 March, 1778, pp. 12–13, Jenkins, *Microfilm*, and Delaware session laws, 22 February, 1777, 20 May, 1778, 9 December, 1778, 12 February, 1781, *ibid.*

[72] *Fortune (Godwin v. Moore)*, 24 June, 1780, #31; *Hawke (Murphy v. Fisher)*, 8 September, 1779, #32; *Sally (Pope v. Schoemaker)*, 1779, #41; *Packet (Caldwell v. Rodney)*, 28 February, 1780, #52; *Betsey (Ridgway v. Earle)*, 14 June, 1783, #77, RCA.

was unique. During the December, 1775, session the Virginia convention appointed three judges to hear cases of capture of British goods imported or Virginia property exported in violation of the Continental Association. The three judges, any two of them constituting a court, received vague but ample jurisdiction "to try and determine on all matters relating to vessels and their cargoes." Owners of captured property could appeal to the local committee on safcty.[73] During the May, 1776, session this ordinance was amended, three new judges appointed, and the court clearly established as a maritime court with jurisdiction "to hear and determine all causes maritime arising within and belonging to the jurisdiction of the admiralty, all offenses committed on the high seas, and all captures of vessels and their cargoes from enemies of America," as well as seizures for violations of the laws of Virginia or the resolves of Congress. The congressional resolutions relative to capture passed on or before April 3 were to be in force in the colony. As in the earlier act, two of the three judges could hold court; both acts insisted on trial by jury.[74]

By December, 1776, the assembly of Virginia found time for a more thorough ordinance, drafted by Thomas Jefferson, regulating the admiralty court. It continued the system of jury trial and one court with three judges presiding to hold office during good behavior. It gave the court jurisdiction corresponding to the scope of the British vice-admiralty court covering "all causes heretofore of admiralty jurisdiction in this country." It specified as the rule of decisions that the court should be

> governed in their proceedings and decisions by the regulations of the continental congress, acts of general assembly, English statutes prior to the fourth year of the reign of king James the first, and the laws of Oleron, the Rhodian and Imperial laws, so far as the same have been heretofore observed in the English courts of admiralty.

If the regulations of Congress should differ from those of Virginia, the congressional ordinances would be observed in cases involving captures taken from enemies with whom the

---

[73] William W. Hening, ed., *The Statutes at Large, Being A Collection of All the Laws of Virginia* (13 v., Richmond, 1809–1823) **9**: pp. 102–105.
[74] *Ibid.*, pp. 130–132.

United States was at war. Otherwise (apparently meaning in non-prize cases) Virginia laws should prevail. Similarly, appeals from the Virginia court could be made to Congress in any case of capture from an enemy with whom the United States was at war according to the regulations of Congress. In all other cases appeals would be to the state court of appeals.[75]

Virginia cleared up the ambiguities of this earlier statute by an act of 1779, prepared by George Wythe, which reconstituted the admiralty court. The assembly added to the list of laws governing the court's decisions the "laws of nature and nations," and dropped from the earlier list "English statutes prior to the fourth year of the reign of king James the first." Besides continuing jury trials in admiralty, this act explicitly applied the common law rules of evidence to trials in admiralty. Where the regulations of Congress conflicted with the laws of Virginia, the state laws would be controlling only in cases involving litigants from the state. In other cases the resolutions of Congress would prevail. Similarly appeals to Congress were allowed except where both parties were citizens of the state.[76]

The South Carolina constitution, by implication continuing admiralty courts already established, confined admiralty jurisdiction to "maritime causes." But the assembly passed an act empowering the court of admiralty to exercise jurisdiction in cases of capture of British ships and establishing jury trial in admiralty. This statute is based on the British prize acts, and whole sections are lifted from the British acts and incorporated into South Carolina law. Much of the act dealt with penalties for excessive fees, for causing delays in court proceedings, or for court officials having interest in any prize cases which came before the court. South Carolina ignored the resolves of Congress specifying the proportion of recaptured vessels to be awarded to the recaptors in lieu of salvage. The statute directed that one-sixth of the value of the vessel and cargo should be allowed the recaptors in all cases where the original American owner proved his right to have his

---

[75] *Ibid.*, pp. 202–206; Julian P. Boyd, ed., *The Papers of Thomas Jefferson* (17 v., Princeton, 1950–1965) **1**: pp. 645–649. The fourth year of the reign of James I was, of course, the year of the founding of Virginia at Jamestown.

[76] Hening, *Statutes of Virginia* **10**: pp. 98–102; Boyd, *Papers of Jefferson* **2**: pp. 572–575.

property restored. No mention is made of appeals to any court. Apparently the assembly saw nothing strange in studiously following British acts and ignoring the resolves of Congress.[77] A subsequent act passed for regulating the court of admiralty cannot now be found.[78] Late in the war South Carolina repealed the earlier act and authorized the admiralty court to make its own rules for procedure. This act made it lawful for the judge to proceed to final sentence and decree of condemnation without a jury.[79]

The Maryland admiralty court presents an anomalous situation. No statute can be found establishing or regulating the admiralty court or the process of appeals to Congress. The constitution of Maryland, completed November 11, 1776, does not explicitly mention the judge of the admiralty as one of the civil officers, but does provide that all appeals from the admiralty court should be to a court of appeals of the state whose judgment would be final and conclusive.[80] The state session laws mention the admiralty court from time to time, but only to provide for the judge's oath, commission, or salary, or to make certain forfeitures recoverable in admiralty. The commission of the admiralty judge does not define the scope of the jurisdiction he is to exercise, but merely instructs him to carry on in his office "according to law."[81] Apparently the assembly merely continued the judicial structure of its colonial days without seeing a need of controlling the procedures. Four cases were appealed to Congress, however, without any sign of a dispute over the restriction of the state constitution requiring all appeals from admiralty to be

---

[77] South Carolina session laws, act passed 11 April, 1776, Jenkins, *Microfilm*; Thorpe, *Constitutions* 6: pp. 3246, 3254; 29 Geo. II, c. 34; 32 Geo. II, c. 25; Ford, *JCC* 5: p. 407. Hugh Rutledge was chosen as admiralty judge. Clark, *NDAR* 4: p. 542. For the committee which prepared this bill, Clark, *NDAR* 4: p. 587.

[78] Act passed 13 February, 1777 is not in the session laws, but is referred to in Thomas Cooper *et al.*, eds., *Statutes at Large of South Carolina* (10 v., Columbia, 1836–1841) 4: pp. 374, 400, 440–441.

[79] South Carolina session laws, act passed 26 February, 1782, Jenkins, *Microfilm*.

[80] Thorpe, *Constitutions* 3: pp. 1689, 1697, 1699, 1700.

[81] Maryland session laws, February session, 1777, chapter V; October session, 1777, chapter X; June session, 1778, chapter III; July session, 1779, chapter VII, Jenkins, *Microfilm*. The brief commission granted for the admiralty judge of the state of Maryland in 1777, giving no description of the scope of his authority, bears no resemblance to the lengthy, elaborate commission of a judge of vice-admiralty in Maryland in 1775, which defines the authority and judicial power of the judge as well as his rights and perquisites. Clark, *NDAR* 2: pp. 1164–1167.

taken to a state court of appeals. In some cases, but not all, the prize trial was by jury.[82]

Even before the North Carolina constitution of 1776 provided for the appointment of admiralty judges, the assembly had acted to establish admiralty courts at the various ports of the state.[83] Merely appointing judges to hear prize cases proved insufficient; the judges had little or no idea how to proceed.[84] The state senate doubted the validity of admiralty jurisdiction over captures and questioned whether the admiralty courts could summon juries for prize cases. It urged, therefore, the passage of a bill to regulate admiralty courts.[85] By November, 1777, the bill was ready and approved. The assembly, basing some passages on the South Carolina admiralty court statute, followed the recommendations of Congress closely in providing for jury trial, for payment of a proportion of the vessel as salvage in cases of recapture, and for appeals to Congress. But it added a phrase which must have made parties reluctant to request appeals: the appellant would have to pay triple costs in case the decree of the state admiralty court should be affirmed. North Carolina, like several other states, specified that the execution of the sentence of the state court should not be suspended because of an appeal, provided that the appellee gave sufficient security to pay the full value of the award to the appellant in case the sentence should be reversed on appeal. The assembly, thinking of the long history of disputes between the common law courts and admiralty courts over instance jurisdiction, tried to define precisely the scope of the admiralty court's non-prize jurisdiction. Through its somewhat clumsy wording, one can detect much reflection on the proper sphere for admiralty authority, undoubtedly derived from experience with colonial courts. The limitation of jurisdiction to *in rem* or voluntary *in personam* appearances is especially enlightening.

And whereas in some Cases properly maritime, the Jurisdic-

[82] The four cases appealed from Maryland are: *Minerva (Rogers v. Wilson)*, 2 June, 1777, #15; *Jane (Fossett v. Foster)*, 18 January, 1780, #48; *Pitt (Courter v. Huntington)*, 13 January, 1780, #63; *Hope (Coakley v. Martin)*, 6 May, 1784, #85, RCA.

[83] Walter Clark, ed., *The State Records of North Carolina* (26 v., Goldsboro, 1886–1914) 10: pp. 542, 634, 644; Thorpe, *Constitutions* 5: pp. 2791, 2792.

[84] Jonathan Ancrum to Governor Caswell, 4 April, 1777, and Sampson Mosley to Governor Caswell, 25 August, 1777, in Clark, *Records of North Carolina* 11: p. 441.

[85] North Carolina Senate Journal, 18 April, 1777, *ibid.* 12: p. 26.

tion of the Court of Admiralty may hereafter be called in Question; Be it therefore Enacted, by the Authority aforesaid, That all Suits for Freight, Mariners Wages, Breach of Charter Parties for Voyages to be made, so as the Penalty be not demanded, and Suits for building, repairing, saving, or the necessary Victualing for a Ship, against the Ship or Vessel, and not against any Party by Name, but such as may choose to make himself a Party, and all Disputes concerning Salvage, and all Matters and Transactions that are in their Nature maritime, shall be tried and determined in the Court of Admiralty.[86]

The Georgia constitution of February 5, 1777, appointed the chief justice to sit as judge of admiralty. Captures were to be tried in the county in which they were brought in. Trial was to be swift, within ten days of the filing of the claims. Appeals to Congress could be requested only after a second trial by a special jury.[87] No session laws can be found establishing or regulating the admiralty court which probably did little business since the British held possession of Georgia for part of the war.

On November 25, 1775, as we have seen, the Continental Congress had approved a series of resolutions. It recommended that each colony should set up some court to hear cases of captured British vessels with the facts tried by a jury. It also urged the states to allow appeals in all cases of capture to Congress or to the persons appointed by Congress to hear such appeals. All the colonies, many of them before they became states upon declaring their independence, established a court with jurisdiction over prize cases. But the variety of limitations placed upon the right of appeal to Congress would seem at first sight to have made the appellate jurisdiction practically useless.

Massachusetts and New Hampshire allowed appeals only when the capture was made by an armed ship commissioned by Congress and fitted out at the expense of Congress. Later they expanded this right of appeal to include cases involving foreign subjects whose country was in friendly relations with the United States. Rhode Island and Connecticut granted appeals in all cases, though both states later hedged this slightly. Rhode Island would not allow appeals requested by the subject of any state which itself limited the right of

[86] *Ibid.* **24:** p. 123 and in general pp. 119–123.
[87] Thorpe, *Constitutions* **2:** pp. 783–784.

appeals to Congress. Connecticut would not grant appeals in cases tried for violation of the laws against illicit trade with the enemy. Pennsylvania restricted appeals to questions of law; all questions of fact were to be determined finally by the jury. Virginia at first granted appeals in cases of capture from an enemy with whom the United States was at war. Later it granted.appeals in all cases except where both parties were from Virginia. The Maryland constitution directed that all appeals from the state admiralty court were to be carried to a state court of appeals for final determination. North Carolina granted appeals in all cases, but if the appellant lost on appeal, he would have to pay triple the costs assessed. Georgia and New York apparently had very few, if any, prize cases, but they placed no restrictions on the right of appeal. Of the states with a substantial number of prize cases only New Jersey, Delaware, and South Carolina placed no limitations on the right of appeal to Congress. With such a confusing array of hesitance and reluctance apparent in the states, it is surprising that the Court of Appeals in Cases of Capture ever functioned effectively at all.

This survey of statutes regulating the state admiralty courts also shows a widespread awareness that prize cases, involving possible disputes with foreign nations, should not be adjudicated merely by state law. Most states explicitly instructed the admiralty judge to use the resolves of Congress and the law of nations in preference to the state laws as the legal norm for deciding cases of capture. It is also apparent that various states had totally different views of the proper scope of instance jurisdiction, probably reflecting widely divergent admiralty practice in civil maritime disputes during the colonial period.

The volume of the prize cases heard by these state admiralty courts is hard to estimate with precision. In most of the states the records of the admiralty court for the years of the Revolution have been lost or destroyed. A study of the admiralty records for the five states where they could be located shows clearly the large number of prize cases heard. During the years of the Revolutionary War very few instance cases came before the admiralty courts, if the extant, often fragmentary, records give a reliable picture.

There can be no doubt, however, that American vessels very early in the conflict took to the seas to protect American coasts, but more especially to capture the often extremely valuable British ships and cargoes. By December, 1775, British military and naval leaders in New England were complaining of the rebel privateers which infested the coast and captured British ships.[88] Silas Deane in October, 1775, estimated that 10,000 seamen were without employment in the northern colonies because of the disruption caused by the British naval force blockading the coast of New England. He felt that most of these would seek employment in privateering.[89] James Warren enthusiastically reported to Sam Adams that "Our Privateers more than answer our Expectations." Thomas Jefferson was amazed at the enterprise and daring of the New England maritime community who were "fitting out privateers, with which they expect to be able to scour the seas and bays of everything below ships of war; and may probably go to the European coasts, to distress the British trade there."[90] The prize business was extensive enough to enrich not only the ship owners but a good number of lawyers as well.[91] Later in the war the lists of captured British ships printed in Massachusetts papers delighted the heart of John Adams in Paris, who felt that these lists showed the rest of the world where American strength lay and demonstrated the weakness of the enemy.[92] Beyond any doubt a large number of American vessels, armed and unarmed, were at sea in spite of the British attempt to blockade the coast. Not all succeeded in their missions. One recent writer has stated, in commenting on the effectiveness of the British blockade, that "an incomplete return of prizes taken [by the British] between March and December [1776] shows 140

---

[88] Vice-admiral Samuel Graves' orders to Captain James Wallace, 13 September, 1775; Graves to Major General William Howe, 13 December, 1775; Howe to Lord Dartmouth, 13 December, 1775, Clark, *NDAR* **2**: pp. 129–130, 81–82. On the fear of American privateers in Britain, see Solomon Lutnick, *The American Revolution and The British Press, 1775–1783* (Columbia, Mo., 1967), pp. 150–155.

[89] Silas Deane, Estimate for Fitting Out Warships for a Three Months Cruise, Clark, *NDAR* **2**: pp. 647–652.

[90] Jefferson to George Gilmer, 5 July, 1775, Boyd, *Papers of Jefferson* **1**: p. 185, and Warren to Sam Adams, 5 December, 1775, Clark, *NDAR* **2**: p. 1286. See also letters of Elbridge Gerry, *ibid.*, pp. 369–370, 1261–1263.

[91] Thomas Cushing to Robert Treat Paine, 9 September, 1776, Robert Treat Paine Papers (Massachusetts Historical Society).

[92] John Adams to the President of Congress, 10 March, 1780, Francis Wharton, ed., *The Revolutionary Diplomatic Correspondence of the United States* (6 v., Washington, 1889) **3**: p. 541.

American vessels taken and twenty-six British recovered."[93]

In spite of many British captures, the number of the captures by American privateers which were tried as British property may have approached 2,000 during the years of the war. Of course, as we shall see in a later chapter, not all of these were actually British vessels or cargoes which could be condemned as lawful prize. The records from five state admiralty courts have been at least partially preserved. A study of these records reveals the following tentative figures for prize cases heard and appealed to Congress:

State Admiralty Court	Approximate number of prize cases heard	Number of prize cases appealed to Congress[94]
Maryland[95]	95	4
Rhode Island[96]	115	10
Pennsylvania[97]	200	13
Connecticut[98]	420	15
Massachusetts[99]	1,000	27

[93] Pierse Mackesy, *The War for America, 1775–1783* (Cambridge, Mass., 1965), p. 100.

[94] For the number of cases appealed to Congress from each state, see RCA.

[95] Maryland Admiralty Minute Books, 1776–1781; Admiralty Court Papers, 1776–1785 (Maryland Hall of Records).

[96] Rhode Island Admiralty Court Minute Book, 1776–1783; Admiralty Papers, 1776–1786 (Rhode Island State House, Archive Room); John Foster Papers 16 (Rhode Island Historical Society).

[97] Pennsylvania Admiralty Court Minute Book, 1776–1777, Admiralty Court Records; Admiralty Court Papers, 1717–1797; Court of Admiralty Papers, 1766–1789, Frederick W. Nicholls Collection (Historical Society of Pennsylvania); notices of trial and sale, *Pennsylvania Gazette*, 1776–1783; Francis Hopkinson (judge of Pennsylvania admiralty during most of the war), *Miscellaneous and Occasional Writings* (3 v., Philadelphia, 1792) 3: *passim.*

[98] Maritime Court Files (Connecticut State Library). Many of these Connecticut cases were trials for seizure of allegedly British property taken on Long Island. Strange libels, therefore, are quite common, for instance, libelling "five oxen," "sixteen barrels of oil," or "eleven yards of striped callico etc." See chapter VII below for a discussion of the plundering of Long Island by Connecticut privateers.

[99] This figure is quite speculative. It is based on the following data: (1) Revolution Prize Cases, 1776–1780 (Massachusetts Archives, State House). These two notebooks give an incomplete list of prize cases heard in the maritime court for the middle district, 1776–1780. All the cases for these years are not listed, but if the numbering and notations in these two notebooks are correct, the middle district heard some 689 prize cases from 1776–1780. The other two districts and the cases from the middle district after 1780 account for the rest of the cases given here as a tentative figure for prize cases in Massachusetts. (2) Ninety cases of prize were appealed from the Massachusetts maritime courts to the Superior Court of Judicature of Massachusetts, and twenty-seven cases were appealed to Congress. About ten of these cases appealed to Congress came from the Massachusetts superior court. So

The prompting of General Washington, who had more pressing concerns than determining prize disputes, and the direct experience of Congress in dealing with prize questions, had brought home to the members of Congress the need for some method of trying the legality of the seizure of ships and cargoes. Even before the delegates in Congress had declared the independence of the colonies from Great Britain, most of the new-born states already had admiralty courts set up to determine prize cases. The states, however, showed their independence of Congress, as well as of Great Britain, by imposing various restrictions and limitations on the jurisdiction of their admiralty courts and on the right of appeal to Congress. The members of Congress had recognized the necessity of assuring a right of review of state court decrees in prize cases. These appeals would often involve questions of the law of nations and would affect parties from different states and from foreign nations. Therefore, months before the Declaration of Independence, Congress had guaranteed, to the best of its ability, the right of appeal from state prize courts to Congress or to the persons Congress would appoint for that purpose.

So it is fitting that the very day Congress issued its famed Declaration to the world, the first prize appeal should be requested of the admiralty court in Pennsylvania. With this appeal in the case of the schooner *Thistle*, the first American federal court was born.

---

about 107 prize cases in all were appealed from the three Massachusetts maritime courts, indicating a large number of prize cases which must have been heard altogether. Minute Book of Appeals from the Maritime Court, 1779–1788, vol. 110; Record Books, Superior Court of Judicature, 1775–1780 (Supreme Judicial Court of Massachusetts, Office of the Clerk); Jedidiah Foster Notebook of Appeals to the Superior Court of Massachusetts, 1777–1779 (facsimile, United States Circuit Court of Appeals, library, Boston).

II. The Commissioners of Appeals in Cases of Capture

C HARLES ROBERTS, captain of the schooner *Thistle*, had been at sea nearly four weeks on a trading voyage from Mobile in West Florida to Jamaica with a cargo of flour and lumber. On April 30, 1776, a strange ship approached, fired on the *Thistle*, and brought it to. Roberts had only a few small arms aboard so he put up no resistance. "Highway robbers" and "pirates," Roberts called his captors as he was forced aboard the American privateer sloop *Congress*. George McAroy, commander of the *Congress*, commissioned by the Continental Congress, which made the capture, had his prize master bring the *Thistle* to Philadelphia.

With the *Thistle* safely in port, McAroy filed a libel in the Pennsylvania admiralty court. He alleged that the *Thistle* and its cargo belonged to inhabitants of Great Britain and that it was carrying supplies to the British army. When Roberts, acting without attorney, denied both points in his answer, McAroy amended the libel, adding the charge that the *Thistle* and cargo belonged to persons who were enemies of the United States. To this Roberts replied that the *Thistle* and cargo belonged to John McGillivray and Company of Mobile. He insisted that the owners, Scottish by birth, had all resided in West Florida for twelve years. But whether or not the owners were enemies of the United States, he said he did not know. (In fact McGillivray, an Indian trader in West Florida, did prove to be a loyalist during the war.[1])

The trial, first set for June 24, 1776, had to be postponed to July 1 because enough jurors did not show up. On the first of July McAroy's attorney read the amended bill and answer to the jury, put in evidence some letters and instructions to

---

[1] Cecil Johnson, *British West Florida 1763–1783* (New Haven, 1943), pp. 175, 195, 209. It is not clear whether this John McGillivray was related to the notorious quadroon Creek chieftain, Alexander McGillivray, who, during the Revolution, led Indian forays against American frontier settlements from Georgia to Cumberland. Frederick W. Marks, *Independence on Trial* (Baton Rouge, 1973), pp. 22–24.

Roberts, taken from the *Thistle,* and presented Roberts's answers to an interrogatory along with several depositions. Roberts also answered under oath in open court. The letters and instructions showed that Roberts had been sent by McGillivray and Company to sell a cargo of lumber and flour in Jamaica and to return as soon as possible with a cargo of rum, sugar, and coffee. Roberts's replies to the interrogatory merely repeated what he had stated in his answer to the libel. The jury also considered several letters of exchange taken from the *Thistle.* Since they were drawn on a London firm, they were apparently meant to show some partial ownership of the *Thistle* and cargo by inhabitants of Great Britain.

Two depositions presented to the jury tended to confirm that the *Thistle* did belong to parties of West Florida. Three other depositions were meant to bolster the case of the libelant. One Cuthbert, otherwise unidentified, swore that a gentleman named Struthers in Georgia belonged to the House of McGillivray and Company, that Struthers was a non-associator, and that Cuthbert had heard that McGillivray and Company were opposed to the American cause. Cuthbert claimed that one of McGillivray's ships had been burnt by the populace at Savannah, Georgia.[2] The other depositions, both by members of the crew of the sloop *Congress*, added practically nothing except that Roberts had called his captors names and that he had four loaded muskets on the *Thistle* when captured.

With such evidence before them, the jury returned a verdict that the *Thistle* and its cargo belonged partly to inhabitants of Great Britain and the rest belonged to persons who were also enemies of the United Colonies. Judge George Ross condemned the schooner with its cargo as lawful prize to be sold for the use of George McAroy and those for whom he had filed his libel.[3]

---

[2] This particular incident is not explicitly mentioned, but it is not at all out of keeping with other activities of American radicals in 1775 and 1776 in Savannah. Kenneth Coleman, *The American Revolution in Georgia 1763–1789* (Athens, 1958), pp. 40–70. On the non-admissibility of this type of evidence according to British admiralty practice, see chapter IV below.

[3] *Thistle (Roberts v. McAroy)*, 19 September, 1776, #1, RCA. George Ross, a signer of the Declaration of Independence, studied law and was admitted to the bar in Pennsylvania. He served for twelve years as a prosecutor for the Crown and for seven years in the provincial assembly. In 1775 and 1776 he was a delegate to the Continental Congress. He played a conspicuous part in the state constitutional convention in 1776. He served as judge of admiralty in Pennsylvania till his death in

Three days later, on July 4, 1776, Roberts, now with William Lewis as his counsel, filed an appeal to the Continental Congress and offered security to prosecute the appeal to effect.[4] Roberts, not sure of proper procedures, sent a petition to Congress on July 16 asking it to hear and determine the appeal as soon as possible. The petition was received by Congress the next day. For the following two months Congress repeatedly postponed consideration of the case.[5] Finally on September 9 Congress appointed a committee of Richard Stockton, Samuel Huntington, Robert Treat Paine, James Wilson, and Thomas Stone, all practicing attorneys, to hear the parties on this appeal. They heard both parties by their counsel on September 16 at the courthouse in Philadelphia. After several days for deliberation, the committee issued its decree reversing the sentence of the trial court and restoring the ship and cargo to Roberts for the owners of the *Thistle*.

The committee styled itself, "The Commissioners appointed by Congress to hear and determine the Appeal of Charles Roberts," undoubtedly thinking of themselves as stepping into the place of the British Lords Commissioners for Prize Appeals.[6] The decree, written in a form which would be used in many of the cases of the first few years, read more like a court decree than a legislative committee report. As in the vast majority of the cases heard on appeal, no reasons were given for the committee's determination.[7] In the case of the *Thistle*, the most likely reason for reversal was that the ship did not belong to inhabitants of Great Britain and was not employed in carrying supplies to the British army, the two categories of captures authorized by Congress in its resolves of March 13. The evidence did not support

---

1779. Allen Johnson and Dumas Malone, eds., *Dictionary of American Biography* (22 v., New York, 1928–1958) **16**: pp. 177–178.

[4] William Lewis studied law and was admitted to the bar in Pennsylvania and became one of the outstanding lawyers of the state. After serving briefly in the Pennsylvania legislature in 1787 and 1789 and in the state constitutional convention in 1789, he was appointed United States district attorney for Pennsylvania. In 1791, he accepted an appointment as judge of the federal court for the eastern district of Pennsylvania. He served for twelve years as a prosecutor for the Crown and for

[5] Ford, *JCC*, 5, 12 and 26 August, 7 September, 1776, **5**: pp. 631, 647, 702, 741.

[6] In chapters IV and VI below a study will be made of the forms and procedures of the Committee on Appeals and the Court of Appeals of the Continental Congress, and those of the Lords Commissioners for Prize Appeals.

[7] *Thistle*, #1, RCA.

these two allegations of the libel. Congress had so far granted permission only to capture vessels belonging to subjects of the British king who were inhabitants of Great Britain. By amending the libel to include the statement that the *Thistle* and its cargo belonged to persons who were enemies of the United Colonies, McAroy showed an awareness of the weakness of the initial assertions. This additional allegation also was drawn from the resolves of Congress of the previous March which authorized Americans in general terms "to fit out armed vessels to cruize on the enemies of these United Colonies." But this provision merely authorized privateering. Only in the next resolve had Congress defined the property liable to capture and condemnation. The *Thistle* did not fit within the two categories described in this next resolve. The libelant, as in most of the cases to follow, based his request for condemnation on the resolves of Congress. The committee assigned to review the lower court sentence reversed it, because McAroy had failed to prove that the *Thistle* came within the scope of the congressional resolutions.[8] There is no record that this determination by the committee was submitted to Congress as a report to be approved or rejected. Roberts's delay was not at an end. To avoid another capture he petitioned Congress and was granted a passport and safe conduct for himself and the schooner. Not till the end of October did Roberts resume his voyage to the West Indies.[9]

The second case Congress considered involved the brigantine *Elizabeth* and its valuable cargo of personal belongings of Boston residents. General Thomas Gage and his successor General William Howe with their British troops had held important but vulnerable positions in Boston through 1775 and into 1776. Washington and his poorly equipped American forces did not have the strength to dislodge the British, even though the British also were short of supplies and the ships expected from England failed to appear. By March the British had less than three weeks' rations of meat in Boston. The Americans forced Howe's decision to evacuate the city by dragging artillery captured at Fort Ticonderoga across the snow-covered hills of New England and installing them on Dorchester Heights in a position to threaten the British

---

[8] Ford, *JCC*, 23 March, 1776, **4**: pp. 230–231.
[9] *Ibid.* **5**: pp. 807, 827; **6**: p. 908.

lines. Howe, therefore, unable to risk storming the Heights, decided to leave while he could. He had seventy-eight vessels loaded to capacity with troops, loyalists, stores, private possessions, and horses. On March 17, 1776, the British army left Boston forever.[10]

In October of 1775 General Gage had commissioned Crean Brush to receive into his care the goods and effects of the inhabitants of Boston, giving them receipts for the safe return of their property. Since Boston was in a state of turmoil and some of the inhabitants were leaving town, Gage thought this authorization necessary to safeguard property. Gage's successor, General Howe, in March, 1776, further authorized Brush to confiscate any property which would help the American rebels carry on war. Brush was to promise the property would be restored to the owners. Anyone refusing to surrender such goods, however, would be considered abettors of the rebels. Brush himself in a memorial captured the atmosphere in Boston during the hectic weeks before evacuation as he tried, with efficiency, if not tact, to carry out his orders.

> In virtue of this Order your Memorialist accompanied by the Assistants he had named . . . removed the Goods answering the description of his Orders which were ready packed in Trunks & Cases and if any Articles were Removed which did not answer the description the Parties are only to blame they being repeatedly called on to declare the Contents of each which they obstinately refused—These People . . . are irritated against him but your Memorialist begs leave to assure your Honor he is fully able to prove that his Conduct toward them was governed with politeness coolness & moderation[.] [T]rue it is that when attempts were made to engage his attention in tedious dissertations on Magna Charta & the rights of British Subjects with intent to retard him in the execution of his Office he did interrupt such Harrangues [sic] & with an Irony which inflamed their resentment complimented them on their Eloquence which had in Town Meetings been so successful as to throw all America into confusion but that I was upon Business which I was determined to execute without interruption. . . . [11]

Some of the goods taken by Brush, mostly woolens and linens, were put on board the brigantine *Elizabeth* which then

---

[10] Mackesy, *War for America*, p. 80.
[11] *Elizabeth (Wentworth v. Hart)*, 14 October, 1776, #2, RCA.

sailed under convoy for Halifax. While most of the owners of
this property watched their goods sailing out of port, a few
embarked with their personal belongings on the *Elizabeth*.
Three of the American naval vessels recently fitted out by
Congress captured the *Elizabeth* and took it to the Piscataqua
River in New Hampshire.

When the *Elizabeth* was tried in the New Hampshire admiralty court, Joshua Wentworth, agent for the United Colonies, filed the libel for the captors. Thinking of the terms of
the congressional resolves of December, 1775, specifying the
amount of salvage due in cases of recapture, he claimed
recapture of an American ship and other American property
which had been in the possession of the enemy more than
ninety-six hours. The owner of the *Elizabeth* and some of the
owners of the goods taken by Crean Brush claimed their
property in court. After trial of the issues the verdict returned by the jury restored the *Elizabeth* and its cargo to the
various claimants. The jurors stated that the brigantine when
taken by the Americans had not been previously made a
lawful prize by the enemy. Furthermore it was not carrying
its cargo for the use of the British army or fleet. The New
Hampshire maritime court restored the ship and captured
property to the claimants and also decreed that these claimants should recover their court costs from the captors.

Undoubtedly feeling that the captors had received no
thanks at all for their efforts, Wentworth appealed to Congress. Since the case involved a capture by ships fitted out at
the expense of the Continental Congress, appeal to Congress
was allowed by New Hampshire law. On September 30, 1776,
Congress appointed a committee of Robert Treat Paine,
Samuel Huntington, Thomas Stone, George Wythe, and
James Smith, all lawyers, to determine the appeal.[12] They
heard the arguments of both parties, studied the lower court
records and the many depositions sent forward. On October
14 the committee reported its findings to Congress. Here the
determination, because it required the special attention of
Congress, was not typically judicial in style, but in the form of
a detailed committee report to Congress with a suggested
mode of settling the dispute. Congress voted to approve the
report.

---

[12] Ford, *JCC* 5: p. 835.

After summarizing the facts of the case, the committee gave its opinion. The *Elizabeth*, it reported, was not included in the description of ships which by resolutions of Congress could be forfeited as lawful prize. It was not an armed or a transport vessel employed in the war against the United States; it was not carrying supplies to the British army or navy within any of the colonies. So it did not come within the congressional resolutions of the previous November 25. The cases of recaptures mentioned in the resolutions of December 5 likewise did not cover this case, since this was not a capture by the British which could, by the law of nations, be condemned as lawful prize to the British. So it could not be considered a case of recapture.

The committee, however, acknowledged that the captors had done their duty in taking the ship. The original owners might otherwise have lost their property entirely, so the owners owed the captors reasonable satisfaction. Therefore the sentence of the New Hampshire court was erroneous and ought to be reversed and annulled. The *Elizabeth* and the parts of the its cargo claimed in the state court should be restored to the claimants. They, however, should pay the captors one-twelfth of the value of the ship and cargo plus costs of the trial and appeal. The case was sent back to the maritime court to carry out Congress's determination.[13]

The cases of the *Thistle* and the *Elizabeth* show the types of cases presented to Congress in the early appeals. Procedurally, the first eight cases follow the general pattern set in these first two. They were all turned over by Congress to *ad hoc* committees to hear and determine the appeals. In these cases the judge in the state admiralty court reached a decision based on a jury verdict. Then one party requested an appeal to Congress from this sentence. When the judge granted the appeal, bond was given by the appellants to prosecute the appeal. The certified records of the trial court were transferred to Congress and lodged with the secretary of Congress.[14] As in the case of the *Thistle*, one other appel-

---

[13] *Ibid.* **6:** pp. 870–873; Josiah Bartlett to John Langdon, 15 October, 1776, Burnett, *Letters* **2:** p. 125.

[14] *Charming Peggy (Keppele v. Glover)*, 24 May, 1784, #3; *Betsey (Kerr v. Barry)*, 23 November, 1776, #4; *Vulcan (Ingram v. Joyne)*, 24 January, 1777, #5; *Kingston Packet (Derby v. Hopkins)*, 18 September, 1777, #6; *Richmond (Craig v. Folger)*, 17 January, 1777, #7; *Phoenix (Darrell v. Peirce)*, 3 September, 1777, #8 & 19, RCA.

lant sent a petition to Congress requesting a hearing on
appeal. The records of this latter case show also that after the
decree of the lower court, a deposition was taken to be used
by Congress in hearing the appeal.[15] This would become
common practice in later cases. In seven of these eight cases
Congress appointed special committees to hear the appeal.[16]
The committee reviewed the records of the state admiralty
court, which usually included a certified copy of all the
pleadings, the depositions and interrogatories, the ship papers from the prize, and the court minutes and decree. It
heard the parties by their counsel and made some determination of the case. One case was continued until 1784 when it
was finally dismissed, neither party appearing.[17]

A case coming from Virginia clearly shows an early committee acting consciously as a review court. After studying
the somewhat confusing records sent forward, it reversed the
sentence of the state court and remanded the case for a new
trial. It instructed the state admiralty court:

> That after Claim or Plea without Oath, a new Trial be had in
> the said Cause, in which separate and distinct Issues be made
> on each material Fact, charged as a Cause of Forfeiture, and
> on each material Fact alledged or pleaded by any Claimant in
> Discharge or Bar of Forfeiture: That Evidence admissible by
> the Rules of the Common Law and no other, be received to
> support each Issue: That the Evidence, offered by the Jury, be
> reduced to Writing, before they retire to give their Verdict,
> and in Case of Appeal, transmitted to Congress and that the
> Libellants be permitted to amend their Libel, and the Claim-
> ants to claim or plead de novo.[18]

This decree gives a clear picture of what the committee

---

[15] *Charming Peggy*, #3, RCA.

[16] Ford, *JCC* **6**: pp. 884–885, 931–932, 964, 985–986; **7**: pp. 13, 30. There is no
mention of a special committee being appointed to hear the appeal in the case of the
Kingston Packet. Congress merely ordered that this case be received and that it be
prosecuted before the Committee on Appeals, apparently meaning the congressmen appointed to hear the preceding case. *Ibid.* **6**: p. 1060.

[17] *Charming Peggy*, #3, RCA.

[18] *Vulcan*, #5, *ibid*. The decree quoted is unsigned and undated, but there is a
notation in the records that the committee to hear this appeal "do adjudge that the
Decree of the Court of Admiralty of Virginia be reversed for the Errors appearing
on the face of the Proceedings. January 24th, 1777, Will Hooper, William Ellery,
Jona D. Sergeant." Although only one of these three, Ellery, had been on the
committee originally appointed to hear this case (Ford, *JCC*, 27 November, 1776, **6**:
pp. 985–986), this notation probably refers to the action taken by the committee in
the unsigned, undated decree referred to in the text.

thought the admiralty courts should do in handling prize cases. The strong overtones of the common law run through the instruction. As we shall see in a later chapter, the general practice in state admiralty courts was to ignore the strict rules of admissible evidence for prize cases insisted on in the High Court of Admiralty in England. Admissibility of evidence was not a serious issue in any cases on appeal to Congress. The state admiralty courts, thinking in terms of common law practice, admitted evidence freely which the High Court of Admiralty would never have allowed. This interlocutory order also shows that these attorneys, sitting as a committee of Congress, viewed themselves as acting in a judicial capacity not only reviewing lower court decrees but at times supervising its procedures.

Some doubts remained, however, in settling on the role of these *ad hoc* committees appointed by Congress. One committee wrote, "The Committee to whom was referred the Appeal in this above Cause beg leave to report, That it is the opinion of this Committee that the Sentence of Acquittal pronounced in this Cause . . . be in all things affirmed with Costs."[19] Here the committee viewed itself as a legislative committee reporting to Congress. There is no record that Congress ever voted on this report.

Perhaps the confusion in the case of the brigantine *Phoenix* helped convince Congress to try a new method of hearing appeals. Though the present records of the *Phoenix* case are incomplete, apparently it took Congress's committees three tries before the case was finally determined. The records were referred to an *ad hoc* committee of five, the same five appointed to hear the previous case.[20] After a hearing the committee affirmed the sentence of the state court. A few weeks later, however, on January 31, 1777, a petition came before Congress from the appellants showing that their appeal in the *Phoenix* case had been heard and decided by the wrong committee. Only two of the members signing the decree had been appointed to hear the appeal. Congress set aside the first decree and referred the appeal to the standing Committee on Appeals established the previous day. This Committee partly affirmed and partly reversed the lower

---

[19] *Richmond*, #7, RCA.
[20] Ford, *JCC* 7: p. 30.

court but apparently without providing for any notice to the
adverse party.[21] Six months later the appellees petitioned
Congress complaining of the *ex parte* character of the second
hearing.[22] The Committee on Appeals reported to Congress
suggesting that the petition for a new hearing be granted,
unless the appellant could show that the appellees had received notice of the previous hearing. Congress approved
the report and granted a second rehearing after the parties
had been notified of the date.[23] No records exist of this
rehearing except a notation that the decree below was reversed on September 3, 1777.[24]

---

[21] *Ibid.*, p. 79; Papers of the Continental Congress (National Archives), Item 42,
II, 267, 271.

[22] *Phoenix*, #8 & 19, RCA. This petition is incorrectly filed under #19, with the
heading "The Greenwich" which was the ship capturing the *Phoenix*.

[23] Ford, *JCC*, 7 and 14 June, 1777, **8:** pp. 427, 467.

[24] The procedure of hearing appeals in all cases heard by *ad hoc* committees
followed the general scheme of the cases of the *Thistle* and the *Elizabeth* with the
ambiguity of the committee's role continuing. Substantively the first eight cases also
were somewhat similar. Two cases, the *Elizabeth* and the *Charming Peggy*, dealt with
aspects of recapture of American property. In the second case the trial court's
condemnation to the recaptors would undoubtedly have been affirmed since the
prize had previously been awarded to the British captors by an admiralty court. The
original American owners no longer could claim restoration according to the resolves of Congress. But neither party prosecuted the appeal. (*Charming Peggy*, #3,
RCA).

The substantive issues of several of these early cases resembled the *Thistle*. The
property captured was claimed as American property, or at least as property not
within the scope of the resolves of Congress allowing capture of British ships. The
Betsey was claimed by the owners, citizens of Virginia and North Carolina, but the
condemnation of the ship to the captors was upheld on appeal. (*Betsey*, #4, RCA.)
The *Vulcan* was claimed by its owners from Virginia as the property of Americans
not hostile to the cause of independence (though, from the records, not too friendly
either). This case was remanded for retrial in the state admiralty court. (*Vulcan*, #5,
RCA.) The *Kingston Packet*, condemned in the Rhode Island admiralty court, had
been claimed by its owner from Massachusetts, though it also carried papers showing a different owner in Jamaica to protect it from capture by British ships. The
committee of Congress reversed the lower court's decree of condemnation. (*Kingston Packet*, #6, RCA. The *Kingston Packet* had previously been captured by Americans on suspicion of trading with the British, but restored to the owner, see Stephen
Moylan to Committee of Safety, Salem, 5 December, 1775, and Richard Derby, Jr. to
Committee of Safety, Salem, 9 December, 1775, Timothy Pickering Papers, XXXIX
(Microfilm, Massachusetts Historical Society). The *Richmond* had sailed to London
in the summer of 1775 to collect debts and settle affairs there for the owners from
Nantucket Island. With the outbreak of hostilities the captain found he could not
clear from London to an American port, so he had the ship and cargo put in the
name of a London firm and cleared for the West Indies and from there to Halifax.
When hailed by an American privateer, the crew was led to believe that the privateer
was British so they destroyed whatever papers they had proving American ownership. (This problem of double papers and privateers sailing under false colors
would lead to many disputes over the legality of captures throughout the war.) The

A more thorough analysis of the procedures and the substantive law followed by the Committees on Appeal and later by the Court of Appeals will be made in subsequent chapters. These few early cases, however, give some slight suggestion of the functioning of these appellate bodies. Congress had already received eight appeals; five had been determined by its *ad hoc* committees. After these first experiences with appeals, Congress took a small step toward more continuity in reviewing lower court judgments. As early as October, 1776, Congress felt the need for revising its resolutions concerning the capture and condemnation of prizes.[25] On January 30, 1777, Congress resolved that a standing committee of five members should be appointed to hear and determine appeals from the sentences of state admiralty courts in cases of captures. Their decisions should conform to the resolutions of Congress. Appeals would still be lodged with the secretary of Congress, the overworked but ever loyal Charles Thomson.[26] When Thomson received the lower court records, he delivered them to the Committee on Appeals for final determination.[27] On most of the appeals in the records there is a notation of the date of lodging, apparently in Thomson's hand.

In May, 1777, Congress settled on a rule of three; though the Committee on Appeals ordinarily consisted of five members, any three of them could hear and determine the appeals referred to them. A few days later Congress authorized the Committee to appoint a register, another step toward transforming a legislative committee into a clearly judicial institution.[28]

The *Journals of the Continental Congress* list the various members of Congress appointed to the *ad hoc* and the stand-

---

commander and crew insisted they had set their course for Nantucket Island. The Rhode Island admiralty court acquitted the ship restoring it to the American claimants. The captors appealed to Congress, only to have the sentence of the lower court affirmed with costs. (*Richmond*, #7, RCA).

[25] 17 October and 27 November, 1776, Ford, *JCC* **6**: pp. 885, 986.

[26] Thomson, a leading radical from Philadelphia, had been chosen by the First Continental Congress as secretary and again selected for that position by the Second Continental Congress. He served as secretary with incredible fidelity throughout the fifteen years of the life of the Continental Congress and at times, in its bleakest years, his presence practically alone breathed some spark of life into the dying Congress. Burnett, *Continental Congress*, pp. 27, 34, 67, 610–613, 720, 723–726.

[27] Ford, *JCC* **7**: p. 75.

[28] *Ibid.*, pp. 336–337, 348.

ing Committees on Appeal. But there are a few strange anomalies when these names are compared with the names of the commissioners on appeal who actually heard a particular case. The problems involved in having the wrong commissioners hear and determine the case of the *Phoenix* have already been mentioned. In two other early cases some of the commissioners who actually heard the appeal do not seem to be the ones who had been appointed for that case.[29] Perhaps once a person had been appointed to the Committee on Appeals, he would feel free to sit on a subsequent appeal, even though other members of Congress had been appointed in the meantime. This comes out most clearly with respect to Thomas McKean who had been appointed to the committee in February, 1778.[30] In the following year there were several changes in membership of the committee and finally on March 9, 1779, Congress mentioned the three members of the committee still active (not including Mc-Kean) and added two new members.[31] But for the rest of 1779 and during the first months of 1780 McKean participated in at least thirteen cases on appeal, although there is no indication that he was ever again appointed to the committee. (During this same period, by the way, McKean was both president of Delaware and chief justice of Pennsylvania.)[32]

The Committee on Appeals continued to serve Congress till February, 1780, when the Court of Appeals in Cases of Capture was established. The members of the Committee on Appeals were all, of course, members of Congress, and so the Committee suffered from the same problems of fluctuating membership that troubled Congress. In the years that the committee functioned, including the few cases heard by the early *ad hoc* committees, at least forty-two appeals were heard and determined. During these same years thirty-seven members of Congress were at one time or another appointed to sit on the Committee on Appeals. Congress usually tried to keep five active members on the committee.[33] In the forty-one

29 *Richmond*, #7; *Sherburne (Swain v. Newman)*, 10 May, 1777, #10, RCA.

30 Ford, *JCC* 10: p. 177.

31 *Ibid.* 13: p. 297.

32 *DAB* 12: pp. 79–81. McKean was at this time active in Congress, especially with questions relating to foreign affairs and establishing a court of appeals in prize cases. Ford, *JCC* 13: pp. 25, 93–94; 14: pp. 894, 898–899, 912, 924–925, 1002; 15: pp. 1021–1025, 1048; 16: pp. 32, 100, 121, 357.

33 Ford, *JCC* 7: pp. 75, 172, 336–337; 9: pp. 800, 936, 1015; 10: p. 177; 11: p. 724; 12: pp. 947, 1064; 13: p. 297; 14: pp. 896, 953, 1004; 15: pp. 1171, 1360; 16: p. 17.

months of Congress's reliance on the committee, this constant turnover of members made it more difficult for clear,
stable judicial policies to be settled upon.

Congress did show, however, an appreciation of the judicial character of the Committee on Appeals. Of the thirty-
seven congressmen appointed to the committee, all but three
had studied law and been admitted to the bar.[34] The three
not known to have been lawyers, Joseph Jones of Virginia,
Henry Laurens of South Carolina, and Benjamin Rumsey of
Maryland,[35] played an insignificant role in the committee's
work. In fact, there is no decision of the committee on record
in which any of these three are known to have taken part. On
the other hand, the most active members of this committee
were all among the best trained lawyers the American states
had to offer. The records are incomplete; some cases on
appeal include no decree or no indication of which members
heard and decided the appeal. But from the records of the
forty-two cases known to have been determined by the
Committee on Appeals, fourteen members of Congress participated in five or more cases. Congress, in choosing these
men, manifested its concern to have the best available legal
talent sitting on the Committee on Appeals.[36]

---

[34] *Biographical Dictionary of the American Congress, 1774–1961* (Washington 1961),
passim.

[35] *Ibid.*, pp. 1138, 1197, 1548.

[36] William Henry Drayton of South Carolina had studied at Oxford. He studied
law privately and under the Crown sat on the council and served as assistant judge in
his colony. Under the new state constitution, while representing his state in Congress, he also sat as chief justice from 1776 till his death in 1779.

William Ellery of Rhode Island had graduated from Harvard, studied law, gained
experience as a naval officer and served on the board of admiralty of Congress.
Appointed by President Washington in 1790 as collector of customs for Newport, he
held this office for thirty years till his death.

Oliver Ellsworth of Connecticut began college at Yale and graduated from Princeton. After being admitted to legal practice, he soon became one of the leaders of the
Connecticut bar. He held various state judicial positions during the war and in 1787
was a delegate to the Federal Convention. He sat in the United States Senate from its
first session till his appointment as chief justice of the United States Supreme Court.
The Judiciary Bill of 1789 was largely drafted by Ellsworth.

Cyrus Griffin of Virginia studied law at the University of Edinburgh and at the
Middle Temple in London. He was elected to the Virginia legislature from 1777 to
1778 and then to Congress, where he represented his state till Congress selected him
in 1780 as a judge of the Court of Appeals in Cases of Capture. President Washington later appointed him federal judge for the district of Virginia, in which position
he served till his death in 1810.

John Henry of Maryland graduated from Princeton, studied law, and completed
his legal training at the Middle Temple. He represented the state in the Continental
Congress and was chosen by Maryland to be its first United States senator. He

From the start some members of Congress saw the need to
take further steps to transform the Committee on Appeals

resigned from the Senate in 1797 to accept the office of Governor of Maryland,
which he held till his death the following year.

Ezra L'Hommedieu of New York graduated from Yale, studied law, and was
admitted to the bar. From 1775 till his death in 1811, he was continuously occupied
in the state's public service. He helped frame the New York constitution of 1777.

Henry Marchant of Rhode Island studied at the University of Pennsylvania, read
law with Edmund Trowbridge, one of the greatest common lawyers of New England, and under the Crown served as colonial agent in London. He was chosen
attorney general of Rhode Island in the last years before the Revolution. He sat in
the Continental Congress and later in the Rhode Island General Assembly. In 1790,
President Washington appointed him United States district judge and he continued
on the bench till his death in 1796.

Thomas McKean of Delaware studied law in the office of his cousin, David
Finney, served in various political and judicial positions before 1776, and also had
the opportunity before the Revolution to complete his legal education at the Middle
Temple. During the war he became acting president of Delaware and at the same
time he sat as chief justice of Pennsylvania. After the war he was elected governor of
Pennsylvania.

William Paca of Maryland graduated from the University of Pennsylvania,
studied law and was admitted to practice. He rounded out his legal training at the
Inner Temple, London. After holding political offices before the war, he was sent to
represent the state in the Continental Congress. Congress chose him in 1780 as judge
of the Court of Appeals in Cases of Capture. Later he was elected governor of
Maryland. In 1789, President Washington named him federal district judge, which
office he held till his death in 1799.

Robert Treat Paine of Massachusetts graduated from Harvard, studied law, and,
being admitted to the bar, was active in state politics. He served as the first attorney
general of his state and helped draft the Massachusetts constitution of 1780. After the
war Paine sat on the Massachusetts supreme court.

Jesse Root of Connecticut graduated from Princeton, studied law, and was admitted to practice. During the war he sat in Congress and on the state council. After the
war he was appointed to the state's superior court and later named its chief justice.

Jonathan Dickinson Sergeant of New Jersey attended Princeton and studied law.
He was active in forming the state constitution of 1776 and was appointed attorney
general of Pennsylvania. After the war he declined public office and devoted his
attention to the practice of law.

James Wilson of Pennsylvania received his training at the Universities of St.
Andrews, Glasgow, and Edinburgh, all in his native Scotland. After studying law in
Pennsylvania he was admitted to the bar and soon became a leading attorney of the
state. He served during the war as the advocate general for France in America and
as legal adviser to Robert Morris in the formation of the Bank of Pennsylvania. He
played a key role in the Federal Convention. In 1789, President Washington appointed him to the Supreme Court.

George Wythe of Virginia attended William and Mary College, studied law, and
was admitted to the bar. He became a professor of law, helped revise the laws of his
state, and sat as judge in the state court of chancery. He participated in the Federal
Convention. After judicial reorganization in Virginia he became chancellor, holding
that office till 1801. (*Biographical Dict. of Amer. Cong.*, pp. 830, 854, 858, 975, 1043,
1217, 1262, 1303, 1417, 1421, 1541, 1581, 1830, 1858; *DAB* **5**: pp. 448–449; **6**: pp.
86, 111–115; **7**: pp. 618–619; **8**: p. 549; **11**: p. 232; **12**: pp. 79–81, 271–272; **14**: pp.
123–124, 156–157; **16**: pp. 148–149, 589–590; **20**: pp. 326–330, 586–589.)

into a clearly established appellate judiciary. James Wilson early in 1777 urged Congress to appoint an official who would manage all admiralty cases on its behalf and give it his opinions on questions of civil and maritime law and the law of nations. Though Wilson's primary interest was to promote his own name to serve in this office of combined advocate general and attorney general, he does show an appreciation of the need for judicial officers to enable state admiralty courts and the congressional appellate jurisdiction to function properly.[37]

By the summer of 1777, the Committee on Appeals proposed that Congress consider the propriety of establishing a court of appeals.[38] The preoccupation of members of Congress with so many other concerns helps explain why the members of the Committee on Appeals desired a court to relieve them of hearing prize appeals. Thereafter the committee was frequently called "the court of appeals."[39] As the committee grew in experience and developed its procedures during its forty-one-month existence, it acted less like a legislative committee and more like an appellate court. By the time the Court of Appeals was born in 1780, the basic procedures and patterns for decisions were already quite well established.[40]

For the first few years of the war, till the beginning of 1780 (and later as well), Congress was continuously occupied with enormous problems seemingly beyond its ability to solve. In these early years after the Declaration of Independence, Congress mulled over the pressing questions of military organization and operations. Amidst many moments of setback and defeat and an occasional day of splendid victory, Congress had to face the need for a well-disciplined, properly led army. Arms, rations, clothing, as well as pay for the troops were usually scarce. The short-term enlistments threatened at times to cause the American forces to disintegrate. And

---

[37] James Wilson to Robert Morris, 14 January, 1777, Burnett, *Letters* 2: pp. 215–217.

[38] Ford, *JCC*, 5 August, 1777, 8: p. 607.

[39] For instance, *ibid.*, 26 May, 1778, 9: p. 533. Though the Committee was often called the court of appeals, in this work that title will be used only for the Court of Appeals established in 1780.

[40] The questions of procedure and substantive law during the period of the Committee on Appeals will be studied in chapters VI and VII together with procedural and substantive questions from the period of the Court of Appeals.

while many in and out of Congress were questioning the leadership of Washington and intriguing against him, Congress had to ponder how the war should be conducted. At the same time Congress debated the complex, emotion-laden issues of forming some type of permanent union for the newly created states. Disagreement over questions of voting, financial contributions, and western land claims sparked the long discussions over the proposed Articles of Confederation. Congress tried courageously to find a way of unifying the wills of thirteen distinct and often antagonistic political entities. On many occasions it could not even maintain sufficient representation of these states to continue the debates effectively or to vote on the various resolves. Then there were the overwhelmingly critical problems of planning for foreign alliances and preparing realistic but acceptable terms for peace with Great Britain. Ministers had to be sent abroad to the geographically and psychologically distant world of Europe; these ministers had to be instructed, their dissensions smoothed over and their indiscretions repaired. And all the while Congress had to face the fact that it had little idea where it would get the money to finance the war or anything else. As it poured out more and more paper money and watched it vanish in a flood of depreciation and inflation, Congress was forced to try to borrow from France or any other friendly nation willing to loan. Often Congress spent the money before the loan was granted. Amidst these immense and urgent problems, Congress on occasion had to flee from place to place because of the threat from advancing British armies. Then there was always the difficulty of the constant turnover of membership in Congress. Frustrations with congressional inability to solve its insoluble problems, as well as the expense and inconvenience of sitting in Congress far from home and personal responsibilities, led many to decide that their time and energy could be better spent in their own states.

During these years before 1780, while Congress staggered under a load it could barely carry and while the Committee on Appeals continued to review state prize judgments, Congress found time to become directly involved in many aspects of maritime matters and prize affairs. For example, claims came to Congress for damages to ships that had been taken into the service of the United Colonies. Congress investigated the facts and paid all just claims.[41] It tried to assure a just share of prizes to the officers and crews of naval ships.[42] When commanders of privateers violated the terms of their commissions, Congress insisted that they be prosecuted. Some of these violations bordered on piracy, causing great distress in Congress whose members expressed an utter abhorrence of all irregular and culpable violations of the law of nations.[43]

Petitions to Congress touching more directly on prize cases continued to receive attention. When the question belonged more properly in a state admiralty court, the petition was dismissed by Congress.[44] When the owners of one privateer appealed to Congress from a court decree in a prize case, Congress dismissed the petition, perhaps because the owners had commenced the suit in a court of common pleas.[45]

One of the state admiralty judges petitioned Congress to remedy an inequity resulting from his own precise interpretation of the resolutions of Congress in a prize case. Some citizens of North Carolina had assisted a congressional vessel in the capture of a British ship, the sloop *Tryal*. The commander of the naval ship promised them the whole prize, releasing his own and his crew's interest in the capture. He had no authority from Congress, however, to release to the joint captors the two-thirds which should have gone to Congress. He made a large number of other captures in which the North Carolinians had assisted, but they had released their shares in all the other prizes to the commander and crew of the naval vessel. When the sloop *Tryal* was libeled, it was condemned as lawful prize. But the admiralty judge in North Carolina felt bound by the resolutions of Congress and decreed two-thirds of the value of the prize to the use of the United Colonies and then requested Congress to rectify what he saw as an inequity. Congress agreed for it decided

---

[41] Ford, *JCC*, 12 July, 1776, 8 August, 1777, 23 October, 1778, **5:** pp. 545–546; **8:** pp. 622–623; **12:** pp. 1057–1059.

[42] *Ibid.*, 4 and 16 October, 1776, **5:** p. 847; **6:** pp. 882–883.

[43] *Ibid.*, 13 November, 1776, **6:** pp. 949–950 and William Hooper to Robert Morris, 31 December, 1776; Hooper to Joseph Hewes, 1 January, 1777; Committee of Secret Correspondence to William Bingham, 1 February, 1777, and Samuel Chase to the Maryland Council of Safety, 6 February, 1777, Burnett, *Letters* **2:** pp. 199, 200–201, 233, 236.

[44] Ford, *JCC*, 21 March, 1777, **7:** pp. 188–189.

[45] *Ibid.*, 28 May, 1778, **11:** p. 533.

that the state captors should receive the share which by law belonged to Congress.[46]

Congress soon discovered that privateering could involve the new-born nation in international complications. This came home dramatically in the case of the Portuguese snow *Our Lady of Mount Carmel and St. Anthony*. An American privateer, the schooner *Phoenix*, with Joseph Cunningham as master, had taken the Portuguese snow as a prize and sent it to Boston to be tried. Cunningham's orders from the owners of the *Phoenix* gave him leave to capture Portuguese ships if he should hear that Portuguese vessels were actually taking American ships.[47] Cunningham went even beyond these dubiously legal instructions. When the case came up for trial in Massachusetts, the snow was acquitted and ordered restored to the Portuguese owners.

In March, 1778, Robert Morris, as part-owner of the schooner *Phoenix*, obviously foreseeing large damage suits resulting from this capture, petitioned Congress to act in the case. Since the captain of the snow had not been brought to America with his ship, there was no one to receive the restored ship and its valuable cargo. Morris urged Congress to preserve the nation's good character by allowing the ship to be sold along with the cargo and to guarantee payment to the original owners whenever they should present their claim. He argued that the owners of the *Phoenix* had not been in any way culpable in the affair and asked Congress to relieve them from the possible legal difficulties the misconduct of their commander had brought upon them.[48] Congress investigated the facts by a committee, allowed the sale of the snow and its cargo, authorized the investment of the net proceeds in public funds of the United States, and provided for notification to the owners through the American commissioners in Paris. Congress made clear, however, that the owners were

---

[46] *Ibid.*, 29 May, 1778, **11:** p. 549; PCC, Item 41, X, 13.

[47] The owners' instructions to Cunningham were perhaps inspired at a time when Congress was expressing strong feelings of resentment against Portugal for forbidding American ships to enter its ports and for ordering those in port to leave as soon as possible. Congress pondered whether these acts of hostility would justify American hostile acts against Portuguese subjects. Ford, *JCC*, 1 May, 1777, **7:** p. 318.

[48] *Ibid.*, 6 March, 1778, **10:** p. 227; Memorial of Morris, PCC, Item 44, 49. Other papers relative to this case, PCC, Item 44, 1–185. Henry Laurens commented with biting sarcasm on Morris's pious concern about the national good faith, Laurens to Samuel Adams, 7 March, 1778, Burnett, *Letters* **3:** pp. 113–114.

not barred from taking any legal action against the owners of the schooner *Phoenix*.[49]

When a claimant for the owners appeared in the person of John Garcia Duarti, Congress discovered it still had not extricated the national good faith. Duarti objected to Congress's settlement, stating that the restitution in American money was useless to the owners. Furthermore, large commissions for the sale of the ship and cargo had been deducted from the proceeds. Since Duarti found that the special damages he sought would take too long to litigate in American courts, he asked that Congress pay him the full value of the ship and cargo in gold or in bills of exchange on any port of Europe together with reasonable damages.[50] This was in June, 1779, a year after Congress first got involved in the case. With the precarious financial situation of Congress ever before their minds, the members of Congress must have shuddered at the thought of paying Duarti some £6,000 sterling. Congress wanted Cunningham, the master, and Carter Braxton of Virginia, the principal owner of the privateer, prosecuted by Virginia for this illegal capture. Thomas Jefferson, governor of the state, however, on the advice of Edmund Randolph, the state's attorney general, informed Congress that the Virginia admiralty court lacked jurisdiction over criminal offenses committed on the high seas.[51] For more than three years after the capture, Congress continued to be troubled with the case till in January, 1781, Duarti finally got a substantial settlement and took the first ship for Cadiz.[52]

Similar violations of neutrality by American privateers came before Congress from time to time. The American ministers in Paris, however, being closer to the irate owners and indignant neutral governments, sensed the dangers even more acutely. They wrote urgently to Congress informing it

[49] Ford, *JCC*, 11 May, 1778, **11:** p. 487, and **13:** pp. 56, 73, 78, 158; PCC, Item 44, 79.

[50] PCC, Item 44, 77.

[51] Ford, *JCC* **14:** pp. 803, 838–842, 856–860. John Jay to Thomas Jefferson, 26 July, 1779; Edmund Randolph to Jefferson, 13 November, 1779; Jefferson to Samuel Huntington, 30 December, 1779, Boyd, *Papers of Jefferson* **3:** pp. 57, 184–186, 249–251.

[52] Ford, *JCC* **14:** pp. 749, 777; **15:** p. 1021; **17:** pp. 528–530, 692–694; **19:** p. 75; PCC, Item 78, II, 317–320, IV, 19, 73.

of the great harm done by a few irresponsible American
privateers.[53]

With all these problems and complications continually con-
fronting it, Congress saw the need to modify the laws regulating captures. Before the Declaration of Independence Congress had authorized capture of ships and cargoes belonging
to inhabitants of Great Britain and any other vessel carrying
supplies to the British army.[54] After the Declaration, Congress found it impossible to distinguish among subjects of the
same sovereign, so it became necessary to consider as
enemies not only the inhabitants of England and Scotland,
but all the subjects of the king of Great Britain wherever they
might dwell. Others who would aid, abet, or adhere to the
British king would also be considered enemies. Therefore,
the previous resolutions allowing capture of ships and cargoes of inhabitants of Great Britain now were extended to
cover the vessels and cargoes belonging to any subject or
subjects of the king of Great Britain, that is, property owned
by residents of the various British colonies or dominions.
Because of petitions from the inhabitants of the Bermudas,
Providence, and the Bahama Islands who needed provisions,
Congress permitted an exception in favor of the property of
residents of these islands.[55]

A new aspect of the seizure of enemy ships developed in
August, 1776, when Congress learned that some crews of
American ships had risen against their captains and seized
the vessels. When one of these ships was taken to England,
Congress expressed shock at discovering that the mutinous
crew was publicly countenanced.[56] Upon further provoca-
tion Congress retaliated a year later. It learned that the

---

[53] Arthur Lee to Committee of Foreign Affairs, 27 November, 1777, and 15
November, 1778; Benjamin Franklin to Ferdinand Grand, 4 October, 1778, Wharton, *Correspondence* 2: pp. 430–431, 784–785, 840.

[54] Ford, *JCC*, 23 March, 1776, 4: pp. 229–232.

[55] *Ibid.*, 24 July, 1776, 5: pp. 605–606. The resolve read: "That all the resolutions
of this Congress, passed on the twenty third day of March last, and on the third day
of April last, relating to ships and other vessels, their tackle, apparel and furniture,
and all goods, wares and merchandises, belonging to any inhabitant or inhabitants
of Great Britain, taken on the high seas, or between high and low water mark, be
extended to all ships and other vessels, their tackle, apparel and furniture, and all
goods, wares and merchandises, belonging to any subject or subjects of the King of
Great Britain, except the inhabitants of the Bermudas, and Providence or Bahama
Islands."

[56] *Ibid.*, 20 August, 1776, 5: p. 692.

British had received into their ports and condemned as lawful prize to the captors several American ships which their masters and crews had delivered to British officials. Now Congress in return encouraged British crews to mutiny and seize control of their ships and bring them into any American port where they could libel the ship and cargo and be considered lawful captors if the ship was condemned as prize.[57]

The case of the capture of the Portuguese ship and other harassment or capture of neutral ships caused such concern in Congress over the violations of the law of nations by its privateers that Congress published a proclamation on May 9, 1778, stating that complaints had arrived of offenses to neutral nations committed by American armed vessels. Neutral ships, flying neutral colors, had been captured contrary to the usage and customs of nations. To end these acts of piracy which brought dishonor on the national character Congress commanded all captains, commanders, and other officers and seamen belonging to any American armed vessel to observe strictly in every detail their commissions and instructions based on the resolutions of Congress. It ordered them especially to pay a sacred regard to the rights of neutral powers and to the laws of civilized nations. On no pretense should they presume to capture any ship belonging to subjects of princes or powers in alliance with the United States unless the ship was carrying contraband goods or soldiers to the British. They must not seize or plunder any ships under the protection of neutral coasts. Captains or crews violating these orders would be punished and held liable for damages. If they should be taken by any foreign power, Congress would give them no protection. They would have to suffer such punishment as might be inflicted on such offenders.[58] With this broadside circulating among the privateers, Congress hoped to hear a little less of the illegal activities of the ships it had commissioned. But privateers had long been an audacious lot; no mere paper commands of Congress would ever suffice to restrain their energies entirely within legal bounds.

Britain had over the years experienced similar problems

---

[57] *Ibid.*, 14 October, 1777, **9**: pp. 802–804.

[58] *Ibid.* **11**: p. 486; see also **10**: p. 196 and President of Congress to President of New Hampshire, 11 May, 1778; Committee of Foreign Affairs to the Commissioners at Paris, 14 May, 1778, Burnett, *Letters* **3**: pp. 225, 236.

controlling the illegal activities or piracies of its privateers. As Congress threatened its privateers with civil or criminal proceedings, similarly in Great Britain civil remedies had long been available to the injured neutral by putting the privateer's surety bond in suit to recover damages. Criminal sanctions had also been imposed in Britain upon privateers indicted for felony or piracy and found guilty by a jury in the special admiralty sessions of oyer and terminer. Privateers, therefore, could go too far with their outrageous behavior and find themselves convicted and sentenced to death. Perhaps such hangings did have some salutary effect on other privateers.[59]

So, as we have seen, Congress had succeeded in establishing an appellate court to review the sentences of the state prize courts. What began as an *ad hoc* committee, with clear traces of its origins as a legislative committee, developed into an appellate judiciary. Decrees of state admiralty courts were reviewed and often reversed. Congress appointed its most qualified lawyer-members to hear and determine these appeals. But because of the irresponsible actions of a few captains, Congress had to struggle with the irate protests of the owners of captured neutral vessels. It, therefore, continued directly to supervise the capture of enemy ships, modifying the regulations and instructions to captains as the situation of the sea war progressed.

When the appellate process broke down completely in the case of the sloop *Active*, Congress had to reconsider and re-evaluate the function of the Committee on Appeals. It was on the question of the power of the central government over a state, the question of federalism, that the inadequacies of the Committee on Appeals became glaring. Did Congress have the final, exclusive authority over prize disputes which could involve the new nation in serious international complications? As Congress faced the problem of establishing a Court of Appeals for prize cases, it also found it necessary to reformulate its regulations controlling the capture of enemy ships. The case of the sloop *Active* helped bring all these issues to a head.

---

[59] Pares, *Colonial Blockade*, pp. 48–52.

III. The Case of the Sloop *Active*— Congress Establishes a Court

GIDEON OLMSTED and three other American sailors from Connecticut had been captured at sea by the British, taken to Jamaica, and put on board the sloop *Active* to help sail it with supplies to New York, then held by the British. About midnight of September 6, 1778, Olmsted and his companions took control of the sloop and ordered the two English sailors on deck to follow their directions while they hauled up the ladder and coiled a cable around the companion to block the passage. John Underwood, captain of the *Active*, awoke and demanded they return the ladder and remove the cables. When Olmsted refused, Underwood started firing through a hole in the wall wounding Olmsted who nevertheless still insisted his men had captured the vessel. The firing continued, so the four captors turned a four pounder into the cabin and fired. This proved rather harmless, so they loaded a swivel gun with shot and fired into the cabin. As this could become dangerous, Underwood stopped firing. In the morning, however, he drove wedges into the rudder to make steering impossible. Olmsted and his men started prying up the stern boards to unwedge the rudder. The passengers in the cabin promised to remove the wedges, if the captors would not tear up the deck and expose those below to the elements. The captain later claimed he had unwedged the rudder only in return for Olmsted's promise that he and his men would restore the *Active* once they had sailed near enough land to escape in the sloop's boat. Two of the captured English sailors, however, and one of the passengers swore that Olmsted could have navigated well enough with oars and sails to bring it to port even if the rudder had remained wedged. By noon on September 7 the rudder was free. Captain Underwood, still irate, threatened to ignite a keg of powder in the cabin and send them all to the bottom, but the passengers in the cabin had no intention of allowing this desperate solution. Olmsted ordered the

101

sloop steered northwest toward Egg Harbor, New Jersey. For
nearly twenty-four hours after the rudder was freed, the ship
sailed under strong wind toward port and by mid-morning
on September 8 land was in sight.

About 10:30 that morning two American ships appeared.
The nearer, the brigantine *Convention*, with British colors
flying, hailed the *Active*, boarded it, and took captive Olmsted
and his men, as well as Captain Underwood. The other ship,
the sloop *Le Gerard*, had agreed to sail with the *Convention*
and to share in the prize money from any captures. Captain
Thomas Houston of the *Convention* brought the captured
Active into Philadelphia and immediately libeled it in the
admiralty court.[1] A local newspaper printed Houston's version of the capture. It stressed that Olmsted and his three
men had been forced to promise to go ashore in the boat
when they neared shore in order to get Captain Underwood
to unwedge the rudder.[2] With this pre-trial publicity favor-
ing the local parties to the suit, Olmsted faced an uphill
struggle in court.

Houston filed a libel in the admiralty court, and James
Josiah claimed for the owners and crew of the sloop *Le Gerard*
as joint captors. Olmsted also filed a claim, but to the whole
of the *Active* and its cargo of rum and coffee, alleging that his
men had captured it to make their escape and to prevent the
cargo from supplying the British army and fleet. He insisted
they had absolute command and control of the *Active* before
the *Convention* and *Le Gerard* had approached and captured
it.[3] This set up a clear question of fact for a jury to determine: was the sloop *Active* an enemy ship when Houston
captured it or was it in the effective control of an American
crew?

---

[1] Depositions of Captain John Underwood, Robert Jackson, and James Taylor, *The
Case of the Sloop Active* (Philadelphia, 1779), pp. 5–14; depositions of James Holmes,
Robert Robson, and George Roberts, Richard Peters, ed., *The Whole Proceedings in the
Case of Olmsted and Others versus Rittenhouse's Executrices* (Philadelphia, 1809), pp.
11–27. No records from the lower court are in the file of the *Active (Olmsted v.
Houston)*, 15 December, 1778, #39, RCA. A vivid, first hand account of the capture,
as well as the earlier adventures of the author, is given in *Journal of Gideon Olmsted*,
Frederick Law Olmstead Collection (LCMss). I am indebted to Mr. Gerald W.
Gawalt of the American Revolution Bicentennial Committee for calling this *Journal*
to my attention.

[2] *Pennsylvania Packet*, 15 September, 1778, and *Pennsylvania Evening Post*, 16
September, 1778.

[3] The libel and claims are printed in Peters, *Whole Proceedings*, pp. 4–11.

The legal basis of Olmsted's claim apparently was never challenged in the trial court or on appeal. Since he and his fellow prisoners had no commission to capture British property at sea, they may have based their claim on the congressional resolve of March 23, 1776, allowing condemnation of British vessels to non-commissioned captors where the capture had been made "near the shores of any of these colonies, by the people of the country." Olmsted's claim stressed that the *Active* was carrying supplies to the British army and navy and that its capture was to prevent the cargo from reaching the British forces. The resolve of Congress of March 23 allowed non-commissioned Americans to capture "all vessels which may be employed in carrying supplies to the ministerial armies." No one thought it worth questioning whether this seizure had been made "near the shores of any of these colonies."[4] The other possible legal basis for awarding the *Active* to the Olmsted claimants was the congressional resolve of October 14, 1777, allowing condemnation to the "master or mariners" of any British vessel brought into an American port by its mutinous British crew.[5] Whether American prisoners impressed to serve on a British vessel would come within this resolve is nowhere discussed.

The Pennsylvania admiralty court, George Ross presiding, heard the case in November, 1778. After listening to the various claims and answers and the lengthy depositions, the jury reached a verdict awarding one-fourth of the proceeds of the sloop and its cargo to Olmsted and his three companions. The remaining three-fourths were to be divided between the second captors, those concerned in the brigantine *Convention* and the sloop *Le Gerard*. Since the *Convention* had been fitted out at the expense of Pennsylvania, a large share

---

[4] Ford, *JCC* **4:** p. 232. The resolve reads:
"That all vessels, with their tackle, apparel, and furniture, and cargoes, belonging to the inhabitants of Great Britain, as aforesaid, and all vessels which may be employed in carrying supplies to the ministerial armies, which shall happen to be taken near the shores of any of these colonies, by the people of the country, or detachments from the army, shall be deemed lawful prize . . . [to be] equally divided among all those, who shall have been actually engaged in taking the said prize."

[5] *Ibid.* **9:** p. 802. The resolve reads:
"That any vessel or cargo, the property of any British subject, not an inhabitant of Bermuda or any of the Bahama islands, brought into any of the ports or harbours of any of these United States by the master or mariners, shall be adjudged lawful prize, and divided among the captors in the same proportion as if taken by any continental vessel of war."

of the prize would go into the state treasury. Judge Ross on November 5 decreed the division of the prize as determined by the jury. Immediately the Olmsted claimants appealed to Congress.[6]

At this point Major General Benedict Arnold entered the scene. Since he had made himself suspect with some vindictive but influential men in Philadelphia just at this time, his involvement in the case of the *Active* only muddied already turbulent waters. Two days after the judgment in the admiralty court, Arnold and Stephen Collins put up £2,000 as security for the appeal by Olmsted.[7] Shortly afterwards Arnold was accused in a Philadelphia newspaper of buying an interest in the claim of the sloop *Active*, a new species of champerty, as the writer termed it.[8] A few months later Arnold was charged by the Pennsylvania General Assembly with various affronts to the civilian population and with using his military position for his own financial gain. One of the articles of the indictment charged him with an illegal and unworthy purchase of the suit of the *Active* at an inadequate price. Apparently Arnold had bought a half interest in Olmsted's claim.[9] Arnold's connection with the appeal certainly did not help matters for Olmsted in Pennsylvania, especially since two of Arnold's personal enemies sat on the state's executive council.

When Congress received the appeal, it referred it to the Committee on Appeals consisting then of William Henry Drayton, John Henry, William Ellery, and Oliver Ellsworth. They heard the parties by their counsel at the statehouse in Philadelphia on December 12. After holding the case under advisement for several days, they decreed on the fifteenth that the judgment of the state court should be reversed. They awarded the whole of the *Active* and cargo to Gideon Olmsted and the three other American prisoners, the first captors, and ordered the Pennsylvania admiralty court to issue process necessary to carry the decree into execution.

---

[6] Peters, *Whole Proceedings*, pp. 27–29.

[7] *Ibid.*, pp. 28–29.

[8] Signed by T[imothy] Matlack, Secretary of the Executive Council of Pennsylvania and one of Arnold's most unsparing critics. *Pennsylvania Packet*, 19 November, 1778.

[9] *Ibid.*, 9 February, 1779; *Pennsylvania Gazette*, 10 February, 1779, and Willard M. Wallace, *Traitorous Hero, The Life and Fortunes of Benedict Arnold* (New York, 1954), pp. 166–167, 180–192.

The appellees, Houston and Josiah, moreover, were to pay the appellants $280 for their costs in supporting the appeal.[10]

The Supreme Executive Council of Pennsylvania, hearing of this reversal, ordered the state attorney general to try to obtain a reconsideration of the case.[11] Judge Ross refused to execute the decree of the commissioners of appeals. He argued that according to state law the facts in a maritime case were to be established by the jury without re-examination or appeal. Therefore as long as the verdict remained in force, the admiralty court could not proceed in any manner contrary to the finding of the jury. He ordered the sale of the sloop and cargo. After deducting court costs the marshal was to bring the rest of the money to the court where it would remain pending further order of the judge.[12]

Late in the evening of January 3, Benedict Arnold wrote desperately to the Committee on Appeals. He had discovered that the marshal of the admiralty court would turn over to Judge Ross the money from the sale. Arnold claimed the judge had positively declared that no order of the Committee on Appeals would take the money out of his hands. Arnold feared that if Ross should pay the money into the state treasury, the claimants would have the whole state to contend with.[13]

Early next morning the Committee on Appeals granted Arnold's request for an injunction to the marshal of the state court commanding him to retain custody of all the money arising from the sale of the *Active*.[14] But the executive council of Pennsylvania, that same morning, directed the marshal to obey the orders of Judge Ross.[15] The marshal, therefore, turned over to the admiralty court £47,981. s2. d4, lawful Pennsylvania currency in congressional loan office certificates from the sale of the cargo. The *Active* itself remained

---

[10] *Active*, #39, RCA.

[11] *Penna. Colonial Records* 11: p. 697.

[12] Order of sale by Judge Ross, 28 December, 1778, *Case of Sloop Active*, p. 22; and Peters, *Whole Proceedings*, pp. 33–35. The statute of 9 September, 1778, had provided that "the findings of said jury shall establish the facts without re-examination or appeal," Mitchell and Flanders, *Statutes of Pennsylvania* 11: p. 279.

[13] *Active*, #39, RCA.

[14] Injunction signed by William Henry Drayton, William Ellery, and John Henry, *ibid.* There is no explanation why Ellsworth did not sign the injunction.

[15] *Penna. Colonial Records* 11: p. 657.

unsold.[16] That evening the commissioners of appeals received word that their injunction had been ignored. Totally
frustrated, they merely recorded the fact adding that they
were unwilling to enter into proceedings for contempt for
fear of the dangerous consequences to the public peace.[17]

The four commissioners drew up a report to Congress,
including all the facts of the trial, appeal, the refusal of the
trial court to execute the decree of the Committee on Appeals, and the futile effort to enjoin the marshal, along with
the pertinent legal papers, so Congress could take whatever
measures might be required by the situation. The Committee
on Appeals concluded by telling Congress it would not proceed further in this case, nor hear any other appeals, till its
authority was settled and its decrees given full effect.[18] Two
days later, on January 21, 1779, Congress appointed a special
committee of five to examine the report of the Committee
and the reasons of the refusal of Judge Ross.[19]

Thomas Burke,[20] chairman of the special committee, in an
exchange of letters with Joseph Reed,[21] president of
Pennsylvania, focused on the basic question, as he saw it, of
whether or not the law of any one state could control the
exercise of the power of Congress to decide finally all cases of
captures. Although he was unmoved by the arguments, Reed
replied with civility as he reminded Burke that Massachusetts

---

[16] *Case of Sloop Active*, p. 22.
[17] The register of the Committee on Appeals reported that he had delivered the
injunction to the marshal before the marshal had turned over the money to Judge
Ross. *Active*, #39, RCA.
[18] Ford, *JCC*, 19 January, 1779, **13:** pp. 86–92; PCC, Item 29, 351, 355.
[19] The members chosen were Thomas Burke, William Paca, Jesse Root, Eliphalet
Dyer, and Meriwether Smith, Ford, *JCC* **13:** p. 97.
[20] Thomas Burke was governor of North Carolina and also a member of Congress
during the Revolution. After practicing medicine he soon decided to give this
practice up for the law. In Congress he represented the strong state's rights position
in opposition to the proposed Articles of Confederation, a position in strange
contrast to the position he had to argue in representing the interests of Congress
against Pennsylvania in these discussions concerning the *Active*. *DAB* **3:** pp. 282–283.
[21] Joseph Reed, a graduate of Princeton, studied law under Richard Stockton and
later at the Middle Temple in London. He was active as a lawyer and in politics in
pre-revolutionary Philadelphia. He served in the state's militia and was military
secretary for Washington. He was elected to the Continental Congress in 1776 and
1777. In 1778 he was chosen president of the Supreme Executive Council of
Pennsylvania, which office he held till 1781. He personally directed the prosecution
of Benedict Arnold for corrupt practice in his military command in Philadelphia.
DAB **15:** pp. 451–453.

and New Hampshire also had laws restricting the right of appeal to Congress in prize cases.[22]

When efforts at compromise bore no fruit, the special committee reported back to Congress in February. These committee members strongly supported the Committee on Appeals, endorsed its authority to hear and determine appeals in all cases of captures and agreed that its power extended to verdicts of juries as well as decrees of judges. For several weeks Congress devoted considerable time to this report, resolving itself into the committee of the whole to allow freer discussion of the issues.[23]

On March 6 Congress finally approved a strongly stated report. After repeating the facts of the judgment by the admiralty court, the reversal by the Committee on Appeals and the subsequent impasse, Congress affirmed that its commissioners necessarily had power to examine questions of fact as well as issues of law. No finding of a jury in any admiralty court could destroy the right of appeal. Congress insisted that it alone was invested by the United States with the supreme power of war and peace. Since the power of executing the law of nations was essential to the power of war and peace, and since the legality of all captures on the high seas must be determined by the law of nations, Congress asserted its sole authority to decide finally on all questions of maritime captures. In order to compel a just and uniform execution of the law of nations, a control by appeal was necessary. This control must extend to verdicts of juries, otherwise juries would have ultimate supreme power of executing the law of nations in all cases of captures. In such a case juries would be beyond any control and could involve the United States in hostilities. Congress would lose its power of giving satisfaction to foreign nations complaining of violations of neutrality or of treaties or any other breaches of the law of nations. In conclusion Congress again stated that the

---

[22] Thomas Burke to Joseph Reed, 26 and 28 January, 1779, Burnett, *Letters* **4**: pp. 43, 45–46, and Joseph Reed to Thomas Burke, 28 and 29 January, 1779, Samuel Hazard, ed., *Pennsylvania Archives*, 1st ser. (11 v., Philadelphia, 1852–1855) **7**: pp. 170, 172.

[23] The report of the special committee with notations of the action of Congress for each paragraph is in PCC, Item 29, 357–359. The report is printed in slightly unreliable form in Ford, *JCC* **13**: pp. 134–137. Discussion of the report is noted *ibid.*, pp. 183, 252–253, 270–271.

Committee on Appeals which reversed the lower court sentence in the case of the *Active* had been properly constituted and had competent jurisdiction to make a final determination of the case. Its decree ought to be carried into effect.[24] Brave words from Congress, but words only would they remain.

A committee from the Pennsylvania legislature had met with the special committee of Congress. Together they had discussed the issues. Congress enacted the basic portions of the report of its special committee. The committee from the Pennsylvania legislature also reported back to ask the legislature for further directions. Pennsylvania's House of Representatives passed three resolves just a few days after Congress had passed its resolves in support of the Committee on Appeals. The Pennsylvania legislature agreed that the power of establishing courts for finally determining appeals in prize cases belonged to Congress according to the Articles of Confederation. Pennsylvania had acceded to the Articles, so its legislature should adopt regulations consistent with the principles of the Confederation. But the law of Pennsylvania stating that the findings of a jury in prize cases should not be reviewable was not repugnant to the resolutions of Congress. Therefore the proceedings of the state admiralty court in the *Active* case had a basis in this state law.[25] With the enunciation of these few principles, the state legislature rejected any compromise solution, deepening the impasse between the state and Congress.

The special committee of Congress, after another month of fruitless discussions with the committee of the Pennsylvania legislature, proposed to Congress two resolutions to cut the knot. The treasurer of Congress would pay to the Olmsted claimants the full amount of the sale of the *Active* and its cargo, plus the court costs assessed by the Committee on Appeals. Congress would then charge Pennsylvania with this sum. This direct solution seemed too risky to try, so it was postponed.[26] Meanwhile Congress received several petitions from Olmsted and the other claimants pleading for payment

[24] Ford, *JCC* **13**: pp. 281–285.
[25] *Journals of the House of Representatives of the Commonwealth of Pennsylvania, 1776–1781* (Philadelphia, 1782), 10 March, 1779: p. 335.
[26] Ford, *JCC*, 9 April, 1779, **13**: p. 435.

of all they had been awarded.[27] Congress finally made the momentous decision not to decide, at least for the moment. It approved a motion postponing further consideration of the *Active* case till the following September 15.[28] For five months it would avoid facing this case. Once again, however, the Olmsted claimants petitioned Congress asking that the amount awarded them be advanced, provided they would put up security to repay it with interest if Congress should so determine. Again Congress merely postponed the question till the following September.[29]

During the spring and summer of 1779 Pennsylvania's side of the case was publicized with telling arguments. In a lengthy newspaper analysis of the case and also in a pamphlet which presented key documents and well-reasoned observations, it became clear that the arguments of Congress in its March 6 resolutions had some weak points. Both these authors (perhaps the same person) argued, with Blackstone as authority, that judicial review of issues of fact destroyed the character of trial by jury. If a case was tried by a judge, as would be done in British admiralty courts, the facts as well as the law could be reviewed by a higher court. But in British common law practice the only review of a jury's verdict was to set aside the verdict and grant a new trial. Both authors referred to a recent, well-publicized case in colonial New York, the case of *Forsey v. Cunningham*. The defendant there in an assault and battery case sought to appeal the verdict of a jury. The lieutenant-governor contended strenuously that judgments in the colonies were reversible "both with respect to law and fact, upon the whole merits." The leaders of the bench and bar in New York had argued just as strongly against the lieutenant-governor's interpretation of the law.[30] The Pennsylvania pamphleteer in his observations on the case of the *Active* quoted from the chief justice of colonial New York, who had stated in commenting on the case of *Forsey v. Cunningham*:

The trial of facts is entrusted to the jury, and the power to

---

[27] *Ibid.*, pp. 320, 424–425, 472. Two petitions dated 19 and 23 April, 1779, are in PCC, Item 41, VII, 247, 251.

[28] Ford, *JCC*, 24 April 1779, **14:** p. 507.

[29] *Ibid.*, 28 April 1779, **14:** pp. 527–529; PCC, Item 42, VI, 25.

[30] *Forsey v. Cunningham* is fully analyzed in Smith, *Appeals*, pp. 390–412.

declare the law upon them to the Judges. These are distinct provinces. The limits between them are guarded by invariable usage, and the most incontestible authorities. The errors of Judges may be corrected by superior judicatories; as for instance—in England those of the King's Bench, in the Exchequer Chamber, and by the House of Peers. But in all these removes, the verdict of the jury suffers no *re-examination*, but is final and decisive.

Both writers in Pennsylvania reminded Congress that it had itself recommended that the colonies employ jury trials in prize courts to be set up in compliance with the resolutions of November 25, 1775. After engrafting common law juries onto prize trials, Congress would undermine the whole institution of trial by jury if it allowed appellate review of a jury's factual determination. These two writers continued by conceding that Congress undoubtedly had never thought of the possible foreign complications when it first authorized privateering and suggested jury trials for prize cases. Perhaps trial by a judge rather than by a jury would have been preferable in cases of maritime captures. (As a matter of fact, Pennsylvania soon after this changed its admiralty court statute eliminating the jury trial requirement.) But since Pennsylvania merely followed Congress's recommendations in tacking juries onto prize trials, Pennsylvania could not be criticized for trying to preserve the integrity of the jury system by refusing any re-examination of a jury's verdict. The whole case in dispute turned on a question of fact: who captured the *Active*? The jury found that both parties aided in the capture. No superior court should be able to overturn its verdict.[31]

Pennsylvania did make one concession to the Olmsted claimants; it paid them their one-fourth share of the proceeds.[32] Olmsted and his attorneys in the fall continued to pressure Congress for the full share of the money as awarded by the Committee on Appeals. Olmsted complained that the value of the money had already depreciated seven-eighths of its nominal value. Again he asked Congress to carry its decree into execution.[33] Another special committee

---

[31] Article signed "An American" in *Pennsylvania Packet*, 22 April, 1779, and *Case of the Sloop Active*, pp. 25–27; see also *Pennsylvania Gazette*, 21 April, 1779.

[32] V.P. Bryan to George Ross, 5 June, 1779, Hazard, *Penna. Archives* 1st ser., 8: p. 468.

[33] James Wilson and William Lewis (attorneys for Olmsted) to John Jay, president

of Congress met with a committee of the Pennsylvania legislature, got nowhere and reported back to Congress. Again its
report supported the authority of the Committee on Appeals. It asserted that Pennsylvania law could not bar the
claimants from a right of appeal to Congress and proposed
that Congress pay Olmsted and the other appellants the
remainder of what had been awarded them, a sum of
£38,250 Pennsylvania currency. The state would then be
charged with this sum and could reimburse itself by using the
judgment of the Committee on Appeals. Congress again
hesitated to adopt this effective but seemingly drastic solution.[34] The delegates pledged they would consider the subject in ten days but the ten days stretched to five months.

Meanwhile the Pennsylvania legislature authorized the
state treasurer to pay Houston and Josiah the three-fourths
of the proceeds that the state admiralty court had awarded
them.[35] More petitions came from Olmsted and his attorneys.[36] One last attempt of Congress in March, 1780, to pay
the claimants from the continental treasury and charge it to
the account of Pennsylvania again met with timid failure.
When the solution came to a vote, only one state supported
it.[37] After a year and a half of special committees, confer-
ences with committees of the Pennsylvania legislature, reports, resolutions, and postponements, Congress finally
dropped the whole question. Olmsted and his three companions still had received only the one-fourth awarded by the
admiralty court. Olmsted, however, never ceased fighting for
his rightful share of the capture and in 1809 the United
States Supreme Court finally saw to it that he reaped the fruit
of his labors.[38]

of Congress, 6 September, 1779, PCC, Item 78, XXIV, 83–85; Olmsted to Samuel
Huntington, president of Congress, 29 September, 1779, *ibid.* Item 78, XVII, 293;
Memorial of Olmsted to Congress, 13 October, 1779, *ibid.*, Item 42, VI, 31; Ford,
JCC 15: pp. 1028, 1122, 1166. For Wilson's participation in this case, see Charles
Page Smith, *James Wilson, Founding Father, 1742–1798* (Chapel Hill, 1956), pp.
124–128.

[34] Ford, *JCC*, 21 October 1779, **15**: pp. 1194–1196; PCC, Item 19, IV, 495.

[35] *Journals of Penna. House of Representatives*, 23 November, 1779: p. 401.

[36] Olmsted to Samuel Huntington, 22 December, 1779, PCC, Item 41, VII, 261,
and James Wilson and William Lewis to Congress, 15 March, 1780, *ibid.*, Item 78,
XXIV, 191–193.

[37] Ford, *JCC*, 21 March, 1780, **16**: pp. 273–274.

[38] *Ross et al. executors of Ross v. Rittenhouse*, 2 Dallas 160 (1792); same case, 1 Yeates
443 (1795[sic]); *Olmsted v. The Active*, 18 Fed. Cases, #10,503a (1803); *United States v.
Peters*, 5 Cranch 115 (1809); *United States v. Bright*, 24 Fed. Cases, #14,647 (1809).
See also J. Franklin Jameson, "The Predecessor of the Supreme Court," in *Essays in*

The first special committee appointed by Congress to study the *Active* case in its initial report noted, with masterful understatement, that it had discovered some imperfections in the system of maritime courts.[39] Some months later a group of prominent merchants of Philadelphia sent a memorial to Congress showing they had observed a few imperfections also. These merchants reminded Congress that certainty in the law is a great source of security for society. This certainty in law comes only from adhering to prior decisions. Since the Committee on Appeals was in a constant state of fluctuation, no fixed legal principles could be established. The merchants also criticized the delays which grew out of the committee's basic character. Since only members of Congress sat on this tribunal, it could hear appeals only where Congress was sitting, leading to great inconvenience and expense for the litigants. Perhaps the reluctance of some states to accede to the full jurisdiction of the committee resulted from these flaws. The privateering business, after all, demanded immediate rewards for the courage of the crews. So the merchants urged Congress to name judges for appeals who were not members of Congress and could thus devote more time to hearing the cases. A court of appeals set up on a lasting and solid foundation would eliminate much of the criticism.[40]

During the months that Olmsted was trying to keep his claim alive, Congress began to consider establishing one or more supreme courts of appeal for maritime cases and appointed a committee of Samuel Huntington, William Paca, and John Dickinson to draw up a plan to revise the appellate system.[41] This committee kept before it the provisions of

the Constitutional History of the United States in the Formative Period, 1775–1789, Jameson, ed. (Boston, 1889), pp. 19–22.

[39] Ford, *JCC*, 2 February, 1779, **13:** p. 137.

[40] PCC, Item 69, II, 65, 69; Ford, *JCC*, 22 May, 1779, **14:** pp. 626–627.

[41] Ford, *JCC*, 26 August, 1779, **14:** p. 1002. John Dickinson of Pennsylvania and Delaware, studied law in the office of John Moland and completed his study at the Middle Temple. Before the Revolution he sat in the Delaware and Pennsylvania assemblies. His pamphlets and articles, especially the *Farmer's Letters* in response to the Sugar and Stamp Acts, gave him prominence in the prewar period. He was a member of the First Continental Congress and was largely responsible for writing the Declaration of the Causes for Taking up Arms. Though he cast his vote in Congress against the Declaration of Independence, he supported the war, served in Congress, and in 1781 was chosen president of the Supreme Executive Council of Delaware. He was a member of the Federal Convention in 1787 and urged the adoption of the new Constitution in his Fabius letters.

Samuel Huntington of Connecticut was largely self educated in Latin and the law.

article nine of the Articles of Confederation, approved by Congress on November 15, 1777, which entrusted to the United States the exclusive right of determining questions of peace and war, of regulating the legality of captures on land or sea, of granting letters of marque and reprisal in times of peace, and of appointing courts for the trial of piracies and felonies committed on the high seas. Article nine also gave Congress sole and exclusive power to establish courts for receiving and determining final appeals in all cases of captures but prohibited any member of Congress from sitting as judge on any such courts.[42] Though article nine clearly gave Congress all the authority it needed to set up an appellate jurisdiction in prize cases, Congress's position was not as strong as it appeared. Not till February, 1781, did all the states ratify the Articles of Confederation. Consequently the committee of Congress appointed to plan for an appellate court system for prize cases could not base its planned courts on a clear constitutional mandate, because the Court of Appeals was destined to be established and functioning for nearly a year before the Articles received final ratification.

The committee reported to Congress at the end of Oc-

After being admitted to the bar, he sat in the colony's lower and upper houses. In 1765, he was appointed the king's attorney for Connecticut. He served as a justice of the peace and as a superior court judge before the Revolution. During the entire war he represented Connecticut in Congress and was president of Congress, 1779–1781. In 1784 he was appointed chief justice of the Connecticut superior court. He was elected governor of Connecticut in 1786 and held that office for eleven years.

William Paca of Maryland studied law in the office of Stephen Bordley and was admitted to practice. He completed his legal training at the Inner Temple. He served in the colonial legislature and was elected to Congress in 1774 and served in Congress almost continuously from 1775 to 1779. He helped prepare Maryland's first constitution in 1779. In 1778 he was appointed chief judge of the Maryland General Court. In 1780 Congress, as we shall see, selected him judge of the Court of Appeals in Cases of Capture. In 1782 he resigned this post when elected governor of Maryland. He was a delegate to the Maryland convention which ratified the Federal Constitution. In 1789 President Washington appointed him federal district judge, which position he held till his death. *DAB* 5: pp. 299–301; 9: pp. 418–419; 14: pp. 123–124.

[42] Ford, *JCC* 9: pp. 915–916. The relevant sections of Article IX read:

"The United States in Congress assembled, shall have the sole and exclusive right and power of . . . establishing rules for deciding in all cases, what captures on land or water shall be legal, and in what manner prizes taken by land or naval forces in the service of the United States shall be divided or appropriated—of granting letters of marque and reprisal in times of peace—appointing courts for the trial of piracies and felonies committed on the high seas and establishing courts for receiving and determining finally appeals in all cases of captures, provided that no member of Congress shall be appointed a judge of any of the said courts." Thorpe, *Constitutions* 1: pp. 12–13.

tober, 1779. Congress then considered and discussed the proposals during November and December. Much of this debate amounted to a steady process of pulling the teeth of the originally strong proposals. At first the committee suggested two courts of appeals, each to sit in two different districts in turn. Judges, learned in the law, were to be commissioned by Congress during good behavior. The courts would have marshals as well as registers and would have all the powers of courts of record for fining and imprisoning for contempt and disobedience. State admiralty court judges and their officers were to be liable for contempt if they disobeyed the decrees or orders of the court of appeals. The state courts would execute the decrees of the courts of appeals and to assure enforcement they were to demand security of the appellee which could be put in suit in case of reversal. Appeals would be allowed only to these congressional courts except where the appellant came from the state of the trial court and represented only interests within that state. Most controversial of all, the initial report had insisted that trial of all captures in state admiralty courts be according to the ancient mode of proceeding, trial by the court and not by jury.[43]

By January 8 the appellate jurisdiction, as then before Congress, still retained some of its initial vigor. Trials in the state admiralty courts would be according to the usage of nations and not by jury. Only one court of appeals was then proposed, but it was to have power to fine or imprison for contempt and disobedience with its own marshal to execute its decrees. But the vote on these resolutions found the states equally divided, so the report could not pass. Congress did defeat efforts to prohibit appeals in cases where all the parties were citizens of one state. A new committee of four, Oliver Ellsworth, Thomas McKean, William Churchill Houston, and Robert R. Livingston, was told to revise the previous committee's work.[44] The report coming from this committee,

---

[43] Ford, *JCC* **15**: pp. 1220–1223, 1349–1350, 1356, 1360; **16**: pp. 13–14, 17–19, 22–24. The powers of the British Lords Commissioners for Prize Appeals will be discussed and compared with the powers of the judges of the Court of Appeals in Cases of Capture in chapters IV and VI below.

[44] Ford, *JCC* **16**: pp. 29–32. Oliver Ellsworth, chapter II, note 36 above; Thomas McKean, chapter II, note 36 above. William Churchill Houston of New Jersey graduated from Princeton and became professor of mathematics and natural philosophy. He sat in the New Jersey Assembly at the start of the Revolution and in

much weaker but able to pass Congress, was adopted on January 15.

This compromise report which Congress accepted established one court to hear appeals from state admiralty courts in cases of capture; three judges, commissioned by Congress, would sit on the court and any two of them could conduct business. The court could appoint a register but not a marshal. Hearings before this appellate court would not be by jury but according to the usage of nations. Though not explicitly provided, the new court apparently could review questions of fact as well as of law. The first session would be held at Philadelphia, but the judges could afterwards hold court at such times and places as they would think conducive to the public good. They could not, however, sit anywhere farther east than Hartford nor farther south than Williamsburg. The judges would receive a salary, but Congress could not yet agree on the sum. To cover its expenses, a charge of one per cent of the value of the prizes tried in the court would be paid into the congressional treasury.

After defeating the proposals that would assure the effectiveness of the court's decrees, Congress merely recommended that the states pass laws directing the admiralty courts to carry into full and speedy execution the final decrees of the Court of Appeals. Finally Congress pointed out to the states that trial by jury in cases of capture was unheard of in any other nation. It urged the states, therefore, to authorize their admiralty courts to decide prize cases without a jury in all cases where the civil law, the law of nations, or the resolutions of Congress provided the rule of decision.[45]

1779 was elected to the Continental Congress where he took a leading part in matters of supply and finance. After studying law he was admitted to the bar in 1781. He held various civil offices in New Jersey and in 1783 resigned from teaching to build a law practice. In 1784 and 1785 he again sat in Congress and was a delegate to the Annapolis Convention and the Federal Convention.

Robert R. Livingston of New York graduated from Columbia and studied law. After admission to the bar he practiced in partnership with John Jay. In 1775 and 1776, 1779 to 1781, and again in 1784 and 1785, he was a delegate to Congress where he was active in committees concerned with financial affairs, foreign affairs, and military questions. In 1781 Congress named him secretary for foreign affairs. He continued an active interest in his state's political issues. From 1777 to 1801 he sat as chancellor of New York. Under President Jefferson he was minister to France and in this position he played a key role in the negotiations leading to the Louisiana Purchase. *DAB* **9**: pp. 267–268; **11**: pp. 320–325.

[45] Ford, *JCC* **16**: pp. 61–64.

The United States had now established its first federal appellate court. True, the Committee on Appeals had acted as a court and had frequently been called the court of appeals. But now a judicial body with appellate jurisdiction over state courts existed outside of Congress, not as a committee of congressmen, impeded by the rush of other pressing congressional concerns. In theory three judges would sit on the new court, but for much of its existence only two judges would be in commission. According to the resolves of Congress the Court of Appeals could hear cases anywhere convenience required between Hartford and Williamsburg. In fact there is no proof the court ever heard appeals outside Philadelphia till near the end of its life in 1786. Part of the final resolutions, passed by Congress on January 15, made two recommendations to the states, obviously a compromise from the original committee report. But these recommendations had little effect. Pennsylvania did drop jury trials in its admiralty courts a few months later and South Carolina followed suit two years later. Apparently the other states which had used juries in prize cases continued to do so. No state passed laws instructing the state court to execute the decrees of the Court of Appeals. Though Congress had failed to give the first federal court all the power many members of Congress had thought necessary, at least it had faced up to the problem of constantly changing membership and lack of continuity in hearing appeals.

Congress then proceeded to the next step of staffing the Court of Appeals. After nominating about a dozen candidates, it chose George Wythe, William Paca, and Titus Hosmer as its first judges.[46] Samuel Huntington, president of Congress, wrote to inform these three of their appointments and enclosed copies of their commissions. The president apologized for the fact that no salary had yet been fixed for the office. This was due to the state of the currency, Huntington explained, but assured them their salary would

---

[46] *Ibid.*, 22 January, 1780, p. 79; and also p. 64; James Lovell to Samuel Adams, 21 January, 1780, and William Floyd to the Governor of New York, 28 January, 1780, Burnett, *Letters* **5**: pp. 12, 19. George Wythe, see chapter II, note 36 above. William Paca, see note 41 above and this chapter below. Titus Hosmer of Connecticut graduated from Yale and after studying law was admitted to the bar. He held various civil offices and sat in the colonial and state general assemblies from 1773 to 1778. In 1778 he was elected an assistant in Connecticut and was reelected until his death in 1780. *DAB* **9**: p. 245.

be decent and satisfactory. Congress would advance each of
them $12,000 for support, so they could immediately start to
work in the new position.[47]

George Wythe of Virginia declined the appointment. Titus
Hosmer of Connecticut accepted, but most likely never
heard a case. He was sick when he accepted and died the
following summer.[48]

William Paca of Maryland previously had experience in
hearing at least eight appeals as a member of the Committee
on Appeals in 1777 and again in 1779. His legal training
included study at the Inner Temple; his practice had continued since 1764 when he was admitted to the bar. He had
served in the Maryland provincial legislature, in the first state
senate and later in the Continental Congress. In 1778 he was
appointed chief judge of the Maryland General Court. He
accepted the office as judge of the Court of Appeals and
served till December, 1782, when he resigned to become
governor of Maryland. In 1789 President Washington appointed him federal district judge, an office he held till his
death in 1799.[49]

On learning that Wythe had declined his appointment,
Congress elected one of its current members to the Court of
Appeals, Cyrus Griffin of Virginia. His background fitted
him well for this office. He had studied at the University of
Edinburgh and the Middle Temple. He had been elected to

---

[47] Ford, *JCC*, 2 February, 1780, **16**: p. 121, and President of Congress to George
Wythe, 2 February, 1780, Burnett, *Letters* **5**: pp. 24–25. The commission reads (the
words in italics were crossed out in the original):

"Know you, that reposing special trust and confidence in your *patriotism* learning,
prudence, integrity, and abilities, we have assigned, deputed, and appointed you
one of our judges of our Court of Appeals, to hear, try, and determine all appeals
from the courts of admiralty, in the states respectively, in cases of capture, *upon the
water* which now are, or hereafter may be duly entered and made in any of the said
states; and to do generally all those things that you are or shall be authorized and
empowered by Congress to do and perform, and which shall be necessary *in and
about the premises* for the execution of the said office, according to the law and usage
of nations and the acts of Congress; to have, hold, exercise, and enjoy, all and
singular, the powers, authorities, and jurisdictions aforesaid; and also the privileges,
benefits, emoluments, and advantages to the said office belonging, or in any wise
appertaining." PCC, Item 29, 383, marked delivered 31 January, 1780, passed, no
date.

[48] George Wythe to President of Congress, 21 February, 1780, PCC, Item 78,
XXIV, 183; Titus Hosmer to Samuel Huntington, 12 April, 1780, *ibid.*, Item 78,
XII, 17.

[49] William Paca to Samuel Huntington, 8 February, 1780, PCC, Item 59, III, 23;
DAB **14**: pp. 123–124.

the Virginia legislature and to Congress. As a member of the Committee on Appeals in 1779 and the beginning of 1780 he had already heard about seven cases. He had to resign his seat in Congress to take his place on the Court of Appeals. Though at first he expected to be a judge of that court for only a short time, he remained on the bench longer and was involved in more decrees than any other judge. He continued as judge till the Court of Appeals faded out of existence in 1787, having heard about fifty cases while on the court. In 1789 President Washington named him a commissioner to prepare a treaty between the Creek Indians and Georgia. Washington later named him to sit as federal judge for the district of Virginia, an office he held till his death in 1810.[50]

With three judges willing to sit on the Court of Appeals, Congress prepared for the start of the new court, although no formal inauguration occurred. In fact the precise dating of the start of the court's work remains somewhat obscure. At the state of the *Active* crisis, the committee stopped hearing appeals during January, 1779, until its authority had been supported by Congress in the resolves of March 6. Immediately thereafter the committee decided several cases and through the rest of 1779 continued to hear appeals. In January, 1780, while Congress was debating the reports on the Court of Appeals, several cases were determined by the committee and in February two more cases were heard. After February no cases are known to have been determined till June. The court records include a notation signed by Griffin and Paca that Andrew Robeson had been appointed register of the Court of Appeals on June 14, 1780. Apparently by that date the two judges had taken their oaths of office. Though the earliest cases do not mention the names of the judges issuing the decrees, the Court of Appeals probably decided its first case on June 23, 1780.[51]

In May, 1780, Congress tidied up details for the newly

---

[50] Samuel Huntington to Cyrus Griffin, 1 May, 1780, PCC, Item 14, 337; Commission for Griffin dated 28 April, 1780, *ibid.*, Item 49, 523; Griffin to Huntington, 4 May, 1780, *ibid.*, Item 78, X, 251; Ford, *JCC* **16**: pp. 322, 397, 411; Griffin to Thomas Jefferson, Governor of Virginia, 9 June, 1780, Burnett, *Letters* **5**: p. 231, and *DAB* **7**: pp. 618–619.

[51] For a partial docket of the decrees of the Court of Appeals, see Miscellaneous Court Records, RCA.

created court. It determined that its name should be "The Court of Appeals in Cases of Capture." It provided an oath of office for the judges and for the register. The judges were to take the oath before the president of Congress, the register before the judges. In the future all appeals would be lodged with the register, not with the secretary of Congress. All matters respecting appeals in prize cases then pending in Congress would be turned over to the register.[52]

With the fluctuation of the value of money, it is difficult to ascertain just how much the judges of the court received for their salaries. The best indication is one civil list in the records which gives the basis for comparing the salary of the judges with other office holders' salaries. For the year 1780 the judges, Paca and Griffin, received $2,250 each. The same year Charles Thomson, secretary of Congress, received $3,000, Robert Morris, superintendant of finance, $6,000, Benjamin Lincoln, secretary at war, $4,000, Robert R. Livingston, secretary for foreign affairs, $4,000, Ebenezer Hazard, post master general, $1,250.[53]

After the death of Titus Hosmer in August, 1780, apparently without ever sitting as judge, Congress resolved to elect a judge to serve in his place.[54] But like all good resolutions, this was soon forgotten. Cyrus Griffin in February, 1781, reminded Congress that the judges on the bench could use the assistance of a third colleague. Congress immediately assigned the next day for electing a judge. Again nothing was done.[55] The office of judge of this court must have been attractive, for several possible candidates maneuvered to win

---

[52] Ford, *JCC*, 24 May, 1780, **17**: pp. 457–459. The oath of office reads (the words in italics were crossed out in the original):

"You do swear or affirm, *that you will take no fee, gift or reward of any one that hath to do before you, nor give counsell to any one in a matter that may touch any cause which shall be brought before you for trial. And that you will do right to every person according to the best of your skill and judgment. So help you God.* [that you will well, faithfully and impartially execute the office of one of the judges of the Court of Appeals in Cases of Capture, according to the best of your skill and judgment. So help you God.]" PCC, Item 29, 389.

[53] PCC, Item 49, 577–579. But the orders for payment of Griffin's salary show he received $40,000 on 5 September, 1780, and $1,000 new emissions on 25 January, 1781, *ibid.*, Item 136, IV, 583, and V, 57. The base salary of $2,250 was clearly translated into current dollar values. Ford, *JCC*, 11 August, 1780, **17**: p. 721.

[54] Ford, *JCC*, 25 August, 1780, **17**: p. 779.

[55] Cyrus Griffin to Samuel Huntington, 22 February, 1781, PCC, Item 78, X, 293; Ford, *JCC* **19**: p. 200. The letter of Griffin mentions that the session after next would be held at Hartford. There is no indication in the records that it was.

the appointment. At the same time an economy-minded congressman favored reducing the court to a single judge until that unlikely day when the public finances could better bear the expense. Congress rejected this move because it realized one judge would have less authority, especially in cases involving litigants from his home state. For about two and a half years, the court would sit with only two judges till Congress was forced to act by Paca's resignation to become Governor of Maryland.[56] On December 5, 1782, two weeks after Paca's resignation, Congress elected George Read of Delaware and John Lowell of Massachusetts as judges of the Court of Appeals.[57]

George Read had begun a long legal career by studying in the office of John Moland, a Philadelphia lawyer. In 1753 he began a law practice in Philadelphia after admission to the bar there. Finding the compensation inadequate he moved to New Castle, Delaware, where he became recognized as a legal authority and a leading political figure of the colony. During the last years before the Revolution, he had served as attorney general. He sat frequently in the state legislature and in Congress and was influential in preparing the Delaware constitution of 1776. As speaker of the legislative council he was the state's vice president and, when the president was captured by the British, the presidential duties fell upon Read. He continued his private law practice even after accepting a position on the Court of Appeals. Before his appointment to this court, he had on occasion acted as counsel in cases of prize appeals. He was a delegate to the Federal Convention in 1787 where he championed the rights of small states. He led the struggle for ratification of the Constitution in Delaware. He was chosen one of the state's first United States senators. In 1793 he was appointed chief justice of Delaware.[58]

---

[56] Samuel Livermore to the President of New Hampshire, 12 March, 1782; David Howell to William Ellery, 10 August, 1782, Burnett, *Letters* 6: pp. 312–313, 439; Madison's Notes of Debates of Congress, 7 November, 1782, Ford, *JCC* 23: pp. 844–845; Paca to Elias Boudinot, President of Congress, 17 November, 1782, PCC, Item 59, III, 55.

[57] Ford, *JCC* 23: pp. 765 and 758, 797 and 862; President of Congress to George Read, 6 December, 1782, and President of Congress to John Lowell, 11 December, 1782, PCC, Item 16, 160 and 163.

[58] George Read to Elias Boudinot, 10 December, 1782, PCC, Item 78, XIX, 439; *DAB* 15: pp. 422–424.

John Lowell after graduation from Harvard studied law in the office of Oxenbridge Thacher, a leading member of the Massachusetts bar, and was admitted to practice. He entered actively into the political affairs of the state before the war and served as a member of Congress and as a delegate to the state constitutional convention of 1779 and 1780. He had a considerable practice in the state maritime courts and had acted as counsel in a number of cases before the Committee on Appeals. He delayed his acceptance of the appointment to the Court of Appeals while he tried to complete some of these admiralty cases. After a warning from a friend in Congress that another Massachusetts delegate to Congress was trying to have Robert Treat Paine, the state attorney general, advanced to the Court of Appeals, Lowell wrote the president of Congress. He accepted the judgeship on condition that he could disqualify himself in several cases with which he had been involved as attorney and which were to be appealed. In 1789 President Washington appointed Lowell federal district judge.[59]

These four judges, therefore, William Paca, Cyrus Griffin, George Read, and John Lowell, constituted the bench of the Court of Appeals in Cases of Capture. They determined more than sixty appeals including several rehearings before the demise of the Court in 1787. Congress had at least solved the problem of constantly changing membership.

During these later years of the war and the postwar years, from 1780 to the end of the life of the Continental Congress in 1789, Congress continued to be preoccupied with more problems than it could solve. Although the Articles of Confederation were finally ratified in February, 1781, the United States in Congress assembled still limped along unable to cope with all the issues and complexities it had to face. Some delegates tried to strengthen the hands of Congress by amending the Articles so that it could exert coercive power to compel state compliance. The Articles had generously conferred on Congress the privilege of asking for anything, but cautiously reserved to the states the prerogative of granting

---

[59] [Member of Congress] to Lowell, 14 March, 1783, Miscellaneous Collection (MHS); James Sullivan to Judge Holten, 9 February, 1783, Personal Papers, Miscellaneous, (LCMss); John Lowell to Elias Boudinot, 12 February, 1783, PCC, Item 78, XIV, 531, and a different letter, Lowell to Boudinot, same date, Old Congress Papers, Gratz Collection (HSP).

nothing. The nation continued on the brink of financial chaos, in spite of the best efforts of Robert Morris and the national bank he managed to have incorporated to introduce some order and stability. French subsidies and Dutch loans were often spent before they were granted. As the paper money Congress persisted in printing plunged into ever deeper depreciation, all efforts to insure stability by new paper issues were defeated by lack of confidence and by the various states' insistence upon different exchange rates between the old congressional dollars and the new. When Congress tried to tidy its finances by requesting the states to grant it the revenue from an import duty, one state was able to frustrate the entire scheme. Somehow, miraculously, amidst this chaos and impotence, America won a war. Congress had to consider the terms for peace negotiations with Britain and to instruct its peace commissioners who were sent to France to conduct the actual discussions. As the negotiations proceeded Congress was greatly embarrassed to find itself the beneficiary of a liberal peace treaty concluded largely behind the back of France, its chief ally and mainstay, at the same time that Congress had been begging further financial aid from France. With actual fighting at an end the army could be disbanded if some way could be found to pay the soldiers. Many in the army, however, had no intention of laying down their arms and going home till they were adequately compensated. Congress had to face near mutiny of the American army and physical threats from the Pennsylvania militia. A great congressional success was achieved in obtaining from several states the cession of their vast western land claims. Congress, after long discussion, made some provision for the disposition and government of these western lands. While Congress meandered from place to place looking for somewhere to call home, it frequently lacked the quorum of members necessary to transact any business at all. Its fervent pleas to the unrepresented states to send delegates immediately were no more effective than its entreaties to the states to send financial requisitions. When Congress decided to adjourn for several months, leaving a caretaker committee of states to sit in its recess, even this rump soon vanished. At times virtually the only visible sign of unity of the states under the Confederation was the secretary, Charles Thomson. When Congress did reassemble it had to wait for a quorum to attend, and then found it difficult to decide where it should sit. Even after the war and peace were settled, Congress had to try to confront pressing problems, none more urgent than the regulation of foreign and domestic commerce. Its failure to deal adequately with this problem contributed largely to the decision of some nationally minded leaders to seek a more perfect union at the Federal Convention of 1787.

During the years of the Court of Appeals in Cases of Capture, 1780 to 1787, Congress occasionally found time from other pressing matters to turn its attention to the court's work. In 1783 some members of Congress indicated a desire that the judges should hold court at various places such as Hartford and Richmond, apparently to make it more convenient for litigants to bring their cases. The various reports brought in, however, never received congressional approval.[60] Congress also contained some economy-minded members who in 1784 tried to have the salaries of the judges stopped. They proposed instead to pay the judges $14 for every day they actually sat on the court, with allowance for travel to and from the place of holding court. Perhaps impressed by the large volume of cases dispatched at the May, 1784, session, Congress did not at this time change the judges' salaries.[61] After this May term, however, Congress thought that the court's business was completed.[62] When the court transacted no business for a whole year, the movement to cut off the judges' salaries gained enough strength to bring Congress to act. Although a committee in June, 1785, had reported that several petitions for appeals or rehearings had been presented to Congress and that in the committee's opinion the judges were still in commission, Congress did not approve its proposed resolution that the salaries of the judges should cease and some unspecified amount be allowed them on a *per diem* basis for completing the court's work. Instead Congress in July passed a blunt resolution,

---

[60] Ford, *JCC* **24:** pp. 98, 185, 212; PCC, Item 19, II, 533; Item 29, 397, 399. A letter from Griffin to the President of Congress, 18 March, 1783, and referred to one of these committees, shows Griffin at this time eager to resign his position on the Court, *ibid.*, Item 78, X, 401.

[61] Ford, *JCC* **26:** pp. 126, 343.

[62] Secretary of Congress to William Churchill Houston, 30 July, 1784, Burnett, *Letters* **8:** p. 852; Hopkinson, *Miscellaneous Works* **3:** pp. 138, 145.

"That the Salaries of the judges of the Court of Appeals shall henceforth cease." Thomson reported to the judges that, as of July 1, their salaries would cease.[63] Stung by this insensitive congressional action, Griffin complained and won from Congress a more tactful statement of its appreciation of the judges' ability and fidelity to their office. Nonetheless, even when clothed in softer words, Congress in February, 1786, thought it necessary to cut off the salaries of the judges.[64]

Early in 1786 Congress had received several petitions for hearings or rehearings in prize appeals. Upon recommendation of a committee, Congress resolved in June that the judges of the Court of Appeals were authorized to grant appeals or rehearings whenever justice and right, in their opinion, required it. The judges would receive $10 for each day of service and necessary travel, and Congress specified that the court was to be held in New York on the first Monday of November. Thomson informed the judges and the state governments of this session.[65] This resolution prepared the way for the court's last two terms, held in November, 1786, and May, 1787.

From the beginning of the court's work, the judges tended to hear and decide cases at definite court terms. Though a few cases were decided at other times, the general pattern of holding court at clearly defined sessions emerges as soon as the decrees are arranged chronologically.[66] In 1782 the court apparently determined only two cases, both in February. Perhaps its failure to conduct other business that year was due to the inability of the two judges then in commission to be free from other occupations at the same time. After Paca resigned in November of that year, Congress quickly appointed two new judges, giving the court a full complement of three judges for the first time. In 1783 the judges heard and determined a large number of cases during the two

[63] Ford, *JCC* **28:** pp. 209, 230, 413–414; **29:** pp. 491–493; Thomson to Griffin, Read and Lowell, 5 July, 1785, PCC, Item 18, A, 106.

[64] Ford, *JCC* **30:** pp. 60–61; Thomson to Griffin, Read and Lowell, 1 March, 1786, PCC, Item 18, B, 31, 32; Read to Thomson, 8 April, 1786, *Ibid.*, Item 78, XIX, 547.

[65] Ford, *JCC* **30:** pp. 26, 291–292, 355–356; Secretary of Congress to Judges of Court of Appeals, 29 June, 1786, Burnett, *Letters* **8:** p. 396; PCC, Item 18, B, 60, 65; Item 28, 201, 215–217.

[66] RCA *passim.* See also Griffin to President of Congress, 22 February, 1781, PCC, Item 78, X, 293, and Read to President of Congress, 5 October, 1783, *ibid.*, XIX, 455.

terms, one in May and June and the other in September and October. In 1784 the judges held court during May, determining about twelve cases. After this May term no cases are known to have been decided for a year and a half. Congress, because of petitions it had received for hearings in prize appeals, insisted upon a session to be held in New York in November, 1786, in spite of the attempt of Judge Read to excuse himself and Griffin because they would be busy attending their state assemblies at that time.[67] At this November session the court apparently cleared one case from the docket by rejecting a petition for a rehearing.[68] The judges also heard arguments in at least two other cases and issued commissions for interrogatories to prepare for a full hearing the following May.[69] In May, 1787, the court held its last session, disposing of five cases. With no more prize appeals to hear, the Court of Appeals ceased functioning after this May term. At that same time, however, many of the men who had been involved with the court's work through the years were gathering in Philadelphia to begin discussing a new frame of government.

During the seven years that the Court of Appeals was established and functioning, Congress continued especially in three ways to remain involved with prize affairs. The delegates to Congress discussed and debated a plan to establish the Court of Appeals on the firmer basis of a fully integrated ordinance. They also revised from time to time the ordinances regulating capture of enemy vessels and tried to collate these into one ordinance. Congress also continued to receive petitions and reports concerning the domestic and foreign complications resulting from privateering activity.

The Marine Committee of Congress in March, 1778, had been directed to revise the privateering commission and the instructions given to commanders of privateers. Congress also wanted it to update the resolutions on captures at sea, which it had previously passed. But apparently not much was

[67] Ford, *JCC* **30:** pp. 291–292, 355–356; Secretary of Congress to Judges of Court of Appeals, 29 June, 1786; Secretary of Congress to George Read, 24 October, 1786, Burnett, *Letters* **8:** pp. 396, 492; Read to Thomson, 7 October, 1786, Read Papers (HSP); Read to Thomson, 3 November, 1786, PCC, Item 78, XIX, 567.

[68] *Hannah (Hepburn v. Ellis)*, 4 August, 1781, petition for rehearing rejected, 14 November, 1786, #74, RCA.

[69] *Hope (Meade v. Hurlburt)*, 3 May, 1787, #103; *Chester (Dubbeldemuts v. Atkinson)*, 3 May, 1787, 2 Dallas 41, RCA.

done besides issuing a proclamation of May 9, 1778, in an attempt to stop attacks on neutral ships.[70] Debate over the stalemate in the *Active* case and attempts to establish a Court of Appeals absorbed much time and energy. In May, 1780, Congress printed new commissions and instructions for the commanders of privateers, based largely on the earlier ones of April, 1776, with modifications to incorporate more recent congressional resolves. Thereafter only those British ships and cargoes belonging to inhabitants of Bermuda or ships bringing settlers to America were exempted from capture. All other ships and cargoes belonging to subjects of the British king could lawfully be seized. These instructions, as the earlier ones, insisted on a sacred regard for neutral rights and tried to assure a fair trial for captured property by directing the commander taking the prize to preserve all papers found on board and to send in with the prize the master and other principal members of the crew, so they could defend their ship in court. Privateers were forbidden to plunder a captured ship or to injure crew or passengers.[71]

The Board of Admiralty, which replaced the Marine Committee, reported to Congress in July, 1780, that it could not comply with the wish of Congress to revise the regulations relative to captures at sea. It complained of being understaffed and overworked, with too few members learned in the law of nations. Congress, therefore, appointed a committee of five to report a system of regulations for maritime captures.[72]

Before this new committee could report, the question of neutral rights was again raised and discussed at the instigation of the empress of Russia who had proposed an armed neutrality in an attempt to protect neutral rights. There were four basic principles of the armed neutrality: that free ships make free goods, that contraband should be narrowly defined, that neutral ships should be allowed free navigation along the coasts of nations at war, and that no port would be considered blockaded unless enough armed vessels were stationed there to make access clearly dangerous. These

---

[70] Ford, *JCC*, 5 March, 1778; **10**: p. 225 and 9 May, 1778, **11**: p. 486.

[71] Instructions, headed "In Congress, May 2, 1780," PCC, Item 37, 511 and 225–240; compare *ibid.*, IV, 253–254.

[72] PCC, Item 29, 398, and Item 37, 277, 283; Ford, *JCC*, 27 July, 1780, **17**: pp. 672–674.

principles fit in with America's long range goals as a prospective neutral in future wars between European powers. Congress, therefore, approved additional instructions in conformity with the armed neutrality, which were sent from the Board of Admiralty to the commanders of all armed vessels commissioned by the United States. Commanders must allow neutral vessels to sail freely even on the coast of America, unless they carried contraband or troops to the British. British property on board a neutral vessel was not liable to capture, except contraband. (By this instruction America accepted the principle of the armed neutrality that free ships make free goods.) The instructions defined contraband narrowly, as in the French treaty, excluding provisions and naval stores from the list. The commander's commission was liable to forfeiture and the commander himself subject to action for breach of the condition of his bond, if he violated these instructions which were to serve as the rule of decision in prize cases in the United States.[73]

James Madison, after the final ratification of the Articles of Confederation in February, 1781, proposed that Congress tighten the laws allowing capture of British vessels. The exemptions previously granted by Congress in favor of British ships carrying settlers or arms to America and in favor of the property of inhabitants of Bermuda had been abused to cover illicit trade, so Madison moved that all these exemptions be removed and that all ships and cargoes belonging to any subjects of the king of Great Britain be liable to lawful seizure. Furthermore Madison proposed that all letters of protection granted by Congress to allow Americans to remove their property from any territory in control of the British be declared void after a certain date. These passports also had aided the enemy by giving a cover for illicit trade. After weighing these proposals Congress passed them with significant additions and more stringent provisions. Thereafter all ships, vessels and goods belonging to any subjects of the British king who inhabited any of the king's dominions or territories could be captured and adjudged lawful prize. Ships coming from Bermuda loaded only with salt could

---

[73] Ford, *JCC*, 27 November, 1780, **18:** pp. 1097–1098, also pp. 864–866, 905–906, 1008; Richard B. Morris, *The Peacemakers—The Great Powers and American Independence* (New York, Torchbook edition, 1970), pp. 164–167.

come to America prior to the first of May. Congress added that the destruction of papers or possession of double papers by captured ships would be considered just cause for condemnation. (In England these offenses would probably have constituted a presumption of guilt of the vessel destroying papers or carrying double papers, but would not have been grounds for condemnation if the claimants of the prize could carry the burden of proving the innocence of their ship.) Moreover the regulations for condemning recaptured vessels were modified. Any American ship recaptured from the British after it had been in possession of the enemy for twenty-four hours would be condemned wholly for the use of the recaptors. If the prize was in enemy possession less than twenty-four hours, the ship should be restored to its original American owners who, in that case, would have to pay one-third of its value to the recaptors as salvage. Americans were warned to avoid all correspondence or dealings with British subjects. State officials were directed to detect and punish all such relations with the enemy.[74]

With the Articles of Confederation fully in effect Congress, by its authority under article nine, established courts for trying piracies and felonies committed on the high seas. Congress was undoubtedly influenced in part by the many reports it had received of violations of neutral rights, abuses committed against crews of captured ships, and acts of piracy by American privateers. No federal courts were set up, but Congress instead gave authority for each state to have the justices of its superior court and the judge of the admiralty court, or any two of them, sit as judges to hear and try maritime crimes according to common law procedures.[75]

Congress in April, 1781, again revised the instructions to commanders of privateers to bring them into conformity with recent changes in the law. The instructions, drafted by the Board of Admiralty, remained basically the same as those of May, 1780, but now all British ships would be liable to seizure with no exception in favor of ships bringing settlers to America or ships from Bermuda. Contraband was defined in the terms agreed on in the French treaty of friendship and

---

[74] Ford, *JCC*, 27 March, 1781, **19:** pp. 314–316, and 270–271; William T. Hutchinson and William M. E. Rachal, eds., *The Papers of James Madison* (6 v., Chicago, 1962–1969) **3:** pp. 22–25; Pares, *Colonial Blockade*, p. 117.
[75] Ford, *JCC*, 5 April, 1781, **19:** pp. 354–356.

commerce of 1778. Neutral vessels were to be permitted free passage on the high seas and in American coastal waters.[76]

Madison during the spring of 1781 tried to stir Congress to establish the Court of Appeals on the basis of a clearer and stronger ordinance. Seeing the need for a more effective federal jurisdiction, he wanted the time and place of the court's sessions specified by Congress and the amount of costs the court could assess and the fees court officials could charge regulated. He suggested common law damage suits and dismissal from office as a way of forcing state admiralty court marshals to execute the decrees of the Court of Appeals. He also proposed that the judges of the court hear cases of piracies and felonies committed on the high seas, which would have introduced the first federal trial court into the states. He suggested that these federal judges hold their commissions during good behavior and that Congress provide them with suitable black robes and with expenses for travel and the purchase of books required for the court.[77]

After Madison's proposals had been referred to a committee of James Mitchell Varnum, Thomas Bee, and Thomas McKean, they were revised to include clauses that would give the court power to fine or imprison for contempt, as well as full authority to admit proctors and advocates to practice and to appoint other officers incident to such courts. Execution of the lower court decree would be allowed, pending appeal, whenever the appellee would give sufficient security to restore the prize or its value, if the lower court sentence should be reversed. (This clause was borrowed practically verbatim from the British prize acts.) By this proposed ordinance Congress would enable the court to appoint marshals, to give exceptions to appellants if the time limit for appealing posed special problems, and to carry into execution any stipulations entered into before it or before any admiralty court judge. But after all the committee work and the debates in Congress, most of this ordinance never passed. The sections approved by Congress merely restated the powers the court already possessed. The Court of Appeals continued on its previous basis without the added power of some means of

---

[76] *Ibid.*, 7 April, 1781, pp. 360–364 and 348; Compare PCC, Item 37, 511.

[77] Ford, *JCC*, 12 April, 1781, **19**: pp. 374–375; Hutchinson and Rachal, *Papers of Madison*, **3**: pp. 66–68.

compelling execution of its decrees.[78] Early in 1782 Congress renewed its interest in an ordinance to establish the Court of Appeals on a firmer basis, but it never got past its second reading.[79]

Prior to this the congressmen had turned their attention to revising and codifying the laws controlling the legality of captures at sea. On December 4, 1781, after considerable discussion, Congress passed an ordinance specifying what captures at sea would be lawful. Building on previous laws it added that after the first of the following March all goods grown or produced in Great Britain would be liable to capture even on neutral ships if found within three leagues of the coasts and destined for any port of the United States, unless this cargo had previously been captured from the British. Ships destined to any blockaded port could also be seized. In cases of recapture provisions were made for special cases, such as recapture of slaves or recapture of other property originally captured on land. Enemy property could be captured by publicly or privately armed ships with commissions from Congress; by private vessels without commissions, if the private vessel had been attacked by the enemy ship; by any body of regular soldiers; by any inhabitants of the country, if made within cannon shot of shore; by armed vessels commissioned by the French government; or by the mutinous crews of British vessels, as long as Britain allowed captures of this kind by American crews. Whenever a ship destroyed its papers or carried double papers, this would be considered evidence for condemnation, unless a good reason could be shown to the contrary. (This softened the conclusive

---

[78] Ford, *JCC*, 18 July, 1781, **20**: pp. 761–764; and 496, 497, 599, 694–695; PCC, Item 29, 397; 29 Geo. II, c. 34, § 9. James Mitchell Varnum graduated from Brown College with honors. He taught a short time and then studied law and was admitted to the bar. He was active in the state militia and in the continental army. In 1780 he was elected to Congress and served intermittently till 1787. In 1787 he accepted an appointment as United States judge for the Ohio territory. *DAB* **19**: pp. 227–228.

Thomas Bee of South Carolina was educated at Oxford, studied law, and was admitted to practice. He was active in colonial politics, sitting for a number of years in the South Carolina lower house. During the Revolution he continued to sit in the state assembly and was chosen speaker of the house in 1777. He also served on the state legislative council and as lieutenant governor, as well as a delegate to Congress for two years. In 1790 President Washington named him federal judge for the district of South Carolina. *Biographical Dict. of Amer. Cong.*, p. 534.

Thomas McKean, see chapter II note 36 above.

[79] Ford, *JCC* **22**: pp. 153–154.

presumption of guilt which Congress, by its act of the previous March, had implied from the destruction of papers and possession of double papers. These present resolves were much closer to the rebuttable presumption which apparently was the practice in England.) All letters of passport or safe conduct for the removal of property from any place held by the British would be void after the first of the following February. Congressional naval vessels would thereafter receive the full value of all British men of war or privateers taken, as an inducement to the American ships to attack armed enemy ships. (This had long been the practice in England, where naval vessels received the full value of all lawful prizes taken, with head money and gun money as an added bonus for the capture of armed enemy vessels.) After specifying the share to be awarded to various members of American naval crews, Congress concluded by stating that the rule of decision in all admiralty courts would be the ordinances of Congress, public treaties and the law of nations. Public treaties were given first place in all trials.[80]

For the remainder of the war Congress from time to time amended this ordinance to clarify or modify some aspect of the law which had presented difficulties. For instance Congress discovered that admiralty courts had been following different norms for judging whether a ship should be considered a joint captor of a prize. Congress determined that only a vessel in sight at the time of the capture and within gunshot when the prize struck would share in the prize as joint captor. The prize would be shared among joint captors in proportion to the number of men and the number and size of guns of the capturing ships.[81]

Congress recommended that the states authorize the seizure of all products grown or produced in any British territory and found on land within the state unless imported before March 1, 1782, or previously captured from the enemy. But on second thought Congress realized that some American ships then at sea could take on a cargo of British goods in some European port without knowing of this new

---

[80] *Ibid.* **21:** pp. 1152–1158 and 861–871, 916, 921, 958, 970, 985, 986, 1109, 1147–1148; Hutchinson and Rachal, *Papers of Madison* **3:** pp. 217–221, 236–243, and Madison to Edmund Pendleton, 8 January, 1782, *ibid.* **4:** pp. 22–24; Pares, *Colonial Blockade*, p. 117; 29 Geo. II, c. 34, § 1.

[81] Ford, *JCC*, 8 January, 1782, **22:** pp. 10–11 and **21:** p. 1172.

ordinance. So it ordained that no American ship which sailed from any friendly port in Europe before the tenth of the following April with British products aboard would be liable to seizure.[82] In July, 1782, Congress modified the rule regarding prize shares for crew members of the ships of war fitted out at congressional expense. Thereafter congressional naval vessels would be awarded the full value of armed prizes taken only if the prize was of equal or superior force to the capturing naval vessel.[83]

Finally Congress continued to receive a steady trickle of petitions, memorials, and reports concerning various domestic or foreign aspects of privateering activity which could not be referred to the Court of Appeals. Many complaints came before Congress from subjects of friendly or neutral nations because of the illegal activity of American privateers. Congress could never forget for long that many privateers are first cousins of pirates. For instance several French subjects complained that they had recovered a judgment against an American privateer commander for injuries they sustained while he was acting under the pretext of his commission from Congress in seizing their property. But the commander had absconded and prevented redress of the injuries. Congress resolved that the bond given when this commander received his commission should be put in suit, that his commission be vacated, and that he should not be allowed to hold another commission till he surrendered himself to justice.[84]

In a clear case of plunder and piracy against a Portuguese ship by an American privateer holding a commission from the governor of Massachusetts, the irate Portuguese subjects were told by Congress that the proper mode to obtain redress of any injuries was by prosecution of the offenders by due course of law in the state courts. Congress sent a letter to the Massachusetts governor requesting his assistance and protection for the Portuguese petitioners. The Board of Admiralty in reporting to Congress called attention to the fact that the commission had been signed by the governor, not by the president of Congress. The Board betrayed its real

---

[82] *Ibid.*, 2 January, 1782, **22**: p. 3 and 26 February, 1782, pp. 99–100, and 96–98.
[83] *Ibid.*, 10 July, 1782, **22**: pp. 379–380 and 377–378; Hutchinson and Rachal, *Papers of Madison* **4**: pp. 373–375.
[84] Ford, *JCC*, 12 August, 1779, **14**: pp. 950–951.

fears of state prejudice against these foreign claimants, even though explicitly denying any such suspicions:

> The Board have mentioned this circumstance, not because they entertain any most distant idea that the *Mars* belonging to the State of Massachusetts, and being Commissioned by the Governor of that State, might influence the conduct of the Supreme Executive thereof with respect to the memorialist, but because the Board humbly conceive that Commissions issueing [*sic*] from different Fountains of Power is a matter which may merit the attention of the United States in Congress assembled, who are the Supreme power of War and Peace.[85]

Congress from time to time had to deal with other facets of prize affairs, as when an American vessel was captured by two American privateers and condemned as lawful prize to the captors by a French court at Cape François, Hispaniola, because the prize carried double papers. Congress was caught in the middle between the American parties and tried to have the affair straightened out by the American ministers in France.[86] When a French vessel, captured by the British, was recaptured by an American privateer, Congress concluded that the French owners, whose ship had been sold in Boston, had no claim against Congress owing to the loss the owners had suffered from depreciation of American currency. Congress insisted that the loss was not because of any arbitrary devaluation in the currency by Congress, "but ensued against the will and the unremitting endeavours of Congress." Therefore Congress concluded that it was not bound to make good this loss resulting from depreciation.[87] And, of course, occasional reminders came to Congress from its ministers abroad of the unfavorable impression created in foreign capitals by American privateers.[88]

The case of the sloop *Active*, as we have seen, had forced Congress to face some unpleasant facts about the Committee on Appeals. Many members of Congress clearly saw the need for some way of assuring uniformity in applying principles of the law of nations. They came to realize that if this nation did not have the final voice in matters which could involve war

---

[85] *Ibid.*, 30 May, 1781, **20**: pp. 578–579; PCC, Item 42, III, 65.

[86] Ford, *JCC*, 22 September, 1783, **25**: pp. 597–601.

[87] *Ibid.*, 11 May, 1784, **27**: pp. 370–372.

[88] B. Franklin to Jay, President of Congress, 4 October, 1779; J. Adams to President of Congress, 6 October, 1780, Wharton, *Correspondence* **3**: p. 365; **4**: p. 83.

and peace or other foreign complications, it could not well survive within the community of nations. But when Congress tried to meet the immediate challenge to the authority of its appellate Committee in prize cases, it could find no way to compel Pennsylvania to acknowledge any higher, ultimate voice. Consequently after pondering the inherent limitations of the Committee on Appeals, Congress sought a stronger, more independent body to determine prize appeals. Though many of its members favored a solidly constituted court with clearly defined power to assure execution of its decrees, Congress simply did not have the strength to give birth to a court with authority over the states and power to act upon individuals within the states. A court was established, however, and qualified judges chosen to carry on in the best way possible.

Congress's concern with prize affairs was not limited to the erection of the Court of Appeals; Congress had to revise the laws which the prize courts would apply. During all the years of the war, Congress continued to modify and adapt its ordinances regulating the capture of enemy property. It used every means available, including increased pressure by privateers, to make the war as costly as possible for the British. But Congress could never for long forget the risks and consequences of violations of neutral rights by the irrepressible privateers.

PART TWO
Legal Analysis

WITH THE HISTORICAL CONTEXT of Part One as a prologue, we can now examine the first federal court as a functioning institution. A mere external description of the origins, development, and demise of this court says little of the procedures it followed or the law it applied in determining prize appeals. Part Two, therefore, focuses primarily upon this court as a live judicial institution; the prize cases decided on appeal are analyzed to illustrate how the court worked and how its bench and bar approached the appeals it heard.

But before we examine the work of this court, we must introduce a further dimension of historical background into this Part, and thus again demonstrate the inadequacy of the book's division into historical and legal segments.

Chapters IV and V are introductory to Part Two; they give the sources of American prize practice. First of all, the system of eighteenth-century British prize practice is sketched, for within this tradition American lawyers learned much of what they knew of prize litigation. Their experience came largely from the vice-admiralty courts at home where all the subtleties of the High Court of Admiralty in England were seldom found. A description of the procedures of the Lords Commissioners for Prize Appeals, on the other hand, shows the stark contrast between the prize appeals they heard, and those, detailed in a later chapter, heard by the appellate prize court of the Continental Congress. Chapter V briefly summarizes the other source of American prize law, the various British and Continental writings on the subject used by American lawyers.

Chapters VI and VII form the heart of Part Two. Chapter VI traces the procedures in prize litigation, in the state courts, through the appellate process, and back to the state courts where the appellate decrees were supposed to be executed. Chapter VII turns to the substantive law applied by the appellate prize court. By grouping the prize appeals according to the legal issues raised, it is possible partially to reconstruct the legal reasoning behind the arguments of counsel and the decrees of the judges.

Chapter VIII considers two aspects of the jurisdiction of the congressional appellate prize court, the scope of its jurisdiction ancillary to a prize case and the constitutional dimensions of its authority over the states. Logically, the jurisdiction of the court should be discussed before its procedures and substantive law. Since the specialized historical background discussed in chapters IV and V, however, is closely related to the questions of procedure and substantive law, it seems appropriate not to separate these four chapters by a treatment of jurisdiction.

Finally, chapter IX looks beyond the appellate prize court set up by the Continental Congress to the federal judiciary established under the Constitution. Some basic themes, federalism, separation of powers, and international relations, interwoven with the study of the first federal court are traced in the years after it ceased to exist, when a new federal judiciary was being created and put into operation. Many who were most influential in establishing the new federal court system had learned from experience the inadequacy of the first federal court. The lessons they learned in dealing with this court must have helped them appreciate the need for a more effective national judiciary.

IV. British Prize Procedure in the Late Eighteenth Century

DURING THE EIGHTEENTH CENTURY the British Parliament set forth the procedural details of prize adjudication in the series of prize acts passed at the outbreak of the various conflicts. These prize acts contained substantially identical language prescribing the procedures to be followed in England and in the colonies for the condemnation of prize vessels and cargoes.[1] In the sections dealing with procedure, the acts first set forth the method of instituting a prize suit. Two initial steps were spelled out in the acts for adjudication of a vessel which had been captured and brought to a suitable British port: the judge of the admiralty or vice-admiralty was to complete the preparatory examination of the key members of the crew of the captured ship and he was to issue monition or public notice to all parties concerned in the trial of this vessel.

> [T]he judge or judges of such court of admiralty, or other person or persons thereto authorized, shall within the space of five days after request to him or them for that purpose made, finish the usual preparatory examination of the persons commonly examined in such cases, in order to prove the capture to be lawful prize, or to enquire whether the same be lawful prize or not; and that the proper monition usual in such cases, shall be issued by the person or persons proper to issue the same, and shall be executed in the usual manner by the person or persons proper to execute the same, within the space of three days after request in that behalf made.[2]

As a third step in initiating prize litigation, the captors had to turn over to the judge all the papers and writings found on board the captured vessel with an affidavit that these constituted all the papers discovered. When these three steps were

---

[1] 6 Anne, c. 37 (1708); 13 Geo. II, c. 4 (1740); 17 Geo. II, c. 34 (1744); 29 Geo. II, c. 34 (1756).

[2] 29 Geo. II, c. 34 § 3.

completed, the judge could proceed to condemn or acquit the vessel if no party filed a properly attested claim with the required security within twenty days of the monition.

> [I]n case no claim of such capture, ship, vessel or goods, shall be duly entered or made in the usual form, and attested upon oath, giving twenty days notice after the execution of such monition; or if there be such claim, and the claimant or claimants shall not within five days give sufficient security . . . to pay double costs to the captor . . . in case the . . . [property] so claimed shall be adjudged lawful prize; that then, the judge . . . shall, upon producing to him . . . upon oath, all papers and writings which shall have been found, taken in or with such capture; or upon oath made that no such papers or writings were found; immediately, and without further delay, proceed to sentence, either to discharge and acquit such capture, or to adjudge and condemn the same as lawful prize, according as the case shall appear to him . . . upon perusal of such preparatory examinations, and also of the . . . papers and writings.[3]

The English High Court of Admiralty followed this simple, three-step procedure for initiating a prize case. When the prize was brought into port, the commander of the capturing privateer or man-of-war delivered to the admiralty judge the papers found on the captured ship. The commander or a chief officer of the captors had to swear that the papers were brought in just as they had been taken, or if any papers were missing, he had to account for them. At the same time the captors presented to the admiralty judge several principal members of the crew of the captured ship. They were examined under oath on standing interrogatories (lengthy series of questions drawn up in advance in general terms and designed to reveal the ownership of the captured ship and cargo). Upon petition of the captor's proctor (the lawyer who played the role in admiralty that the attorney or solicitor played at common law), the judge decreed the usual monition or public notice that any party with an interest in the captured ship or cargo should present a claim within twenty days. The judge had to proceed to sentence if within these twenty days no claimant appeared and put up proper security to pay double costs in case of condemnation of the property.[4]

---

[3] *Ibid.*

[4] The procedure of the High Court of Admiralty is described in Arthur Browne,

To lawyers experienced in English prize practice, this section of the prize acts seemed clear, and these procedures were carefully and precisely followed in England. In the context of vice-admiralty court prize practice, however, the prize acts apparently were not clear enough to induce colonial lawyers and judges to adhere to the procedures as understood and practiced in England. In the colonies as in England, there were always the monitions or public notice to interested parties to defend their rights in the captured property. But the practice in the American and Jamaican vice-admiralty courts varied significantly from the other two of these three steps for bringing suit in a prize case. In the first place, it was the universal practice in America and Jamaica for the captors to file a libel, which was a highly stylized bill in admiralty comparable to the plaintiff's complaint at common law.[5] The libel was a common way of initiating suit in admiralty on the instance (non-prize) side. As will become apparent through much of this chapter, the American and Jamaican vice-admiralty courts followed instance procedures in many details in their prize practice, whereas in England prize procedures were clearly distinct from the instance practice of the High Court. The use of a libel in prize cases in the vice-admiralty courts is only one symptom of a basically different approach to prize adjudication in America and in England.

A Compendious View of the Civil Law (2 v., 2d ed., London, 1802) **2**: pp. 445–447. Although written a generation after the American Revolution (the first edition came out in 1798), the prize procedures had not changed significantly in the intervening years. The printed cases used for prize appeals during the Seven Years' War also indicate that the procedures in the High Court of Admiralty closely followed the details of the prize acts. For instance, see, *Jesus Maria y Joseph* (Ezenarro), HCA, 45/3; *Maria* (Vande Velde), HCA, 45/1; *Maria Theresa* (Byaart), HCA, 45/2; and *Novum Aratrum* (Steekling), HCA, 45/2 in the Public Record Office (London). In general all cases from the High Court of Admiralty during the Seven Years' War indicate the same procedures, see HCA 45/1–5. The cases appealed to the Lords Commissioners for Prize Appeals will be cited by the name of the prize vessel with the name of the master or commander of the captured ship in parentheses, which is the standard mode of citation in the Public Record Office materials.

[5] In the printed cases presented in prize appeals during the Seven Years' War, it appears that in every case coming from a vice-admiralty court in America or Jamaica a libel was filed in the court below, whereas in no case coming from the High Court of Admiralty or the Irish vice-admiralty court was there mention of a libel. HCA, 45/1–5 (PRO). The rule must have been that no pleadings were proper before the judge considered the evidence of the ship's papers and the preparatory examinations. The Lords Commissioners for Prize Appeals issued an order, 27 March, 1760 condemning such pleadings. HCA, 43/15 (PRO).

The form of the libel in prize cases followed a definite pattern wherever it was found in this period. Though the order of the contents of a libel might vary, each one generally included most of the following points: The libel was addressed to the judge of the vice-admiralty court where the captured property was to be tried. The libelant (often the master or commander of the capturing ship) gave his own name, the name of the vessel in which he made the capture and then he mentioned the other parties (the owners of the privateer, its officers, and crew) for whom he libeled. (This *qui tam* form, "who for himself as well as for . . ." was common in prize libels.) The libel also described the captured property by naming the vessel and briefly mentioning its cargo. The facts of the capture were then stated. War had been declared with a certain enemy, the captors had been properly commissioned to seize as lawful prize the property of this enemy, this particular vessel or its cargo belonged to the enemy at the time it had been seized. The time and place of the capture were given. The legal basis of the capture was made clear, for instance, that it was enemy property or the cargo was contraband. The libel concluded with a prayer for the condemnation of the captured property for the use of the libelant and those for whom he libeled. Though at times made out and signed by the libelant himself, many libels were prepared and signed by the proctor for the libelant.[6]

The vice-admiralty court in Jamaica had an apparently unique local practice. At the time of the Seven Years' War the advocate general of the island seems to have exercised the right to bring suit for all captors, even though the Crown had

---

[6] Typical examples of libels can be found in *Reports of Cases in the Vice Admiralty of the Province of New York and in the Court of Admiralty of the State of New York, 1715–1788*, Charles M. Hough, ed. (New Haven, 1925), p. 267 and in *Records of the Vice-Admiralty Court of Rhode Island, 1716–1752*, Dorothy S. Towle, ed. (Washington, 1936), p. 562. See also: Maryland Court of Vice-Admiralty Proceedings, 1754–1775 (Maryland Hall of Records); South Carolina Vice-Admiralty Court Records, 1716–1763 (LCMss); Pennsylvania Vice-Admiralty Court Records, 1735–1759 (LCMss). Though in the eighteenth century no formularies of admiralty instruments existed, the various courts and attorneys undoubtedly kept files of such legal forms and copied the proper form when occasion required. Perhaps the uniformity in prize libels was ultimately due to a brief, scholastic analysis of libels, "A Brief Discourse, Shewing the Order and Structure of a Libel or Declaration," in Henry Conset, *The Practice of the Spiritual or Ecclesiastical Courts* (3d ed., London, 1708), pp. 400–405. The form of a libel in ecclesiastical courts was basically the same as a libel in admiralty.

no interest in the prize. The libel was filed in the name of the advocate general and the captors were named as relators.[7]

Another divergence between the procedures in England and in the colonies, more significant than whether or not a libel was filed, was the use in the vice-admiralty courts of evidence that would not have been admitted in England. In the High Court the prize acts were interpreted to mean that the only evidence ordinarily admitted in a prize case was to be the papers found on board the captured vessel and the preparatory examinations, based on standing inter-rogatories, of the principal members of the crew of the captured vessel. The general rule in England was:

> The evidence to acquit or condemn, with or without costs or damages, must, in the first instance, come merely from the ship taken, viz. the papers on board, and the examination on oath of the master and other principal officers; for which purpose there are officers of Admiralty in all considerable sea ports of every maritime power at war, to examine captains and other principal officers of every ship brought in as prize, upon general and impartial interrogatories.[8]

Again and again, however, the vice-admiralty courts were found to have admitted evidence which ordinarily would have been rejected by the High Court of Admiralty. In a good number of cases brought from the colonies to the Lords Commissioners for Prize Appeals, the advocates (the lawyers, comparable to barristers at common law, who argued admiralty cases in court) contended that interrogatories had been taken of improper parties or not on the standing inter-rogatories. Objections were particularly vehement against interrogatories drawn up by the captors and then adminis-tered to the crew of the captured ship, instead of questioning them on the standing interrogatories prepared in advance in England. For instance, in a prize appeal from New York the advocates for the claimant, in the printed case presented to the Lords Commissioners, contended that:

> [S]everal other Witnesses were at sundry Times after produced and

---

[7] Vice-Admiralty, Rough Minutes of Prize Court, 1758–1759 (Jamaica Archives). See also, "Case concerning the Court of Vice-Admiralty in Jamaica," 24 March, 1745/6, Sir George Lee, Admiralty Opinions, 2 (HSP).

[8] *Report of the Law Officers of the Crown*, in Marsden, *Law of the Sea* 2: p. 351. This very significant Report is discussed briefly in the next chapter.

examined by the Captor upon *Five other different Sets of Interrogatories* . . . [and the captor] *examined the said Captain Seymour
and William Smith, on Interrogatories prepared for that Purpose,* and
administered to them, on behalf of the Captor, with a View to
make these Papers, if they could, Evidence in this Cause,
*contrary to the express Directions of the Act of Parliament, and the
most solemn Determinations.*

The Appellants cannot suppose that the Respondent will
presume to state or offer to read any of these subsequent
irregular Examinations, or the Papers which he did so improp-
erly introduce in the first Instance of this Cause; or that, in
case he should attempt it, they will be received or have any
Weight; but, on the contrary, the Appellant hopes that they
will be rejected, and that no other Evidence shall be read upon
the hearing of this Appeal, but that which the Act of Parliament has made such in Prize Causes; viz. the *Preparatory Examinations, regularly taken, upon the usual standing Interrogatories,
and the Papers that were actually on board the Ship, at the Time of the
Capture thereof.*[9]

In other prize appeals the advocates argued against the
admissibility of interrogatories because taken several weeks
after the preparatory examinations were completed and
taken of common crew members, not the principal members
of the crew as required by English practice.[10] In one case
from Jamaica the Lords Commissioners, in their final decree,
agreed with the advocates for the appellant that the captors'
evidence was irregular because based on several sets of interrogatories drawn up by the captors and administered to
members of the crew of the captured vessel at different
times. The Lords Commissioners stated that the proceedings
in the court below had been irregular and they "declared that
no Depositions ought to be read out of such Persons as might

---

[9] Appellant's case, *St. Fernando* (Hilkes), HCA, 45/2. Italics in original. See also,
Amstel (De Witt), HCA, 45/2; *Anna Margarita Galley* (Hellison), HCA, 45/2; *Charming
Elizabeth* (Davis), HCA, 45/1; *Florence* (Breakill), HCA, 45/1; *Spanish Galley*
(Malmstrom), HCA, 45/1; *Vryheidt* (Feteris), HCA, 45/1; *Vryheid* (Hop), HCA, 45/1
(PRO); Pares, *Colonial Blockade*, pp. 110–111.

[10] *Vrouw Clara Magdelena* (Van Houten), HCA, 45/1 (PRO). The same objections
were raised in *San Joseph* (Gallardo), HCA, 45/1, and in *San Antonio e Almas* (da
Costa), *Appeal Cases in Prize Causes* (4 v., Library of Congress, Law Division) 1, which
were both appealed from the High Court of Admiralty. (The vice-admiralty courts
apparently did not have a monopoly of procedural irregularities.) Other examples
of these same procedural irregularities in vice-admiralty courts can be seen in *Il
Santo Christo* (del Valle), tried in New York, and *Vreede* (Boon), tried in Jamaica,
Appeal Cases (LC Law) 1.

have been examined in preparatorio."[11] In a case appealed from New York the appellant's advocates contended that the chief evidence presented by the captors had been inadmissible because based on the examination of a person who had not been on board the captured vessel at the time of the capture. The Lords Commissioners reversed the court below and condemned the proceedings as irregular and illegal.[12] But in another case appealed from New York, the advocates for the claimant argued vigorously against the admission of evidence irregularly taken.

> But the Captor, not thinking the Examinations on the Standing Interrogatories would be alone sufficient to justify the Seizure, or to obtain a Condemnation of this Ship and Goods, prepared *another Set of Interrogatories,* upon which the aforesaid *Surgeon* and *First Mate* of the *Dutch* Ship were *again examined,* in a very improper and irregular Manner, about *Three Weeks after their first Examination:*—But as the Appellant conceives, and humbly hopes, from former Determinations, that these second Examinations will not be suffered to be read, but will be rejected as irregular, he has not stated them here, and avoids making any further Observations on them, or on the improper Steps taken by the Captor, and countenanced by the Judge Below, in order to obtain a Condemnation of this Ship and Goods.[13]

In spite of the feigned shock of these advocates, the Lords Commissioners in this case apparently ignored the issue of irregular interrogatories and affirmed the decree of the court below. (This passage just quoted, by the way, also illustrates the general use of precedent—"from former Determinations"—in arguments before the Lords Commissioners.)

A complete study of the records of the various American vice-admiralty courts would undoubtedly show that interrogatories prepared by one of the parties were frequently used instead of the standing interrogatories.[14] The prize practice in the colonies of using interrogatories drawn up by

---

[11] *Hoop* (Keetel), HCA, 45/1, 43/15 (PRO).

[12] *Virgin del Rosario yel Sancto Christo de Buen Viage* (Ybanes), HCA, 45/1, 3 (PRO).

[13] *St. Marcus* (Mulder), HCA, 45/2 (PRO). Italics in original.

[14] Innumerable examples of depositions based on specially prepared interrogatories are given in Towle, *Records, passim.* An example of a standing interrogatory is given, *Ibid.,* pp. 566–570.

one of the parties probably reflected the ordinary practice of the vice-admiralty courts in their instance proceedings. Even in England, and certainly more so in the colonies, the examination of witnesses on the instance side of admiralty was less stringently regulated than on the prize side.[15]

There were also occasional irregularities in colonial vice-admiralty courts in the admission as evidence of papers not found on the vessel captured. In a number of cases heard in the New York vice-admiralty court, the judge admitted letters or other papers discovered on board other vessels, or the captors were allowed to deliver only some selected papers from the captured vessel and only later turned over to the court the rest of the papers.[16]

Rules for evaluating evidence remained vague in England as well as in the colonies. Any court which had to deal with prize cases became necessarily involved in the often impossible task of discerning the truth in a context of frequent perjury and repeated use of false ship papers. Captors often contended that the papers found on board the vessel they had captured were forged, that the true papers had been burnt or thrown overboard in order to conceal the true ownership of the vessel or cargo, that the captured vessel carried double papers, one set sufficient to obtain free passage from either nation involved in the hostilities. The officers of the captured vessel, in turn, claimed that the papers were authentic, that no papers had been destroyed, or that the true papers had been lost or carried off by some previous captor, or that some of the ship's papers had been destroyed by the captors who wanted to suppress evidence favorable to the captured ship.[17] Undoubtedly, all these practices, and many others besides, were engaged in by captors and captured alike. In England and in the colonies there were no clear rules of evidence in prize cases to assist the admiralty judge in piercing through the charges and coun-

---

[15] Browne, *Compendious View* **2**: pp. 419–425.

[16] *Spanish Galley* (Malmstrom), HCA, 45/1; *Vrouw Clara Magdelena* (Van Houten), HCA, 45/1; *Vryheidt* (Feteris), HCA, 45/1 (PRO); see also Hough, *Reports*, pp. 94–100, 131–137. See also similar objections to use as evidence of papers not found on board the captured vessel in *Peter John* (Le Moyne) HCA, 45/2 (PRO), a case appealed from Antigua, and also Pares, *Colonial Blockade*, pp. 112–113.

[17] *Amstel* (De Witt), HCA, 45/2; *Geregtigheit* (Daal), HCA 45/2; *Hoop* (Bakker), HCA, 45/1; *Hoop* (Keetel), HCA, 45/1; *Juffrow Maria* (Vander Velde), HCA, 45/1 (PRO).

tercharges or in discovering forgeries among the confusing collection of ship papers. The cases speak of presumptions of guilt based on certain types of conduct or falsified documents.[18] The Lords Commissioners for Prize Appeals, as well as the admiralty judges, had to evaluate these factual questions in the light of all the evidence produced before them.[19] The system of presumptions, however, seems to have been little more than common sense rules which might sway a judge, or the Lords Commissioners, one way or the other, but must have done little to help the court feel confident it had discovered the truth in a context so often charged with deceit. One author lists the presumptions which weighed against the captured vessel, but says nothing of the various wiley practices of privateers which should have been weighed in the balance also, nor of the fact that such suspicious conduct was so widespread as to cast doubt on most maritime commerce in wartime.

> Some of the grand circumstances, which, if proved, go strongly to condemn the ship, or at least to excite strong suspicion, are the want of complete and proper papers, the carrying false or colourable papers, the throwing papers overboard, prevarication in the master and officers examined in preparatorio, spoliation of papers, the master not knowing who the owners are, or not being able to give an account whose property are the ship and cargo, the national character and domicile of the master; his conduct, and that of the vessel herself; the time when the papers were composed, with many others creating greater or less degrees of suspicion according to their nature.[20]

In theory, if any of these suspicious acts of the officers of the captured vessel had been proven, they should have gone far in convincing a judge to condemn the vessel. But where both captors and captured were consistently engaged in deceitful practices, where bribery and intimidation of witnesses were all too common, it must have been frequently impossible for

---

[18] *Good Christian* (Plow), HCA, 45/1; *Marie Theresa* (Byaart), HCA, 45/2, 43/13; *San Antonio e Almas* (da Costa), HCA, 45/1 (PRO); Hough, *Reports*, pp. 88–92; Pares, *Colonial Blockade*, pp. 115–131.

[19] *San Vincente* (Pellot), HCA, 45/1, 2 (PRO); same case, *Appeal Cases* (LC Law) 1.

[20] Browne, *Compendious View* 2: pp. 451–452. See also Philip Jessup, ed., *Neutrality—Its History, Economics and Law* (4 v., New York, 1935–1936) 1: pp. 224–246.

a judge, even with this list of presumptions, to know what documents or which individual's sworn testimony to believe.

One rule of evidence apparently was insisted on in the colonies as well as in England. Witnesses who had some financial interest in the outcome of a case could not be admitted to testify. Such witnesses might divest themselves of their interest and thereby render their testimony admissible. But as long as they had an interest in the litigation, their testimony could be objected to. In one case involving joint capture appealed to the Lords Commissioners, the advocates for the alleged joint captors stated in the printed case:

> The rest of the Witnesses, examined on both Sides, were all interested, consisting of divers Officers and others, of the Company of the several contending Ships, none of whom do appear from the Process, to have released their Interests in the Prize in Question. It is therefore submitted that the Evidence of such interested Persons cannot be read by either Side.[21]

Although in some cases this rule rejecting evidence presented by interested parties might have been wise, it is hard to imagine where the parties could obtain testimony in a case of joint capture if not from the crews of the various ships claiming to have shared in making the capture. Impartial bystanders must have been rare indeed. Of course, the officers and crew of the captured ship might testify as to which vessel made the capture. Bribes and intimidation, however, must have been common enough to call such evidence in question in many cases. These rules against testimony by interested parties must have led often to various subterfuges by which the interested parties signed statements releasing their share in the prize in order to have their testimony admitted, but received some assurance of payment of their share nonetheless. One gets the impression that perjury was a way of life for some eighteenth-century seamen.

Therefore, we can see that the vice-admiralty courts followed the general pattern of the British prize acts for the initiation of a prize case and the admission of evidence, but

---

[21] *Mars* (le Ray), HCA, 45/2 (PRO); *Hannah of London* in: *Sir George Lee Prize Appeals* (2 v., New York Public Library, Rare Book Room) 1; *Il Santo Christo* (del Valle), *Appeal Cases* (LC Law) 1; Pares, *Colonial Blockade*, p. 114; William E. Nelson, *Americanization of the Common Law* (Cambridge, Mass., 1975), pp. 24–25.

with significant variations from the practice of the High Court of Admiralty. One further detail of colonial practice strengthens the impression that the colonial courts employed in prize adjudication the general admiralty procedures, appropriate in instance (non-prize) suits. There are indications in all the colonial vice-admiralty court records consulted of a system of proclamations and defaults used in prize cases.

In the High Court of Admiralty the party bringing an instance suit, for example, an action for seamen's wages or collision, presented an affidavit of the debt and sought from the court a warrant directed to the marshal commanding him to arrest the ship or cargo. All those having an interest in the vessel were cited to appear in court on a certain day to answer the allegations and defend against them. If the interested parties failed to appear, the court proceeded by way of defaults. The proctor for the promovent or plaintiff, after the marshal had executed the warrant arresting the vessel, and the court had three times made proclamation for all interested parties to appear, moved for the first default if no one appeared to defend. The next court day the same procedure would be followed, the three proclamations, the motion for default, and the court-ordered second default. After the fourth default had been incurred the court assigned a day for summary hearing.[22]

This same basic system of the threefold proclamation in open court followed by a default for nonappearance can be seen more or less clearly in prize cases in practically all the colonial records consulted.[23] These records fre-

---

[22] Browne, *Compendious View* 2: pp. 397–401. Again it should be stressed that Browne, though first published in 1798, gives an accurate picture of late eighteenth-century admiralty procedure. See also, F.L. Wiswall, Jr., *The Development of Admiralty Jurisdiction and Practice Since 1800* (Cambridge, 1970), pp. 12–14, and Beawes, *Lex Mercatoria*, p. 249.

[23] For example, New York Vice-Admiralty Court Minute Book, 1753–1770 (New York Public Library, Manuscript Division); Vice-Admiralty Court of the Province of New York, Minutes, 1701–1774 (National Archives); Jamaica Vice-Admiralty Rough Minutes, Prize Court, 1758–1759 (JA); Massachusetts Vice-Admiralty Court Record Book, 1740–174__ (last number not clear) (Massachusetts Supreme Judicial Court, Office of the Clerk); Rhode Island Admiralty Court Minute Books, 1727–1743 (Rhode Island State Archives). Pennsylvania Vice-Admiralty Court Records (LCMss); South Carolina Vice-Admiralty Court Records (LCMss). Colonial admiralty practice on the instance side (and indirectly on the prize side) was undoubtedly influenced by Francis Clerke's, *Praxis Supremae Curiae Admiralitatis* (1667), which went through several editions in the seventeenth century and was inadequately translated into English in 1722. On defaults, see titles 22 and 35. See also *The Practice*

quently referred to proclamations and a series of defaults followed by the assignation of a day for a hearing and sentence. With the exception of New York and South Carolina, even the instance procedures in the vice-admiralty courts appear to have been simplified variations of English instance practice with overtones of the common law.[24]

We have seen, therefore, that the colonial vice-admiralty courts did not follow the clearly set forth procedures of the British prize acts for initiating a prize suit and bringing it to judicial sentence where no claim, with proper security, was filed. Significant variations between English and colonial practice suggest that the continental American and Jamaican courts employed their own peculiar adaptation of instance procedures for prize adjudication. The court in England clearly regarded its prize jurisdiction as distinct from its instance jurisdiction and recognized that the prize procedures were entirely controlled by parliamentary statutes renewed at the outbreak of each war. Lord Mansfield, in a case reported with *Le Caux v. Eden*, decided during the American Revolution, expressed the English attitude when he stated that:

> The whole system of litigation and jurisprudence in the prize court, is peculiar to itself; It is no more like the court of Admiralty [instance procedures], than it is to any court in *Westminster* Hall [common law procedures].[25]

This statement could not have been made of prize procedures in American vice-admiralty courts. Judge Francis Hopkinson of the Pennsylvania Admiralty Court shortly after the American Revolution stated that lawyers and judges grasped the difference between the instance and prize practice of admiralty courts only when they had read Mansfield's recent decision. Hopkinson wrote:

---

of the Court of Admiralty in England and Ireland (Dublin, 1757), titles 30 and 31. Both of these books deal only with instance procedures.

[24] L. Kinvin Wroth, "The Massachusetts Vice-Admiralty Court," in: *Law and Authority in Colonial America*, George A. Billias, ed. (Barre, Mass. 1965), pp. 38–40; Maryland Court of Admiralty Proceedings (MHR); Records of the Courts of Admiralty and Vice-Admiralty of Massachusetts Bay, 1718–1772 (LCMss); New York Vice-Admiralty Court Minutes (NA); South Carolina Vice-Admiralty Court Records (LCMss). A fairly typical uncontested prize proceeding can be seen in *Seymour qui tam v. Ship Le Raphael and Lading*, in New York Vice-Admiralty Court Minutes (NA).

[25] In *Lindo v. Rodney and Another*, Douglas, 591 at 592; 99 *English Reports*, 385 at 386.

Then [on reading Mansfield's decision in *Le Caux v. Eden*], for the first time, did the distinction occur, between the *prize* court and the *instance* court of admiralty.[26]

Whereas the English High Court of Admiralty regarded its prize jurisdiction and procedures as defined by the prize acts, the colonial vice-admiralty courts apparently looked at prize procedures as merely one facet of their general admiralty practice.

The British prize acts, therefore, set forth the procedural details already seen for bringing suit in a prize case and for determining the right to captured property if no claim with proper security was filed. The acts then gave detailed prescriptions for those situations where a claimant did appear and provide the required security. The acts distinguished two situations if a claim was properly filed: where there was no need to examine witnesses at a distance from the court, and where the case appeared doubtful to the judge so that he thought it necessary "to have an examination, upon pleadings given in by the parties, and admitted by the judge, of witnesses that are remote from such court of admiralty." In the first situation the court was to proceed to examine witnesses for each party, as where no claim was filed, and then give its sentence. The judge was given ten days in such a case to reach a final determination. But if a claim was properly filed and the court still remained doubtful about true ownership of the property after studying the ship papers and the usual examination on standing interrogatories, it could order the parties "to plead and prove." This technical phrase in English prize practice called for a series of formal pleadings in which the parties alleged proof in support of their respective positions. The judge could grant a commission for the examination of witnesses who were at a distance from the court and could not be questioned in the usual preparatory examinations.[27] The parties obtaining the com-

---

[26] *Dean et al. v. John Angus*, Bee, *Reports*, 369, 372 (1785). This case is discussed in chapter VIII below.

[27] 29 Geo. II, c. 34, § 3. The statute stated that: "[I]n case such claim shall be duly entered or made, and security given thereupon, according to the tenor and true meaning of this act, and there shall appear no occasion to examine any witnesses, other than what shall be then near to such court of admiralty, that then such judge or judges shall forthwith cause such witnesses to be examined within the space of ten days after such claim made and security given, and proceed to such sentence as aforesaid, touching such capture; but in case upon making or entering such claim,

mission to examine witnesses could prepare interrogatories on which they would be questioned. The prize cases appealed from England indicate that in the High Court of Admiralty the parties did follow this practice of filing formal pleadings, given different names in various cases. One case speaks of the captor's allegation, the claimant's allegation, the captor's reply, and the claimant's answer.[28] Another case speaks of the captor's allegation, the claimant's plea, the captor's reply, and the claimant's rejoinder.[29] The terminology in another case changed to the claimant's allegation, the captor's allegation, and the claimant's dissent and denial.[30] Perhaps this difference in terminology reflected slight differences in the form the pleading took.

In the colonial vice-admiralty courts the claims filed were frequently lengthy arguments, on oath, to prove that the property was not lawful prize.[31] In England the claim was generally a short, general statement signed by the claimant himself, accompanied by an affidavit stating the facts of the ownership of the property to show it should not be condemned as prize. In the vice-admiralty courts the tendency was to combine these two forms into the claim itself, sometimes called a claim and answer.[32] The formal pleadings used in the High Court of Admiralty were apparently the exception

---

and the allegation and oath thereupon, or the producing such papers or writings as shall have been found or taken in or with such capture, or upon the said preparatory examinations, it shall appear doubtful to the judge or judges of such court of admiralty, whether such capture be lawful prize or not, and it shall appear necessary, according to the circumstances of the case, for the clearing and determining such doubt, to have an examination, upon pleadings given in by the parties, and admitted by the judge, of witnesses that are remote from such court of admiralty, and such examination shall be desired, and that it be still insisted on, on behalf of the captors, that the said capture is lawful prize, and the contrary be still persisted in on the claimants behalf, [such examinations shall be ordered]."

[28] *Maria Theresa* (Byaart), HCA, 45/1, 2; see also *Joanna Arnoldina* (Churchill), HCA 45/1, 2 (PRO).

[29] *Juffrow Maria* (Vander Velde), HCA, 45/1 (PRO).

[30] *Jesus, Maria y Joseph* (Ezenarro), HCA, 45/1, 3. In another case the terminology was: the captor's allegation, the claimant's allegation, and the captor's replication. *Novum Aratrum* (Steekling), HCA, 45/1, 2 (PRO).

[31] A published example of a claim is given in Hough, *Reports*, p. 270; see also Towle, *Records*, pp. 92, 191, 198, and *Grande Juste* (Duplessis), Massachusetts Admiralty Court Record Book, 1740–174__ (MSJC).

[32] Many examples of claims are given in HCA, 45/1–5. The differences between claims in England and Jamaica are discussed in "Case concerning the Court of Vice-Admiralty in Jamaica," Sir George Lee Admiralty Opinions, 24 March, 1745/6, 2 (HSP).

in most vice-admiralty prize cases, though there are examples of cases in which answers, replications, and rejoinders were filed in New York, Pennsylvania, and South Carolina. The pleadings in the South Carolina vice-admiralty court became highly formal and repetitious, with frequent examples of replications, duplications, prayers for a time probatory, or for apostles and letters dimissory.[33] The vice-admiralty judges as the English admiralty judges, issued commissions for the examination of witnesses at a distance from the court.[34]

The prize acts continue by ordering the judge, in cases where the parties must further plead and prove, to have the vessel and cargo appraised, and to have the cargo inventoried and stored in a warehouse under separate locks by the collector of customs. This process was necessary to prevent the ship or cargo from being damaged during the more lengthy trials where the parties had to obtain further evidence. The prize acts further provided that the judge could order the release of the ship and cargo to the claimant pending trial, if the claimant could give sufficient security to pay the captor the full appraised value of the property in case the final decree should condemn it as prize to the captors. If the claimant could not give such security, the judge could release the property to the captors if they could give adequate security to pay the full appraised value in case the vessel and cargo should be acquitted.[35] Apparently the vice-admiralty courts rarely followed these procedures set forth in the prize acts. Though the colonial courts often used more expeditious procedures for trials than the formal pleading and proof used in England, on occasion it was necessary to have the vessel and cargo appraised pending trial and to seek

---

[33] *Santo Christo* (de Valle), New York Vice-Admiralty Court Minute Book, 1753–1770 (NYPL, Mss); Hough, *Reports*, pp. 100–111; New York Vice-Admiralty Court Minutes (NA); Pennsylvania Vice Admiralty Court Records (LCMss); South Carolina Vice-Admiralty Court Records (LCMss).

[34] *Santo Crucifixo e Nostra Seniora Della Misericordia e San Nicola* (Issuardo y Benedetto), Jamaica Prize Papers before 1776 (JA); *Geregtigheit* (Daal), HCA, 45/2 (PRO); in *Capt. Jacob Roome et al. agt Ship St. Fernando & Lading,* Hough, *Reports,* p. 131, the New York vice-admiralty judge used his discretion to refuse to issue such a commission, stating: "The Court having considered the Motion for a Commission to Examine Witnesses in Holland is of Opinion that by the Act of Parliament, no commission can issue unless the Judge is in Doubt & then must be Applied for in Ten days." He went on to explain why he was not in doubt.

[35] 29 Geo. II, c. 34, § 3, 4.

security from one party or the other for its immediate release.[36]

The next section of the prize acts applied only to the vice-admiralty courts in America. The acts provided that all captured property brought into a port in America should be under the joint custody of the collector of customs (or naval officers of the port if there was no collector) and the captors pending adjudication. The admiralty judge had authority to give orders for the care of the property or for its release to one party or the other.[37] Though the New York Vice-Admiralty Court followed these requirements of the prize acts for custody pending trial,[38] the records from most American vice-admiralty courts give the impression that ordinarily the captured property remained in the sole custody of the captors. The collectors of customs, perhaps because they received no fee, do not seem to have been involved in keeping the vessel or cargo safe and protecting it from theft or damage pending trial.

This precise point was raised in a formal question presented to Sir George Lee, a leading civilian in England. The questioner, perhaps the governor or vice-admiralty judge in Jamaica, stated that the collector of customs never took custody of prizes since they received no fees for their trouble. The admiralty judge in Jamaica never enforced this section of the prize act, even though at times the common sailors of the captor's vessel suffered great loss because the prize remained in the custody of the officers of the capturing vessel who stole freely before the property was condemned and as a result the rest of the crew was deprived of a large part of their share in the prize. The questioner asked Lee for his opinion as to the proper remedy to assure that the collectors of the customs did their duty in taking joint custody of the captured property. Lee answered:

> I am of opinion the Judge of the Admiralty will subject himself to the Penaltys [sic] in the Act if he delays proceeding till the

---

[36] One clear example of this procedure for appraisal and release pending trial, with security provided, is *Juffrow Anna Maria*, Jamaica Rough Minutes Prize Court, 1758–1759 (JA).

[37] 29 Geo. II, c. 34, § 5.

[38] New York Vice-Admiralty Court Minutes (NA). Apparently, it was also the practice in Maryland for the vice-admiralty court to order the vessel arrested, but perhaps these are all cases brought for violations of the Acts of Trade. Maryland Court of Vice-Admiralty Proceedings (MHR).

Prize is in the hands of the Collector & Comtroller of the Customs[.] [I]t seems to be an omission [in the prize acts] but I doubt as the Act is Penned no Power is given to the s[ai]d Judge to oblige the Captors by any Compulsory method to put the Prize into the Custody of the Custom or Naval officers or to give them a reward for their trouble, nor can he compell [sic] the making of a division[.] [I]f any one is aggrieved by an unfair division I conceive he must seek his Remedy by an Action at Common Law ag[ain]st the Wrong Doer.[39]

This opinion, which would subject the vice-admiralty judge to penalties for enforcing this section of the prize acts and make no provision for fees for the collectors, undoubtedly explains why captured vessels and cargoes remained in the sole custody of the captors. If this opinion, written in 1745, was widely shared, this section of the prize acts certainly must have become a dead letter.

The next section of the prize acts, referred to by Lee, subjected the vice-admiralty judges to a possible fine of £500 for delaying the procedures for adjudicating prize cases. One half the fine would go to the informer who revealed the judge's neglect or delay in performing his duties. The next section set a limit on the fees the vice-admiralty judges could collect for hearing prize cases.[40] Both these provisions, for fines and for fees, had been in the prize acts since the first one in 1708, with only one amendment. In the section dealing with fines for delaying judicial process, the 1740 prize act added "in any of his Majesty's plantations or dominions abroad," apparently to make sure that admiralty judges at home would not be liable to such fines.[41] Since the vice-admiralty courts in America had existed only a short time at the start of the eighteenth century, it seems unlikely that this provision for heavy fines was orginally due to reported abuses abroad. A few of the cases in America give the impression of needless delay, but it is possible that this section dealing with fines was not carefully enforced. If desirable, the lawyers for either party could have found many ways to have the case delayed with the judge's approval, without the risk that the judge would be subjected to this fine.

The prize acts did not mention, though clearly took for

[39] "Case concerning the Court of Vice-Admiralty in Jamaica," 24 March, 1745/6, Sir George Lee Admiralty Opinions, 2 (HSP).
[40] 29 Geo. II, c. 34, § 6, 7; 13 Geo. II, c. 4, § 6, 7.
[41] 6 Anne, c. 37, § 6, 7; 13 Geo. II, c. 4, § 6, 7.

granted, the presentation of various motions by counsel and the oral arguments before the admiralty courts. The court records from America and Jamaica do indicate the various roles played by counsel for the libelant and the claimant, but only with cryptic notations. When the case came on for oral argument, counsel for each party read the pleadings and the evidence and apparently presented some legal argument to support their request that the property be condemned as lawful prize or acquitted as belonging to a subject of a friendly nation. Undoubtedly the issues were generally factual and frequently involved the court in trying to discern the truth in a situation fraught with deceit.

In England the lawyers in admiralty and ecclesiastical suits were called proctors and advocates, comparable to solicitors and barristers in common law litigation. Sir George Lee stated the roles of proctors and advocates in eighteenth-century English admiralty practice (and, by the way, also mentioned the distinction already discussed between the claims filed in England and those common in the colonial vice-admiralty courts).

> It is the usage in the adm[iral]ty Court in England for Advocates to sign Libells & pleas, but the Claims here are general & short, given in by the Party or his agent with an Affidavit & not sign[e]d by an Advocate[.] [T]he Claims used at Jamaica I have observed are specifick [sic] & articulate upon which witnesses are examined[.] [S]uch Claims I am of Opinion ought to be signed by an Advocate as well as Libells & other pleas & Interr[ogatorie]s; with us the Proctors make their Petitions *in Court* and allegations but all matters are moved & spoke to by Advocates regularly admitted & that method I think should be observed in all Courts where the assistance of Advocates can be had[.][42]

Probably all the vice-admiralty courts generally relied on the services of common lawyers as counsel, but in most courts the English terminology of proctor and advocate was used. The roles played by proctors and advocates in the colonies, however, were quite confused. In Jamaica, where the most active vice-admiralty court existed, proctors were recorded to

---

[42] "Case concerning the Court of Vice-Admiralty in Jamaica," 24 March 1745/6, Sir George Lee Admiralty Opinions, 2 (HSP). The words in the text in italics were crossed out in the original.

have presented the following motions: that the marshal seal the hatches of a captured vessel and properly secure it to preserve its cargo; that the claim be read; that the captors be at liberty to unload the captured ship and land its cargo; that a party be at liberty to stipulate for a bond and file a claim. The advocates at Jamaica were recorded to have made the following motions: that witnesses be examined; that monitions issue; that the libel be read; that the court order defaults; that publication pass and the case be set down to be heard; that the libel be dismissed and the vessel acquitted; that the case be adjourned; that the captors be at liberty to stipulate for a bond and to prosecute an appeal; that the party have leave to appeal. The advocates at Jamaica also conducted the oral arguments; in the terms of the records, they opened the libel and read the proofs or opened the claim or opened the plea and exception.[43]

In the New York vice-admiralty court, the records indicate that the proctors filed most of the motions and occasionally also argued the case. For example, proctors are recorded to have made the following motions: that proclamations issue; that the claimant be admitted to defend and give security; that publication might pass and a day be assigned for a hearing; that leave to amend the libel be granted; that the libel be read; that the answer be filed by a set date; that the property be condemned where no claim was filed; that the court proceed to sentence; that the other party be ordered to pay costs; that a party have leave to appeal. The advocates in New York are recorded to have moved for proclamations for a hearing or to have the owners of a vessel give security for costs. They also read the depositions and exhibits, argued the case, and argued the motion to appeal.[44]

In the Massachusetts and Rhode Island vice-admiralty courts, it seems that the lawyers were ordinarily called attorneys, but there were occasional references to proctors or advocates.[45] The terminology appears to be interchangeable.

---

[43] Jamaica Vice-Admiralty Rough Minutes Prize Court, 1758–1759 (JA).

[44] New York Vice-Admiralty Court Minute Book, 1753–1770 (NYPL, Mss); New York Vice-Admiralty Court Minutes (NA); Hough, *Reports*, p. 92, where the same lawyer is listed as proctor and advocate; see also p. 101.

[45] Massachusetts Vice-Admiralty Record Book, 1740–174__ (MSJC); Rhode Island Admiralty Court Minute Books, 1727–1743 (RISA); Wroth, "Massachusetts Vice-Admiralty," in: *Law and Authority*, p. 40; Frederick B. Wiener, "Notes on the Rhode Island Admiralty, 1727–1790," *Harvard Law Rev.* **46** (1932): p. 48.

After the judge heard the pleadings and the oral arguments of counsel and had studied the interrogatories and the various ship papers, he frequently took some time to reflect and prepare the final sentence or decree. The form of the decrees in the vice-admiralty courts vary from brief statements of acquittal or condemnation to lengthy discussions of the case. In one six page decree from Massachusetts, the judge summarized the minutes of the trial and the pleadings, gave his own factual statement of the case, evaluated the evidence, answered point by point the arguments of claimant's counsel, and then, after determining that the vessel and cargo should be adjudged lawful prize, gave his reasons, including various presumptions, for the condemnation.[46] Many other cases decided in American vice-admiralty courts have lengthy decrees in which the judge seems to be trying to justify his determination with a view to possible appeal.[47] Vice-admiralty judges could show anger and impatience, as the New York judge who wrote in his decree: "I do not remember to have met with so bare faced Perjury in any case that ever came before me."[48] A judge from Massachusetts reacted strongly to some of the commercial practices frequently engaged in during wartime, such as carrying double papers. He stated in his decree:

> [F]or my part till I am better Informed from Home I shall never Ballance in Cases so Wickedly Contrived & contrary to the Conduct of plain Trading & simple Honesty[.] But in Justice to my King & Country always Condemn and if this Mackay was in Court notwithstanding all his subtley & Double Dealing & his pretended naturalization Certifyed [sic] from Teneriffe as in the Case I should order him in Custody till delivered up to the Government.[49]

The prize acts conclude the sections on procedure with provision for appeal "to the commissioners appointed, or to be appointed, under the great seal of *Great Britain*, for receiving, hearing and determining appeals in causes of prizes."

---

[46] *Grande Juste* (Duplessis), Massachusetts Vice-Admiralty Court Record Book, 1740–174__ (MSJC).

[47] Towle, *Records*, pp. 143–145, 192, 209–211, 222–223, 242–243, 276–278; Hough, *Reports*, pp. 88–92, 96–99, 108–110, 117–118, 131–137, 286–288.

[48] *Spanish Galley* (Malmstrom), HCA, 45/1 (PRO).

[49] *Amsterdam Post* (Mackay), Massachusetts Vice-Admiralty Record Book, 1740–174__ (MSJC).

The appeal had to be requested within fourteen days after sentence. The appellant had to give security that he would "effectually prosecute such appeal, and answer the condemnation, and also pay treble costs, as shall be awarded, in case the sentence of such court of admiralty be affirmed."[50] The prize acts provided that the decree of the admiralty court could be executed pending appeal, if the appellee gave sufficient security to restore the vessel and cargo or its full value in case the sentence appealed from should be reversed.[51] The privateering act of 1759, however, slightly modified this section. The admiralty judge by this act of 1759 was authorized to deliver the captured property to either party, pending appeal, provided the party give sufficient security to restore the full appraised value of the property. If neither party gave security acceptable to the other, the judge could have the vessel and cargo sold at public auction and deposit the proceeds in public securities to be held in trust for the party in whose favor the Lords Commissioners for Prize Appeals would finally decide.[52]

Many cases in the vice-admiralty courts indicate that the procedures of these acts were closely followed in requesting appeals. After the judge pronounced his sentence, the party dissatisfied with the decree could orally in open court, or by written notice of appeal, move for leave to appeal to the Lords Commissioners. If the motion was made within the fourteen days allowed by the prize acts, and if the moving party provided security to go forward with the appeal and to pay whatever costs might be assessed for the appeal, the court routinely granted the motion. Frequently the prize property was appraised so that one party could take possession of the property pending appeal upon providing adequate security to pay the full appraised value to the other party, should the other party prevail on appeal.[53] Where the appeal was not requested within the fourteen days allowed, the court could refuse to grant the appeal, even though counsel for the moving party alleged that he had not known

---

[50] 29 Geo. II, c. 34, § 8. Italics in original.
[51] *Ibid.*, § 9.
[52] 32 Geo. II, c. 25, § 24.
[53] Towle, *Records*, pp. 148, 160, 184, 209, 221–222; New York Vice-Admiralty Court Minutes (NA); Hough, *Reports*, pp. 77–79, 99–100, 288; Jamaica Vice-Admiralty Rough Minutes Prize Court, 1758–1759 (JA).

of the decree till after the time allowed for appeal.[54] Both parties could be given leave to appeal.[55] In one case the vice-admiralty judge refused to allow the appeal because the party requesting it by his own pleadings was not entitled to any more than he had received by the final decree and so could not be aggrieved by the sentence.[56] One claimant who had been granted leave to appeal requested the New York vice-admiralty court to have the prize cargo stored under proper security pending appeal, since the appraised value of the cargo at New York was "vastly below the Value of the said Goods, if sold at *Amsterdam*, the Place of their Destination." The judge refused this request and although the claimant prevailed on appeal, he apparently could only recover the New York appraised value of the cargo, plus interest from the time the cargo had been sold.[57] This case, decided in New York in 1759, illustrates the need for the provision of the privateering act of that same year allowing the court to restore the prize property to either party, if that party provided adequate security pending appeal.

One final section of the prize acts, first added in 1744, prohibited anyone, not a party to the original suit, from intervening in a prize appeal unless he filed a claim, apparently to be filed with the Lords Commissioners.[58]

This analysis of the prize procedures of the colonial vice-admiralty courts has shown some basic similarity to the procedures prescribed in the British prize acts and practiced in the High Court of Admiralty, but at the same time has indicated significant differences between the practice of the colonial courts and the English court. The colonial variations point to a strikingly different attitude in viewing prize jurisdiction and prize procedures. In England it was clear that prize jurisdiction was specially granted to an admiralty court in time of war and the procedures were entirely within the control of Parliament which conferred the power to hear prize cases. In the American vice-admiralty courts, however,

---

[54] Hough, *Reports*, p. 184. The interesting point in this case is that the counsel for the two parties were father and son, William Smith and William Smith, Jr. Apparently the son had concealed the decree from his father, who represented the other party, till it was too late to appeal.

[55] Towle, *Records*, pp. 193–194.

[56] *Ibid.*, pp. 222–224.

[57] *Dolphin* (Spin), HCA, 45/1, 3 (PRO).

[58] 17 Geo. II, c. 34, § 10; 29 Geo. II, c. 34, § 10.

the attitude seems to have been that, although some special authorization might be needed to hear prize cases, the procedures to be followed were the same as in any other case brought before the vice-admiralty courts. The tradition of prize practice in America, within which American lawyers were trained, was already different from English practice before the American Revolution. When the Americans came to establish their own prize courts during the Revolution, it was very natural for them to continue the type of procedures (probably thinking them to be standard English procedures) with which they had become familiar in their own vice-admiralty court. This, as we shall see, is just what they did.

Although it is quite clear that many American lawyers and lawmakers had direct experience with prize practice before the Revolution, it is doubtful that most Americans knew much at all about the intricacies of appellate practice before the Lords Commissioners for Prize Appeals. The statistics for appeals to the Lords Commissioners give one indication of the limited experience American lawyers must have had with prize appeals. During the Seven Years' War, just fifteen years or so before the Revolution, the Lords Commissioners received about 253 appeals. The printed cases submitted to the Lords Commissioners exist for 234 of these appeals. Although 88 of these 234 appeals came from Jamaica, only 34 came from all the thirteen American colonies. Twenty-three cases were appealed from New York, three from Rhode Island, two each from Pennsylvania and Virginia, and one each from Massachusetts, North Carolina, Maryland, and Georgia.[59] Apparently no appeals were heard by the Lords Commissioners from the five other colonies. Therefore, outside of the colony of New York, an appeal to the Lords Commissioners must have been an extremely rare occurrence in America. It is likely, however, that considerably more appeals were requested and granted than were actually carried to the Lords Commissioners. Even if an American lawyer had been associated with a prize case that

---

[59] These statistics were compiled from the four bound volumes of *Appeal Cases in Prize Causes* (LC Law). This collection of printed cases from the Seven Years' War period is more complete and more systematically compiled than the five volumes of printed cases for the same years in the Public Record Office, London. The volumes in the Library of Congress probably belonged to an officer of the court of prize appeals, perhaps the register.

went up on appeal, he would have had to obtain special counsel in England to act as proctors, barristers, and advocates for the handling of the case. It is quite unlikely, therefore, that the American lawyers who established an appellate prize court during the Revolution were greatly influenced by the procedures of the British court of prize appeals. A brief study of the practice before the Lords Commissioners for Prize Appeals, when compared with the procedures established for appeals in prize cases in America during the Revolution, will amply confirm this *a priori* judgment.

Only a few members of the Lords Commissioners for Prize Appeals heard and decided most of the cases. Although more than forty commissioners are mentioned as being present at sessions of prize appeals during the Seven Years' War, most of them merely put in an appearance once or twice. Only eleven individuals seem to have attended with any regularity, and only six of these were present at more than twenty sessions. These six, who apparently did the bulk of the work of the Lords Commissioners, were: John Earl Granville, who was supposed to be present at all meetings of sections of the Privy Council because of his office as Lord President of the Council, George Earl Cholmondeley, John Lord Berkeley of Stratton, Hugh Viscount Falmouth, Samuel Lord Sandys, and William Lord Mansfield, chief justice of King's Bench. These six each took part in at least half and probably three-fourths of the meetings of the Lords Commissioners and undoubtedly carried much weight in the deliberations, even when several other commissioners happened to be present at one or other session. Of these six most active members of the Lords Commissioners, only Mansfield had legal training and experience.[60] With the exception of Mansfield, whose influence must have been considerable, and perhaps Granville, minor ministers and would-be amateurs of prize law carried on much of the work of the Lords Commissioners.[61] Probably these five lay councillors,

[60] John Carteret, 1st Earl of Granville, 1690–1763; George Cholmondeley, 3rd Earl of Cholmondeley, 1703–1770; John Berkeley, Lord Berkeley of Stratton, 1697–1773; Hugh Boscawen, 2d Viscount Falmouth, 1707–1782; Samuel Sandys, 1st Baron Sandys, 1695–1770; William Murray, Earl of Mansfield, 1705–1793. Lord Hardwicke also assisted the Lords Commissioners with some frequency. HCA, 45/1–5 (PRO).

[61] Pares, *Colonial Blackade*, p. 105. See also the observations of Blackstone on the influence of "a judge [Mansfield], whose masterly acquaintance with the law of

from their frequent attendance at the oral arguments of the civilian advocates and barristers, did become somewhat more than amateurs in prize law, but just how much more is hard to say.

During the Seven Years' War, at least after 1759, the Lords Commissioners tended to decide groups of cases at the same time, indicating that there must have been court terms during which they heard the various motions of the proctors and the arguments of the advocates and then gave their determination. A large number of decrees (for instance, eighteen, twenty, twenty-three, and thirty-one) were dated the same days. On some of these days the lords were recorded also to have heard and granted a number of petitions by proctors in other cases. Apparently the Lords Commissioners had court days on which they heard motions and arguments over a period of several days or weeks and then issued their sentences on the same day.[62]

Much of the routine work in prize appeals was taken before the surrogate of the Lords Commissioners. The surrogate was a doctor in the civil law and a member of Doctors Commons, the professional association of the civilian advocates. The surrogate's court was held at Doctors Commons. During the Seven Years' War Andrew Coltee Ducarel served most frequently as surrogate, although from time to time some other member of Doctors' Commons was mentioned as

---

nations was known and revered by every state in Europe." William Blackstone, *Commentaries on the Laws of England*, (1st ed., 4 v., Oxford, 1765–1769) **3**: p. 70.

[62] The dates on which cases were decided are listed below, with the number of cases determined on that date given in parentheses:

1758	29 June (1)				
1759	29 March (1)	12 April (1)	24 May (1)	28 June (1)	12 July (1)
	19 July (1)	2 Aug. (1)	14 Dec. (1)	20 Dec. (1)	
1760	29 Feb. (1)	6 March (1)	13 March (1)	20 March (4)	24 March (2)
	25 March (2)	26 March (3)	27 March (3)	3 June (3)	12 June (5)
	19 June (4)	8 July (5)	9 July (4)	10 July (5)	14 July (6)
	15 July (6)	20 Nov. (3)	27 Nov. (7)	19 Dec. (4)	20 Dec. (6)
1761	5 Feb. (3)	5 March (6)	14 March (10)	23 June (8)	27 June (6)
	29 June (3)				
1762	16 March (3)	13 July (15)	17 Dec. (6)		
1763	5 March (23)	12 March (1)	9 July (20)		
1764	1 May (31)	28 July (5)			
1765	15 July (18)	14 Aug. (4)			
1766	8 July (4)				

Appeal Cases (LC Law) **4**. On Saturday, 9 July 1763, besides issuing final decrees in twenty cases, the Lords Commissioners are recorded to have heard and acted upon eight petitions of proctors in other cases. HCA, 41/5 (PRO).

surrogate. The proctors, who made the various motions and filed the highly stylized and verbose pleadings, could expedite much of their court business before the surrogate. As had been mentioned, the role of the proctor in admiralty was similar to the role of the attorney or solicitor in eighteenth-century common law practice.[63]

After the proctors had finished the formal process of pleading, whether before the Lords Commissioners or the surrogate, the advocates presented a printed case to the lords. The printed case for each party contained the factual background of the vessel that had been captured, the details of the trial in the court below, printed copies or excerpts of relevant documents, with each side concluding the case with a statement of the legal reasons why the sentence of the lower court should be affirmed or reversed. During the Seven Years' War the cases included the names of counsel for each party. In the vast majority of these printed cases, counsel was composed of a civilian advocate and a common law barrister. Occasionally the civil law advocate appeared alone or with two barristers, or in a few cases two advocates appeared with one barrister. Presumably both the barrister and the advocate presented the oral arguments for the appeal before the Lords Commissioners.[64] Sessions of the Lords Commissioners were held at the Cockpit, Whitehall. This representation of a client on appeal by a small group of proctors and advocates experienced in the formalities of prize appeals and knowledgeable, as we shall see, in the precedents of former prize decrees, clearly distinguished appeals to the Lords Commissioners from the later appeals to the Court of Ap-

---

[63] The pleadings and motions will be discussed more fully below, but in general, see HCA, 41/4–6; 43/12–18 (PRO).

[64] HCA, 45/1–5. The advocates frequently named in the printed cases were: John Bettesworth, George Hay, Richard Smalbroke, William Wynne, James Marriott, William Burrell, Peter Calvert, and George Harris. The first three each appeared in a very large number of prize appeals during the Seven Years' War. The barristers frequently mentioned in the printed cases were: Charles Yorke, Charles Pratt, Alexander Forrester, Henry Dagge, Alexander Wedderburn, Fletcher Norton, William De Grey, John Dunning, William Blackstone, Beaumont Hotham, and John Gardiner. Yorke and Pratt appeared most frequently. For a list of civilian advocates, see Ernest Nys, *Le Droit Romain, Le Droit des Gens et le College des Docteurs en Droit Civil* (Brussels, 1910), pp. 152–154. Most of the barristers are listed in *Register of Admissions to the Honourable Society of the Middle Temple* (3 v., London, 1949) 1: *passim*, or *A Calendar of the Inner Temple Records* (5 v., London, 1896) 4 and 5: *passim*.

peals in Cases of Capture set up in America during the Revolution.

A detailed study of the legal forms and procedural formalities for appeals before the Lords Commissioners further confirms the conviction that American lawyers and politicians who established an appellate court for prize cases during the Revolution had little or no knowledge of the intricacies of the British system of prize appeals. In the records of cases before the judges of appeals authorized by the Continental Congress to hear prize appeals, there is practically no trace of the procedural details or terminology employed in cases brought before the Lords Commissioners.

The proceedings for a prize appeal began in England with a proctor exhibiting his proxy before the surrogate. A proxy was a warrant giving the proctor power of attorney by which he came to represent a party to the suit and to control the litigation. The proctor "made himself party for" his client. The proctor for the appellant then by proper form or orally requested the inhibition, citation, and monition. The surrogate routinely granted this petition by issuing a writ ordering the lower court judge and officials and the respondent, as well as all other persons in general, not to interfere with the prosecution of this appeal. This inhibition was accompanied with a citation for the adverse party to appear before the Lords Commissioners a certain number of days after service of this process. The judge of the lower court and the respondent were ordered to transmit the whole process of the original trial within a certain number of days. The forms show that the lower court officials were regularly given ten days to forward the proceedings from the High Court of Admiralty, thirty days from the vice-admiralty court in Ireland and one hundred days from Gibraltar or any of the American or West Indian vice-admiralty courts. The petition for the inhibition, citation, and monition contained a statement that the appeal had been made from various grievances or complaints of nullity of the appellant in general and especially (the "praesertim" of the appeal) from that part of the decree of the lower court which had condemned this vessel or its cargo or had acquitted it. The petition always included the caution or production of a surety for the appellant who would guarantee payment of treble costs if such should be awarded against the appellant. The surrogate received the caution only after he had received a report of an official of the High Court of Delegates that the surety was sufficient to pay the amount of the bond.[65]

When the appellant's proctor returned the inhibition, citation, and monition with proof of service, a proctor for the respondent presented his proxy and became party for his client. The respondent's proctor then petitioned for the filing of a libel by the appellant's proctor, which the surrogate ordered.[66] If the respondent could not be served personally, the appellant's proctor petitioned the Lords Commissioners (or sometimes the surrogate) for an inhibition and citation by ways and means. This meant that if the respondent could not be personally served, the writ could be fixed to one of the pillars of the Royal Exchange in London to provide public notice to him.[67] If the proctor could produce an affidavit of personal service on the respondent and he failed to appear, after a threefold proclamation for the respondent to appear, the Lords Commissioners could pronounce him to be in contempt and order him to be attached or arrested for his contumacy.[68]

The proctor for the appellant presented a libel of appeal, one of the typical repetitive and highly stylized pleadings filed in a prize appeal.[69] If the respondent intended to cross-appeal, his proctor filed an adhesion of appeal which stated the parts of the sentence below from which he was appealing and which he wanted reversed.[70] When one of these forms was presented to the court, the opposing proctor is recorded to have confessed subscription and identity,[71] perhaps a means of avoiding a contest over the authentication of the form or accompanying affidavit.

---

[65] HCA, 43/12–18. Examples of these forms can be seen in the following cases: *Vast Betrouwen* (Hensing), HCA, 41/4; *St. Jacob* (Vander Moor), 43/13; *Good Christian* (Plow), 43/13; *Hoop* (Bakker), 42/70; *Jonker Allard* (Doets), 41/14 (PRO).

[66] Minute Book, Surrogate's Court, HCA, 43/13 (PRO).

[67] *Alexandria* (Cullum), HCA, 41/5; *Elizabeth* (Vigeron), HCA, 41/5 (PRO).

[68] *Ranger* (Crowninshield), HCA, 41/5 (PRO).

[69] *Hoop* (Bakker), HCA, 42/70 (PRO).

[70] *St. Fernando* (Hilkes), HCA, 45/2. In *Maria Johanna* (Lindeboom), the adhesion of appeal was not admitted by the Lords Commissioners because the respondents had acquiesced too long in the sentence below. HCA, 45/2 (PRO). Perhaps a doctrine similar to laches was applied in prize appeals.

[71] *St. Juan Baptista* (de Arteaga), HCA, 43/14; *St. Jacob* (Vander Moor), HCA, 43/13; *Felicite* (Bernos), HCA, 43/13 (PRO).

During the course of an appeal the proctors made a variety of motions, some before the surrogate's court and some before the Lords Commissioners. The limits of the surrogate's authority are not clear, but some idea of the types of routine motions disposed of by the surrogate emerges from a brief list of motions made before him, most of which are recorded again and again. The surrogate regularly granted the proctor's petitions. Proctors, for instance, petitioned the surrogate: to have monitions issued to the executors or administrators of the estate of the respondent, who was deceased;[72] to relax the inhibition where the appellant could not further prosecute the appeal;[73] to cite the respondent personally to appear before the Lords Commissioners under pain of contempt, since his proxy had died;[74] to monish (order) the vice-admiralty judge to transmit certain ship papers since the records sent forward were incomplete.[75] Many petitions addressed to the surrogate were presented to secure full execution of a final decree of the Lords Commissioners. For example, proctors petitioned the surrogate: to cite and monish appellants or their sureties to pay respondents the costs of appeal where the sentence of the lower court had been affirmed by the Lords Commissioners;[76] to cite and monish the executors and administrators of the respondent (deceased) to jointly and severally pay liquidated costs and damages and order them arrested till they paid;[77] to confirm the deputy register's report on the value of the ship and cargo and to monish appellants and their sureties to pay respondents this sum since the Lords Commissioners had affirmed the decree of the lower court;[78] to attach respondents for contempt in not restoring the ship and cargo or its value pursuant to a restitution or monition by ways and means (by public notice where personal service was impossible).[79]

Occasionally a proctor would make a motion before the

---

[72] *Young Abraham* (Hassell), HCA, 41/5 (PRO).

[73] *Fra Anna Catharina* (Pietersen), HCA, 41/5 (PRO).

[74] *La Ville de Bilboa* (Placentia), HCA, 41/5; *Jonker Allard* (Doets), HCA, 41/5 (PRO).

[75] *Amherst* (Maddocks), HCA, 41/5 (PRO).

[76] *Peggy* (Haddon), HCA, 41/5 (PRO).

[77] *Virgin del Rosario yel Sancto Christo de Buen Viage* (Ybanes), HCA, 41/5 (PRO).

[78] *Quebeck* (Pew), HCA, 41/5; *Pieter and David* (Boef), HCA, 41/5, 43/14 (PRO).

[79] *Maria Francina* (Cadis), HCA, 41/5; *Victoria* (Potenza), HCA, 41/5 (PRO).

Lords' Commissioners which apparently he could have made
before the surrogate, for instance, to order the vice-
admiralty judge to send forward all the papers concerning
the case appealed.[80] The lords refused a request to have the
captured vessel (that is, the principal members of its crew)
re-examined by preparatory examinations.[81] The Lords
Commissioners did grant proctor's motion to have witnesses
who live at a distance from the court examined on prepared
interrogatories;[82] or to have the opposing party personally
appear before the lords to answer questions on oath.[83] The
lords also granted the request of proctors to have vessels
appraised, unloaded, and sold, because of the allegation that
they were in perishing condition.[84] In at least one case a
party personally, without a proctor, petitioned the Lords
Commissioners to declare the appeal deserted for failure to
prosecute and to order the vice-admiralty judge to execute
his original sentence.[85]

The Lords Commissioners, as just mentioned, issued
commissions to have witnesses remote from the court examined on interrogatories prepared by the opposing parties.
They also supervised the examination of the opposing party
who was ordered to appear before them to answer questions
on oath. Clearly they were not limited to the record below in
considering an appeal, but could, for special reasons, admit
new evidence and, in effect, try the case *de novo*.[86]

The advocates and barristers, who argued the appeals
before the Lords Commissioners, in their printed cases (and
presumably in their oral arguments) made general references to the law of nations without citing any particular
authors. They also referred specifically to particular treaties
of Great Britain and quoted from them at length to prove a
point in their client's case. From time to time they argued
from precedent, mentioning in general "many determina-

[80] *Vast Betrouwen* (Hensing), HCA, 41/5 (PRO).

[81] *San Joseph* (de Alamo), HCA, 41/5 (PRO).

[82] *Jesus Maria y Joseph* (Ezenarro), HCA, 41/5; *Novum Aratrum* (Steekling), HCA, 41/5 (PRO).

[83] *San Joseph* (de Alamo), HCA, 41/5; *Jonker Allard* (Doets), HCA, 41/5 (PRO).

[84] *Constantia* (Toft), HCA, 43/13; *Resolutie* (Johannesz), HCA, 43/14 (PRO).

[85] *Maria* (Ellis), HCA, 42/80 (PRO).

[86] For example, see *Saint Jacob* (Vander Moor), HCA, 45/1; *San Joseph* (de Alamo), HCA, 41/5; *Juffrow Maria* (Vander Velde), HCA, 45/1 (PRO); Pares, *Colonial Blockade*, pp. 133–134.

tions of the Lords Commissioners of Appeal in Prize Causes." Only rarely did they mention a prior case by name as precedent for the legal position they wanted the Lords Commissioners to adopt.[87] Since no reports of decrees in prize cases were yet published, this occasional use of precedents reflects the intimate familiarity with the work of the Lords Commissioners shared and exchanged by a small clique acquainted with the esoteric practice of prize appeals. The prize acts of Parliament were frequently referred to as the norm for proceeding in prize cases. Many irregularities in prize trial practice were condemned by the advocates as opposed to the procedures prescribed in the prize acts.[88]

The decrees of the Lords Commissioners, issued from the Privy Council Chamber at the Cockpit, Whitehall, were always in the name of all the lords present and never signed by any individual. The language, as in all the forms connected with prize appeals, fit into general patterns, suggesting that the Lords Commissioners often merely said, "affirmed with costs," or "reversed, ship and cargo restored," and the court officials completed the wording of the decree by using the proper form. The decrees were generally brief but at times became fuller and more complex when it was necessary to distinguish various parties or different parts of the cargo or to award or deny costs or damages. Occasionally the decree included a brief statement of the reasons for the determination.[89]

The decrees of the Lords Commissioners frequently mentioned costs and damages, more frequently to deny them to an aggrieved neutral whose property had been unjustly taken than to award them. Some examples of the reasons given in the decrees for granting or denying costs and damages will make possible a better appreciation of the nuances of the decrees themselves. The lords found various reasons

---

[87] *Jonge Hendrick Brouwer* (Engels), HCA, 45/3; *Juffrow Maria* (Vander Velde), HCA, 45/1; *San Antonio e Almas* (da Costa), HCA, 45/1; *St. Marcus* (Mulder), HCA, 45/2; *Vriendschap* (Laurensen), HCA, 45/2; *Vryheid* (Hop), HCA 45/1 (PRO).

[88] *Anna Margarita* (Hellison), HCA, 45/2; *Dolphin* (Spin), HCA, 45/1; *Elizabeth* (Pleen), HCA, 45/1; *Joanna Arnoldina* (Churchill), HCA, 45/1, 2; *Mars* (le Ray), HCA, 45/2; *Novum Aratrum* (Steekling), HCA, 45/1, 2; *Peter John* (Le Moyne), HCA, 45/2; *St. Fernando* (Hilkes), HCA, 45/2; *Vryheidt* (Feteris), HCA, 45/1. See also order of Lords Commissioners, 27 March, 1760, HCA, 43/15 (PRO).

[89] The printed cases in the Library of Congress regularly include a handwritten notation of the final decree, often called "final interlocutory decree." *Appeal Cases* (LC Law).

for making both parties pay their own costs and for refusing to allow damages, even when the property was restored on appeal to the claimants. If they could read the evidence to suggest the captors had probable cause for the seizure, costs and damages would usually be denied. For instance, costs and damages were denied because the evidence indicated that the property of the ship at the start and during most of the voyage belonged to the enemy, or that the pass of the vessel did not come up to all the requirements of the treaty with Spain and was not on oath.[90] Where the ship and cargo were restored to the claimant and the captor condemned in costs, the lords might refuse to grant damages because of the claimant's delay in making the appeal.[91] In one case the advocates for the claimants had listed cogent reasons for granting costs and damages: that the crew of the privateer was guilty of plundering and robbing part of the cargo; that the captors caused delay in the trial by not examining all the witnesses at the same time, that the captors had held the mate on the privateer to prevent him from testifying. Nevertheless, the Lords Commissioners, though reversing the sentence and restoring the ship and cargo, refused to grant costs or damages.[92] The claimants, moreover, had to consider the possibility that costs could be awarded against them, as where the claimant was found to have been guilty of perjury and of concealing some of the ship's papers. The claimant not only lost the ship and cargo, but was condemned in costs from the time of first filing his claim in the court below.[93] Probably this fear of having to pay costs explains why some claimants withdrew their appeal before the final hearing.[94] But there were enough cases in which the captors were condemned in costs and damages to make the owners of privateers think twice about some of the unwarranted captures their crews made.[95]

---

[90] *Felicite* (Bernos), HCA, 43/13 (PRO); see also *St. Juan Baptista* (Arteaga), *Appeal Cases*, (LC Law) 1; Pares, *Colonial Blockade*, pp. 143–144.

[91] *Maria Theresa* (Byaart), HCA, 43/13 (PRO).

[92] *Vast Betrouwen* (Hensing), HCA, 45/1, 3 (PRO).

[93] *Juffrow Maria* (Vander Velde), HCA, 45/1 (PRO); same case, *Appeal Cases* (LC Law) 1.

[94] *San Joseph* (de Alamo), HCA, 45/3 (PRO).

[95] *Joanna Arnoldina* (Churchill), HCA, 45/1, 2; *Pieter and David* (Boef), HCA, 45/2; *San Joseph* (Gallardo), HCA, 45/1, 3; *Vryheid* (Hop) HCA, 45/1 (PRO); same case, *Appeal Cases* (LC Law) 1.

In one case the captors, on appeal, were not only condemned in costs and damages for making an illegal seizure, the Lords Commissioners also decreed that they should have been prosecuted as pirates and that the privateer's bond should be put in suit to be applied for the benefit of the injured claimants.[96] Where the ship after capture had been lost in a storm, the Lords Commissioners decreed that the cargo which had been saved should be restored to the claimants, condemned the captors in costs and damages resulting from the illegal capture, but refused to grant the claimant damages due to the wreck of the vessel since the captors had manned it better after the capture than the owners had before. The loss of the ship did not appear to have resulted from the fault of the prize crew put on board at the time of the capture.[97]

As has already been mentioned, when an appeal was filed in the trial court, the property in dispute (usually the captured vessel and its cargo) was turned over by the court to one or other party who had to provide sufficient security to restore it or its value to the other party if that party should prevail on appeal. Some of the decrees of the Lords Commissioners, after affirming or reversing the sentence of the court below, ordered this bond to be given up.[98] If the parties to the appeal were in England, the decree of the Lords Commissioners could be carried into effect by the deposit of the value of the property in the registry of the court of prize appeals. The proctor for the party in whose favor the lords had decreed, appeared before the surrogate and acknowledged receipt of this amount.[99] These simple, direct methods undoubtedly assured that most of the decrees of the Lords Commissioners achieved their full effect.

Execution of the decrees on appeal could, however, be much more difficult to secure in some cases. When the Lords Commissioners reversed the decree of the court below which had condemned the prize to the captors and restored the property to the claimants, the decree directly ordered the

[96] *Virgin del Rosario yel Sancto Christo de Buen Viage* (Ybanes), HCA, 45/1, 3 (PRO).
[97] *Jonge Hendrick Brouwer* (Engels), HCA, 45/2 (PRO).
[98] *Geregtigheit* (Daal), HCA, 45/2, 3; *Young Moses* (Lopez), HCA, 41/5 (PRO). The Lords could also order the privateer's surety bond given up. *San Joseph* (de la Rosa), HCA, 45/1, 3 (PRO).
[99] *St. Jacob* (Vander Moor), HCA, 43/14 (PRO).

captors to restore the property or its value. But if the commander of the capturing privateer could not be located, the
proctor for the claimants had to return to the Lords Commissioners or their surrogate for further process to obtain
full execution of the decree. The proctors could obtain a
monition by ways and means against the commander, which
made public notice, where personal service was impossible,
sufficient for contempt proceedings. The proctors also obtained monitions against the owners of the privateers and the
sureties who had put up a bond when the privateers were
given their commission. The owners and the sureties were
held jointly and severally liable to the claimants for the full
amount of the property restored, plus costs and damages.
The lords used threat of attachment for contempt to obtain
full payment of the judgment from the owners and
sureties.[100]

A summary of two particular cases will show some of the
more complex problems involved in obtaining execution of
the decrees of the Lords Commissioners. The Dutch ship
Christophilus, with Menketer Kamp as commander, was captured in 1758 by the privateer *Resolution*, David McKie (or
Macky or McGhee), master. A prize master and seventeen
other members of the privateer crew were put on board to
bring it to port. The *Christophilus* was carried to Baltimore in
Ireland and there was wrecked in a storm. The captors had
not started the process of adjudication of their prize in the
vice-admiralty court at the time of the wreck. Kamp, therefore, filed a claim to the vessel and cargo several months later
in the English High Court of Admiralty. In December, 1759,
the admiralty judge, acting on the preparatory examinations
and the ship papers, decreed that the vessel belonged to the
neutral claimants and should be restored to them but without
costs or damages since there was just cause for the seizure.
He held that most of the cargo was doubtful and that the
claimant should plead and prove that it belonged as claimed.
Kamp appealed to the Lords Commissioners who, in 1761,
decreed that the ship and the whole cargo belonged to the
claimants and the full value of this property should be paid

---

[100] *Notre Dame de la Conception et St. François de Paulo* (Fereira), HCA, 45/3; 41/5;
Aventure (Groen), HCA, 45/2 (PRO); same case, *Appeal Cases* (LC Law) **1**; *San Thomas*
(Pieter), *Appeal Cases* (LC Law) **2**.

to them. The proctor for the claimants returned the decree of restitution with an affidavit that McKie had died some months before on the coast of Africa, intestate, insolvent, and without any legal representative. The sureties for McKie, when he had been given the privateer's commission, had been personally served with the decree as had a number of the owners of the privateer, as well as the assignees in bankruptcy of another owner. The proctors for Kamp brought in to the lords an account of the value of the wrecked property, worth some £13,635. They prayed attachments for contempt to be ordered against the parties who had been personally served. Proctors for some of the owners appeared before the lords and stated that their parties owned only small shares of the privateer (1/64 or 4/64). The Lords decreed that the bonds of the sureties be forfeited and that the sureties themselves should be attached for non-payment of the amount of their bond. They also decreed that those owners who had been personally served should be held in contempt. The last notation of the case, in July 1762, shows that some of the owners deposited in court an amount proportional to their share in the privateer. The proctor for the claimant accepted this amount, but without prejudice to his claim on each of the owners for the whole of the unpaid judgment. The claimant's proctor then obtained a monition against the other owners.[101] The *Christophilus*, besides serving as a good summary of some of the procedural details previously discussed, brings out the long and costly process of wringing payment out of the parties when a decree on appeal went against them. Clearly owners and sureties for privateers could be held jointly and severally liable for injuries caused by the lawless conduct of the privateer. The length of time between the initial capture (1758) and the settlement of claims (1762) was not at all unusual. The persistence of the proctors and the contempt powers of the Lords Commissioners must have gone far to assure some payment to the injured neutral claimants, although many must have had to settle for far less than full payment for their loss. Since the Lords Commissioners seemed reluctant to award damages

---

[101] *Christophilus* (Kamp), *Appeal Cases* (LC Law) **2.** The printed cases include extensive handwritten notes of the decree and the various proceedings to secure its execution. This case is briefly discussed in Pares, *Colonial Blockade*, p. 135n.

against the offending privateers, the claimants must have suffered significant loss even when they managed to obtain and have executed a decree of restitution.

If the process of appeal and execution of decrees was lengthy and costly in Britain, the complexities and delays in appeals from America were even greater. The long story of the piratical seizure of property from on board the *Virgin del Rosario* shows that even with stubborn proctors in London and the contempt powers of the Lords Commissioners, a clearly injured neutral party had difficulty getting any recovery at all. This one example will suffice to indicate the inherent limitations of the British prize appellate system where it had to deal with distant colonies.

The Spanish vessel *Virgin del Rosario yel Sancto Christo de Buen Viage*, with Philipe Ybanes (or Vanes or de Francis or de Francais) as master, sailed in May, 1756, from Trinidad to Havana and from there to Port Royal, Jamaica. Captain Ybanes carried all the documents necessary to prove it a Spanish vessel. The *Virgin del Rosario* was hailed and boarded by Americans from the privateer *Peggy*, Richard Haddon, commander. Haddon, although shown the Spanish papers and a passport, forcibly took everything of value from on board, which included several bags of money, some jewelry, arms, gunpowder, and indigo, all of which was later valued at £2,409. Haddon also took all the ship's papers and two of its passengers whom he detained for six weeks and then abandoned on the coast of Jamaica. He brought the stolen property to New York where he libeled it as French property. He produced only one witness who swore that the *Virgin del Rosario* "had no regular Commander, no Dispatches or Papers of any kind from any Port or Place, and . . . that had the said Vessel been taken by any Vessel of any Nation, she would have been a lawful Prize, and had she been taken by a *Spanish* Guarda Costa, the whole Ship's Crew would have been hanged as Pirates." On the basis of this perjured testimony alone the vice-admiralty judge in New York, the same day, condemned the stolen property as lawful prize for the use of the captors. He did place one limitation on the sentence, that no just and rightful claim be made to the property within a year and a day. This sentence of March 31, 1757, was challenged in less than a year by a claim filed by the colony's advocate general, William Kempe, dated March 10, 1758.

Kempe acted because of vigorous letters of complaint from the governor of Jamaica to the governor of New York. Haddon's counsel demurred to this claim, arguing that the British king had no interest in the property claimed so his advocate general had no right to file a claim. Furthermore a suit by the advocate general would not bar a subsequent claim by the owners, thus exposing Haddon to the risk of double recovery. On April 19, 1758 (more than a year and a day after the original sentence), the vice-admiralty judge decreed that the demurrer was good and therefore dismissed the claim filed by the advocate general.

The following September Ybanes filed a libel and claim (apparently to cover all possibilities), but the New York judge decreed in February, 1759 that, although he would be very willing to do anything in his power to enable Ybanes to get the justice he demanded, he did not know how he could reverse his own decree which had become final when the year and a day had expired. So the sentence of the court must be allowed to stand till reversed by a court having proper jurisdiction to reverse it. Ybanes therefore appealed from this decree to the Lords Commissioners, who in December, 1760, reversed the decree of the court below, condemned the proceedings and sentence of condemnation of March 31, 1757, as irregular and illegal, restored the property or its value to Ybanes, condemned the captors in costs and damages, and suggested that the captors be prosecuted as pirates. This must have been heartening to Ybanes, but it was still merely an elaborate piece of paper until he could secure its execution in New York.

When Ybanes tried to have this decree against Haddon and the owners of the *Peggy* executed, the New York vice-admiralty judge, in July, 1761, refused to act. He objected that the final sentence of the Lords Commissioners presented to him was not under seal. The judge protested that he was very willing to aid Ybanes in carrying the sentence of reversal into execution in any way consistent with law and justice. But, he objected, "to proceed by execution against Bail discharged by a sentence unreversed (for aught any proof as yet produced) cannot be right." He added insult to injury by claiming to be suspicious of Ybanes's agents in England, suggesting that they were negligent in conducting his cause there or in transmitting proofs of the sentence to

New York. When Ybanes again moved the judge for execution of the Lords Commissioners decree, the judge this time argued that his first decree of March 31, 1757, had not been appealed from. Ybanes had appealed from the sentence on his libel much later. The judge argued that these were separate and distinct suits and therefore that the reversal of one sentence could not effect the reversal of the other. (The decree of the Lords Commissioners had explicitly reversed the decree of March 31, 1757, perhaps anticipating the perverse reasoning of the New York judge.)

Ybanes, or his agents, returned to England and obtained an order revoking Haddon's privateering commission. In February, 1764, Ybanes's proctor appeared again before the court of prize appeals. The proctor presented a report of the liquidated damages sustained by Ybanes and stated that the owners of the *Peggy* had been personally served with process. On motion the surrogate decreed that Haddon and the owners of the *Peggy* (or their executors since one had died) be cited and monished jointly and severally to pay Ybanes the full amount of the liquidated damages. On further motion, the surrogate decreed that these parties be held in contempt until they paid the full amount due.[102] With this decree the case vanishes from the records, and the odds are better than even that Ybanes never recovered fully for his loss. With vigorous debates and violence in the colonies over the Sugar Act and the Stamp Act, this was not a good time to seek enforcement of such a decree in America.

Although this case undoubtedly was extraordinary, it does suggest that even with coercive contempt powers in London, the orderly system of prize appeals could crumble if a colonial judge was determined to listen to local interests rather than obey the central authority in England, so remote in time and distance. Even if Ybanes had recovered finally, the delay of eight or ten years was intolerable in any system of justice, especially where the rights of foreign parties were involved. Such delays in prize appeals to the Lords Commissioners were all too common.[103]

---

[102] *Virgin del Rosario yel Sancto Christo de Buen Viage* (Ybanes), HCA, 45/1; 41/5; 42/88 (PRO); same case, Hough, *Reports*, pp. 112–122; Pares, *Colonial Blockade*: pp. 47, 48n, 51n, 55n. For a decree of reversal which was properly executed by the New York vice-admiralty court, see *Maria* (Vander Kroom), New York Vice-Admiralty Court Minute Book, 1753–1770 (NYPL, Mss).

[103] Pares, *Colonial Blockade*, pp. 144–147. In a case appealed from Rhode Island,

These details of British prize procedure on the trial court level and on appeal to the Lords Commissioners serve two purposes here, one positive and the other largely negative. In subsequent chapters it will be suggested that the American lawyers and politicians who established prize courts during the Revolution closely followed the patterns they were familiar with, the prize practice of the vice-admiralty courts. Although the colonial prize practice was already significantly divergent from prize practice in England's High Court of Admiralty, the colonial lawyers (mostly trained in the common law) probably knew little of the difference. Traditionalists that they were, they most likely thought they were being faithful to long-existing prize procedures in setting up their own prize courts—and so they were, but to colonial variations of prize practice, not to the prize practice as it existed in England. The study of the procedures of appeals to the Lords Commissioners, however, has produced a largely negative result. The technical terminology of pleadings and motions before the Lords Commissioners and their surrogate was, as we shall see, just about totally absent from the records of appeals to the committees on appeals or the Court of Appeals in Cases of Capture. But since American lawyers had little or no experience of British prize appellate practice, this is not surprising. What was a good *a priori* hunch becomes confirmed as a hypothesis, when it appears in later chapters that practically no trace of the procedures and practices of the British court of prize appeals can be discovered in the forms and procedures used in the American appellate prize court.

But, although American lawyers were undoubtedly formed largely by their first hand experience with the local courts, they were also deeply influenced by the books they read. Some brief description of the legal literature relied on by American lawyers at the time of the Revolution will fill out the picture of the sources of American prize law and prize practice. The subsequent chapters based on a study of the records of prize appeals during the Revolution will confirm that American prize law did stand upon these two legs, the

---

for instance, the capture had been made in 1745, the decree of the Lords Commissioners reversing the court below in 1752, the decree of execution in Boston in 1755, and a petition for attachment for contempt for noncompliance brought to the Lords Commissioners in 1763. *William Galley* (Couwenhoven), HCA, 41/5 (PRO).

local legal institutions with which the Americans were inti-
mately familiar and the published sources on prize law which
the Americans studied and from which they derived their
arguments in prize cases.

V. Published Sources of Prize Law
Used by American Lawyers

THIS BRIEF EXCURSUS describes the authorities relied
on at the time of the Revolution by American lawyers when
they were preparing for prize litigation. It will provide some
necessary aspects of the background for the main chapters of
this section concerning the procedural and substantive law of
the Committees on Appeals and the Court of Appeals in
Cases of Capture. Of course, men do not live by books alone;
the extremely important tradition of prize practice with
which the American lawyers were acquainted has already
been discussed at length. This chapter, however, merely describes the published sources which were found in the colonies in the 1770's and 1780's and which were actually used
by lawyers in their prize practice.

Merely listing the books available on prize law would not
convincingly indicate whether or not they were used by
lawyers in America. It is necessary to try to establish from
contemporary legal writings which authorities on prize law
actually influenced American legal thinking. The fact that
certain books had been published at that time, or even that
they were found in some lawyer's libraries, is not always
satisfactory evidence that they were used in the day-to-day
business of serving a client or deciding a case. It is possible,
however, to give some direct, though inadequate, evidence
from contemporary court records to show which legal authorities were relied on by lawyers in prize cases. In a small
number of Revolutionary War cases there are references in
the lawyer's arguments or in the judge's opinions to those
authors who were consulted to determine questions of prize
law and procedure. These few scattered references give a
faint glimpse of the sources actually used by American
lawyers as they studied prize law. As each authority is described here, a reference will be given to the case or cases in
which eighteenth-century American lawyers or judges cited
this work. Though only a tiny fraction of the Revolutionary

War prize cases contain such citations, it is a thesis of the chapters on procedural and substantive law that, even where no citation of authorities has been given, some slight hint or suggestion of such published works can be detected beneath the surface of prize litigation.

One group of authorities can be classed together as English writers who discussed commercial or admiralty law and in the process treated the law of captures at sea in some detail. First among these because of its scope and usefulness is Wyndham Beawes, *Lex Mercatoria Rediviva or the Merchant's Directory*, published in 1751.[1] This bulky folio volume, intended to be a "complete guide to all men in business," was popular enough to go through three editions by 1771. Beawes treated all aspects of maritime commerce such as the navigation acts, fisheries, freight, charter parties, bills of lading, bottomry, pilots, wrecks, salvage, safe conduct passes, foreign consuls, insurance banks, contracts, bonds, brokers, bankruptcy, to list only a few of the widely varied topics in the volume. He devoted several chapters to privateering, admiralty courts, letters of marque and reprisal, and the law of captures at sea. He gave in full or in summarized form several of the key statutes and examples of commissions and instructions for privateers.

An earlier volume also dealing with maritime and commercial law, as well as aspects of the law of nations, Charles Molloy's *De Jure Maritimo et Navali*, was first published in 1676 but had reached a tenth edition by 1778.[2] Molloy's brief but clear treatment of a wide range of questions of interest to merchants and lawyers explains the book's long-lasting popularity. Under the heading, the law of nations, Molloy treated privateering, alliances and treaties, treatment of neutrals and

---

[1] Referred to in the notes of counsel's legal arguments in *St. Antonio (Debadie v. Russell)*, 28 May, 1783, #95, RCA. Beawes was also referred to in the judge's opinion in *Purviance v. Angus*, decided by the High Court of Errors and Appeals of Pennsylvania, 1 Dallas, 180 at 184 (1786). This case, treated by the court as within the state admiralty court's instance jurisdiction, concerned an action by owners of a privateer against its master for recovery of damages they had to pay because of his tortious capture of a vessel already taken as prize.

[2] Cited in counsel's argument in *Rice v. Taylor* (1779), Francis Hopkinson, *Miscellaneous Essays and Occasional Writings* (3 v., Philadelphia, 1792) **3**: p. 17. Hopkinson was judge of the Pennsylvania admiralty court during much of the Revolution, 1779–1789. Molloy was also cited in a number of instance cases, *ibid.*, pp. 164, 179, 181, 190, 199.

neutral property, and the prize jurisdiction of the British admiralty court.

The two-volume treatise, *The Laws, Ordinances, and Institutions of the Admiralty of Great Britain, Civil and Military*, published anonymously in 1746, touches on various aspects of maritime and commercial law, with sections dealing with the jurisdiction of the admiralty, letters of marque and reprisal, and privateers.[3] It also includes a number of statutes relating to the admiralty, naval affairs, and commerce and the second volume is largely a compilation of maritime treaties from 1661 to 1728.

Another volume covering similar topics of the law merchant and the law of nations, though less substantial than Beawes, is Giles Jacob's *Lex Mercatoria: or the Merchants' Companion*, published in 1718 and reaching a second edition in 1729.[4]

One slender volume treated only questions relating to privateering and prize law, Richard Lee's *A Treatise of Captures in War*, published in 1759.[5] Since it focused exclusively on topics related to captures, Lee could discuss these subjects at greater length than such authors as Beawes or Molloy who dealt with the law of captures at sea as only one among many of the questions of concern to merchants. Lee's book, however, provided only a superficial and inadequate treatment of questions of prize, largely parroting the opinions of the Dutch jurist Cornelius van Bynkershoek's *Quaestionum Juris Publici*. Lee in general did not utilize the wealth of material available in the prize cases determined by the Lords Commissioners for Prize Appeals in England. He did summarize at length, however, the highly authoritative *Report of the Law Officers of the Crown*, to be discussed next. As a result of his heavy reliance on Bynkershoek, Lee's work had more of an international, than specifically British flavor. With all the

---

[3] Cited in the judge's opinion in *Purviance v. Angus*, 1 Dallas 180 at 184.

[4] I could not find any citations in contemporary prize cases to Jacob, but it was undoubtedly available to American lawyers. See note 16 below.

[5] Cited in counsel's arguments in *Lusanna* (*Doane v. Penhallow*), 17 September, 1783, #30; *Mary* (*Smith v. Hinson*), 6 May, 1784, #73, RCA; in counsel's arguments in the cases of the *Valenciano* and *Holy Martyrs* before the Massachusetts Superior Court of Judicature, Jedidiah Foster Note Book, pp. 414–415 (facsimile, United States Circuit Court of Appeals library, Boston), in the judge's opinion in *Purviance v. Angus*, 1 Dallas 180 at 184 and *Pray v. Brig Recovery* (1780), Hopkinson, *Writings* 3: p. 49.

limitations of this treatise, however, Lee did draw a simple, straightforward sketch of the law of nations relative to captures which gave American lawyers more information on the subject, even if lacking in depth or originality, than any other source written by an Englishman. All the indications point to the conclusion that American lawyers did rely on this inadequate little volume more than any other English source on prize practice.

In a class by itself because it spoke with such unusual authority was the *Report of the Law Officers of the Crown*, a remonstrance drafted and published in 1753 against the action of Frederick II of Prussia in withholding the money due to British subjects on the Silesian loan because he objected to the losses Prussian subjects had suffered due to captures by British privateers.[6] The *Report* was written by Sir George Lee, a civilian advocate and Dean of the Arches, Dr. George Paul, a civilian advocate and advocate general, Sir Dudley Ryder, a barrister and attorney general, and William Murray, later Lord Mansfield, a barrister and solicitor general. Montesquieu termed it a "réponse sans réplique." This pamphlet-length *Report* treated briefly, but with definitive clarity and authority, several basic questions of British prize procedure and the law of capture of neutral property.

Several other British legal sources were occasionally cited in American prize cases, but none of them had much to say about prize practice. Of course, William Blackstone's *Commentaries on the Laws of England* was familiar to American lawyers, and his few comments on prize courts were referred to in various cases.[7] T. Rutherforth's *Institutes of Natural Law*

---

[6] Referred to in counsel's argument in *Chester* (*Dubbledemuts v. Atkinson*), 3 May, 1787, 2 Dallas 41, RCA. Also cited in judge's opinion in *Talbot v. The Commanders and Owners of Three Brigs*, decided by the High Court of Errors and Appeals of Pennsylvania, 1 Dallas 95 at 101, 103, 106 (1784). This case focused mainly on the jurisdictional issue whether a maritime trespass to a previously captured prize vessel was within the instance or prize jurisdiction of the state admiralty court, and therefore whether appeal should lie to the congressional Court of Appeals in Cases of Capture, or (if an instance case) to the state High Court of Errors and Appeals. Not surprisingly, the state court decided this was instance jurisdiction and so upheld its own appellate jurisdiction. This case is discussed in chapter VIII below. The *Report of the Law Officers of the Crown* (London, 1753) was available to American lawyers either in its 1753 original quarto edition, or as republished in Nicolas Magens, *An Essay on Insurances* (2 v., London, 1755) 1: pp. 429–509. It was also summarized at length in Richard Lee, *A Treatise of Captures in War* (London, 1759), pp. 238–243.

[7] Cited in counsel's argument in *Lusanna*, #30, RCA and in the judge's opinion in *Talbot v. Commanders and Owners of Three Brigs*, 1 Dallas 95 at 98, 99, 101, 105.

was mentioned in at least one case, even though the two volumes dealt mainly with jurisprudence and have only one chapter on international law.[8] There are also a number of citations in these American prize cases to various volumes of published reports of British cases. No reports of admiralty or prize cases had yet been published; all these citations referred to cases heard at common law relating only tangentially to questions of prize law.

The second general grouping of authorities used by American lawyers includes the various continental writers on the law of nations. These writers have been briefly discussed in chapter I. Most popular among these was Emmerich de Vattel, whose classic, *The Law of Nations*, was available in English translation by 1760.[9] This Swiss diplomat approached the law of nations as a cultured internationalist who sought to teach the principles of the philosophy of his day to those in charge of public affairs. He viewed the law of nations as simply the law of nature applied to nations. He wrote with such a humane and intelligible style on many facets of war, neutrality, and the law of captures in war, that his easily grasped philosophical opinions often became the basis of legal arguments.

Hugo Grotius's *The Rights of War and Peace* was, of course, well known in America as a basic source on the law of nations.[10] Grotius's classic, originally published in 1625, had gone through six English editions by 1750. This wide-ranging, monumental work was referred to by American lawyers in prize litigation, but its sections on the law of captures at sea were not much more than brief hints of the legal issues and so were less helpful to lawyers than Vattel.

Baron Samuel von Pufendorf's substantial volume *Of the Law of Nature and Nations* had been popular enough to require five English editions before 1750.[11] Most of this work is devoted to questions of jurisprudence and moral philosophy

---

[8] Cited in counsel's argument in *St. Antonio*, #95, RCA.

[9] Cited in counsel's argument in *Lusanna*, #30; *St. Antonio*, #95; *Chester*, 2 Dallas 41, RCA, in cases of the *Valenciano* and *Holy Martyrs*, before the Massachusetts Superior Court of Judicature, Jedidiah Foster Note Book, pp. 414–415 (facsimile, United States Circuit Court of Appeals library, Boston), and in the judge's opinions in *Miller v. the Resolution* (1781), Hopkinson, *Writings* 3: p. 81 and *Talbot v. The Commanders and Owners of Three Brigs*, 1 Dallas, 95 at 103, 105, 106.

[10] Cited in counsel's arguments in *St. Antonio*, #95, and *Chester*, 2 Dallas 41, RCA.

[11] Cited in counsel's argument in *St. Antonio*, #95, RCA.

with only a comparatively small section treating the law of nations. The law of captures at sea received little attention.

Another philosophical treatise on the law of nature was J. J. Burlamaqui's *The Principles of Natural and Politic Law*, translated into English in 1752.[12] Only one section is concerned with the basic topics of the law of nations: war, treaties, and ambassadors. A lawyer searching for arguments to use in a prize case, however, would find only general philosophical principles with little directly related to the issues of captures in time of war.

An author nowhere referred to in contemporary American prize cases is Cornelius van Bynkershoek who in his *Quaestiones Juris Publici* treated in detail from a non-philosophical, historical point of view the main topics of the law of captures in war.[13] No writer at that time had considered so many aspects of the customary usages of nations in the area of maritime prizes as Bynkershoek. Although there is no direct evidence that American lawyers used Bynkershoek in prize litigation, perhaps because no English translation of his difficult Latin had yet appeared, they did know something of his work as filtered through the often-blurred lens of Lee's *Treatise of Captures in War*.

Besides these British and continental authorities on prize law and prize practice, American lawyers and judges had access to the basic British admiralty and prize statutes and the various commissions and instructions to privateers which brought much of the existing prize law to bear on those directly involved in making the captures.[14] We have already seen that Congress and the state assemblies during the Revolution at times borrowed ideas or whole sections from the British models when they prepared prize acts or privateers'

---

[12] Cited in counsel's argument, *ibid.*

[13] Anthony Stokes in *A View of the Constitution of the British Colonies in North America and the West Indies, At the Time the Civil War Broke Out on the Continent of America* (London, 1783), pp. 277–278 mentions Bynkershoek, along with Grotius, Vattel, and the *Report of the Law Officers of the Crown*, as books useful to a lawyer in America studying questions of captures at sea. Stokes, a loyalist, had practiced as a lawyer in Baltimore and held office in Georgia prior to the Revolution.

[14] The statutes were available as separately published session laws or in *A Collection of All Such Statutes, and Parts of Statutes, As Any Way Relate to the Admiralty, Navy and Ships of War . . . Down to the 14th Year of King George the Second* (London, 1755), or in *A Collection of the Statutes Relating to the Admiralty, Navy, Ships of War, and Incidental Matters, to the Eighth Year of King George the Third* (London, 1768).

instructions.[15] Some of the basic statutory material, as well as examples of privateers' instructions and commissions were included in Beawes's *Lex Mercatoria*, and undoubtedly many printed copies of these instructions and commissions were still in circulation after the Seven Years' War, during which privateering had been widely practiced.

This listing of the sources on prize law drawn from citations in specific prize cases seems inadequate since so few extant cases give any direct citations of the authorities relied on by counsel and the judges. But these sources which were cited in prize cases are in general the same books collected in contemporary private law libraries in the colonies.[16] With the exception of a few pamphlets of little use to American admiralty practice, this list of books cited in American cases includes the best sources in English on prize law the colonial lawyers could have obtained.[17]

As a further hint of the use of these published sources in late colonial America, we can analyze what they say about prize procedures and compare this with the procedures of the American vice-admiralty courts. As we have seen in the last chapter, the practice of prize courts in the American colonies differed markedly from the practice of the High Court of Admiralty. Procedural details in the American and English courts of admiralty have already been compared and contrasted. The published sources on prize law which have been described here gave the American lawyers and vice-admiralty judges very little help in understanding the distinctive characteristics of English prize procedures. These books and prize statutes were undoubtedly read in England and in America in the light of the tradition of prize practice with which the practitioners in each place were acquainted.

From a thorough reading of the published authorities on

---

[15] See chapters I and II above.

[16] Charles Warren, *A History of the American Bar* (Boston, 1911), pp. 181–186; James Madison's "List of Books to be Imported for the Use of Congress," 24 January, 1783, Ford, *JCC* 24: pp. 83–92; Hutchinson and Rachal, *Papers of Madison* 6: pp. 62–117; *Catalogue of the Library of Thomas Jefferson*, E. Millicent Sowerby, ed. (5 v., Washington, 1952–1959) 2: pp. 67–88, 228, 357–375; *A Catalogue of the Books Belonging to the Library Company of Philadelphia* (Philadelphia, 1789), pp. 218–235; Paul M. Hamlin, *Legal Education in Colonial New York* (New York, 1939), pp. 173–195.

[17] Holdsworth, *History* 12: pp. 105–107, 626–639, 646–676.

the law of captures at sea, American lawyers and judges
could have learned that the prize jurisdiction of admiralty
courts was exclusive, and that the common law courts could
not issue prohibitions to stop admiralty proceedings in a
prize case.[18] These books, of course, also made clear that any
property captured from the enemy had to be brought before
an admiralty court to determine whether it was a lawful prize
or not.[19] The captors were forbidden to break bulk before
proper adjudication.[20] These authorities repeated the clear
injunction of the privateers' instructions that the captors
bring in with the captured vessel the principal members of its
crew to be examined on interrogatories and deliver to the
admiralty judge all the papers found on board the vessel.[21]
The rule of decision in prize cases was to be the law of
nations and the treaties entered into between the nations
from which the litigants came.[22] Various presumptions of
unneutral conduct by the captured vessel were mentioned as
factors in determining the lawfulness of the capture.[23] Any
party seeking recovery of the captured property had to file a
claim supported by oath.[24] If the case was doubtful after
studying the ship papers and preparatory examinations, the
admiralty judge could allow further proof by the parties.[25]
The admiralty judge could award costs or damages against
the captors if they made an illegal capture without probable
cause for the seizure.[26] In case one or other party was dissatisfied with the sentence of the admiralty court judge, he

---

[18] Beawes, *Lex Mercatoria*, p. 212; *Report of Law Officers,* Marsden, *Law of the Sea* **2:**
p. 350; Charles Molloy, *De Jure Maritimo et Navali, or a Treatise of Affairs Maritime and
of Commerce* (7th ed., London, 1722), p. 41.

[19] *The Laws, Ordinances, and Institutions of the Admiralty of Great Britain, Civil and
Military* (2 v., London, 1746) **1:** p. 222; Lee, *Treatise of Captures*, p. 239.

[20] Beawes, *Lex Mercatoria*, p. 213; Molloy, *De Jure Maritimo*, p. 44.

[21] Beawes, *Lex Mercatoria*, pp. 213, 221; Molloy, *De Jure Maritimo*, p. 44.

[22] *Report of Law Officers*, Marsden, *Law of the Sea* **2:** pp. 350, 369; William
Blackstone, *Commentaries on the Laws of England* (4 v., 1st ed., Oxford, 1765–1769) **3:**
p. 69; **4:** p. 67; Lee, *Treatise of Captures*, p. 242.

[23] *Report of Law Officers*, Marsden, *Law of the Sea* **2:** p. 351; Lee, *Treatise of Captures*,
p. 240.

[24] *Report of Law Officers*, Marsden, *Law of the Sea* **2:** p. 351; Lee, *Treatise of Captures*,
p. 240.

[25] *Report of Law Officers*, Marsden, *Law of the Sea* **2:** pp. 351–352; Lee, *Treatise of
Captures*, pp. 239–241.

[26] *Report of Law Officers*, Marsden, *Law of the Sea* **2:** pp. 352, 356–357; *Laws of the
Admiralty* **1:** p. 220; Molloy, *De Jure Maritimo*, p. 43; Lee, *Treatise of Captures*, pp.
226–232, 240.

could appeal to the Lords Commissioners for Prize Appeals upon giving bond to prosecute the appeal to effect.[27] The claimant could obtain execution of a decree in his favor pending appeal if he provided security for return of the property to the captors upon reversal. According to two authors (but contradicted by later parliamentary acts), the captors could not obtain execution of the admiralty court decree pending appeal if the decree condemned the property to them.[28]

These meager procedural details told American lawyers and judges little about the distinctive features of prize practice before the High Court of Admiralty. Read within the context of American admiralty practice, the vice-admiralty judges or lawyers could say that these details were all ordinarily followed in American prize cases. None of these published authorities gave a full description of prize practice in England and none explicitly stated that English prize procedures were sharply different from the instance procedures in the High Court of Admiralty. Nothing in these books or in the prize statutes told the American lawyers that libels were unnecessary or improper in prize cases. The published authorities on prize practice and the British prize statutes were read in America or in England against the background of traditions of prize adjudication which differed widely. While English prize practitioners undoubtedly read the prize acts and these various authors as describing English prize procedures, colonial lawyers and judges, acquainted with a different system of prize procedures, found little to convince them that they were not proceeding properly in their prize cases.

The most significant divergence of colonial prize practice from the practice in the High Court of Admiralty involved the rules of evidence insisted on in England. As we saw in the last chapter, the English advocates, arguing before the Lords Commissioners for Prize Appeals, frequently objected strenuously to the introduction of improper evidence in the vice-admiralty courts. The colonial courts permitted the use of depositions taken on specially prepared interrogatories,

---

[27] *Report of Law Officers*, Marsden, *Law of the Sea* **2**: p. 352; Lee, *Treatise of Captures*, pp. 241–242; Beawes, *Lex Mercatoria*, pp. 211, 241; Blackstone, *Commentaries* **3**: p. 69.

[28] Molloy, *De Jure Maritimo*, p. 49; Beawes, *Lex Mercatoria*, p. 211; 29 Geo. II, c. 34 §9; 32 Geo. II, c. 25, §20.

not on the standing interrogatories used in England. Papers were occasionally introduced from other vessels than the one being tried as prize. The clearest statement of English rules of evidence in prize cases, clearer than anything in the prize acts, was in the *Report of the Law Officers of the Crown*, already quoted in the last chapter.[29]

American lawyers or judges, familiar with the colonial practice of using interrogatories drawn up by the captors, probably could have read even this passage without sensing that their prize practice was out of line with English practice. They did, after all, introduce evidence in the first instance coming from the ship taken, namely the papers on board and the examination on oath of the master or other officers. The specially prepared interrogatories, which seemed to English civilian advocates patent violations of the rules of admissible evidence, probably appeared to any American lawyers or judges who might have read this passage as "general and impartial interrogatories."

Therefore the general, vague suggestions of prize procedure found in the published sources on prize practice fit quite well with the level of prize practice in the vice-admiralty courts. The lawyers and judges in the American colonies did carry out the provisions of the prize acts and the hints of prize procedures found in the available books on the subject, but without the careful differentiation of procedural details characteristic of prize practice in England. There was a general conformity between the hazy, inadequate description of prize procedures found in the published sources and the functionally undifferentiated prize procedures, confused with instance procedures and even common law procedures, which characterized the prize practice of the vice-admiralty courts. This conformity, of course, does not by itself prove that American lawyers read these published sources, but it is a further hint in this direction. It would be impossible to

---

[29] In Marsden, *Law of the Sea* 2: p. 351; quoted verbatim in Lee, *Treatise of Captures*, p. 239. This passage stated:
"The evidence to acquit or condemn, with or without costs or damages, must, in the first instance, come merely from the ship taken, viz. the papers on board, and the examination on oath of the master and other principal officers; for which purpose there are officers of Admiralty in all considerable sea ports of every maritime power at war, to examine the captains and other principal officers of every ship brought in as prize, upon general and impartial interrogatories."

show that the tradition of prize practice in the vice-admiralty courts was entirely shaped by these writings. More likely some of these American peculiarities and aberrations, like Topsy, just growed. But at least there is nothing in the tradition of American prize practice which jars or conflicts with the hypothesis that some lawyers and judges in the colonies were acquainted with the chief contemporary writers on prize law. Probably American lawyers and judges did read such books and study the few comments on prize procedure when they were involved in prize adjudication. Quite likely they made sure that their prize practice did conform to the procedural details, inadequate though they were, given in these books. Not until a generation after the American Revolution would a book appear which studied with some adequacy the procedures of the High Court of Admiralty and carefully distinguished its instance practice from its prize practice.[30] Without such a book American lawyers and judges who took the trouble to read what was then available could only find a hazy picture of prize procedures which must have closely resembled the prize practice they could see in their own vice-admiralty courts.

The next two chapters will discuss the procedural and substantive law of cases appealed to the Committees on Appeals or the Court of Appeals set up by the Continental Congress. An effort will be made to discover some influence from the procedural and substantive law described in the published sources on prize law, as well as from the tradition of prize practice in the vice-admiralty courts. This brief overview in the present chapter of the published materials available to American lawyers in their prize practice fits side by side with the earlier study of the tradition of prize law and prize adjudication within which American lawyers in the late eighteenth century were trained. Together these two chapters describe the general sources of prize law and prize practice in America during the Revolution. The next chapters will analyze the procedures and substantive law in American prize adjudication during the Revolution. The tradition of

---

[30] Arthur Browne's *A Compendious View of the Civil Law and the Law of the Admiralty* (2 v., 1st ed., London, 1798). See also Admiralty Judge Hopkinson's contemporary comments on the distinction between instance and prize procedures, chapter VIII below, note 8.

vice-admiralty prize practice, along with the often brief and inadequate treatment of prize law in the available published sources, provides a framework for analyzing American prize practice during the Revolution.

VI. Procedural Prize Law in America During the Revolution

THE LAST TWO CHAPTERS have discussed in some detail the basic sources of American prize law at the time of the Revolution: the tradition of prize adjudication in the colonies and the published writings on prize law. During the Revolution the states, acting in their own way and at their own pace, set up courts to determine the legality of the numerous captures made by American privateers and naval vessels. The procedures of these state prize courts, as we shall see, drew heavily on the experience of the colonial prize practice. Before analyzing in detail the procedures followed by the appellate prize court established by the Continental Congress, the main topic of this chapter, it will be helpful to discuss the prize procedures followed at the trial court level by these various state maritime courts.

The most accurate model to use as a starting point in describing the procedures in American prize courts after 1775 is the procedural structure of the American vice-admiralty courts prior to 1775. In chapter IV the prize procedures of the colonial courts were distinguished from prize practice in England, where the terms of the parliamentary prize acts were meticulously followed. The American prize courts during the Revolution resembled their vice-admiralty predecessors and fit well into the undetailed, hazy procedural framework vaguely described by the English legal authors read in America.

From whatever American prize court one consults the extant records, one finds libels used to initiate the proceedings. Though these libels show some slight variations in terminology and style, they are remarkably similar in structure whether they come from New England, the Middle States, or the South. They closely resemble the libels filed earlier in prize cases in the vice-admiralty courts. But, as already indicated, no libels were ordinarily filed in prize cases in England. The records also suggest a universal practice of issu-

191

ing monitions to give notice, often by publication in a newspaper, to all interested parties that the named vessel was to be tried at a certain time and place by one of the state maritime courts. The claims presented to the prize courts likewise generally resembled the form of the claim and answer commonly used in prize practice before the vice-admiralty courts (but not the much simpler form of claims filed in England). The ship papers turned over to the admiralty judge, the numerous depositions and interrogatories (usually taken on questions prepared by the opposing counsel and not on standing interrogatories as in England) all follow the pattern of American colonial prize practice.

The strikingly new feature of prize practice during the Revolution was the introduction of juries in most states to determine the facts of the case. Apparently Delaware (and Pennsylvania after 1780) did not employ juries at all in prize cases, and several states, such as Maryland, North Carolina, and Massachusetts did not always use juries in prize suits.[1] Juries apparently were not used where no claim was filed and the libel was uncontested. In contested cases in the three states just mentioned, the parties perhaps had the option of jury or non-jury trials. Though not universally used, juries were definitely the rule and not the exception in prize litigation.

The pattern for juries was the common law jury with which American lawyers and judges were well acquainted. Often the jury merely returned a general verdict, such as, that the facts set forth in the libel were not true and the captured vessel and its cargo were not British property.[2] The jury might return a verdict in which it settled the crucial fact question on which the case turned, such as, "We find that the aforesaid Vessel has been employed in carrying and Supplying the Enemies of the United States of America contrary to the Resolves of the Congress the Laws of this State and the Law of Nations,"[3] or "We find the Vessel and Cargo to be the

---

[1] This general description of prize procedures in the trial courts is based on a thorough study of the Records of the Court of Appeals in Cases of Capture. For some examples of prize appeals in which there was no mention of a jury in the trial court, see the cases numbered: 20, 31, 32, 71, 72, 76, 77, 79, 85, 89, 98, 102, 103, 104, RCA. For the legislative basis of the state prize courts, see chapter I.

[2] For example, *Richmond* (*Craig v. Folger*), 17 January, 1777, #7, RCA.

[3] *Frank* (*Alsop v. Rutenbourgh*), 20 May, 1777, #11, RCA.

Property of Aaron Lopez."[4] Some juries returned special verdicts with separate findings of fact on each of the principal allegations of the libel and claim.[5] There are some instances where the judge's charge to the jury was written down and remains part of the record,[6] but in most cases the absence of the charge must mean that it was not recorded, not that none was given. Jury verdicts could bring other common law elements into the trial, such as a motion to set aside a verdict and grant a new trial because improper evidence had been admitted.[7]

For some unknown reason, the juries in Pennsylvania were particularly troublesome. There are several notations that the admiralty court had to postpone cases because a sufficient number of jurors did not appear, in spite of a warrant to the marshal to impanel a jury.[8] In one case the jurors, unable to reach a verdict, escaped forcibly from the custody of the tipstaff before they came to any agreement.[9] Another Pennsylvania jury returned a judicial decree rather than a verdict. It read:

> that the Brigantine or Sloop of War now called the Hope her Tackle Apparel and Furniture shall be restored to the Claimants they paying to the Capt[ain] & Crew of the private Ship of War Gen[era]l Pickering one half of the Value thereof in lieu of Salvage and also delivering up the Guns and Warlike Stores to the said Capt[ain] & Crew.

The admiralty judge noted that he disagreed with this verdict, although his decree followed its terms.[10]

The admiralty judge ordinarily wrote a decree or sentence, often summarizing the proceedings and adjudging the captured property to the captors or to the claimants depending on the jury's verdict. If there was no verdict on which to base the decree, the judge might prepare an opinion stating his reasons for condemning or acquitting the captured vessel

---

[4] *Hawke* (*Tredwell v. Lopez*), 29 March, 1779, #37, RCA.

[5] *Pitt* (*Courter v. Huntington*), 13 January, 1780, #63; *Bermudas* (*Cooke v. Conckling*), 23 December, 1780, #50; *Victoria* (*Ignatio v. Board of War for Massachusetts*), 8 November, 1779, #59, RCA.

[6] *Good Intent* (*Ploy v. Gurney*), 13 November, 1779, #44, RCA.

[7] *Bermudas*, #50, RCA.

[8] *Polly* (*Bunch v. Taylor*), 22 November, 1779, #33; *Good Intent*, #44, RCA.

[9] *Richmond*, #7, RCA.

[10] *Hope* (*Harraden v. Blewer*), 26 February, 1780, #62, RCA; Hopkinson, *Writings* **3**: pp. 14–15.

and cargo.[11] The judge often joined to the decree an order of sale at public auction of the prize property and an order of distribution of the proceeds of the sale to the parties in certain specified proportions.

These few comments suffice for a general description of prize procedures on the trial court level during the Revolution. Except for the innovation of jury trials, there is a clear resemblance between the colonial prize practice and the procedures used by the various state admiralty courts.

When procedural details are brought into sharper focus, however, it becomes clear that some state admiralty courts had their own peculiarities in prize practice. It is not always clear that these apparent procedural nuances among the states reflect different practices in the various courts, or merely differences in what the court clerks considered worth recording, or what chanced to survive. Probably the extant records do reflect quite accurately the procedural details of the different courts. Of course, a full study of distinctive state prize practice is hampered because of the loss of most state court records. The more or less complete records of only a few state admiralty courts during the Revolution are known to exist: Massachusetts, New Hampshire, Rhode Island, Connecticut, Pennsylvania, and Maryland. A few records for the other state admiralty courts survive among the papers sent to Congress for appeal. From the records that do exist, some preserved separately as trial court records, some as the records of the trial court sent forward for appeal, a few procedural characteristics distinctive of various state admiralty courts will be pointed out.

Although most state prize courts apparently followed the vice-admiralty practice of leaving the captured property in the custody of the captors pending trial, the Pennsylvania admiralty court at times issued writs of attachment ordering the marshal to take custody of the captured vessel and its cargo pending trial.[12] Perhaps this had been the regular practice in Pennsylvania, or else it reflected the orders of a new judge. In 1779 Francis Hopkinson, the admiralty judge

---

[11] *Two Friends (Young v. Penny)*, 23 December, 1780, #72, RCA; Hopkinson, *Writings* 3: pp. 50–54.

[12] Admiralty Court Papers (HSP). There are occasional references in other states to custody by the marshal, e.g., *Hanover (Coor v. Hussey)*, 7 August, 1778, #16 & 17; *Diamond* and *Dolphin (Jackson v. Forman)*, 21 May, 1784, #91 & 92, RCA.

there, ordered that henceforth the marshal should go on board all captured vessels brought into the state's ports in order to demand that the prize master bring all the ship's papers as well as the key members of the original crew of the vessel to the admiralty court, so that the judge could conduct the preparatory examinations.[13]

The Pennsylvania admiralty judge also examined witnesses in open court, issued commissions for the examination of witnesses at a distance from the court and ordered vessels to be unloaded and their cargo sold because they were alleged to be in perishing condition. (These routine orders were probably made by other admiralty judges also, but they are better attested in Pennsylvania.) In at least one case (where the marshal had been roughly treated by the captors who, under color of a common law writ of replevin, forcibly took the captured vessel out of the marshal's custody), the Pennsylvania admiralty judge issued a writ of attachment for contempt against the unruly captors. He fined them and ordered them committed to prison till they paid the fine and restored the vessel. After they had been arrested and held in custody by the marshal, the state's executive council intervened ordering the captors released and the fines remitted. Apparently the marshal did regain custody of the vessel.[14]

In Connecticut the five county common law courts were authorized to hold maritime sessions at which the legality of captures were tried, so it is not surprising that the maritime records there have especially strong common law overtones. The attorneys there (sometimes called proctors or advocates) occasionally interjected demurrers and pleas in abatement in prize proceedings. There are reminders also of earlier vice-admiralty prize practice in the frequent use of a series of proclamations for interested parties to appear and defaults for nonappearance, followed by the decree of condemnation. There are occasional references to warrants for the sheriff (not the marshal) to arrest the vessel. The voluminous maritime court records in Connecticut abound in the usual libels and claims (often filed without aid of counsel), depositions, occasional interrogatories and, of course, the papers

---

[13] *Pennsylvania Gazette*, 18 August, 1779.

[14] Admiralty Court Papers (HSP). See especially the case of the *Fame* in these papers.

from the captured ships.[15] The peculiar problems resulting from Connecticut seamen plundering the inhabitants of Long Island will be discussed in the next chapter.

The most distinctive trait of the Massachusetts and New Hampshire maritime courts was the allowance of appeals to the state superior court in prize cases. These two state superior courts tried the facts *de novo*, admitting new evidence where it was presented. Juries in these superior courts returned new verdicts based on all the evidence presented. The practice of a new trial by jury on appeal in prize cases followed the practice of appeals from common law courts in these states to these same superior courts.[16] The problems involved in appeals, whether from the Massachusetts and New Hampshire trial courts or their state superior courts, to the appellate judiciary of Congress, will be discussed later in this chapter and the constitutional aspects of these appeals will be treated in a later chapter.[17]

Although in general, written pleadings in the state admiralty courts were rare except for the libels and claims, there are occasional examples of slightly more sophisticated pleadings, especially in Rhode Island, Maryland, and South Carolina. But these replies and replications seldom added much to the legal argument beyond what the initial libels or claims already contained.[18] Common law pleadings, such as demurrers or pleas in abatement, were sometimes used by attorneys, again indicating their own background in the common law.[19]

---

[15] Connecticut Maritime Court Records (CSL).

[16] Massachusetts, Court Files, Suffolk; Minute Book of Appeals from the Maritime Court; Record Books, Superior Court of Judicature; Suffolk Minute Books (MSJC). Revolution Prize Cases, 1776–1780 (MA). New Hampshire, Superior Court Minute Books, 1777–1784 (Rockingham County Court, Office of the Clerk). The cases appealed from these two states to the appellate judiciary of Congress are: #3, 9, 14, 21, 47, 54, 56, 57, 58, 59, 60, 66, 67, 75, 78, 86, 88, 93, 94, 95, 96, 98, 99, 104, 107, 108, and 2 Dall. 34 (Mass.) and #2, 30 and 97 (N.H.). See also, Goebel, *Antecedents*, pp. 25–35, and Nelson, *Americanization of the Common Law*, pp. 16, 23, 28–30, 165–171. Nelson also discusses the lawfinding role of juries in Massachusetts, which would undoubtedly also be true of the juries in the maritime courts of the State.

[17] Chapter VIII below.

[18] Rhode Island, Admiralty Court Minute Book; Admiralty Papers (RISA); Maryland, Admiralty Court Papers; Admiralty Court Minute Books (MHR). The cases appealed from these three states are: #6, 8 & 19, 11, 18, 34, 37, 68, 90, 100, and 2 Dall. 40 (R.I.); #15, 48, 63, and 85 (Maryland); #24, 25, and 2 Dall. 41 (South Carolina).

[19] E.g., *Adventurer* (*Boitar v. Young*), 17 August, 1781, #106, RCA.

Just as the prize procedures in the Revolutionary War admiralty courts followed closely the model of colonial prize practice, so the rules of evidence in American prize courts remained basically unchanged from the colonial through the Revolutionary periods. Depositions and interrogatories of any persons (not just the principal members of the crew of the captured vessel, as was the rule in England) were freely admitted with one key limitation. The testimony of any person with financial interest in the outcome of the suit could not be admitted unless he signed a release of all his interests in the prize property.[20] In one case the judge refused to admit the deposition of an interested party even though he had signed a release. Perhaps the judge suspected that the release was fraudulent.[21] The judge determined whether the person whose testimony was challenged really did have an interest in the outcome of the litigation.[22] But in a case where evidence of an interested person had been admitted without objection, the judge overruled a motion after the verdict was returned to set aside the verdict and grant a new trial.[23] The judge, as in a trial at common law, could also refuse to admit hearsay evidence.[24] The trial judge had it within his discretion to delay the trial to allow time for witnesses to appear.[25] Although many judges would probably have admitted as evidence papers found on board vessels other than the one being tried (contrary to the rule in England), in at least one case the judge did follow the English rule and sustain an objection to such evidence.[26]

The usual tricks and deceits of privateer captains as well as merchants made the evaluation of evidence just as difficult for the court as it had ever been. Even though there are just two cases in which bribery or intimidation of a witness were clearly charged,[27] such conduct must have been a rather frequent occurrence. After all, the interested party needed some inducement to sign a release so that his testimony could

---

[20] *John and Sally* (*Stevens v. Henderson*), 11 March, 1779, #35; *Polly* (*Gibbons v. Davis*), 23 March, 1779, #43; *Good Intent*, #44, RCA.

[21] *Fame* (*Johnston v. Taylor*), 23 December, 1780, #45, RCA.

[22] *Polly*, #33, RCA.

[23] *Bermudas*, #50, RCA.

[24] *Hannah* (*Hepburn v. Ellis*), 4 August, 1781, #74, RCA.

[25] *George* (*Jennings v. Griffin*), 23 December, 1780, #40, RCA.

[26] *Ibid.*

[27] *Ibid; Diamond* and *Dolphin*, #91 & 92, RCA.

be admitted. If a witness's testimony could not be coerced or bought, the key witness himself could be illegally detained far from the place of the trial.[28] But with all the difficulties in obtaining and evaluating evidence, there are no indications that the American courts at this time used the various presumptions to acquit or condemn a vessel as the High Court of Admiralty did. The use of the common law rules of evidence in the appellate court, undoubtedly paralleling the usage in the trial prize courts, will be briefly discussed later in this chapter.

The evidence clearly indicates that the final decrees of the admiralty courts were ordinarily carried into execution with no difficulty. Sometimes the captured vessel or cargo was itself delivered to one or other party, or frequently the property was sold by order of the court at a public auction under the watchful eye of the marshal and the proceeds distributed to the parties according to the court's decree.

If one or more of the parties were dissatisfied with the final decree, they could appeal to the Committee on Appeals or the Court of Appeals in Cases of Capture, the appellate judiciary of the Continental Congress. The following analysis of procedures for appeals to this appellate judiciary will make mention of the similarities with the procedures for review by the Lords Commissioners for Prize Appeals discussed in chapter IV. In general, however, there is little to indicate any reliance of Congress or the appellate judges on the procedural structure of the court of the Lords Commissioners. The trial court procedures in prize cases closely paralleled the experience of the vice-admiralty courts and not the practice of the High Court of Admiralty. The appellate procedures before the Lords Commissioners, however, were little known by American lawyers; there were no published sources which would have given them an accurate picture of these procedures.

In most cases the appeal to Congress was made by oral motion to the state admiralty judge shortly after he had issued the definitive decree. Occasionally the attorney for the dissatisfied party filed a written notice of appeal with the trial court.[29] The resolutions of Congress required that the ap-

---

[28] *Pitt*, #63, RCA.
[29] E.g., *Thistle* (*Roberts v. McAroy*), 19 September, 1776, #1, and *Sherburne* (*Swain v. Newman*), 10 May, 1777, #10, RCA.

peal be demanded within five days after the definitive sentence and filed with the secretary of Congress (later with the register of the Court of Appeals) within forty days. The appellant had to give security to prosecute the appeal.[30] When the appellant fulfilled these requirements and when the judge had no special reason for refusing the appeal, the motion was routinely granted and the stipulation or recognizance (the bond to prosecute the appeal) was accepted by the judge. In these cases the register of the admiralty court provided the appellant with a certified copy of the full court records and other papers, often sending forward the original ship papers, not copies. In cases where the authenticity of various ship papers was questioned, only the originals would be adequate for the appeal. The appellant filed these papers with the secretary of Congress or, after the Court of Appeals was established, with its register within the forty days allowed. The mere lodging of the file papers and lower court records sufficed to enter an appeal.

Slight variations of this mode of appeal occurred, as when both parties appealed to Congress,[31] or two parties representing separate interests in a multiparty suit appealed. In this latter case the court considered the appeals individually, but both were eventually dismissed.[32] There is record also of an objection by the opposing party to the motion for an appeal to Congress which the trial judge overruled, granting the appeal.[33] In another case the judge of the Rhode Island maritime court granted the appeal to a party from North Carolina, but as required by state law, only on the condition that the laws of North Carolina did not prevent out-of-state litigants in their admiralty courts from appealing to Congress.[34]

A second procedure for bringing an appeal was by petition. Congress's appellate judiciary for prize cases clearly distinguished these two methods of appealing. In the table of

---

[30] Ford, *JCC*, 25 November, 1775, **3**: p. 374.

[31] *Jane (Fosset v. Foster)*, 18 January, 1780, #48; *Victoria*, #59; *Pitt*, #63; *Hepsabeth and John (Anthony v. Deshon)*, 5 April, 1781, #69 & 70, RCA.

[32] *Good Fortune (Allen v. McConnell)*, 14 June, 1783, *(Howell v. McConnell)*, 11 May, 1787, #87, RCA.

[33] *Lark (Johnson v. Prebble)*, n.d., #86, RCA.

[34] *Speedwell (Bain v. Brown)*, 24 May, 1784, 2 Dall. 40, RCA. North Carolina did not in fact have any restriction on appeals to Congress. *Rhode Island Session Laws*, November session, 1780, pp. 18–19.

fees of the register of the Court of Appeals only these two procedures are listed: "Entry of Proceedings on a rehearing or appeal granted on Petition" and "Entry of an Appeal."[35] Appeals on petition came before Congress or the court when the trial court had refused to grant the appeal, or when the appeal was requested or filed with Congress after the time allowed, or when no bond had been given.

Perhaps the source of this clear distinction between appeals granted by the court below and appeals granted by the appellate court of Congress on petition derived from the colonial experience of appeals to the Privy Council (probably more familiar to American attorneys than appeals to the Lords Commissioners for Prize Appeals). Appeals to the Privy Council from colonial common law or admiralty courts (but apparently not in prize cases) could be made either where the lower court granted the appeal or by *doléance*. The *doléance* procedure involved a petition for a review of a decree not brought before the Privy Council in the ordinary course of appeal, as when the request for an appeal had been refused by the court below.[36] The term *doléance* does not appear in the records of the Court of Appeals in Cases of Captures, but the twofold procedure for appealing, by appeal granted by the court *a quo* and by petition to the court *ad quem*, resembles the *doléance* procedure for bringing cases before the Privy Council. No examples of appeals by petition to the Lords Commissioners for Prize Appeals were discovered.

Admiralty court judges found a variety of reasons for refusing to grant an appeal to Congress. The most obvious reason was a state law which forbade appeals in the type of case before the court. The cases coming from Massachusetts and New Hampshire will be more fully discussed in chapter VIII in connection with the debate over the jurisdiction of the congressional appellate judiciary. In three of these cases the decree of the maritime court had been appealed to the state superior courts, but these courts, after the verdict and decree on appeal, refused to allow an appeal to Congress because of the limitation in the state laws. Both Massachusetts and New Hampshire at the time of these three cases

---

[35] For some reason the appeal on petition cost less ($10) than the entry of an appeal ($15). Miscellaneous Court Records, RCA.

[36] Smith, *Appeals*, pp. 27–28, 96–98.

allowed appeals to Congress only where the vessel making the capture was a naval vessel fitted out at the expense of Congress.[37] These cases came before the Committee on Appeals by means of petitions addressed to Congress. The petitions were referred to the committee, which in the first two cases reported back an order, approved by Congress, for the opposing party to appear and show cause why the prayer of the petition should not be granted. In the third case, the one from New Hampshire, the committee itself, acting on the confirmation of its authority by Congress of March 6, 1779 (after the case of the sloop *Active*), ruled that the appellant should give at least thirty days' notice of the hearing to be held before it.[38]

In a Connecticut case the maritime court refused to allow an appeal to Congress. The party seeking the appeal first petitioned the Connecticut legislature to review the refusal of the court. The upper house of the legislature (made up mostly of judges of the various courts) summoned the adverse party to appear before the general assembly to show cause. But after a hearing the assembly resolved that the petition of the appellant should be dismissed since it concerned maritime matters which by the state law were reserved to the jurisdiction of Congress. The appellant thereupon sent a petition to Congress asking it to take cognizance of the case. The petition was referred to the Committee on Appeals but probably was never further prosecuted since there are no papers on file for the case among the court records.[39]

After this case had been referred to Congress, Connecticut tightened its laws preventing illicit trade with the enemy, a special problem for Connecticut because of the presence of the British on Long Island. As part of this revision of the state laws, the legislature forbade appeals to Congress or any superior court in cases of vessels or cargoes proceeded against for violating the state laws against this illicit trade. So

---

[37] *Acts and Resolves of Massachusetts* **5**: p. 477; Batchellor, *Laws of New Hampshire* **4**: p. 31.

[38] *Countess of Eglinton (Jones v. Babcock)*, 14 September, 1783, #9; *Anna Maria (Bucklin v. White)*, 18 August, 1780, #21; *Lusanna (Doane v. Penhallow)*, 17 September, 1783, #30, RCA; Ford, *JCC* **8**: pp. 602–603; **12**: pp. 1022–1023, and PCC, Item 44, 189.

[39] *Peggy (Hart v. Griffing)*, n.d., #26, RCA; PCC, Item 42, III, 357–365; Ford, *JCC* **11**: p. 789, and Revolutionary War Collection, 1st ser., X, 367–368, 237 (CSL).

subsequently when the losing party in the case of the sloop *Sally* requested an appeal to Congress, the proctor for the opposing party objected because of the state law. The issue presented to the trial court was precisely whether this was a lawful prize taken by the captors, or illicit importation from Long Island by collusion between the alleged captors and the crew of the captured ship. The court, after hearing both parties on the objection to the appeal, determined that the motion for an appeal should be denied and no appeal was granted. The appellant (the alleged captor) addressed a petition to the judges of the Court of Appeals praying that he be allowed to prosecute his appeal. The court, without reference to Congress, heard the petition, gave notice to the adverse party and finally reversed the decree of the lower court. The Court of Appeals here ignored the jury's verdicts below which had found that the vessel was not a prize at all, but was involved in illicit importation of British goods from Long Island. Presumably if the case involved illicit importation, it was not a true prize case at all, and Congress's appellate court would not have jurisdiction. The main point here, however, is that the Committee on Appeals and the Court of Appeals, on petition of the aggrieved party, reviewed lower court sentences, even though the lower court had not allowed the appeal. In the case of the *Sally* the state maritime court had the last word; it refused to execute the decree of the Court of Appeals.[40]

A slightly different procedure was followed in the case of the schooner *Liberty* because of the special circumstances of the case. It involved the recapture of an American ship after less than twenty-four hours in possession of the enemy. The original owner, a citizen of Virginia, appealed to Congress from a sentence restoring the property to him but ordering him to pay one-eighth the value to the recaptors. The North Carolina admiralty judge had refused to grant an appeal to Congress without assigning any reason. The appellant's petition was referred by Congress to a special committee of three, not to the Committee on Appeals, perhaps because of the interstate aspects of the dispute. The committee recom-

---

[40] *Sally* (*Spencer v. Peters*), 12 June, 1783, #84, RCA; New London County Maritime Court Files (CSL). This refusal to execute the decree will be discussed below. For the state law see, Connecticut Session Laws, 29 November, 1780, p. 563, Jenkins, *Microfilm*.

mended, and Congress approved, granting an appeal. Congress agreed to issue an order, upon application of the appellant, to the register of the North Carolina admiralty court to send forward a copy of all the proceedings in the case. The case also involved the theft of the ship and its cargo after the maritime court decision while it was within the custody of the captors. The captors had made no effort to resist the robbers and apparently were in collusion with them. In October, 1778, Congress sent this report to the executive authority of North Carolina to have some measures taken to prosecute the parties guilty of stealing the property and to make compensation to the original owner. A copy of the report was also sent to the legislature of Virginia, the home of the owner. In August, 1779, the governor of Virginia forwarded to Congress a memorial from the owner, complaining of the loss of £17,750 Virginia currency due to the theft of the *Liberty* and its cargo. The memorial further claimed that the North Carolina delegates in Congress had obtained postponement of the former resolves of Congress so that their state could make voluntary reparation for the theft, but nothing had been done and there was little prospect anything would be. The memorial prayed the governor of Virginia to take some steps to redress the injury. Virginia's governor sent the memorial to the Virginia delegates in Congress who laid the question before the members. Congress referred this memorial to the Committee on Appeals, which ordered the North Carolina admiralty judge to receive the appeal, accept the proper security for prosecuting the appeal, and transmit the proceedings and testimony to the committee. The lack of documents from the court below suggests that the North Carolina admiralty judge did not comply with this order. Neither party ever appeared so the appeal was dismissed in 1784.[41] Such cases clearly demonstrated the need for a more effective judiciary for the central government.

In the case of the sloop *Polly* an appeal on petition was made to the Court of Appeals from an interlocutory judgment of the Rhode Island admiralty court on a demurrer to a plea taking exception to the jurisdiction of the court. (A good example of common law pleading in a prize case). The peti-

---

[41] *Liberty (Harper v. Ansill)*, 6 May, 1784, #105, RCA, and Ford, *JCC* **11**: p. 837; **12**: pp. 1087–1089; **14**: p. 941.

tion to the Court of Appeals alleged that the *Polly* belonged to Richard Smith of Connecticut, who was bringing it and another ship, the sloop *Little Dick*, from Long Island with his personal property with permission of the Connecticut legislature. Thomas Wickham, also of Connecticut, commander of the privateer sloop *Hampton Packet*, captured both ships in Long Island Sound and was proceeding with the *Polly* to some unknown destination when a friendly ship retook the *Polly* off the coast of Rhode Island. Because of the wind and weather they had to anchor near the shore of Rhode Island but with favorable weather they returned to New London, Connecticut. Though the *Polly* was no longer within Rhode Island waters, Wickham libeled it in the admiralty court there. The judge of admiralty there received the libel, but Smith, the owner, appeared by counsel and pleaded by way of exception to the jurisdiction of the admiralty court, since the *Polly* had never been in possession of the court or of any court officer. Even then the *Polly* was at New London, so the Rhode Island court had no jurisdiction to hear or determine the facts alleged in the libel. The captors demurred to this plea of the owner and Smith joined in the demurrer. The judge determined that the plea to the jurisdiction was insufficient in law to preclude the court from taking cognizance of the libel. Smith then requested an appeal to the Court of Appeals from this interlocutory decree, but the court refused to grant one. The judge further refused to allow him to enter a claim in order to be heard on the merits and then proceeded to render judgment by default against the *Polly*. Smith petitioned the Court of Appeals to hear the case. After reviewing the records and hearing the arguments of counsel for both parties, the Court of Appeals determined that the Rhode Island admiralty court had never had cognizance of the case since it did not arise and was not within the jurisdiction of the court. (Jurisdiction apparently was only *in rem*, and if the *res* was not within the power of the court, there was no jurisdiction.) The decree of the state court was reversed and annulled.[42] Perhaps the harshness of the judge's action in Rhode Island appears in a somewhat better light when one realizes that Smith's other ship, the *Little Dick*, had also been captured and Wickham claimed a share of this

---

[42] *Polly (Smith v. Wickham)*, 26 May, 1784, #100, RCA.

prize in the Connecticut maritime court. The judgment there went for Smith, and when Wickham asked for an appeal to Congress, Smith objected. So two weeks before the case of the *Polly* was heard in Rhode Island, Smith (who would request an appeal in Rhode Island), had objected in the Connecticut court that the appeal requested there by Wickham should not be granted as against the law of the state. The Connecticut court had refused to grant Wickham an appeal.[43]

If the appellant requested the appeal more than five days after the trial court passed definitive sentence or filed the appeal with Congress more than forty days after the request, then the appeal (like a *doléance* procedure) was ordinarily by petition. If some peculiar circumstances made the delay unavoidable or reasonable, the Committee on Appeals reported to Congress that the appeal should be received and heard, and Congress so ordered.[44] (Though the committee took on

[43] *Little Dick (Broome, Libellant v. Wickham, Claimant and Smith, Claimant)*, June, 1783, session, New London County Maritime Court File (CSL). There is no record that this case was ever brought before the Court of Appeals.

The case of the *Success* was an exception to the ordinary rule. Here the judge of the South Carolina admiralty court refused to grant an appeal, but the case came before the Committee on Appeals without any petition. The admiralty judge had expressed in a decree his reasons for not granting the appeal requested by the unsuccessful claimant. In this decree the judge, whose actions appear to have been prejudicial to the claimant at trial, objected to the form of the request for appeal, "for that it was not only highly Indecent and Indelicate in the mode of Expression, but was also fraught with many palpable falsehoods and if admitted he [the judge] would very justly have merited the Opprobrious Epithets which were therein illiberally heaped upon him." Precisely what the judge found so objectionable is not clear from the records. The written notice of appeal and the various motions of the claimant to obtain an appeal all appear moderate and quite routine. The judge stated also that he would not grant an appeal because no appeal could be made from interlocutory decrees. Though the appellant did object to various interlocutory orders, the request for appeal was made only after the final decree. The judge further refused to allow the appellant to have copies of the court proceedings since he had not granted the appeal. There is no explanation how the appellant secured the full records of the court with copies of the ship papers and testimony. The records were filed with the secretary of Congress and referred to the commissioners of appeals, who received and heard the case as if an appeal had been granted by the trial court and finally reversed the lower court sentence. Unfortunately, no records tell of the admiralty judge's reaction when asked to execute this decree. (*Success (Arthur v. Weyman)*, 7 August, 1778, #24, RCA; Ford, *JCC*, 12 September, 1777, 8: p. 738).

[44] *Polly (Knight v. White)*, n.d., #12, RCA; Ford, *JCC* 7: p. 171; 8: p. 647, and PCC, Item 29, 347–348. For a similar case of unavoidable delay, where the officers of the captured ship were forceably kept by the captors from filing any claim till after their ship was condemned, see *Sally (Mifflin v. Powers)*, 1779, Miscellaneous Case Papers, RCA; Ford, *JCC* 9: p. 1052, and PCC, Item 42, V, 59, 67, 112, 114.

much of the style of a court, it never fully lost its original
characteristic of a legislative committee.) In a case where the
delay in lodging the appeal was due to the failure of the
secretary of Congress to enter receipt of the court papers
and the loss of these records, the Committee on Appeals
itself granted the petition of appellant to have the case heard.
The commissioners ruled that the appellant give to the appellee thirty days' notice of the time appointed for the hearing.[45] But where the party claiming ownership of the prize
ship had not received notice of the original trial and could
not make an appearance or enter a claim till after the trial,
the Committee on Appeals ruled that the adverse party appear to show cause why the prayer of the petition should not
be granted. When the committee received an affidavit of the
admiralty judge, however, that the claimant had never even
requested an appeal though he had been present and discussed the case two days after the trial, the committee dismissed the appeal.[46]

When Congress established the Court of Appeals, it
transmitted to the court all the cases then pending before the
committee. The court received with these records a petition
for a hearing on appeal which had been filed late with the
secretary of Congress. The petition merely alleged unavoidable accidents without specifying the causes for the delay.
The court dismissed the appeal without giving reasons and
assessed costs against the petitioner.[47] But even after the
Court of Appeals had been established, some petitioners
referred their cases to Congress to obtain a hearing for
appeals lodged late. In two cases from Connecticut the reason for delay in filing the appeal with the court was that the
court had not been held at Hartford, as had been advertised.
The petition to Congress for a hearing went to a specially

---

[45] *Charming Sally (Edwards v. Elderkin)*, 5 January, 1780, #46, RCA. The same type
of unavoidable delay led to the granting of an appeal by petition by the Committee
on Appeals, *LeVern (de Valnais v. Tucker)*, 25 July, 1780, #56, RCA.

[46] *Success (Doane v. Price)*, n.d., #51, RCA. In a case where a Massachusetts
claimant could not find any sureties in a distant state (North Carolina) and therefore
could not give a bond to appeal, a petition to Congress was referred to the Committee on Appeals, which reported, and Congress resolved, that notice should be rved
on appellee to show cause. *Roseanna (Hussey v. Fowkes)*, n.d., #20, RCA; Ford, *JCC* 8:
pp. 472, 486.

[47] *Sandwich Packet (Bradford v. Brimmer)*, 14 August, 1780, #66, RCA; PCC, Item
19, VI, 569; Item 41, X, 440, and Ford, *JCC* 16: pp. 401, 410–411; 17: pp. 457–459.

appointed committee which reported in favor of authorizing the Court of Appeals to hear the cases.[48] In another case the court itself followed strictly the time limitation for lodging an appeal with the register. In 1786 Congress had given the court authority to grant rehearings or new hearings wherever justice required, but the judges dismissed this case because it had originally been lodged late with no excusing cause.[49] The cumbersomeness of this procedure requiring congressional approval for each appeal filed late is obvious.

The case of the brigantine *Gloucester* showed most clearly the attitude of Congress toward the time limitations. It involved an appeal from Pennsylvania in which the appellant's bond had not been properly registered for more than five days after the final sentence of the admiralty court. The delay occurred because of the illness and death of the court's register. In spite of this adequate explanation, the Court of Appeals, conscious of the precise limits imposed by Congress on its power to review, had refused to grant a hearing because the bond for appeal had been executed after the time allowed. The appellant petitioned Congress, and the special committee appointed to study the petition reported: "That although Congress ought not to relieve in any case relievable by the Court of appeals, yet in instances of peculiar hardship, in which the sufferer had not been in fault, and that Court is incapacitated by strictness of law to interpose, Congress should prevent a defect of Justice." Congress instructed the Court to receive and hear the appeal.[50]

The general policy, therefore, was to hear cases in which the lower court had granted the appeal, or else where the appellants petitioned for a hearing. Though at times the Committee on Appeals granted the petition on its own initiative, the judges throughout the period took a strict view of the limitations imposed by Congress on the right of appeal. In most cases, even under the court, Congress had to grant special authorization to hear a petitioner whose appeal had

---

[48] *British Goods* (*McCluer v. Ston*), 21 September, 1783, #80 & 101, and *British Goods* (*Gardiner v. Johnson*), 21 September, 1783, #81, RCA; Ford, *JCC* 11: p. 72, and PCC, Item 41, VII, 75.

[49] *Hope* (*Meade v. Hurlbert*), 3 May, 1787, #103, RCA, and Ford, *JCC*, 19 May, 1786, 30: p. 291.

[50] *Gloucester* (*Keane v. Mahon*), 5 February, 1783, 2 Dall. 36, RCA; Ford, *JCC* 21: pp. 935–936, and PCC, Item 19, III, 323; Item 41, IV, 87.

not been made within the proper time limits. If the lower court judge had granted the appeal, however, even if requested after the time limit, the appellate judges heard the case without a petition from the appellant.[51] The judges of appeal[52] apparently had no discretion to refuse a case if the lower court granted an appeal.

In the records of the Court of Appeals it is possible to identify one hundred and thirteen cases which came before the committee or the court. This most likely is an accurate estimate of the number of cases, though a few could have completely disappeared from the records. Several of these cases were never heard on appeal. About twenty came before the judges of appeals by petition. The state court records show that other cases were appealed to Congress and bond was given, but there is no record that they were ever lodged with the secretary or register.[53] The appellant, it seems, could avoid forfeiting the bond without too much difficulty, probably by a settlement of the claim. Lower court records also indicate cases where the request for an appeal had been refused and the appeal was not pursued by petition.[54]

After a case was properly before the committee or the court, the judges of appeals required that the adverse party receive due notice of the time and place of the hearing. Often the appellant had already given notice to the adverse party or his agent and presented the judges with an affidavit proving the fact.[55] In some cases the judges of appeals ruled that a party should give thirty or forty days' notice of the day

---

[51] *John and Sally*, 35, RCA. In this case the appellees petitioned to object to the hearing on appeal, because appellants had requested it late, but Congress and the Committee on Appeals treated the case as if the appeal had been regularly granted. Ford, *JCC* **12**: p. 1055; **13**: p. 96.

[52] This term, judges of appeals, though not used in the records, will be used to apply both to the members of the Committees on Appeals, often referred to in the records as commissioners of appeals, and also to the judges of the Court of Appeals.

[53] For example, *Chaffy v. Schooner Sally*, April, 1783, session and *Mayhew v. Boat Rainbow*, November, 1783, session of Massachusetts Superior Court of Judicature, in: Minute Book, Appeals from Maritime Court (MSJC); *Read v. Sloop Fair American*, 17 July, 1783, Rhode Island Admiralty Court Minute Book, 1776–1783 (RISA), and *Joseph Hull v. Boat Bathsheba*, January, 1782, and *Ebenezer Dayton v. Schooner Delight*, July, 1782, New Haven County Court Record Book, 1774–1783 (CSL).

[54] *Little Dick*, New London County Maritime Court File (CSL); *Brown v. Brigantine Little Porgey*, April, 1781, session and *Donaldson v. Brigantine Lark*, April, 1783, session, Massachusetts Superior Court, Minute Book (MSJC).

[55] *Industry (Perkins v. Coit)*, 8 September, 1777, #14, and *British Goods (Wells v. Judson)*, 21 September, 1783, #79, RCA.

set for the hearing.[56] The form of these rulings remained basically the same, whether issued by the committee or the court, though by the last year of the court's life the style became more formal.[57] In cases coming to the attention of Congress by petitions for a hearing, Congress likewise required the adverse party or his agent to be served with a copy of the petition and a notice of the time of the hearing.[58] Delays of hearings and continuances were frequent,[59] but there were limits to the patience of the judges of appeals. In a case that had been postponed twice already, the Committee on Appeals peremptorily ruled that the appeal be heard on a certain day. But even here the final determination was not made for eight more months.[60] Throughout the life of the committee and the Court of Appeals, justice was seldom swift or easy to come by.

The practice of requiring notice of the appeal for the opposing party bears only remote resemblance to the formalized inhibitions, citations, and monitions used for appeal to the Lords Commissioners for Prize Appeals. There is no indication of proctors submitting their proxies to become parties to the appeal in place of their clients, as in English prize appellate practice. For appeals to the congressional appellate judiciary, generally there were none of the stylized pleadings (libel of appeal, adhesion of appeal) which characterized prize appeals in England.

No distinction apparently was made between proctors and advocates in America and the appellate records use these terms interchangeably with attorney. No separate bar developed in America for prize appeals, as far as the records indicate. It seems that in many cases the attorney who handled the case in the trial court argued the appeal also. But the

---

[56] *Countess of Eglinton*, #9; *Mermaid* (*Gleason v. Mapes*), 24 August, 1780, #53, and *LeVern*, #56, RCA.

[57] Compare ruling of committee, 5 May, 1779, *Lusanna*, #30, and a similar ruling of the court, 8 December, 1786, *Chester* (*Dubbeldemuts v. Atkinson*), 3 May, 1787, 2 Dall. 41, RCA.

[58] *Roseanna*, #20, RCA.

[59] *Two Brothers* (*Stanton v. Champlin*), 30 August, 1779, and 29 May, 1783, #18; *Anna Maria*, #21, RCA, and Thomas McKean to Thomas Rodney, 10 April, 1778, Gratz Collection, Old Congress Papers, (HSP).

[60] *Fortune* (*Godwin v. Moore*), 24 June, 1780, #31, and Miscellaneous Court Records, RCA. The repeated delays were caused by other business and by illness of one of the attorneys. George Read to C. Rodney, 11 August, 1779, in H. L. Brown Collection (Historical Society of Delaware).

lack of pleadings on appeal most often makes it impossible to tell who did argue the case before the judges of appeals. The list of attorneys who argued prize cases in the trial court and presumably often on appeal also, includes many of the well-known lawyers of the day. Some of these same lawyers also sat as judges of appeals for a brief period during the years the appellate prize court existed.[61]

With a case before them for review, the judges of appeals did not often have the benefit of a full written statement of the legal arguments. Indeed the crux of most appeals was in the interpretation of the facts at least as much as in the application of the law. The applicable substantive law, studied in the next chapter, was in general either the statutory law of Congress or the law of nations, a vague and variously interpreted collection of principles for dealings between nations. It will be remembered that the Lords Commissioners for Prize Appeals invariably received copies of a printed case which stated the facts and trial court proceedings of the suit and briefly gave the legal reasoning for affirmance or reversal. Where petitions for appeals came to Congress or the court, they usually set forth in a summary way the facts, the lower court proceedings and at least suggested the legal issues of the case, but not in a form resembling the printed cases presented to the Lords Commissioners.[62] One case coming from South Carolina, where the procedures and pleadings were highly formalized, included among the records a lengthy notice of appeal that had been

---

[61] The attorneys most frequently involved in prize cases which were appealed to the appellate judiciary of Congress, with the approximate number of cases in parentheses, are: Richard Bassett, Del. (3); Phineas Bond, Penna. (3); William Bradford, R.I. (3); William Channing, R.I. (4); John Cole, R.I. (4); John Cooke, N.C. (7); Francis Dana, Mass. (3); Pierpoint Edwards, Conn. (3); Oliver Ellsworth, Conn. (4); R. J. Helme, R.I. (3); Benjamin Hichborn, Mass. (8); Jared Ingersoll, Penna. (6); William Lewis, Penna. (19); John Lowell, Mass. (13); Luthur Martin, Md. (3); Thomas McKean, Del. (3); Perez Morton, Mass. (9); Abner Nash, N.C. (4); George Read, Del. (5); Bowes Reed, N.J. (9); Richard Ridgely, Md. (3); Jesse Root, Conn. (3); Jacob Rush, Penna. (8); Jonathan Dickinson Sergeant, N.J. (6); Gold Selleck Silliman, N.J. (3); Richard Stockton, N.J. (8); James Sullivan, Mass. (5); William Tudor, Mass. (6); Nicholas Van Dyke, Del. (4); Marvin Wait, Conn. (3); James Wilson, Penna. (5). It should be repeated that it is not clear from the records that these attorneys were the ones who argued the case on appeal. In some cases the names of the attorneys for the appeal are indicated, but most often they are not. We can only guess that some of these attorneys whose names appear on the trial court pleadings also appeared before the judges of appeals, while others obtained counsel (such as William Lewis) closer to the place where the court sat.

[62] For example, *Sally*, #84, RCA.

presented to the trial judge to request the appeal. The notice stated the facts of the case, the applicable law, and the alleged errors of the judge in interpreting the law.[63] In another case the libelant addressed to the commissioners of appeals a full, hand-written argument, clearly modeled on the English printed cases, discussing the factual issues and the legal significance of the various ship papers.[64] The petition to the Court of Appeals for a hearing in another case also took the form of a detailed and highly formal presentation of the factual issues.[65] But these few examples of written arguments for an appeal and assignments of error were exceptions. Ordinarily the judges of appeals received only the records from the court below, depositions, interrogatories, and ship papers. Whatever legal argument was presented by counsel was oral, not written.

The lower court records usually included depositions and interrogatories, similar in form to the interrogatories and occasional depositions used in the American vice-admiralty courts. There had never been any strict insistence on the use of standing interrogatories in the colonial courts as there was in England. The widespread practice of using depositions and written copies of in-court testimony in the Revolutionary War state admiralty courts carried these courts even further from the English prize practice. Counsel appearing before the judges of appeals apparently made no objections to these depositions and interrogatories which would have been objected to by advocates arguing before the Lords Commissioners.

As the Committee on Appeals took on more the form and style of a court, the commissioners received depositions specially taken for the appeal or had additional depositions taken before themselves specifically for the appeal.[66] When the Court of Appeals began hearing cases, the judges continued to have depositions taken before themselves as a

---

[63] *Polly and Nancy* (*Norris v. Porter*), 14 August, 1778, #25, RCA.

[64] *Mary* (*Smith v. Hinson*), 6 May, 1784, #73, RCA.

[65] This petition for appeal also involving a South Carolina case, was written by Alexander Hamilton. *Chester*, 2 Dall. 41, RCA; Julius Goebel, Jr., ed., *The Law Practice of Alexander Hamilton, Documents and Commentary* (2 v., New York, 1964–1969) **2**: pp. 892–903.

[66] *Hope* (*Lopez v. Brooks*), 10 April, 1779, #28; *Lark* (*Jennings v. Taylor*), 28 January, 1780, #36; *George*, #40, RCA.

source of fuller evidence on which to base their decree.[67]
They also issued commissions to state officials to take depositions of various witnesses at a distance from the court.[68]
These commissions generally were limited to a set of interrogatories sent by the court, probably prepared by opposing
counsel. The register of the court could also attest depositions.[69] But the judges of the court had the discretion to
accept or reject depositions taken for the hearing before
them,[70] and, in at least one case, the depositions rejected by
the court below were admitted by the Court of Appeals.[71]
This introduction of new testimony on appeal shows that the
appellate judiciary of Congress, like the Lords Commissioners for Prize Appeals, considered its proceedings a trial *de
novo*, and did not feel constrained by the record of the court
below.

The records do not give much basis for ascertaining the
rules of evidence followed by the judges of appeals. Ordinarily the issue was not raised at all. As we shall see in the next
chapter in the detailed analysis of the case of the brigantine
Lusanna, one attorney arguing before the judges of appeals
thought it appropriate to base part of his oral argument on
Geoffry Gilbert's treatise on the common law rules of evidence, *The Law of Evidence*, published in London in 1754. It
will also be recalled that in one of the first cases appealed to
Congress, the *ad hoc* committee ordered the trial court to
rehear the case and to admit evidence only according to the
common law rules. "That Evidence admissible by the Rules
of the Common Law and no other, be received to support
each Issue: That the Evidence, offered to the Jury, be reduced to Writing, before they retire to give their Verdict,
and in Case of Appeal, transmitted to Congress."[72] The
Court of Appeals, however, did on one occasion state a rule
of evidence derived from the law of nations to be followed in
determining whether a ship was prize or not. In the case of
the ship *Resolution*, one of the few cases in which the judges
articulated the reasons for their determination in a full opinion, the judges stated:

---

[67] E.g., see *Hannah*, #74, RCA.
[68] *Betsey (Olds v. Bradley)*, 21 September, 1783, #71, RCA.
[69] *Hope*, #103, RCA.
[70] *Dolphin* and *Diamond*, #91 & 92, RCA.
[71] *Nonesuch (Garret v. Fellows)*, 13 May, 1783, #94, RCA.
[72] *Vulcan (Ingram v. Joyne)*, 24 January, 1777, #5, RCA.

The national interest of every commercial country requires, that some mode or criterion be adopted to ascertain the ship, cargo, destination, property and nation to which such ship belongs; not only as a security for a fair commerce according to law; but as a guard against fraud and imposition in the payment and collection of duties, imposts and commercial revenues. The peace also and tranquillity of nations equally require, that the like criterion should be adopted, to distinguish the ships of different countries found on the high seas in time of war; to prevent an indiscriminate exercise of acts of hostility, which may lay the foundation of general and universal war. Hence it is, that every commercial country has directed, by its laws, that its ships shall be furnished with a set of papers called ship papers: and this criterion the law of nations adopts, in time of war, to distinguish the property of different powers, when found at sea; not indeed as conclusive, but presumptive evidence only. Bills of lading, letters of correspondence, and all other papers on board, which relate to the ship or cargo, are also considered as *prima facie* evidence of the facts they speak; because such papers naturally accompany such a mercantile transaction.

Such then is the evidence which the law of nations admits on a question of prize or no prize; and it is on this evidence, that vessels with their cargoes are generally acquitted or condemned. And therefore, if, in this case, the papers on board affirm the ship and cargo to be such property as is not prize, there must be an acquittal, unless the captors are able, by a contrariety of evidence, to defeat the presumption which arises from the papers, and can show just grounds for condemnation. On the other hand, if the papers affirm the ship and cargo to be the property of an enemy, there must be a condemnation, unless they who contest the capture can produce clear and unquestionable evidence to prove the contrary.[73]

Probably the judges of appeals, as well as the better-educated state admiralty judges, as occasion offered, blended this accurately stated rule from the law of nations with common law rules of evidence. (In this same case of the ship *Resolution*, as we shall see in the next chapter, the judges of appeals relied in part on the common law principle of possession as good title against all the world, except the right owner, thereby displaying their common law bent.)

As we have seen, the rule of admissible testimony before

---

[73] *Resolution* (*Miller v. Ingersoll*), 25 January, 1782, 2 Dall. 19 at 23.

the Lords Commissioners interpreted the parliamentary prize acts strictly and allowed only the testimony of the key members of the prize vessel's crew. There is no indication that the judges of appeals ever considered such a restriction on the admission of testimony. In many cases the testimony of persons, not members of the prize vessel's crew, was admitted by them without objection.[74]

From what has been said of the process of bringing a prize appeal to the congressional appellate prize court, the similarity with the somewhat amorphous common law appeals within the colonies is apparent. Appeals in prize cases were brought, orally or by simple written notice, without any assignment of errors, except occasional statements of the reasons for appeal in the petitions to Congress. The entire certified record of the trial court (in a few cases referred to as apostles), including depositions, interrogatories, and transcribed in-court testimony, were carried forward for appeal without any order from the appellate court; the appellant apparently had the responsibility to secure the record for the reviewing court, and, it seems, seldom had difficulties obtaining it even if the trial court had denied the appeal; and facts as well as law were subject to review. The intermingling of common law and prize procedures did not seem strange to a judicial system which incorporated jury trials in prize suits.[75]

Besides the full records from the lower court, the judges of appeals also relied on the oral arguments of counsel for both parties. Since many cases involved considerable sums of money, two or three attorneys might represent each party. Though oral arguments were heard in most cases, notes outlining arguments are preserved in only a few. These notes, taken apparently by one of the judges or attorneys, give a brief statement of the arguments used by the attorneys with a marginal notation citing the legal authorities to prove each point. The attorneys referred to the standard English writers discussed in chapter IV: Lee, Beawes, Blackstone, Rutherforth, as well as the continental writers on the law of nations, Vattel, Pufendorf, Grotius, and Burlamaqui.[76] From

---

[74] E.g., *Anna Maria*, #21; *Hope*, #28; *Polly*, #33, and *Fame*, #45, RCA.

[75] For a description of colonial common law appeals, see Goebel, *Antecedents*, pp. 9–49, esp. 25–35.

[76] These notes were preserved in *Lusanna*, #30; *St. Antonio* (*Debadie v. Russell*), 28 May, 1783, #95, and *Chester*, 2 Dall. 41, RCA. These published works are discussed

a study of the citations, it is possible in part to reconstruct the argument as presented to the court. In the next chapter the oral argument, based on the notes from one of these cases and the sources cited there, will be reconstructed to assist in the analysis of the substantive legal questions. In one appeal the records include a written statement of the facts agreed to by the consent of the attorneys for both parties.[77] There is little indication, however, that counsel frequently stipulated the facts.

Congress in 1780 had considered bestowing upon the court the power to fine and imprison for contempt (powers associated in the minds of congressmen with a court of record). In the end, however, Congress failed to grant these coercive powers[78] which the Lords Commissioners regularly exercised. The judges of appeal did issue various rulings, however, which were necessary if the court was to function at all. The boldest order of the Committee on Appeals was the injunction issued in the case of the sloop *Active* commanding the marshal of the Pennsylvania admiralty court to sell the sloop and cargo and to keep custody of the money, awaiting further order of the committee. The results, already discussed at length, showed that the committee did not have the power to back up such an order.[79] Shortly after Congress had reaffirmed the authority of the committee by the resolves of March 6, 1779, the committee did rule that a state admiralty court should send forward a complete record of the case,[80] and remanded another case to the trial court for a definitive sentence,[81] far cries from an injunction against the marshal of a state court. After the Court of Appeals began hearing cases, it continued issuing routine orders but nothing as strong as an injunction except in one case. When execution of the final decree of the court had been frustrated by one party, the court issued an order to apprehend and

---

in chapter V above. For an analysis of another oral argument in a prize appeal, see Henry J. Bourguignon, "Incorporation of the Law of Nations During the American Revolution—The Case of the *San Antonio*," *Amer. Jour. International Law* **71** (1977): pp. 270–295.

[77] *Hawke*, #37, RCA.

[78] Ford, *JCC*, 29 October, 4 December, 1779, 4, 5, 6, 7, 8, 15 January, 1780, **15**: pp. 1220–1223, 1349–1350; **16**: pp. 13–14, 17–19, 22–24, 29, 32, 61–64.

[79] *Active* (*Olmsted v. Houston*), 15 December, 1778, #39, RCA, and chapter III above.

[80] *Bermudas*, #50, RCA.

[81] *Hawke* (*Murphy v. Fisher*), 8 September, 1779, #32, RCA.

arrest the parties guilty of contempt. This case of the brigantine *St. Antonio* will be discussed more fully later in this
chapter as an example of the problems of assuring execution
of the decrees of the court.[82] The effect this writ of attachment achieved is very doubtful. This writ, in the effect it
sought to achieve, if not in its form, resembled the use of
contempt power by the Lords Commissioners to assure
execution of their decrees.

The other orders issued by the Court of Appeals were
more modest in the power they asserted. The court ordered,
for example, that a ship, the subject of an appeal then pending, should be sold because it was in perishing condition.[83]
Here the court adopted ordinary admiralty practice. But
when a party to another case was imprisoned as a British
subject, the court had to ask Congress to have the prisoner
paroled so that he could consult his attorney in preparation
for the appeal. Since the determination of the appeal would
also settle the question whether he was an enemy and should
remain in jail, the court asked Congress for authority to
discharge him finally or remand him into custody, depending on the outcome of the appeal.[84] Without specific authorization of Congress, the court did not have this power.

After a case came before the judges of appeals, therefore,
they made every effort to acquaint themselves with the facts.
They studied the record from the trial court, the file papers
and the depositions sent up to them, and those specially
taken for the hearing on appeal. They also heard the parties
by their counsel, and occasionally granted a motion to continue the proceedings or to suspend execution of its decree
pending rehearing, and undoubtedly other routine motions.[85] But only rarely, if the present records are a reliable
index, did they issue injunctions or writs of attachment for
contempt, and then only under extraordinary circumstances
and with questionable effectiveness. There must have been a
good number of merchants and lawyers during these years,

---

[82] *St. Antonio*, #95, RCA.

[83] *Squirrel (Stoddard v. Read)*, 1 October, 1783, #90, RCA.

[84] *Seahorse (Gardner v. Lynch)*, 14 August, 1780, #64; William Paca and Cyrus
Griffin to Samuel Huntington, President of Congress, 26 June, 1780, PCC, Item 78,
XVIII, 307.

[85] *Two Brothers*, #18; *Liberty*, #105; and *Adventurer*, #106, RCA.

however, who reflected on the need for a truly effective national judiciary with power to reach individuals and to reverse state court judgments.

The final decrees of the Committee on Appeals and the Court of Appeals differ slightly in their style, the former being somewhat wordier. But they ordinarily followed a set form, naming the vessel and parties, the fact of a hearing, the decision to affirm or reverse the sentence of the court below, and the costs assessed to one party. They were not modeled on the decrees of the Lords Commissioners, which were generally an even briefer statement of affirmance or reversal with or without costs. In nine cases the final decree was issued after hearing only one party, but after evidence had been given of sufficient notice to the adverse party. In several of these cases the appellee did not make an appearance and the lower court sentence was reversed with costs to be paid by appellees.[86] There are cases, however, where no one appeared to argue for the appellee, but still the judges affirmed the decree of the lower court, dismissed the appeal, and ordered the appellant to pay costs.[87] In one case the appellant failed to appear, so the committee dismissed his appeal, affirmed the lower court decree, and ordered appellant to pay costs.[88] The Lords Commissioners, as we have seen, occasionally awarded costs and damages, although they apparently did so with some reluctance. The American judges of appeals awarded damages in only one case. It involved the capture of a neutral ship within Spanish waters in the Mississippi while protected by a flag of truce. The Court of Appeals ordered the captors to pay $1,000 damages besides the costs of the trial and appeal. This decree, however, was not executed, which led to the court's issuance of its only writ of attachment for contempt.[89]

The judges of appeals affirmed the lower court decree in about thirty-nine cases, reversed in about forty-nine, in a few cases partly affirmed and partly reversed and dismissed several appeals after a settlement by the parties or their nonappearance. In cases of reversal or altering of the lower court

---

[86] Frank, #11; Charming Sally, #46, and British Goods, #80 & 101, RCA.
[87] Industry, #14; Four Sisters (Robinson v. Rogers), 21 September, 1783, #76, RCA.
[88] Nancy (Babcock v. Bradford), 9 August, 1779, #47, RCA.
[89] St. Antonio, #95, RCA, discussed more fully below.

decree, the Court of Appeals added one phrase to its final decree which the committee had ordinarily not used. The court ordered the state maritime court to "issue all necessary process for carrying into Execution the Decree of this Court."[90] The need for cooperation from the state admiralty courts in executing the appellate decrees had become obvious, especially in the case of the sloop *Active*.

These decrees of the judges of appeals did not ordinarily give the reasons for their decision to affirm or reverse. They merely decreed affirmance or reversal of the lower court, and ordered the ship and cargo to be restored to the appellant, if the lower court sentence had been reversed. But in six of the cases decided by the Court of Appeals, the judges wrote opinions explaining their reasons for the decision. Five of these opinions of the Court have been collected in the second volume of Dallas, *Reports*.[91]

At the very beginning of Congress's involvement with prize appeals in 1776, as discussed in chapter II, there were several cases in which the *ad hoc* committee appointed for each case acted more like a legislative committee than a court. The committees drew up reports which Congress then approved. This procedure did not outlive the brief period of *ad hoc* committees. After those first eight cases, and even in most of them, the Committee on Appeals wrote judicial decrees, not committee reports. But Congress in various ways continued to interact with the committee and the Court of Appeals. Since Congress had placed various restrictions on the right of appeal, it usually had to act upon petitions for hearing where special circumstances had made these limitations an unreasonable burden. In April, 1777, Congress had to intervene also in the case of the brigantine *Sherburne*

---

[90] E.g., *George*, #40, RCA.

[91] *Hope*, #103; *Resolution* (*Miller v. Ingersoll*), 15 August, 1781, and 25 January, 1782, 2 Dall. 1 and 19; *Eersten* (*Darby v. Thompson*), 5 February, 1782, 2 Dall. 34; *Gloucester*, 2 Dall. 36, and *Chester*, 2 Dall. 41, RCA. These five cases with opinions, and two other cases with only decrees were reported in A. J. Dallas, ed., *Reports of Cases Ruled and Adjudged in the Several Courts of the United States and of Pennsylvania*, (4 v., Philadelphia, 1790–1807) **2**: pp. 1–41. Unfortunately the records of five of these cases in the Records of the Court of Appeals are not numbered consecutively with the other cases, but are listed under the reference to the page number in 2 Dall. Other cases, however, as the *Hope* above, are in 2 Dall. but have been numbered in the Records as are all the other cases. There are seven cases in all reported in 2 Dall. from the Court of Appeals. See bibliography for a fuller explanation of the method of citation.

in which the Committee on Appeals had divided equally, three members in favor of affirming and three for reversing the lower court. Congress appointed an *ad hoc* committee of five which affirmed the trial court. But after this decree Congress received a petition from the captain of the *Sherburne,* a British whaling vessel which had been awarded as a prize. He asked Congress to revise the decree of the committee so as to allow the seamen on the vessel a share of the profits of the voyage as their wages. It had been a policy of Congress to grant to seamen of prize ships their wages to the time of capture, but the committee had made no such allowance in this case. The response of Congress is very significant as an expression of the basic policy toward the decrees of the judges of appeals. Congress would not act as a super-court to revise the decrees of the committee it had established. On recommendation of the Marine Committee, Congress decided:

> That the matter on which the petitioners pray to be relieved, depends on the construction of promulgated resolutions of Congress, which make part of the code of the laws of maritime war; which laws ought to be construed and applied by the courts of admiralty and commissioners of appeals in their judicial capacity, and not by Congress: That the case of the *Sherburne* having already received a judicial determination before the said courts, where the parties had an opportunity of availing themselves of the full effects of the said laws, it is improper for the Congress to come to any resolution relative thereto.[92]

This policy of refusing to review the decrees of the judges of appeals remained constant through the entire period of the Continental Congress. In 1783 Congress again stated that the final decree in all cases of prize appeals rested with the Court of Appeals, over which Congress had no control except to remove the judges for corruption or misdemeanor.[93] Perhaps the lessons of the *Active* case had taught Congress the wisdom of minimal involvement in settling prize disputes. Or perhaps implicit in the refusal of Congress to intervene in judicial matters was the unspoken doctrine of

---

[92] *Sherburne,* #10, RCA, and Ford, *JCC* **7**: pp. 259–260; **8**: pp. 383–384.

[93] *St. Antonio,* #95, RCA, and Ford, *JCC* **25**: pp. 546–548; **21**: pp. 1170–1171, where Congress also refused to interfere with the judges of appeals acting in their judicial capacity.

the separation of powers, the widely proclaimed principle of good government accepted by so many Americans of that period.[94] Although Congress measured carefully the powers it gave to the Court of Appeals, it did not try to interfere with the court's exercise of properly judicial powers.

Congress did consider petitions for hearings on appeal and also petitions for rehearings. But it was reluctant to grant any exceptions to its own resolves. In a case where the appeal had been lodged with the court after the time limit due to negligence of the party, Congress refused to allow an appeal outside the explicit scope of the law, even though the French counsul at Boston, Joseph de Valnais, had been the negligent party. Congress in rejecting this petition pointed out the difficulties arising from granting any exceptions to the laws in particular cases.[95] The closest Congress came to any interference with the decrees of the court was in a case involving a captured Prussian ship, the *Minerva*. The trial court had declared it not a lawful prize, and the Court of Appeals had affirmed this sentence but awarded special costs to the captors amounting to £680 Massachusetts currency. Congress received a memorial complaining of this large award, referred the memorial to the court, and ordered the judges to report to it the proceedings, proofs, and judgment in this case. Apparently the judges ignored the order, for a year later Congress received another complaint from the neutral party. This time Congress referred the memorial to John Jay, secretary for foreign affairs, who proposed that Congress should inquire whether the judges had ever received its previous order. If they had, Congress should schedule a hearing for the judges to explain why they had not obeyed it.[96] There is no further indication of any action on Jay's suggestion.

The appellate prize court set up by Congress had begun its eleven-year life quite unsure of its own role, but ended with considerable judicial independence. Congress might exert a little pressure on the court in an important case involving a neutral ship, but the ordinary policy of noninterference with judicial decrees clearly set the pattern for the period.

---

[94] Wood, *American Republic*, pp. 446–453.
[95] *Mars (Mitchell v. de Valnais)*, 1781, #78, RCA; Ford, *JCC* 22: p. 43, and PCC, Item 41, X, 589.
[96] *Minerva (Derby v. Koler)*, 27 May, 1783, #96, RCA; Ford, *JCC* 26: p. 12; 29: p. 661, and PCC, Item 41, IV, 119; VI, 412.

Even after the final decree of the committee or the Court of Appeals, the case was usually not completed. Two further problems could still confront the judges of appeals in cases in which they had already issued a decree. A number of petitions for rehearings came to the judges of appeals, and then there was the more serious problem of execution by the state admiralty court of the final appellate decree. From the English records consulted, it does not appear that the Lords Commissioners for Prize Appeals ever reheard a case, but perhaps further study would reveal occasional rehearings. At least, they must have been infrequent. Some of the complex problems facing the Lords Commissioners in obtaining execution of their decrees (especially in the colonies) were suggested in chapter IV. But the Lords Commissioners had at their command far greater and more effective coercive power than the American judges of appeals ever enjoyed.

The principal case which raised the question of the authority of the Court of Appeals to rehear cases already decided by them involved the ship *Resolution*. The ship was Dutch property, sailing in March, 1781, from the Island of Dominica, formerly British but recently captured by the French. The British citizens of the island had been made secure in possession of their property by their capitulation. The cargo on the *Resolution* was the property of some of these capitulants shipped to Amsterdam and consigned to the Dutch owners of the vessel. On the voyage to Amsterdam the ship was three times captured by the British, once released, but twice taken from the British by Americans. The American privateer brigantine *Ariel* finally brought the *Resolution* into Philadelphia where the ship and cargo were libeled as lawful prize. After careful study of the case the admiralty judge, in a well-reasoned opinion, declared the cargo lawful prize to the libelants but restored the ship to the Dutch owners. Both parties appealed this decree to the Court of Appeals. On August 15, 1781, the court, writing a long opinion to explain its decree, affirmed the lower court's judgment restoring the ship to its original owners but reversed that part dealing with the cargo. The judges restored the cargo to the party who claimed it for the original shippers. Immediately after this decree counsel for the captors, James Wilson and Gouverneur Morris, requested a new hearing on the grounds that they had discovered new evidence. The Court of Appeals issued an order to the Pennsylvania admiralty court staying its previous decree till it gave further order. The libelants, according to this interlocutory decree, had to give security within three days to pay all costs and charges occasioned by the stay if the rehearing should not be granted or their decree should not be reversed. The claimants were ordered to show cause at the next session of the Court of Appeals why the rehearing should not be granted. William Paca and Cyrus Griffin, the judges, both signed this order. Paca also sent an undated note to the admiralty judge stating that he and Griffin thought the appellate decree might be executed as it stood. The cargo should be delivered to the claimant, provided he had given security and his bond was lodged in the Court of Appeals. Paca concluded the note, "at a future Day we will make some Rules with regard to Orders of this Nature," an ambitious promise that never materialized, but which does suggest that the appellate judges thought they had the authority to supervise the trial prize courts in the execution of appellate decrees.

The Court of Appeals took depositions in the case during December and January, and on January 25, 1782, issued another decree, again accompanied by a lengthy opinion. As to the ship, the judges discharged their stay order and affirmed their first decree restoring it to the Dutch owners. The libelant was to pay the costs of the rehearing. But from a careful analysis of the new evidence the Court now awarded a large part of the cargo as lawful prize to the captors.[97]

At this point, after the second hearing and decree, Robert R. Livingston, the secretary for foreign affairs, forwarded to Congress letters and documents showing the concern of Anne Caesar Chevalier de la Luzerne, the French minister to America, over the decree of the Court of Appeals.[98] Livingston, who had been Luzerne's personal choice for secretary and remained firmly loyal to the French alliance, urged Congress to press the court for a rehearing of the case. The committee appointed to report on these letters recommended that the proceedings in this case and also in the

---

[97] *Resolution*, 2 Dall. 1 and 19, RCA; Admiralty Court Papers and Nicholls Collection, Court of Admiralty Papers (HSP).

[98] Luzerne to Livingston, 18 February, 1782; Bouillé to Luzerne, n.d.; Memorial of the Council of Dominica; Livingston to Luzerne, 20 February, 1782, and Livingston to President of Congress, 21 February, 1782, Wharton, *Diplomatic Correspondence* 5: pp. 176–179, 190–192.

companion case of the brigantine *Eersten* should be suspended till further orders from the judges of the Court of Appeals, who were not then sitting, and from the state admiralty court judges. Congress passed this resolve and also gave one judge of the Court of Appeals power to stay execution of any decree as long as necessary, but not after the first day of their next session. The initial committee report, reiterating the general policy of Congress, had stated, "that the United States in Congress assembled, have not by [article nine] or any other article of confederation any judicial, but only a Legislative authority in causes of prize." There is no indication of any further action by either party in the case of the *Resolution*. After Yorktown many Americans felt considerably less dependent on the French; thus Luzerne's influence waned.[99]

The Committee on Appeals had never granted a rehearing, except in the early case where the wrong *ad hoc* committee had heard the appeal.[100] The committee did reject a petition for a rehearing, stating that the reasons given in the petition were insufficient in law to justify a new trial.[101] But apparently the committee did not think that granting a rehearing would be completely beyond the scope of its power.

The Court of Appeals, six months after its final action in the *Resolution* case, did grant a rehearing of a case previously heard and determined by the Committee on Appeals in 1779. The appellees petitioning for a rehearing complained that they had not received sufficient notice of the original appeal and therefore had not appeared. The Court in August, 1782, granted the petition, and after hearing both parties and reviewing the entire record, dismissed the original appeal and affirmed the sentence of the state admiralty court which the committee had reversed. The appellant had to pay all costs of appeal and rehearing.[102] The Court of Appeals in another case, on motion of petitioner, suspended the execution of its decree of August, 1781. Three years later

---

[99] Ford, *JCC*, 7 March, 1782, **22:** pp. 116–118, and PCC, Item 25, II, 85, 87, 89; Item 45, 421; Item 59, 285; *Eersten*, 2 Dall. 34, RCA. William C. Stinchcombe, *The American Revolution and the French Alliance* (Syracuse, 1969), pp. 183–195.

[100] *Phoenix* (*Darrell v. Peirce*), 3 September, 1777, #8 & 19, RCA.

[101] *Hope*, #28, RCA, and James Wilson [counsel] to Aaron Lopez, 22 February, 1780, telling his client of the committee's refusal to grant a rehearing, Dreer Collection (HSP).

[102] *Two Brothers*, #18, RCA.

it reheard the case and revised its first decree in light of new evidence then submitted.[103]

Two important cases came at the same time before Congress and the court for rehearings, namely the case of the sloop *Hannah*, decided on appeal in August, 1781, and the case of the brigantine *Eersten*, decided in February, 1782. In both cases the party losing on appeal petitioned the court for a rehearing alleging that new evidence had been discovered which warranted a new trial. The court refused to grant rehearings in either case. Both petitioners got the impression that the judges thought they did not have power, without authorization of Congress, to rehear cases they had once determined. (Since the court had previously reheard two cases on its own authority, the judges probably had no such doubts about their power.) In March, 1782, the court did order the suspension of execution of its previous decree in the case of the *Eersten*. In both cases the petitioners turned to Congress, asking the members to grant the court authority to rehear their cases. Since the *Eersten* was claimed as neutral property, John Jay, secretary of foreign affairs, also wrote Congress, urging it to grant a rehearing in this and other cases. In April, 1785, the committee appointed to study the two petitions reported a resolution, in terms suggested by Jay, that the Court of Appeals should be authorized in these two cases and in every other case before it to grant a rehearing whenever in its opinion justice might require. The resolves, approved by Congress, further provided that an order for a rehearing should in no case suspend the execution of the first decree, if the party in whose favor the first decree had been granted gave sufficient security to pay damages and costs in case the first decree should be reversed on rehearing. After all this, however, the court refused to rehear either case. No reason explained the refusal in the *Hannah* case, but in the case of the *Eersten* the judges, in May, 1787, found that the petitioners had been culpably negligent of not giving notice to the adverse party of the suspension of execution they had ordered in March, 1782. Without this notice the other party had proceeded to sell the *Eersten* and its cargo and distribute the money to all parties involved in the capture. The judges, therefore, refused to rehear a case

---

[103] *Adventurer*, #106, RCA.

five years after they had decreed the ship and cargo lawful prize to the captors.[104]

These cases of rehearings show the judicial independence of the Court of Appeals. The judges at times granted rehearings and reversed former decrees on their own authority, but when Congress obviously wanted them to rehear cases involving neutral property, they could in some instances reject the petitions for rehearings. They apparently granted rehearings according to the merits of the petition, though with a strong inclination against reopening a case.

One final phase remains to be discussed to complete the picture of the procedure of the Committee on Appeals and the Court of Appeals. After the final decree on appeal, the successful party had to secure its execution. This extremely important stage of appellate practice completes the whole process of appeals, hearings, decrees, and rehearings which would be little more than a game if the litigant ended up with merely a paper telling him he had prevailed on appeal. Unless the state admiralty courts regularly executed the decrees of the judges of appeals, the entire effort of prosecuting an appeal would be futile. Unfortunately the loss of most records from the state admiralty courts makes it impossible to analyze this facet of appellate procedure with full satisfaction. Furthermore the argument from silence does not carry the weight it might in other facets of the procedural spectrum. Since all indications point to the substantial integrity of the records of the Court of Appeals, it is highly unlikely that the judges were frequently issuing injunctions or contempt citations, for instance, when the records leave trace of only one injunction and one writ of attachment for contempt. But if a litigant presented a decree of the court to the local admiralty judge, only to have it ignored, it is not clear that he would always retrace his steps to Philadelphia for another piece of paper, perhaps just as meaningless. So it is possible that no records remain from a number of cases in which the appellate decree could not be put into effect. With this initial *caveat* the evidence that does remain from the state courts and the Court of Appeals can be properly assessed.

Some evidence indicates that the admiralty courts, in some

---

[104] *Hannah*, #74; *Eersten*, 2 Dall. 34, RCA, and Ford, *JCC* **28**: pp. 209, 230, 413–414.

states at least, executed the decrees of the judges of appeals as a matter of course. For instance, James Wilson, a lawyer who often represented parties before the judges of appeals and had been a member of the Committee on Appeals in some early cases, wrote a letter in 1780 to Aaron Lopez, a client. The Court of Appeals had just heard, debated, and dismissed a petition for a rehearing in the case. In the original hearing the court had reversed the Connecticut admiralty court and restored the ship and cargo to Lopez. Wilson, after the dismissal of the adverse party's petition for a rehearing, warned Lopez that some efforts might be taken in Connecticut to prevent him from obtaining the full effect of the decree of the Court of Appeals. If this should be the case, Wilson wanted to be informed so he could let Congress know of the difficulties. Wilson concluded by telling his client how to obtain execution, apparently the ordinary procedure followed. He promised Lopez an authenticated copy of the decree of the court. This should be presented by Wilson or by Lopez himself to the Connecticut maritime court with a motion that the decree of the Court of Appeals be carried into effect.[105] This procedure closely followed the ordinary mode of obtaining execution of the decrees of the Lords Commissioners for Prize Appeals.

In an earlier case from Pennsylvania a bill of costs shows an entry for receiving, reading, and filing a decree of the Committee on Appeals. But in this case the sentence of the Pennsylvania admiralty court had been affirmed, so there would be little resistance expected from the admiralty judge.[106] In another Pennsylvania case there is a writ from the admiralty judge, ordering the marshal to carry the original decree of that court into execution, but stating that the appeal granted in the case had been dismissed and the admiralty court sentence affirmed by the commissioners of Congress.[107]

[105] Wilson to Lopez, 22 February, 1780, Dreer Collection (HSP). This letter dealt with *Hope*, #28, rehearing rejected 19 February, 1780, RCA. The case of the *George*, #40, RCA, also shows that the successful party on appeal ordinarily moved in the state admiralty court for execution of the decree of the Court of Appeals. In the case of the *George*, no measures were ever taken to enforce the decree of the Court of Appeals restoring the sloop and cargo to its owner, Jennings from St. Eustatia. In 1790 Jennings tried in the Federal Courts to have the sloop restored, but was ultimately unsuccessful. *Jennings v. Carson*, 4 Cranch 2 (1807).

[106] *Sherburne*, #10, RCA, and bill of costs, n.d., Admiralty Court Papers (HSP).
[107] *Polly*, #33, RCA, and Admiralty Court Records (HSP).

In North Carolina a petition came to the governor from the successful party to an appeal with the complaint that the admiralty judge had defected to the British leaving the office vacant. Therefore the decree of the Court of Appeals could not be executed or enforced.[108] This again indicates that the usual procedure was to present the appellate decree to the state admiralty court and move its execution.

Two Connecticut cases perhaps best illustrate the ordinary course of procedure, as well as the pitfalls, in obtaining execution of a decree of the Court of Appeals. In both cases the extant records include the written motion for execution, a certified copy of the decree of the Court of Appeals, and the order of the admiralty court on the motion. In one case the state court had originally granted the appeal, the Court of Appeals had reversed, and the state court, on motion, ordered full execution of the appellate court decree.[109] The other case, however, coming back to the same court a year earlier, had involved an appeal on petition. The state maritime court had refused to grant the appeal because of the state law (the Connecticut law forbidding appeals in cases of seizure of goods illegally imported into the state from Long Island). So when the Court of Appeals, on petition, heard the case and reversed the lower court sentence (thereby treating the case as one of prize, not illegal importation), the successful party returned to move that the maritime court issue all necessary process to carry the appellate decree into execution. But the maritime court refused to grant the motion. The judge stated that he did not have the power, consistent with the laws of the state, to issue any process to carry the decree of the Court of Appeals into execution.[110] There is no record of what further steps, if any, the party took to have the decree executed. Apparently he did not return to the Court of Appeals or to Congress.

Problems of execution arose in two cases decided on appeal about the same time and involving the same party as

[108] Petition to Governor Thomas Burke from Marshal Bostair, n.d., Clark, *Records of North Carolina* **16:** p. 220. This refers to *Adventurer*, #106, RCA.

[109] *British Goods* (*Hart v. Foster*), 21 September, 1783, #82, RCA, and order of state court dated, 18 June, 1784, New London County Maritime Court Files (CSL).

[110] *Sally*, #84, RCA, and order of state court, 25 June, 1783, New London County Maritime Court Files (CSL). See also Connecticut session laws, May session, 1780, 553–557 and November session, 1780, 563; Governor Trumbull (of Connecticut) to the President of Congress, 24 April, 1782, PCC, Item 66, II, 218.

appellee. One case originally had been decided in the Rhode Island admiralty court in favor of Samuel Champlin, the claimant. In August, 1779, the Committee on Appeals reversed. Apparently the successful appellant could not secure execution against Champlin and the other claimants. The appellate records include a writ of attachment against Champlin and others, issued by the court of common pleas of South Kingston, Rhode Island, in an action of trover and conversion of certain goods, not specified, belonging to the plaintiff, to the value of £500,000. The return of the writ shows that the sheriff attached a ship, not the one originally in dispute, belonging to one of the defendants. Several years later Champlin got a rehearing of the case before the Court of Appeals on the grounds that he had not received sufficient notice of the original hearing on appeal. The court reversed the prior decree and restored the prize to Champlin and the other claimants.[111] The fate of the suit in the common law court remains unknown. This case, though quite unclear in the records, does suggest that litigants might turn to the common law courts in a *quasi in rem* proceeding to attempt to have the captured property or its value restored, even after a decree of the judges of appeals had awarded it to them. Such an action at common law would be unnecessary if the decree of the appellate court were fully executed in admiralty.

Samuel Champlin was also party to an appeal taken from a judgment of the admiralty court of North Carolina. In September, 1779, the Committee on Appeals reversed the lower court sentence and restored the ship and cargo to the claim-

---

[111] *Two Brothers*, #18, RCA. Further records from the suit at common law could not be located. An action of trover could be brought where there was alleged a finding of plaintiff's property by the defendant, even though the finding, as in this case, was fictitious. The action further had to allege that the defendant had converted plaintiff's property to his own use. Plaintiff could recover damages. An eighteenth-century law dictionary defined trover and stated the reasons why it was preferred to the older action of detinue: "An action of trover lies wherever one man, who came to the possession of any of the goods of another by actual finding, does convert the same: And an action of trover does likewise lie wherever one man, who came to the possession of any of the goods of another by delivery, does convert the same; for altho' there be not in this case an actual finding, there is such a finding in law as is sufficient to found this action upon. . . . It is in the general true, that where an action of trover lies, an action of *detinue* does also lie; but the latter action is very seldom brought, because the defendant therein may wage his law . . . [and because] in the latter, the plaintiff can only recover the goods in specie, whereas in the former he may recover damages for the conversion thereof." T. Cunningham, *A New and Complete Law Dictionary* (2 v., London, 1764–1765) **2:** no page numbers.

ant. Here again Champlin had been appellee and had lost his case on appeal. But the party who prevailed on appeal could not get Champlin to abide by the Committee's decree. When Champlin was personally served with a copy of the decree, he refused to comply with its order. There is no known record of any attempt to secure execution by any state court, perhaps because the original admiralty court in North Carolina had no jurisdiction over Champlin or his property in Connecticut. The other party therefore returned to the Court of Appeals several years later and narrated on oath before Judge Griffin his efforts to get Champlin to comply. But there are no further records of the case.[112]

Appeals from Massachusetts presented special problems for execution. Even after the legislature had changed the law to allow appeals to Congress in cases of ships claimed by friendly foreign nations, there still remained doubt whether the state maritime courts could execute the appellate decrees in such cases. Three cases from Massachusetts had been decided by the Committee on Appeals in November, 1779. All three involved vessels and cargoes claimed as Spanish property. The committee partially or completely reversed the state court in all three cases. But John Holker, a French consul and marine agent in Pennsylvania, had to present a special petition on behalf of the Spanish claimants to ask the state legislature to authorize the maritime court to carry these decrees into effect. The legislature served notice on the three captors to show cause why the petition should not be granted.[113] Since no further records of two of the cases could be found, presumably the maritime courts were given power to execute the decrees of the judges of appeals. In the third case, however, a petition came to Congress in August 1780 from Holker who claimed to be legal representative and agent of the Spanish owners of the captured brigantine *Santander y los Santos Martires*. He alleged that the parties who had originally claimed the brig for the Spanish owners, and to whom the property was restored by the Committee on Appeals, did not have proper power of attorney, but

---

[112] *Sally*, Miscellaneous Case Papers, RCA.

[113] *Acts and Resolves of Massachusetts*, 18 September, 1780, **21**: pp. 604–605; *Nuestra Senora de Merced (Cabot v. Sagarra)*, 6 November, 1779, #57; *Valenciano (Luca v. Cleveland)*, 1 November, 1779, #58, and *Santander y los Santos Martires (Tracy v. de Llano)*, 6 November, 1779, #60, RCA.

nonetheless had gotten possession of the cargo. Holker had brought suit both in the state admiralty court and at common law in an action of trover. The common law court refused to recognize him as legal representative and the admiralty court claimed that its jurisdiction did not extend to the case. Nevertheless Congress assured Holker that the Massachusetts courts were adequate to provide justice and transmitted his petition to the state requesting the executive to take immediate and effective measures to ensure speedy justice to the parties concerned.[114] Again the records consulted do not tell of the further steps, if any, taken in the case. Congress gave its assurances to Holker and urged Massachusetts to provide justice. Congress's hollow words, in fact, were confessions of the inadequacy of its power to settle finally and effectively all prize appeals.

The Portuguese schooner *Nostra Seigniora da Solidade e St. Miguel e Almas* had been captured by the American privateer schooner *Sally* in October, 1781. The *Nostra Seigniora* was brought to Massachusetts and sold, along with its cargo, even before George Randall, master of the *Sally*, had libeled the schooner and cargo as British property. About a month after Randall had libeled the prize in the Massachusetts maritime court, the Portuguese parties brought two suits in the court of common pleas of the state against the captors for trover and conversion of the ship and cargo. But when these actions came to trial, the plaintiffs did not appear, so the judgment went for the captors by default. Vincenti Doo, master of the *Nostra Seigniora*, had in the meantime filed a claim in the maritime court for the schooner and cargo as Portuguese property, not liable to forfeiture. After a full trial in the maritime court, the jury's verdict restored the schooner to Doo but awarded the cargo as lawful prize to Randall and those for whom he had libeled. Both parties appealed to Congress. The Court of Appeals in May, 1783, decreed that the schooner and all the cargo should be restored to Doo and that Randall should pay costs of the appeal. But apparently Doo was still not able to get possession of the schooner or the value of the cargo. In July, 1783, he began another action in the Massachusetts common law court against the captors on a writ of trover and conversion, claiming damages of £10,000

---

[114] PCC, Item 41, IV, 127, and Ford, *JCC* 18: pp. 933–934.

due to the loss of the *Nostra Seigniora* and its cargo. Along
with various depositions, Doo presented a copy of the decree
of the Court of Appeals as part of his case at common law.
But the jury in the court of common pleas returned a verdict
that Randall and the other captors were not guilty. Doo
appealed to the Massachusetts superior court where he presented more depositions for the trial on appeal. At the February, 1784, term the jury of the superior court found Randall and the other captors guilty and assessed damages for
the appellant of £2,880. s9. d6. Randall moved for a review of
the case and gave bond, but the records do not indicate any
further proceedings.[115] Apparently only by this common law
suit could Doo obtain partial restoration of the value of his
captured property which the Court of Appeals had previously decreed.

A few words of background will be helpful in discussing
the next Massachusetts case. It will be remembered that the
Spanish at the time of the Revolution controlled the Louisiana territory at the mouth of the Mississippi. In spite of all
American diplomatic efforts to establish the principle of free
navigation of the Mississippi, Spain remained adamant in
insisting on control of both banks of the river, at least to the
thirty-first parallel. During the war a Spanish garrison captured the British positions in West Florida at Mobile and
Pensacola. The Spaniards had angered many Americans
when, on capturing Pensacola, they allowed the British garrison to proceed to New York where it reinforced the British
troops.[116] The case of the *St. Antonio* unfolded in this context
of Spanish control of the lower Mississippi.

The Spanish brigantine *St. Antonio* had been seized below
New Orleans in November, 1782, by the American privateer
brigantine *Patty*. William Hayden, commander of the *Patty*,
had the prize brought to Boston, where he and the owners of
the privateer libeled it as British property captured on the
high seas that had been employed in shipping British cargo
even though sailing under a flag of truce. The captors alleged that the *St. Antonio* was carrying on an illicit and contraband trade and had false and double papers on board.
Pierre Debadie, commander of the *St. Antonio*, claimed the

[115] *Nostra Seigniora da Solidade e St. Miguel e Almas (Randall v. Doo)*, 29 May, 1783,
#88, RCA; Court Files Suffolk, #103371, and Suffolk Minute Book (MSJC).
[116] Morris, *Peacemakers*, pp. 219–222, 241; Marks, *Independence on Trial*, pp. 21–33.

ship and cargo in the Massachusetts maritime court. He
alleged that the ship had been captured within the territorial
jurisdiction of Spain in the Mississippi River, not on the high
seas, and that the ship and cargo were the property of
Spanish subjects, not liable to forfeiture. (Capture of neutral
vessels, unless carrying contraband, or of any vessels within
neutral waters, was strictly forbidden by Congress to American privateers.)[117]

The *St. Antonio* had been freighted to certain British subjects of Pensacola in the province of West Florida who had
surrendered to the Spanish. Pursuant to their capitulation
agreement, they had chartered the *St. Antonio* to transport
themselves and their property, under flag of truce, from
West Florida to Great Britain. At the time of capture the brig
was returning from Great Britain, still under flag of truce, to
New Orleans with a cargo belonging to Spanish subjects, not
contraband, nor destined for the use of the British. Don Juan
Francisco Rendon, *chargé d'affaires* of Spain in the United
States also filed a claim on behalf of the Spanish king alleging
that the brig had been taken within the dominion and jurisdiction of Spain. After trial in the maritime court, the jury in
Massachusetts returned a verdict that the *St. Antonio* was the
property of British subjects and was employed in carrying on
an illicit and contraband trade with the British. The judge
therefore awarded the brig and cargo to the captors. (Here
was a glaring example justifying the fears that local juries in
admiralty cases could involve the United States in serious
international incidents.) After the maritime court in April,
1783, had ordered the prize sold for the use of the captors,
Debadie appealed to Congress. Luzerne, the French minister
to the United States had, prior to the maritime court verdict,
forwarded to the secretary for foreign affairs two letters
from Spanish officials in New Orleans giving the details of
the capture. Congress reviewed these letters and resolved
that the proper mode for the owners of the captured brig to
obtain redress for the "criminal contempt of public faith and
a violation of the law of Nations alledged to have been committed" by the captors, was to prosecute the case by due

---

[117] Ford, *JCC* 11: p. 486; 18: pp. 864–866, 905–906, 1008, 1097–1098; PCC, Item
37, 233–238. Of course, at the time of capture, Spain was at war with Great Britain,
though no alliance existed between Spain and America. The Spanish claimants
contended that Spain was neutral *vis-à-vis* the United States. *St. Antonio*, #45, RCA.

course of law. Congress wrote to the Governor of Massachusetts sending along copies of the various documents received and asking him to assist the Spanish parties to obtain full satisfaction in the Massachusetts courts. Perhaps this letter did not arrive before the decree of the maritime court.

The Court of Appeals promptly reviewed the facts of the case, heard the oral arguments, and entered a decree on May 28, 1783, that the sentence of the maritime court should be reversed and the *St. Antonio* and its cargo should be restored to Debadie, the claimant. The court also ordered the captors to pay the costs of the maritime court as well as the appeal, and the captors were assessed $1,000 as damages for the capture and detention of the vessel and cargo. As already mentioned, this was the only case in which the judges of appeals awarded damages. (It will be recalled that the Lords Commissioners occasionally awarded damages for an illegal capture made without probable cause.) It is impossible to measure the extent of Luzerne's influence on the court. Two years earlier, during the desperate months before Yorktown when Congress looked to Luzerne and the French for survival, a word from the French minister might have swayed the court's judgment. There is adequate basis in the record, however, even without Luzerne's intervention, to explain the court's action. Although Americans by May, 1783, were still elated at the news of the preliminary peace treaty and felt less dependence on the French, the court and Congress could not well ignore the serious allegations of violations of neutral rights.

A month after the decree of the Court of Appeals the captors sent a petition to Congress arguing that they had captured the prize on the high seas, not within the jurisdiction of Spain. They objected to having the verdict of a jury set aside by two judges of the Court of Appeals and claimed that their case was prejudiced before these judges by the letters from the Spanish officials of New Orleans who had accused the captors of piratical conduct. Furthermore, the judges had exceeded their authority by decreeing damages, which had never come before them on argument and which were not even hinted at during the entire hearing. The captors therefore asked Congress for a rehearing of their case to give them a chance to defend their actions free from all charges that might bias the minds of their judges.

While Congress pondered this petition, the Court of Appeals, in July, 1783, received a complaint from Debadie that the captors had refused to obey the decree of the court. The judges therefore issued a writ of attachment, ordering the owners of the *Patty* to be apprehended and brought before the court to answer for their trespass and contempt. During the summer of 1783, Francisco Rendon and the owner of the *St. Antonio* again wrote Congress complaining of the refusal of the captors to comply with the decree of the Court of Appeals. (The Lords Commissioners, it will be recalled, often used their contempt powers to assure the effectiveness of their decrees.)

Congress appointed a committee to review the letters and the petition it had received from both parties. The committee reported that the captors' complaints of irregular proceedings by the Court of Appeals had no substantiating evidence. After stating that the committee believed Congress had no judicial power in any prize appeal, it concluded that the final decision in all cases of capture rested with the Court of Appeals over which Congress had no control except to remove the judges for corruption or misdemeanor. Congress, therefore, recommended that the executive of Massachusetts give such assistance as necessary to obtain due execution of the decree of the Court of Appeals.[118] Once again Congress, by this recommendation, had to implicitly admit its impotence to assure full justice in prize cases without the free cooperation of the states—and cooperation of the states was never an item in abundance. But Congress, in this action, did not object to the court's assessment of damages or issuance of a writ of attachment.

During that same summer of 1783 Andrew Dumont, captain of the *St. Antonio*, brought an action for trover and conversion of his personal property taken from the ship by the captors. In the court of common pleas in Massachusetts the verdict went for Dumont, but the captors appealed to the superior court, and after several continuances, obtained a verdict in their favor. So Dumont's efforts to obtain £700 for the loss of his personal property met only with failure after a lengthy legal struggle.[119] The records consulted fail to

---

[118] *St. Antonio*, #95, RCA; Ford, *JCC* **24:** pp. 386–387; **25:** pp. 546–548, and PCC, Item 19, V, 267; Item 42, VII, 165–168; Item 78, XIX, 443–453.

[119] Court Files Suffolk, #104090, and Suffolk Minute Book, February, 1786, term, (MSJC).

tell whether the owners of the *St. Antonio* ever obtained full compliance with the decree of the Court of Appeals.

Another neutral ship, the *Minerva*, had been captured and brought into Massachusetts to be libeled. Elias Haskett Derby, a well-known merchant of Salem, owned the *Grand Turk* which had seized the *Minerva*. Jochem Koler, commander of the prize ship, filed a claim to the ship and cargo as belonging to subjects of the king of Prussia and other states, all neutrals. The jury in the trial court found that Derby had not proved his libel, so the *Minerva* and cargo were restored to the claimant. Derby appealed to the Court of Appeals, but in May, 1783, the court affirmed the decree of the maritime court. Since the *Minerva* at the time of capture by the *Grand Turk* had been in the hands of British captors, the Court of Appeals ordered that Koler should pay court costs and all costs of the safe-keeping of the *Minerva*. This was not considered a case of recapture requiring salvage because the ship was not American property and perhaps also because the British court could not have decreed this neutral vessel as lawful prize to British captors. But nevertheless the American captors had taken the vessel out of British hands, thereby meriting in the eyes of the court at least the payment of the costs of the American privateers. The Prussian owners were outraged by the costs assessed at £680 Massachusetts currency. In July, 1783, Koler brought an action against Derby in the court of common pleas in Massachusetts for the loss of the *Minerva* and its cargo. Koler claimed damage to the extent of £1,000. Apparently Koler's suit was only for damage caused by the captors to the rigging and cargo. This complaint at common law, however, does have the appearance of a suit to offset the special costs assessed by the Court of Appeals. The common law court found Derby not guilty, and on appeal to the superior court, Derby was again found not guilty.[120] Apparently the Prussian owners did have to pay the special costs before obtaining restitution of the *Minerva* and its cargo.

These various cases dealing in one way or another with the problem of execution of the decrees of the judges of appeals show that merely obtaining a favorable decree from the Court of Appeals did not end all disputes. In some cases,

---

[120] Court Files Suffolk, #103389, and Suffolk Minute Book, February, 1784, term, *ibid.*, and *Minerva*, #96, RCA.

probably the largest number, the appellate decree could be presented to the state admiralty court, and the court would grant a motion to carry it into effect. But at least one maritime court in Connecticut refused to execute a decree. It had previously refused to grant the appeal as against the state law, so it accepted the logic of the situation and refused to take any steps to execute the appellate decree as beyond the power granted by state law. The same question was raised in Massachusetts by a petition to the legislature requesting that it grant the maritime courts power to execute the decrees of the Court of Appeals in three cases. These cases recall the difficulties encountered by Congress in the cases of the sloop *Active* and the brigantine *Lusanna* (the latter to be discussed in chapters VII and VIII.) Without voluntary cooperation of the states, which perhaps occurred in most cases, the judges of appeals had few resources to guarantee enforcement of their decrees. Whereas the Lords Commissioners had behind them the elaborate machinery of an efficient government to assure the execution of their decrees (at least in Great Britain), the judges of appeals could only look to Congress, which was at times all but submerged by its own insoluble problems.

In several Massachusetts cases involving neutral property, the foreign litigant had to turn to the common law courts to obtain full justice. At least in one case involving the schooner *Nostra Seigniora da Solidade*, the suit in the common law court appears to have been an attempt to secure in fact what had been awarded on paper by the Court of Appeals.

These details give a picture of how the Court of Appeals functioned. With the exception of a few early cases, the committee and the court were clearly judicial institutions and, within the narrow scope of the authority Congress gave them, the judges decided the cases independent of any outside influences. Though the relationship with Congress remained necessarily close, Congress did not attempt to exercise any judicial power to revise the decrees of the judges of appeals. Of course, Congress showed an understandable sensitivity about cases of neutral ships captured by Americans. Many complaints came to Congress from foreign governments. But the court was allowed to handle each case on its own merits. Whether this refusal of Congress to interfere with the judicial determinations of its judges of appeals was due to a philosophical commitment to the principle of the separation of powers, or to a deep unspoken awareness of Congress of its own inadequacies in solving such problems, or to a recollection of Congress of its impotence in trying to settle such cases as the sloop *Active,* is difficult to say. Cowardice and wisdom can easily be confused.

The various state admiralty courts, as we have seen, closely resembled their colonial vice-admiralty predecessors in many procedural details. The procedures for appeal to the congressional judges of appeals, however, resembled the procedures before the Lords Commissioners for Prize Appeals only in the most general sense. This is not surprising since American lawyers must have known very little of the work of the Lords Commissioners. Perhaps the lawyers and lawmakers who set up the congressional appellate jurisdiction were thinking in terms of appellate practice before the various colonial common law courts when they incorporated some of the procedures and practices for appellate prize cases. But they probably read and tried to adapt to American needs the vague and inadequate descriptions of the Lords Commissioners' court found in the few published sources available.

The biggest obstacle to the smooth operation of this appellate court of Congress always remained the same, the states' power to ignore its orders and decrees. The merchants and lawyers who turned to the judges of appeals to settle prize disputes, or who merely observed the work of this appellate court, must have come to realize that a strong central court with effective power over individuals and the states would be a great asset to a new nation. Suits involving interests of citizens of different states, or of foreign nationals and American citizens, or disputes between the states and the central government, could not always be finally and fairly settled without a more effective federal judicial system.

VII. Substantive Prize Law in America During the Revolution

A DETAILED ANALYSIS of the substantive law applied by the congressional appellate prize judiciary must encounter several basic difficulties. In the first place most of the pleadings and evidence presented in the trial court and brought forward on appeal focused on questions of fact far more than on legal issues. In the vast majority of libels, the legal grounds for condemnation were stated in terms of the various prize statutes of Congress. Evidence was then presented to determine whether the captured property came within the scope of these prize statutes. Clearly one primary legal basis for condemning or acquitting the captured vessels and cargoes lay in these resolves of Congress already discussed.[1] But if the resolves and ordinances of Congress were the sole basis for the substantive law applied by the judges of appeals, this could be a brief chapter indeed. We shall see in this chapter some examples of the application of congressional norms, but in general the crucial issues in most of these cases will be factual not legal.

Other norms, however, had to be applied by the judges of appeals. Congress itself had stated that the rule of decision in all American admiralty courts should be the ordinances of Congress, public treaties, and the law of nations "according to the general usages of Europe." Public treaties were to be ranked first by the prize courts.[2]

Cases determined by the judges of appeals involving issues of treaty interpretation were necessarily rare, so the second ingredient of the congressional rule of decision seldom came into play. The only treaties the Americans entered into during the war were the commercial treaty and the treaty of alliance with France in 1778 and the commercial treaty with

---

[1] Chapters I, II, and III; Ford, *JCC* **3**: pp. 371–375; **4**: pp. 229–232; **5**: pp. 605–606; **9**: pp. 802–804; **18**: pp. 1097–1098; **19**: pp. 314–316; 360–364; **21**: pp. 1152–1158; **22**: pp. 10–11, 99–100.

[2] Ford, *JCC* **21**: p. 1158.

the Netherlands, concluded just six months before the cessation of hostilities. The judges of appeals received only two cases involving French vessels and, as we shall see, applied the terms and the spirit of the French treaties.

A large number of the prize appeal cases in Britain during the Seven Years' War would have furnished the American lawyers and judges with few helpful precedents, even if they had been available in America in published reports. Many of these British prize appeals precisely centered on questions of treaty interpretation. Various British treaties had guaranteed to both signatory nations the right, as a neutral, to carry enemy cargo during any war involving one of the parties to the treaty ("free ships make free goods"). During the wars preceding the American Revolution, the Lords Commissioners for Prize Appeals had gradually worked out restrictions on neutral treaty rights by the rule of 1756 (neutral vessels which were allowed by Britain's enemy to trade with the enemy's colonies in time of war, although not permitted to engage in such trade in time of peace, were to be condemned with their cargoes as enemy property) and by the doctrine of continuous voyage (enemy property from its colonies destined for an enemy port was liable to capture by the British, even though carried on a neutral vessel which had not touched at an enemy port, but was merely continuing a voyage begun on an enemy vessel).[3] The British court of prize appeals during the eighteenth-century colonial wars had effectively rewritten prior treaties and greatly restricted the neutral's rights to carry enemy goods by the rule of 1756 and its corollary, the doctrine of continuous voyage.

These live issues of international relations in European wars struck no resonant cord in the American court of prize appeals. The lack of American commercial treaties and the nature of the American Revolution made these recently developed doctrines of little significance in American prize litigation, even if they had been widely known in America. These two British rules of prize law had developed in a context of the eighteenth-century colonial wars in which Britain, with its sea power, hoped to deprive the enemy's colonies of essential trade carried in neutral bottoms. Colonial trade, closed to neutrals in time of peace, could not be

---

[3] Pares, *Colonial Blockade*, pp. 180–225; Jessup, *Neutrality* 1: pp. 152–156.

opened to neutrals in time of war, the British reasoned, without rendering the neutral vessels enemy property. The American Revolution was a totally different kind of colonial war in which Americans were far more concerned with independent survival than with the unlikely prospect of stopping the neutral carriage of goods to Britain's colonies. As we shall see, the issue in many American prize cases was rather that the vessel, claimed as American property, had been accused of engaging in trade with British colonies in the West Indies or Nova Scotia. If such allegations were proven, it would require no treaty analysis to justify the condemnation of the captured American vessel and its cargo for trading with the enemy.

The third element of the rule of decision, as required by Congress, the law of nations, likewise presents some difficulties for one analyzing the substantive law of the American appellate prize court. Prize courts, in America as elsewhere, were expected to apply the law of nations where treaties or statutory law did not apply. During the Revolution Lord Mansfield, in a significant British decision, stated that:

> Mutual convenience, eternal principles of justice, the wisest regulations of policy, and the consent of nations, have established a system of procedure, a code of law, and a Court for the trial of prize. Every country sues in these Courts of the others, which are all governed by one and the same law, equally known to each.[4]

The celebrated *Report of the Law Officers of the Crown* in 1753 had also clearly stated that the law of nations was to be the rule of decision in all prize courts in England and elsewhere.[5]

---

[4] *Lindo v. Rodney*, 2 Douglas, *Reports*, 613, 616; 99 *English Reports*, 385, 388.

[5] *Report of the Law Officers of the Crown*, in Marsden, *Law of the Sea* 2: pp. 350, 353, 369; see also Blackstone, *Commentaries* 4: pp. 66–67:

"The law of nations is a system of rules, deducible by natural reason, and established by universal consent among the civilized inhabitants of the world; in order to decide all disputes, to regulate all ceremonies and civilities, and to insure the observance of justice and good faith, in that intercourse which must frequently occur between two or more independent states, and the individuals belonging to each. This general law is founded upon this principle, that different nations ought in time of peace to do one another all the good they can; and, in time of war, as little harm as possible, without prejudice to their own real interests. And, as none of these states will allow a superiority in the other, therefore neither can dictate or prescribe the rules of this law to the rest; but such rules must necessarily result from those principles of natural justice, in which all the learned of every nation agree: or they depend upon mutual compacts or treaties between the respective communities; in

In spite of this glowing lip service to the law of nations, however, it would have been impossible for anyone to say with assurance just what it taught about many crucial aspects of prize law. Each writer, and each nation's prize courts, interpreted this law on occasion in different ways. The natural law of reason applied to dealings between nations led to vague principles expressed in different maxims in the various sources of the law of nations. The difficulty of the natural law doctrine is that everyone can claim to listen to the voice of reason, but no one can agree on what it says.[6] We shall see, however, that there were some widely accepted principles of the law of nations which were applied in American prize cases.

Even if the law of nations had been clear and universally agreed upon, some of its key doctrines would have had no application in American prize appeals. The writers of the day discussed contraband and blockade at length, but no cases turning on these two issues ever came before the judges of appeals.[7] Although there were differences between nations in specifying just what was to be considered contraband, there was general agreement that a belligerent had the right to intercept and confiscate war materials, owned and carried by neutrals, if going to an enemy. Nations in the eighteenth century continued to dispute Britain's efforts to include provisions or foodstuffs and naval stores in the lists of contraband.[8] Congress, as we shall later discuss, hoping America would one day be a neutral carrier nation, wanted contraband to be liberally interpreted with provisions and naval stores excluded from the forbidden list. But the judges of appeals were confronted with no cases requiring an interpretation of the law of nations on contraband. By the law of blockade in the eighteenth century, all cargo carried to a blockaded enemy port was considered contraband and was liable to condemnation as prize,[9] but there was never any occasion for the judges of appeals to apply this aspect of the law of nations either.

---

the construction of which there is also no judge to resort to, but the law of nature and reason, being the only one in which all the contracting parties are equally conversant, and to which they are equally subject."

[6] Pares, *Colonial Blockade*, p. 157, and in general, pp. 152–162.

[7] Contraband and blockade are discussed in Jessup, *Neutrality* 1: pp. 50–124.

[8] *Ibid.*, pp. 79–85.

[9] *Ibid.*, pp. 116–123.

With all these obstacles in mind, we can turn to a consideration of the substantive law which the American appellate prize judiciary did apply. Although this analysis will be limited by the inherent difficulties, already indicated, some hints of the substantive legal thinking behind the judgments of the judges of appeals can be gleaned from the court's records as well as from a few of its decrees or from its few opinions.

The first and largest category of cases coming before the judges of appeals are peculiarly characteristic of the type of war in which the Americans were engaged. In a civil war allegiances of individuals can be divided and difficult to ascertain. In a war which converts normal commercial patterns into hostile acts, many merchants will find themselves in very compromising positions. Such were the numerous cases involving capture of vessels and cargoes claimed as American property but libeled by the captors as British.

Because of the difficulties of commerce immediately before and during the war, an American merchant often found his property liable to capture by both the British and the Americans. The merchants resorted to many ruses such as double papers to protect their property and therefore, when discovered engaging in suspicious activities, at times were forced to give complicated and implausible explanations of their conduct. Furthermore many American privateers sailed under British colors, thus tempting American merchant vessels to destroy their American papers when hailed by a privateer under British colors and thereby risk capture with British papers aboard. Though at times these merchants lost their property by condemnation to the captors in state courts, they generally received sympathetic treatment from the judges of appeals. In practically every such case decided on appeal, the judges restored the captured property to the original American owner. The judges of appeals did not express the reasons for their decrees in any of these cases dealing with the capture of property claimed by Americans. But in one case, that of the brigantine *Lusanna*, it is possible to approach somewhat closer to the reasons behind the appellate decree. In this case the records include some notes of the oral arguments before the judges.

The *Lusanna*, with its cargo of whale oil, staves, and wood, had sailed from Massachusetts early in September, 1775, just a week before the Continental Association banning commerce with Great Britain went into effect. Elisha Doane, owner of the brig and its cargo, had sent his son-in-law, Shearjashub Bourne, as supercargo to sell the cargo, to collect the large accounts owed Doane by Lane, Son, and Fraser, London merchants, and to return with a cargo or the cash. Bourne's instructions left wide latitude for discretion, since the whole situation of commercial relations with Britain was so cloudy in the summer of 1775. The *Lusanna* ran into a severe gale shortly after embarking and had to put in at Halifax for repairs. A British ship at Halifax seized the brig and detained it there for months. Bourne finally had to take out a new registry listing the ship as belonging to the British port of Halifax. Upon arrival in London in March, 1776, Bourne began the necessary negotiations for sale of the cargo, but this could not be completed quickly. While waiting for the cargo to be sold, Bourne agreed to charter the *Lusanna* to carry cargo, at least partially military, to the British post at Gibraltar and it sailed there with a London registry made out in Bourne's name. When word arrived in London that another of Doane's ships had been taken by the British and condemned late in 1775 in the British vice-admiralty court in Massachusetts, Bourne tried to obtain a reversal of the court's decree. In these negotiations he posed as an American loyalist who had fled from the wrath of the rebels at home. Though he was unable to recover the condemned ship for Doane, he did leave some written records portraying himself as a loyalist in flight which would later be used against him in the trial of the *Lusanna*. In spring of 1777 Bourne began planning another voyage for the *Lusanna*. He later claimed that his intention was to recover as much of Doane's credits as possible, take on a cargo and clear out for Halifax. Once in Halifax he hoped to be able to obtain cash for the substantial bills of exchange he had from Lane, Son, and Fraser, clear out for a British port and then slip into some port in Massachusetts. Such a scheme would be necessary to escape the watchful British fleet. Unfortunately, however, the *Lusanna* was captured by an American privateer from Portsmouth, New Hampshire, the brigantine *McClary*, on October 30, 1777, while on the voyage to Halifax. Doane and Bourne tried to defend the *Lusanna* from condemnation in the New Hampshire maritime court, but the jury found it lawful prize. The principal grounds for condemnation asserted by the captors were that the vessel and its cargo belonged to inhabitants or subjects of Great Britain and that the vessel was carrying supplies to the British military forces. These were two of the primary categories of captures authorized by Congress.[10]

Since the trial court denied Doane leave to appeal to Congress, he carried an appeal to the state's superior court, which affirmed the judgment of the maritime court. When Doane requested an appeal to Congress, the superior court also refused to grant one. The New Hampshire law, already discussed, forbade appeals to Congress except in limited categories of cases. Doane petitioned Congress to review these New Hampshire decrees. For several years the case remained on the docket of the judges of appeals. Finally, with the Court of Appeals established, the Articles of Confederation approved and the war ended, the court in September, 1783, heard this case.[11]

On September 11, 1783, the Court of Appeals began hearing the oral arguments in the case of the Lusanna. Judges Griffin and Read sat in this case, Judge Lowell obviously having disqualified himself since he had acted as counsel for the brig's owners before the trial court six years earlier. Both parties obtained excellent counsel for the appeal. Jacob Rush, William Lewis, and James Wilson argued for the appellants, while Jonathan Dickinson Sergeant and Jared Ingersoll represented the appellees. All these attorneys had reputations as among the top lawyers of the day and all had frequently argued before the judges of appeals. Wilson and Sergeant had also served as members of the Committee on Appeals in a number of cases. The hearing began on September 11 with an argument as to the court's jurisdiction. This aspect of the case will be discussed in chapter VIII. When the judges decided in favor of their jurisdiction, Ingersoll moved for a continuance, but the court would not delay the case any longer. On September 13 the merits of the appeal came up for oral argument. Presumably by that time the judges had reviewed the voluminous depositions, interrogatories and other written evidence presented. Among the

---

[10] Lusanna (Doane v. Penhallow), 17 September, 1783, #30, RCA, and L. Kinvin Wroth and Hiller B. Zobel, eds., Legal Papers of John Adams (3 v., Cambridge, Mass., 1965) 2: pp. 356–372; Ford, JCC 3: p. 373; 4: pp. 230–231; 5: p. 606.

[11] Lusanna, #30, RCA.

records there are three pages of notes from the oral arguments on the thirteenth. Apparently taken by one of the judges or a court officer, these notes give a brief summary of the main arguments used by each attorney, with marginal references to the legal authorities cited in the course of the argument.[12] By tracing these citations it is possible to reconstruct partially the oral arguments in an attempt to discover what reasoning the judges found convincing in deciding this case.

Jacob Rush opened the argument for the owners of the *Lusanna*. The captors had originally obtained the condemnation of the *Lusanna* by supporting with evidence the two main allegations of their libel: that the brig and the cargo belonged to inhabitants of Great Britain, subjects of the king of Great Britain; and that the brig at the time of capture was carrying supplies to the enemies of the United States. Rush began by taking up the contention that the vessel was British property. Here he had to counteract the effect of the ship's registry and other papers taken on board, all of which indicated British ownership. Rush probably insisted that ownership must have remained in Doane throughout the time of the voyage, since Bourne had no power to effect a change of ownership. He must have contended that all the evidence showing British ownership had been used by Bourne to deceive the British as a means of bringing the ship and other property back to Doane. He also tried to answer the argument used by the captors that the insurance taken out in London to protect the vessel in case of capture by Americans was also a cause of forfeiture. Another argument used in the previous trials of the *Lusanna* was that the chartering of the vessel to carry supplies to Gibraltar had justified condemning the ship as prize. Rush met this argument by contending that whatever misconduct there might have been on a former voyage could not affect the ownership of the vessel and cargo on a later voyage. He quoted Richard Lee, who had written a treatise on captures, widely used by lawyers in prize cases in America. Lee had stated that a ship which had been liable to capture, for instance because of violating a blockade, was no longer subject to confiscation after it had returned to its home port. "[F]or if they are come into the Port to which they

---

[12] *Ibid.*, and Minutes of the Court, Miscellaneous Court Records, RCA.

were bound, the Voyage is deemed completed, and Confiscation is at an End."[13] Perhaps this argument clinched the point, for the trip to Gilbraltar was not mentioned again. Rush then turned his attention to the other major contention of the captors, that the *Lusanna* had been carrying supplies to the enemy at Halifax. He first referred to Vattel, whose readable volume on the law of nations was well known in America. Vattel had argued that a sovereign who declared war could not detain any subjects of his enemy who happened to be within his territory at the time of the declaration, nor could he seize their property. Since they had come in reliance on the public faith, Vattel reasoned, the sovereign by permitting them to enter his territory implicitly promised them full liberty and security to return home, with a suitable time allowed to withdraw their property. Vattel showed that the king of England had followed this policy when at war with the French.[14] Rush then quoted a conflicting passage from Lee which probably stated the customary law of nations more accurately than the section from Vattel he had just referred to. Lee stated that all enemy property, corporeal and incorporeal alike, was liable to confiscation in time of war.[15] Therefore, Rush concluded, Doane's credits in the hands of Lane, Son, and Fraser were subject to confiscation by the British as enemy property. Apparently Rush argued that Bourne had the natural law right (indicated by Vattel) as well as the practical necessity (as shown by Lee) of recovering all of Doane's property in Britain and bringing it back to its proper American owner, even though the only means by which he could accomplish this was to risk sailing to the enemy port at Halifax. Though the British could have confiscated Doane's accounts in England (Lee), they had not and thus it remained American property. So Bourne had a right (Vattel) to remove what he could in the hope of restoring it to Doane, even by creating the appearance of carrying supplies to the British. False coloring of cargoes, as we have seen, was a common mercantile practice in war.

---

[13] Lee, *Treatise of Captures*, pp. 176–177.

[14] Emmerich de Vattel, *Le Droit des Gens, ou Principes de la Loi Naturelle, Appliqués à la Conduit et aux Affaires des Nations et des Souverains*, Charles G. Fenwick, tr. (3 v., Washington, 1916) 3: p. 256. The reference in the notes of the oral argument is to p. 24, Bk. III, sec. 63, which refers to the English edition of Vattel (2 v. in 1, London, 1759–1760).

[15] Lee, *Treatise of Captures*: pp. 113–114.

Jonathan Dickinson Sergeant following Rush presented the basic arguments for the captors. He repeated the contentions which had been decisive for the captors in the trial court: that the vessel was bound on a voyage from London to Halifax at the time of capture; that it was carrying supplies to the enemy there; that it was registered at London, showing British ownership, and had British subjects on board. Sergeant conceded that the insurance alone could not cause forfeiture of the ship and cargo. It did, however, create a strong presumption of British ownership. (Presumptions, one will recall, played a large part in British prize litigation.) Sergeant also turned to Lee to confirm his arguments. In discussing what property could lawfully be captured, Lee had written, "But in dubious Cases it is always to be presumed that what we find in the Enemy's Country, or in their Ships, is deemed to belong to them."[16] Lee continued that this presumption, however reasonable in itself, could be destroyed by proof to the contrary. But, Sergeant insisted, all the documentary evidence only confirmed the presumption that the *Lusanna* and its cargo belonged to British subjects. Again quoting Lee, Sergeant showed that the law of nations required trial of prizes first and foremost on the basis of the evidence of the ship papers. "The Evidence to acquit or condemn . . . must, in the first Instance, come merely from the Ship taken, viz. the Papers on board. . . ."[17] Of course, Sergeant admitted, other factors had to be weighed, such as the testimony of the captain and crew and affidavits of the owners,[18] but by the accepted rules of evidence, the best evidence a thing is capable of was always required. Here Sergeant referred to Gilbert, an authority on the common law rules of evidence, that the first rule was that a man must have the utmost evidence the nature of the fact was capable of.[19] Sergeant again turned to Lee to show that in time of war all commerce with the enemy must cease. It would be absurd to continue commerce between nations at war, only to have the traders imprisoned and the goods confiscated.[20] All the

---

[16] *Ibid.*, pp. 83–84.
[17] *Ibid.*, p. 239.
[18] *Ibid.*, pp. 239–242.
[19] Geoffry Gilbert, *The Law of Evidence* (London, 1760), p. 4; Sergeant also referred to pp. 16–17.
[20] Lee, *Treatise of Captures*, pp. 68–70.

evidence pointed to the fact that Bourne had been carrying on trade between two enemy ports; one who claimed to be an American had been making profits by aiding the enemy.

After Sergeant sat down, William Lewis rose to press the case for the owners. He began by showing the good character of the owners of the property seized, Isaiah Doane and James Sheppard, two of the claimants of parts of the cargo of the *Lusanna*. There were depositions in the record to prove the owners were true Americans, loyal to the cause of independence. Lewis then reviewed the evidence which tended to show British ownership of the property. Undoubtedly he tried to persuade the court that all the evidence from the ship papers only showed the clever scheme of Bourne to cover the ship and cargo against the inevitable risk of capture by the British. Lewis then turned to the conduct of Bourne, who had been in charge of Doane's affairs in Britain. Bourne had shown himself a true friend of his country, Lewis argued, by attempting to bring back the property owned by an American. It would be a harsh judgment to condemn this property precisely because of Bourne's desperate efforts at restoring it to its true owner. Furthermore Bourne was an American citizen and his voyage to England could not have changed his domicile. So the property, even though in the name of Bourne, must be presumed American until the captors clearly proved the contrary. Here Lewis tried to counteract the effect of the presumptions on which Sergeant had relied. He tried to shift the burden of proof to the captors. But, Lewis continued, even if Bourne had been guilty of criminal activity in his various attempts to secure Doane's property from confiscation by the British, his offense was not such as would work a forfeiture of the property. Lewis then focused on what he considered the central point of the case, whether a subject of a nation at war could transport his property from the enemy's territory into his own. He discussed the customs of various nations which he claimed demonstrated a willingness to permit enemy merchants present within their territory at the outbreak of a war to withdraw with their property. Lewis referred to Lee, who had given examples of agreements between states "that if a War should break out between them, that the Goods of the Subjects of one State, found in the other state, should not be confiscated; but that it should be lawful for them to carry them away within six months." This right to remove property from an enemy country after the start of war necessarily included the right to remove incorporeal property such as Doane's credits.[21] In this context, however, Lee clearly had discussed only treaty agreements. On the page immediately preceding that cited by Lewis, Lee had stated the customary law of nations, that "No Princes or States when a War suddenly breaks out, are accustomed to declare, to the Subjects of their Enemies, that they might carry away their Effects, which will be otherwise confiscated; none have ever expected it . . . such has been the general Consent of all Nations, unless it is otherwise agreed, by Treaty or some other kind of Compact." Lewis probably passed over this passage in silence, turning to more solid confirmation of his position in a passage from Vattel previously used by Rush. Vattel does confirm Lewis's argument that the person or the property of an enemy happening to be within hostile country at the time of a declaration of war may not lawfully be detained.[22] Lewis also relied on the authority of Blackstone to show that the English could not rightfully have confiscated Doane's property in England. English law, Blackstone had written, paid particular regard to foreign merchants. By *Magna Carta* all merchants had safe conduct to enter, travel in, or depart from England without any unreasonable imposts, except in time of war. If a war should break out, Blackstone wrote, merchants from the enemy country would be attached without harm of body or goods till the king was informed how English merchants were treated in the enemy country.[23] Lewis could conclude from these authorities that property belonging to a merchant such as Doane did not become enemy property merely because it was found within the enemy territory at the outbreak of a war. If Doane's property in England had actually been confiscated or declared legally forfeit, then there would have been no basis for seeking restoration if it had been subsequently seized by an American privateer. As it was, Lewis concluded, the property remained

---

[21] *Ibid.*, pp. 30–31, 114.

[22] Vattel, *Droit des Gens*, Fenwick, tr., **3**: p. 256.

[23] Blackstone, *Commentaries* **1**: p. 260; **4**: p. 69. In the notes the second reference is mistakenly given as page 60. It appears that many of the early editions of Blackstone followed the same pagination, so it is impossible to determine which early edition was referred to in these notes of the oral arguments.

Doane's, and Bourne had every right and duty to take whatever steps were necessary to restore it to Doane when possible.

Jared Ingersoll took the rostrum when Lewis finished. In final summation for the captors, Ingersoll again went through the evidence which provided the factual grounds for presuming the *Lusanna* and its cargo were enemy property. He then reiterated the other key argument of the appellees, that the *Lusanna* when captured was in the service of the enemy. With quotations from Vattel he tried to show that by the law of nations the *Lusanna* should be condemned as a lawful prize. Vattel had written that an ally of an enemy makes himself likewise an enemy. "It matters little whether a person makes a war upon me directly and in his own name," Vattel wrote, "or whether he does so under the flag of another." Anyone who aided an enemy Vattel considered an ally of that enemy.[24] Though Vattel was primarily thinking of nations, not individuals as allies, Ingersoll argued that Bourne's conduct had put him into the service of the British by attempting to supply their forces at Halifax. He again turned to Vattel to show that even neutral property could be seized when necessary to prevent goods useful to war from coming into the hands of the enemy.[25] The passage in Vattel referred to contraband goods, but it is doubtful that Ingersoll argued that the cargo of the *Lusanna* was strictly contraband. The captors had tried to show, however, that the goods were intended for the enemy forces stationed in Halifax, which was one of the grounds for condemnation authorized by Congress. Ingersoll closed the case for the captors with a quotation from the resolves of Congress which stated that all transports carrying to the British forces stationed in America any troops, arms, ammunition, clothing, provisions, or military or naval stores of any kind at all were liable to seizure. If the ship itself belonged to an inhabitant of one of the American states, it should be confiscated along with the cargo.[26] This was the strongest

---

[24] Vattel, *Droit des Gens*, Fenwick, tr., **3**: pp. 264–265. The reference in the notes is to Bk. III, sec. 95, 96 and 97, which are on these pages of the Fenwick translation.

[25] *Ibid.*, pp. 270–271. The reference in the notes is to Bk. III, sec. 111.

[26] Resolves of Congress, 25 November, 1775. The notes referred to *Journals of Congress containing the Proceedings from September 5, 1774 to January 1, 1776* (Philadelphia, 1777), p. 260; see Ford, *JCC* **3**: p. 373.

point in the case for the captors and with this argument Ingersoll sat down.

James Wilson spoke last. His position as final speaker indicates that he must have been counsel for the owners, although the brief summary of his arguments gives no indication of what side he spoke for. If these notes were taken by one of the judges, perhaps by the time Wilson spoke the judge had made up his mind that the vessel and cargo should be restored to the original owners. Wilson did not have a reputation for such brevity. The notes merely show that he went over the now-familiar points of the case of the captors: whether the ship and cargo were British property and if not, whether they should be forfeit because of the voyage to Halifax.

Judges Griffin and Read held the case under advisement till September 17 when they published their decree. They reversed the sentence of the New Hampshire maritime court and superior court and restored the property to the claimants, Elisha Doane, Isaiah Doane, and James Sheppard. Each party to the appeal, however, was to pay his own costs. The judges did not add the phrase commonly used when they reversed a trial court decree, that the lower court should issue all necessary process to carry the decree of the Court of Appeals into effect.[27] Perhaps a mere oversight. Judging from the long subsequent history of the case, it would not have helped anyway. Griffin and Read gave no indication of the reasoning behind the decree. There certainly was enough evidence to justify the opposite decision. But the owners had made out a good case to show that the vessel and cargo had remained American property and had not freely been employed in carrying supplies to the British forces at Halifax. As in other cases dealing with property claimed by Americans, the judges showed an appreciation of the difficulties in which American merchants had found themselves during the war. The judges tended to accept the arguments of the interested parties to explain away the incriminating evidence present at the time of the capture of their property. The subsequent history of the case of the *Lusanna* extending over twelve more years will be discussed in the next chapter.

---

[27] *Lusanna*, #30, RCA.

As already stated, in none of the prize cases concerning
property claimed as American did the judges of appeals state
their reasons for restoring the captured property to the
American claimants. In the case of the *Lusanna* we can get an
insight into the legal arguments used by counsel. Although
the case turned largely on factual questions, the opposing
attorneys argued from some of the standard sources of prize
law available in America. In one other case, notes, likewise
probably taken down by one of the judges during oral argument, have been preserved showing the legal arguments
raised by counsel before the judges of appeals.[28] These two
sets of notes, along with the notes of an attorney apparently
for use in argument before the Court of Appeals,[29] suggest
that, at least in more important cases, the attorneys delved
into whatever writings they could find that might touch on
the law of nations on captures in time of war. Such notes of
legal arguments help us come much closer to the type of legal
reasoning that must have swayed the judges of appeals. Similar arguments, derived from the various authorities who
discussed prize law, must have been considered by the judges
in many cases.[30]

The other cases involving capture of property claimed as
American can now be briefly summarized. The available
records give only the factual issues with the final appellate
decree. Legal arguments similar to those raised in the case of
the *Lusanna* most likely were part of the appeal. Although
the precise legal arguments used in each case cannot now be
reconstructed, the consistent pattern of the decrees of the
judges strongly suggest that the ultimate basis of restoring
practically all these prizes to the American claimants was not
derived solely from substantive legal arguments, but from a
realistic appreciation of the plight of American merchants
caught in a war in which only highly suspicious conduct
could assure them of some protection for significant property interests. This attitude of the judges of appeals, ready to
listen sympathetically to the long, complex stories of the
owners and masters, tells us something of the way in which
the law was applied, even if it says little about the substantive

---

[28] *St. Antonio (Debadie v. Russell)*, 28 May, 1783, #95, RCA.

[29] *Chester (Dubbledemuts v. Atkinson)*, 3 May, 1787, 2 Dall. 41, RCA; Goebel, *Law Practice of Hamilton* **2**: pp. 892–903, esp. p. 896.

[30] These authorities have been discussed in chapter V.

law itself. In all these cases the captors asserted that the capture was authorized by some resolve of Congress. In most of them there were sufficient grounds for strong suspicion that the owner had engaged in illegal activity. Yet in all these cases but one, the judges of appeals restored the captured property to the American owner who had claimed it.

The schooner *Frank* was at Montego Bay in Jamaica when the commander, Sylvanus Waterman, heard of the skirmish at Lexington and the battle of Bunker Hill. He knew that American property could be captured by the British, so without orders from the owner of the schooner he made a bill of sale to a merchant of Jamaica, took out a new register and cleared to Newfoundland. He later stated that he had intended to sail directly to Connecticut where he had originally sailed from. British ships, however, forced him to proceed to Newfoundland and return to Jamaica. There he had to procure a bond to carry his cargo to Newfoundland or some other place in possession of the British. To save his bondsman he again proceeded to Newfoundland and after clearing from there was captured by an American privateer. The captors libeled the *Frank* in Rhode Island where the first trial in the admiralty court resulted in acquittal of the ship and cargo. A retrial was granted and the schooner and cargo were condemned as prize to the captors. The conduct of the commander of the *Frank* raised serious doubts whether the ship had not been regularly supplying the British army and navy as the libelants had charged. The owner, a citizen of Connecticut, nevertheless, appealed to the commissioners of appeals who reversed the trial court and restored the property to him as the true owner.[31]

---

[31] *Frank (Alsop v. Rutenbourgh)*, 20 May, 1777, #11, RCA.

Two similar cases, both involving vessels owned by Aaron Lopez of Rhode Island, were also appealed to the Committee on Appeals. Before the war Lopez had carried on an extensive trade with the British West Indies. After the war began and the British took possession of parts of Rhode Island, Lopez moved to Massachusetts. He tried to recover part of the large property interests he had in Jamaica resulting from his earlier trade. But during the summer of 1778 he received news of the capture of two of his ships which he claimed were returning with his property from Jamaica. Lopez had placed Benjamin Wright in charge of his interests in Jamaica. Wright, who had befriended many American sailors held captive on the island, prepared the schooner *Hope* for a voyage with a secret understanding that the ship would sail to some port of Massachusetts. Wright chose a crew made up entirely of American prisoners, but he had to register the ship in Jamaica making it appear as property of the subjects of the British king and he had to clear for Halifax. A British man-of-war hailed the *Hope* and brought it to, so the Americans threw overboard all papers

The Court of Appeals followed this pattern of decisions set by the Committee on Appeals. Where American privateers had captured vessels and cargoes claimed as the property of American citizens, the court ordinarily restored the property to the original owner.[32] The case of the schooner *Fame* stands

---

which showed the real design of their voyage. The British ship released them, but as the *Hope* drew near the coast of Rhode Island it was captured by American privateers. The commander of the *Hope* later claimed that he had a defective mast, which he planned to use as an excuse to sail toward Newport, then in possession of the British, to evade British ships. When near land he had intended to bring the schooner into some port in Massachusetts. The captors libeled the *Hope* as British property in the service of the enemies of the United States. The Connecticut maritime court decreed it lawful prize to the captors. But Lopez appealed to the Committee on Appeals, where the lower court was reversed and the ship and cargo restored to Lopez. *Hope* (*Lopez v. Brooks*), 10 April, 1779, #28, RCA.

The other ship belonging to Lopez, the schooner *Hawke*, had also been fitted out and loaded at Jamaica by Benjamin Wright. The registry and clearance indicated it was British property. American privateers captured the *Hawke*, but the admiralty court in Rhode Island, Lopez's original home, declared that the ship and cargo were not lawful prize. This time the captors appealed to Congress, but the Committee on Appeals affirmed the sentence of the lower court. *Hawke* (*Tredwell v. Lopez*), 29 March, 1779, #37, RCA.

Other cases of ships, claimed as American property and eventually restored to the American claimants by the commissioners of appeals, although captured under suspicious circumstances, are: *Minerva* (*Rogers v. Wilson*), 2 June, 1777, #15, and *Fancy* (*Payson v. Jenckes*), 3 December, 1778, #34, RCA.

[32] The clearest example of such a case heard by the Court of Appeals involved the *Hannah*. The *Hannah* had a Pennsylvania registry and in February, 1781, obtained a clearance from the customs collector of New Jersey for a voyage to the island of St. Eustatia. But after the sloop was laded with a cargo of lumber and ready to sail, it was captured by a group of citizens of New Jersey. In their libel the captors alleged that the *Hannah* was carrying supplies to the British troops at New York. They produced depositions to show that the sloop was not adequately rigged or provisioned for the long voyage to St. Eustatia. The unseaworthy condition of the *Hannah* and the fact that the commander and crew had taken inadequate provisions and no change of clothes on board led the jury to decide for the captors. After the judge of the New Jersey admiralty court condemned the sloop as prize to the captors, the owner appealed. Judges Griffin and Paca took various depositions which went to show that the *Hannah* had enough food aboard and was in good enough condition for the voyage to St. Eustatia, while others testified that they had been to sea in much worse vessels than the *Hannah* and that the owner was a good whig and friend to the American cause. The Court of Appeals reversed the sentence of the lower court and restored the sloop and cargo to the owners.

Several years later, in May, 1784, and again in May, 1785, the captors petitioned the Court of Appeals for a rehearing, claiming to have new evidence to prove that the *Hannah* had been fitted and laded for a voyage to New York to supply the British there. Among the new evidence was a deposition of the commander of the *Hannah*, who changed his story and now admitted that the sloop was bound for New York. He stated that when he entered on board the sloop he did not know it was bound to New York but later he discovered the true intention of the owner. But in spite of this new evidence, the Court of Appeals refused to reopen the case. The court stood by its previous decision to restore the sloop to the original owner. Perhaps the court's reluctance to grant any rehearings, long after the original capture and trial, played a

out as an exception to this tendency shown in many cases to restore property to American claimants if they could give a plausible explanation of the circumstances of their capture. Samuel Johnston and William Hubbard of Connecticut filed a claim for the schooner, libeled in the New Jersey admiralty court. Johnston, formerly a resident of Rhode Island, recently had been forced to flee the British who plundered and destroyed his property. Since he had before the war engaged in trade with Jamaica, he still had substantial accounts owed to him there. In November, 1777, he sailed on a prisoner ship to Jamaica and on arrival collected a large part of the debts owed him and with William Hubbard, the other claimant, purchased the *Fame* and its cargo. They had to take out a Jamaica registry, which made the property formally liable to capture by Americans as belonging to subjects of the British king. They cleared out for New York to prevent seizure by the British.

Johnston had befriended some American prisoners in Jamaica and took them on board as a crew. Johnston insisted later in court that he had planned to sail to some American port such as Nantucket, New London, or Boston. But due to shortage of water he was forced to sail up the Delaware toward Philadelphia just as the British were leaving the city. One British man-of-war gave him some water and ordered him to follow to New York. When the *Fame* had managed to get out of sight of this British ship, it was captured by two American privateers sailing under British colors and taken into New Jersey as prize. Testimony in the admiralty court by a passenger and a crewman from the *Fame* was quite damaging to the claim of the owners. These witnesses contended that Johnston had intended to land at Philadelphia because he thought the British were still in possession of the city, or else to land at New York. Even when captured by the Americans, according to these witnesses, Johnston expected help from some British ship. Another passenger on the *Fame*, however, testified strongly and in great detail that Johnston

---

large part in this final disposition of the appeal. *Hannah* (*Hepburn v. Ellis*), 4 August, 1781, rehearing denied, 14 November, 1786, #74, and Miscellaneous Court Records, RCA.

In two other cases the Court of Appeals decreed the restoration of ships to American claimants: *Lovely Nancy* (*Ingersol v. Shewell*), 22 August, 1780, #38, and *Betsey* (*Ridgway v. Earle*), 14 June, 1783, #77, and Miscellaneous Court Records, RCA.

wanted to get to some port in possession of the Americans. This witness was not allowed to testify in the admiralty court, but the Court of Appeals received a long deposition he made in support of the claimants. The admiralty court adjudged the schooner and cargo lawful prize and, when the claimants appealed, the Court of Appeals heard the case, dismissed the appeal, and affirmed the lower court sentence.[33]

Though the ship had certainly been taken under very suspicious circumstances, the judges of appeals had reviewed such cases before and had regularly restored the property to the American claimant not to the captors. Though the testimony in the case of the *Fame* is conflicting, the story of the owners is not utterly beyond belief. It might be that one deciding factor in this case was a letter found on the *Fame* at the time of capture from a resident of Jamaica to Lord Drumond (*sic*) apparently intended for the Scottish nobleman Thomas Lord Drummond, who had served as an intermediary carrying to members of Congress an abortive peace plan from Lord North on the eve of the Revolution. Drummond remained in New York till the end of 1778 as an unofficial adviser to Lord Richard Howe and stayed in close contact with the loyalists there. Little wonder Drummond was regarded as a loyalist.[34] The letter found on the *Fame* addressed to Drummond expressed strong opposition to the American cause. For instance this letter vented the hope that America might be brought to a sense of its real interest and happiness, which the writer could "never suppose would follow were they to effect their Standard of Independency and which would only bring on Anarchy and confusion among them."[35] Possibly this letter, along with the adverse testimony, tipped the scale against the American owners of the *Fame*. According to the law of nations, the primary evidence to acquit or condemn a vessel was to come from the ship itself, the papers found on board, and the interrogatories taken of its principal officers.[36] Whatever the reason, this case was an exception to the general rule. The

---

[33] *Fame* (*Johnston v. Taylor*), 23 December, 1780, #45, RCA.

[34] Milton M. Klein, "Failure of a Mission: The Drummond Peace Proposal of 1775," *Huntington Library Quarterly* 35 (1972): pp. 343–380.

[35] *Fame*, #45, RCA.

[36] *Report of the Law Officers*, Marsden, *Law of the Sea* 2: p. 351; Lee, *Treatise of Captures*, p. 239.

judges of appeals apparently listened carefully to the attorneys for the parties as they presented their oral arguments based, undoubtedly, on apt quotations from the writers on prize law. But the judges understood the plight of American merchants during the Revolution; they tended to believe the long, involved explanations of the compromising situations in which the merchants' property had been captured.

A unique group of cases involving the capture of property claimed as American brings another problem of the Revolutionary War into focus. These cases do not concern the merchants and their problems owing to a war which disrupted their normal trading patterns with former sister colonies. They concern rather the difficulties involved in determining what was enemy property when the enemy was in possession of large parts of a nearby state. In all of these cases citizens of Connecticut had crossed the Sound and seized property belonging to persons living on Long Island, then in the possession of the British. In the end we may conclude that these cases of Connecticut plundering on Long Island tell us little of the substantive law of the appellate judiciary of Congress. But an analysis of these cases, within the framework of the political realities of Connecticut during the Revolution, will fill out the picture of the types of cases presented to the judges of appeals, and will reveal again the attitude of the judges toward cases involving captured American property. The problems of federalism and the frictions between states which regarded themselves as sovereign also are highlighted.

Early in the war the officials in Connecticut felt compelled to take measures to stop illicit trade with Long Island which was under British control.[37] Since British manufactured goods were scarce in all the American states, imports from Long Island offered great profits to imaginative adventurers. No real criticism could be leveled at these efforts to stop illicit trade with parts of the country in British possession. Complaints started arriving, however, that crews of armed boats, with commissions from the Connecticut governor, had landed on Long Island and plundered the inhabitants of their livestock, clothes, and personal property. In August,

---

[37] Hoadly, *Records of Connecticut* 1: pp. 337, 340, 528–529. For economic conditions in Connecticut during the war, see, Christopher Collier, *Roger Sherman's Connecticut* (Middletown, Conn. 1971), pp. 110–180.

1778, Governor Jonathan Trumbull of Connecticut made an attempt to control those accused of attacking the inhabitants of Long Island. He tried, or claimed he tried, to suppress the plundering of innocent persons.[38] George Washington also tried to stop these attacks which made no distinction between loyal citizens and tories.[39]

In early 1779 the Connecticut government tightened still further the laws to discourage all illicit trade with the British on Long Island. All safe-conduct passes previously granted to refugees from Long Island to bring their property into Connecticut were revoked since these had been used as a means of importing British merchandise. Any goods seized and libeled in the maritime courts of the state as illegally imported from Long Island would be considered forfeit and prize to the captors. The goods would be condemned even though the libelants could only establish a probability that the property had been imported from a place in the possession of the enemy. This law put upon the owner the burden of proving that the property was legally imported. Those commissioned by the governor to capture enemy property on Long Island had to give sufficient bonds not to plunder any inhabitants on the island, a technical nicety which apparently did little to prevent the plundering.[40]

Congress tactfully recommended to the states, especially those adjacent to Long Island, to do whatever they could to stop the plundering of the inhabitants of places under British control. Washington strongly supported Congress's recommendations and wrote to Governor Trumbull urging him to prevent all these depredations on Long Island.[41]

But in 1780 citizens of Connecticut still complained that

---

[38] Hoadly, *Records of Connecticut* 2: p. 110; Samuel Brown to Trumbull, 1 April, 1779; Trumbull to Deputy Governor Bowen, 9 August, 1779; Trumbull to Major General Wolcott, 24 August, 1779, Jonathan Trumbull Papers (CHS).

[39] Washington to Brigadier General Charles Scott, 31 October, 1778; to Major General Israel Putnam, 27 November, 1778, and 21 March, 1779, Fitzpatrick, *Writings of Washington* 13: pp. 187, 340–341; 14: p. 273; Trumbull to Washington, 24 September, 1779, Jonathan Trumbull Papers (CHS).

[40] Connecticut Session Laws, 7 April, 1779, 514, and 13 May, 1779, 531, Jenkins, *Microfilm,* and Hoadly, *Records of Connecticut* 2: pp. 346–347.

[41] Ford, *JCC*, 22 June, 1779, 14: pp. 758–759; Washington, General Orders, 1 July 1779; Washington to Governor Trumbull, 30 September and 4 November, 1779; to Major Benjamin Tallmadge, 2 November, 1779; to Governor George Clinton, 3 November, 1779, Fitzpatrick, *Writings of Washington* 15: pp. 358–359; 16: pp. 361–363; 17: pp. 62–63, 67, 70–71.

British goods were being openly sold within the state, imported into the state illegally, or obtained by plundering the defenseless inhabitants of Long Island. Strong rumors connected unnamed parties in high places with this illicit trade.[42] The Connecticut General Assembly passed another act to prevent this illicit trade, imposing severe penalties and summary judicial procedures on the violators.[43] It also tried twice to pass an act to prevent plundering and robbing of the inhabitants of Long Island. But the bill could not pass both houses. The assembly did, however, pass an act which forbade appeals to Congress in any cases of seizures made pursuant to the act to prevent illicit trade.[44]

Governor Trumbull, indicating his attitude toward Congress, in 1780 complained strongly that Congress had granted a permit to Doctor George Howell to bring all his property from Long Island. Howell was suspected of being a tory and an emissary of the British. Trumbull expressed amazement that Congress would grant permission without any restrictions to bring property from within the area controlled by the British. "I could not conceive," he wrote indignantly, "that Congress, under the *proposed* articles of Confederation have a right to, or much less in the present *unconnected, unfederated* state of the *union*, would assume such diction as the permission conveys—'Commanding all Governors, Generals, etc.'—to afford protection in pursuance of his said permit."[45]

In January, 1781, Governor Trumbull and the state council revoked all previously granted commissions to make captures from the enemy and to prevent illicit trade with the enemy.[46] But the inhabitants of Long Island continued to complain of the depredations and plunder perpetrated by citizens of Connecticut under color of newly granted commissions of the governor.[47] Governor Clinton of New York

---

[42] Letters signed "Detector" and "A.Z.", *Connecticut Courant*, 29 February and 16 May, 1780.

[43] Connecticut Session Laws, 11 May, 1780, 553–557, Jenkins, *Microfilm*.

[44] *Ibid.*, 29 November, 1780, 563, and Revolutionary War Collection, 1st series, XIX, 58, October, 1780 and 59, n.d. (CSL).

[45] Trumbull to Huntington, 21 August, 1780, PCC, Item 66, II, 91 (Italics in original), and 95, 99, 103; Ezra L'Hommedieu to John Morin Scott, 27 August, 1780, James Duane Mss. (NYHS).

[46] Hoadly, *Records of Connecticut* 3: pp. 292–293.

[47] Affidavit, 22 June, 1781, Jonathan Trumbull Papers, XV, 27 (CSL).

and the New York assembly took up the cause of these Long
Island citizens. Clinton wrote to Trumbull and to the president of Congress enclosing a resolution of the New York
legislature vigorously condemning the plundering of Long
Island residents.[48] Congress referred the question to a committee and, in August, 1781, passed a resolution expressing a
desire that the governor of Connecticut revoke the commissions in so far as they authorized seizure of goods on Long
Island.[49] Clinton was not satisfied with this resolve of Congress. It had made the revocation of commissions optional
for Trumbull, whereas Clinton wanted a clear decision that
the commissions were void. Clinton forwarded to Congress a
letter he had received from Trumbull justifying the commissions he had granted as necessary to preserve the country
from evil and artful men who were trying to undermine the
nation by introducing large quantities of British goods.
Trumbull, whose letter speaks volumes of the wartime furor
in Connecticut, had written to Clinton, "These pernicious
Tools, with the allurements furnished them, spread the con-
tagion of Corruption, Falsehood, unreasonable Jealousies, a
cry of intolerable Taxes and artfully seduce young men to
enlist and join the associated Loyalists." Since Trumbull had
argued so fervently in support of the commissions he had
granted, Clinton strongly suspected that more decisive inter-
vention by Congress would be necessary to stop the plundering.[50]

Congress hesitated to act on Clinton's letter since it believed, or hoped, that Trumbull would follow its previous
recommendations. One delegate in Congress from New
York correctly predicted that the law of the land was clearly
against the plundering on Long Island. He was sure that

---

[48] *Ibid.*, XIV, 316, and PCC, Item 67, II, 390, 398, 406, 408, 416.

[49] Ford, *JCC* **21**: p. 835. For covering letters from the president of Congress to
Governors Clinton and Trumbull, see Thomas McKean Papers (HSP). See also
L'Hommedieu to Clinton, 31 July, 1781, and Connecticut Delegates in Congress to
Trumbull, 14 August, 1781, Burnett, *Letters* **6**: pp. 164 and 182.

[50] Clinton to President of Congress, 25 August, 1781; Trumbull to Clinton, 20
July, 1781; Clinton to Trumbull, 20 August, 1781, PCC, Item 67, II, 422, 430, 434;
Clinton to James Duane and Ezra L'Hommedieu, 25 August, 1781, James Duane
Mss (NYHS); Trumbull to Colonel Samuel Canfield and Thaddeus Burr, 26 March,
1781, Trumbull to Samuel Bishop, same date, Jonathan Trumbull Papers (CHS). It
is interesting that Clinton, who in a few years would oppose the ratification of the
Constitution, suggested in 1781 that the commissions of Trumbull were void as
against the Articles of Confederation.

there would be no difficulty obtaining reversals in the Court of Appeals of any decrees obtained in the state admiralty court that might condemn British goods from Long Island to the captors.[51] The patience of Congress was rewarded. The governor and council of Connecticut revoked the commissions previously granted so far as they related to the crews of armed ships landing on Long Island.[52] Shortly after Trumbull had revoked the commissions, he received another complaint from Long Island residents of plundering by a Connecticut crew acting under one of his commissions.[53] But these acts of plunder had been committed before Connecticut had revoked the commissions. After September, 1781, there do not seem to be any complaints from Long Islanders, so perhaps the revocation of the commissions helped solve the problem.

This discussion of the activities of Connecticut privateers on Long Island provides the background for a number of cases which came before the Court of Appeals, all originally tried in the maritime courts of Connecticut. As mentioned earlier, the Connecticut county courts, in their maritime sessions, heard over four hundred libels, many of them involving goods captured from Long Island or goods allegedly imported from Long Island. Strange libels occur in the maritime court files, such as libels of five oxen, or eleven yards of calico, or sixteen barrels of oil.[54] Such were the kinds of "British goods" seized from Long Island residents.

The first case to come before the Court of Appeals involving British goods captured on Long Island concerned a libel by the captor who had acted under a privateering commission ironically from Governor Clinton of New York. Captain William Scudder, leader of the captors, acted directly against the orders of General Washington in seizing property within the British lines. Lieutenant Colonel Eben Gray of the United States Army filed a claim to the property in the Connecticut court, since he had previously warned Scudder not to land on Long Island but only to cruise in the Sound.

---

[51] L'Hommedieu to William Floyd, 28 August, 1781, Burnett, *Letters* **6:** pp. 201–202. See also L'Hommedieu to Clinton, 8 September, 1781, and New York Delegates to Clinton, 9 September, 1781, *ibid.*, pp. 212 and 214.

[52] 15 September, 1781, Hoadly, *Records of Connecticut* **3:** p. 513.

[53] Representation to Trumbull, 21 September, 1781, Jonathan Trumbull Papers, XV, 148 (CSL).

[54] Connecticut Maritime Court Records (CSL).

Gray asked the maritime court to order that the goods remain in his hands to be disposed of according to law. But the trial court condemned most of the property captured to Scudder and the other captors. Gray appealed to Congress and the Court of Appeals reversed the lower court and condemned the captured goods for the use of the United States. Apparently the goods did belong to British subjects, since owners did not file claims to all the property. A letter of Governor Clinton is in the case file stating that his commissions did not authorize plundering on Long Island. The court by its decree upheld the authority of Washington. The judges undoubtedly needed little legal authority to conclude that Scudder's activities on Long Island were illegal.[55] The temper of the times is shown by the fact that the Connecticut court had considered Scudder's seizures legal.

The Court of Appeals decided four other cases involving claims of a large number of Long Island residents. Probably they were argued together for they were all decided the same day. In all four cases Connecticut crews commissioned by Trumbull had captured property from these Long Islanders. The claimants produced testimony to show that the captors had seized by force of arms large quantities of personal property from their homes and stores. In all cases the Connecticut maritime courts had awarded the seized property to the captors but granted appeals to the claimants. The trial court in all cases had acted in 1781 or early 1782, but the Court of Appeals did not determine the cases till the war was over and the passions and fears generated by war had begun to subside. On September 21, 1783, the court reversed the Connecticut courts in all four cases and restored the property to the claimants from Long Island.[56]

The judges of appeals, as usual, gave no reasons for their decrees restoring this property to the claimants. There are no records of the arguments of counsel. But perhaps counsel for the Long Islanders had called to the judge's attention an early resolve of Congress stating that "all persons abiding within any of the United Colonies, and deriving protection from the laws of the same, owe allegiance to the said laws,

---

[55] *British Goods (Gray v. Scudder)*, 13 December, 1780, #49, RCA.
[56] *British Goods (Wells v. Judson)*, #79; *(McCluer v. Ston)*, #80 & 101; *(Gardiner v. Johnson)*, #81; *(Hart v. Foster)*, #82, all decided 21 September, 1783, RCA.

and are members of such colony." Though ambiguous as to
the status of persons dwelling within occupied territory, the
resolve further makes clear that only those proven by open
deed to have levied war against any of the colonies, or who
adhered to the king of Great Britain or other enemies, or
gave aid or comfort to the enemy, should be deemed guilty
of treason.[57] Certainly these residents of Long Island, without further proof, should be considered citizens of New
York, not British subjects whose property could be condemned to American captors.

Counsel for the claimants might well have cited a passage
from Lee explicitly showing the illegality of these captures on
Long Island:

> It is further necessary, in order to appropriate a Thing by
> the Right of *War*, that it belong to the Enemy; for Things
> belonging to People who are neither his Subjects, nor ani-
> mated with the same Spirit as he against us, cannot be taken by
> the Right of *War*, even though they are found in the Enemy's
> Country.[58]

The judges of appeals had consistently restored property
to American claimants even though taken from parties
caught in suspicious circumstances. They must have had
even greater sympathy for these Long Island residents whose
only fault had been their misfortune to dwell within territory
occupied by the British. The judges refused to consider their
property as belonging to the enemy.

Another group of cases, however, shows that the Court of
Appeals would not upset a judgment against an American
party where strong evidence indicated fraud or collusion in
the original capture. The best example of collusive capture
involved the schooner *Dolphin* and the sloop *Diamond*.
Nathan Jackson, along with some citizens of New Jersey,
conceived a scheme for making a quick profit. Toward the
end of the war, apparently with the encouragement from
influential friends in New Jersey, Jackson hired some hands
and took them to New York where he formed a partnership
with some New York merchants. They purchased two ships,
the *Dolphin* and the *Diamond*, and a valuable cargo of British

---

[57] Ford, *JCC*, 24 June, 1776, **5:** p. 475.
[58] Lee, *Treatise of Captures*, p. 83 (Italics in original); see also pp. 71–72; Molloy, *De
Jure Maritimo*, pp. 13–14; Vattel, *Droit des Gens*, Fenwick, tr., **3:** p. 259.

cloths, crockery, and other merchandise which was scarce in New Jersey. The ships were registered in the names of the New York merchants and cleared for Halifax. Jackson then returned to New Jersey, obtained a whaleboat, and, at the beginning of December, 1782, set out to capture his own two ships which had just sailed from New York. They anchored off Governor's Island waiting for Jackson to come and take them. When he arrived with his small crew, he boarded them, and announced, in mock seriousness, that they were his prisoners. He then took the *Dolphin* and the *Diamond* into Egg Harbor as prizes where he libeled them in the state admiralty court. But General David Forman of New Jersey discovered the fraud and took control of the two ships. By long and hard questioning of one of the sailors Jackson had hired, Forman finally got the full story. The state admiralty court sentenced the property to Forman, but Jackson was granted an appeal. The Court of Appeals, in the spring and summer of 1783, conducted a thorough inquiry into the facts of the case, including some interrogatories with over a hundred questions and answers and one deposition which covered more than twenty-five pages. The court also received testimony that the brokers who had insured the two ships in New York refused to pay the claim to the New York merchants who appeared on the registry as owners. The brokers were convinced that the capture had been collusive and fraudulent. In May, 1784, the Court of Appeals dismissed Jackson's appeals in both cases and affirmed the decree of the lower court.[59] Two other cases involving collusive capture came before the court. In both cases the state courts, Connecticut and Massachusetts, condemned the ships as prize to the claimants, not to the fraudulent captors. The Court of Appeals affirmed both decrees.[60]

In one other case, however, the allegation of collusive capture was rejected by the Court of Appeals. Samuel Spencer of Connecticut, with a commission as a commander

---

[59] *Diamond* and *Dolphin* (*Jackson v. Forman*), 21 May, 1784, #91 & 92, RCA.

[60] *Four Sisters* (*Robinson v. Rogers*), 21 September, 1783, #76, and *Good Intent* (*Elkins v. Plaisted*), 23 May, 1784, #108, RCA. The confusing case of the *Polly* (*Gibbons v. Davis*), 23 May, 1779, #43, RCA, might also involve collusive or fraudulent capture, although the final decree of the Committee on Appeals awarded part of the cargo to the captain, who would have been the party guilty of the fraud. This decree does not seem to fit any hypothesis.

of the privateer schooner *Weazel*, claimed to have captured the sloop *Sally* which had sailed from New York. After the cargo had been taken ashore in New London, Nathan Peters and some members of the state militia reported the goods to the sheriff who took custody. Both Spencer and Peters filed libels in the maritime court. The jury found Spencer's libel unsupported, but it found the facts alleged in Peter's libel true. Peters had based his case on the allegation that Spencer had been engaged previously in illicit trade with Long Island and that this supposed capture of the *Sally* was part of his illegal activity. The depositions show that some people in Connecticut thought Spencer had been carrying on an illicit trade with Long Island, but other testimony supported the contentions of his libel. The trial court refused to allow an appeal by Spencer, but he petitioned the Court of Appeals to hear his case. After a hearing the court reversed the decree of the Connecticut maritime court and awarded the *Sally* and cargo lawful prize to Spencer. In this case, however, the Connecticut court refused to execute the decree of the Court of Appeals.[61]

These cases of collusive capture clearly turned on questions of fact; the judges of appeals needed no citations to convince them that collusive captors should not profit from their fraud. In the three clear cases of collusive capture, the judges assessed costs against the captors who had prosecuted the appeal.[62]

Turning now from these cases of capture of property claimed as American and cases of collusive captures, we can consider several of the other issues presented to the judges of appeals. One group of cases involved the recapture by Americans of American vessels which had previously been taken by the British.

Writers on the law of nations seemed in agreement that the original owner was entitled to have his property, captured by the enemy, restored if a fellow citizen retook it from the enemy before there had been firm possession by the enemy sufficient to make the enemy the rightful owner. If the original owner had lost all hope of recovery, the ownership had

---

[61] *Sally (Spencer v. Peters)*, 12 June, 1783, #84, RCA; Trumbull to president of Congress, 24 April, 1782, PCC, Item 66, II, 218, and New London County Maritime Court Files (CSL).

[62] *Four Sisters*, #76, *Diamond* and *Dolphin*, #91 & 92, *Good Intent*, #108, RCA.

passed to the enemy captor and any one who took it from him could have it condemned as prize just as any other enemy property. The writers discussed what constituted firm possession and it was generally thought that the captured property, to be really within the power of the enemy sufficient to change ownership, had to come within enemy territory or into some enemy place of security such as his fleet. Of course, condemnation of a captured enemy vessel by an admiralty court was thought clearly to pass title to the captors. Some earlier authors had even suggested that possession of the property by the captors for twenty-four hours was enough to change ownership and deprive the original owner of all property rights in the captured vessel or cargo.[63]

This customary law of nations had been modified by statute in Great Britain. During the Seven Years' War the prize act in force ordered that all vessels and cargoes belonging to British subjects which were captured by the enemy and later recaptured by a British vessel, whether naval vessel or privateer, should "in all cases" be restored to the original owner. The owner had to pay a privateer-captor a certain per cent of the value of the property in lieu of salvage: one-eighth if in enemy possession for twenty-four hours, one-fifth if held by the enemy between twenty-four and forty-eight hours, one-third if in enemy possession between forty-eight and ninety-six hours, and one-half if held longer than ninety-six hours. If a naval vessel recaptured the property, regardless of the time it had been held by the enemy, the recaptor always received one-eighth in lieu of salvage.[64] The Lords Commissioners took the phrase "in all cases" seriously. They restored vessels to the original British owners even though they had been taken to an enemy port and condemned in a court of admiralty.[65]

When Congress considered the problems of recaptures shortly after its resolves recommending that the thirteen colonies establish prize courts and that all prize appeals

---

[63] Lee, *Treatise of Captures*, pp. 86–101, 207–217; Vattel, *Droit des Gens*, Fenwick, tr., 3: pp. 307–308, 313; Molloy, *De Jure Maritimo*, pp. 9–11, 41; *Laws of the Admiralty* 1: p. 219.

[64] 29 Geo. II, c. 34, §24 (1756). Salvage was the allowance made for saving the ship or cargo from the risk of loss, e.g., from the hands of the enemy. Cunningham, *Dictionary* 2: no pagination.

[65] *Charming Elizabeth* (*Davis*) and *Florence* (*Breakill*), HCA, 45/1, 3, PRO.

should be to Congress, it merely adopted the exact provisions of the British prize act of 1756. The same proportion of the value of the recaptured property, depending on the length of time the enemy had held it, would be paid to the American recaptors in lieu of salvage. Congress did make one significant change, however, probably with a thought of conforming more closely to the usual doctrine of the law of nations. It provided that if the recaptured vessel or cargo had been condemned as prize in a court of admiralty, the recaptors would receive the whole of the prize they took and the original American owner would receive nothing.[66] This resolve of Congress remained in effect through most of the war, till March 27, 1781. It was then revised so that the recaptors would receive the entire value of any vessels or cargo retaken from the enemy if in possession of the enemy more than twenty-four hours. If the enemy held the vessel less than twenty-four hours before recapture, the recaptors would receive one-third of its value as salvage when the property was restored to the original owner.[67] The judges of appeals in all cases of recapture coming before them followed exactly the norms which Congress had prescribed.

The final decree respecting the brigantine *Bermudas* shows the policy of the Court of Appeals in this type of case. The *Bermudas* had been run aground and captured near Nantucket by the British sloop *Tryon*. On Sunday, February 28, 1779, the American privateer sloop *Eagle* recaptured the *Bermudas* and brought it into Connecticut for trial. In the state maritime court conflicting evidence indicated that the *Tryon* chased and seized the *Bermudas* on Wednesday, February 24, while other evidence pointed to Thursday, February 25. The jury, in a special verdict, determined the initial capture by the British had taken place on Wednesday at four P.M., which meant that the *Bermudas* was in possession of the British for ninety-nine hours. So the judge decreed one-half the value of the brig and cargo to the recaptors as salvage. On appeal, however, the Court of Appeals reversed and decreed only one-third to the recaptors. Obviously the judges had reviewed the evidence and decided that, notwith-

---

[66] Ford, *JCC*, 5 December, 1775; **3**: p. 407.
[67] *Ibid.*, **19**: p. 315. The ordinance of 4 December, 1781, retained this same proportion for salvage in cases of recapture, *ibid.*, **21**: p. 1156.

standing the verdict, the facts showed that the *Tryon* had made the capture on Thursday, not Wednesday, and that the *Bermudas* was in possession of the British only seventy-seven hours, as the claimants had stated. Therefore, according to the proportions allowed by Congress, the court awarded one-third to the recaptors. The weight of the evidence, including depositions of eyewitnesses on Nantucket, was against the verdict of the jury. This is one of the clearest cases of the review of the facts which a jury had previously determined.[68] Even after the furor of the sloop *Active* case, the judges of appeals were not reluctant to review the jury-tried facts *de novo*. This case shows that the judges of appeals carried out the exact prescriptions of the congressional resolves whenever they applied. Even when the vessel had been in possession of the British for three months, without being condemned in an admiralty court, the judges of appeals reversed the lower court which had granted the whole ship as prize to the recaptors. The recaptured vessel was restored to the original owners who were required to pay to the recaptors one-half the value of the ship and cargo.[69] After Congress changed the proportion to be awarded to the recaptors, the Court of Appeals, of course, followed the modified ordinance.[70]

In another category of cases, joint capture, the decrees of the judges of appeals, as usual, give us little indication of the substantive law the judges were applying. The British writers on questions of prize law took a variety of positions on joint capture and the continental authors read in America said nothing at all.[71] When two or more privateers shared in making a capture, obviously they should share in dividing the prize after its condemnation. But precisely what type of

---

[68] *Bermudas* (*Cooke v. Conckling*), 23 December, 1780, #50, RCA.

[69] *Charming Sally* (*Edwards v. Elderkin*), 5 January, 1780, #46, RCA. Other cases of recapture involved: *Nancy* (*Babcock v. Bradford*), 9 August, 1779, #47; *Pitt* (*Courter v. Huntington*), 13 January, 1780, #63; *John* and *Hepsabeth* (*Anthony v. Deshon*), 5 April, 1781, #69 & 70; *Adventurer* (*Boitar v. Young*), 17 August, 1781 and 21 May, 1784, #106, RCA.

[70] *Polly* (*Hathaway v. Ingersol*), 21 May, 1784, #107, RCA, and Minute Book, Appeals from Massachusetts Maritime Courts (MSJC). Perhaps this case turned on the dubious loyalty to America of the original owner.

[71] Cornelius van Bynkershoek, *Quaestionum Juris Publici, Libri Duo*, Tenney Frank, tr., (2 v., Oxford, 1930) 2: pp. 105–107. The author did treat the question of joint capture, but there is no indication that his impenetrable Latin was read by American lawyers in the eighteenth century.

activity by a privateer made it share in the capture? Some British writers suggested that mere presence of a privateer at the place of the capture, even though the other privateer by itself had engaged the prize and took possession of it, made both privateers joint captors.[72] "In case two Ships of the same Nation, having Letters of Marque, are at Sea in Company, and one of them taken [sic] a Prize before the other can come up, nevertheless the last Ship being ready and prepar'd for Battle, has a Right to a Moiety [half] of that Prize."[73] Another writer restates the same rule, requiring merely that the one privateer was in sight at the time the other made the capture in order for both to share equally in the prize. He states the rationale for this seemingly inequitable rule: "yet the other being in Sight shall have an equal Share of the Prize, though he afforded no Assistance in the Capture; because his Presence however struck Terror in the Enemy; and made him yield, which perhaps he would not have done, had his Conqueror been single."[74] Lee, the British author probably most relied on by American lawyers in prize cases, rejected the opinion that mere presence sufficed to make a privateer merit a share in the prize. Lee followed the continental author Bynkershoek and stated that only those ships which actually engaged the enemy should share in the prize: "what is taken by Means of their common Force, may be in common between them." The prize should be divided proportionately according to the size and strength of each captor.[75] Lee also discussed (as usual, parroting Bynkershoek) the legal effect of agreements between privateer captains to sail together and divide all prizes taken by either, or by both together. Lee concluded that the captains could not thereby bind the owners of the privateers, so the agreement would have no legal effect. "[W]hatever, therefore, the Captain did, he did without Order, and therefore it could not bind his Employer."[76]

This variety of opinions in the standard works relied on by American lawyers led to utterly irreconcilable court decrees in the various state prize courts. Congress acted, therefore, to

---

[72] Molloy, *De Jure Maritimo*, pp. 42–43.
[73] *Laws of the Admiralty*, pp. 219–220
[74] Beawes, *Lex Mercatoria*, pp. 212–213.
[75] Lee, *Treatise of Captures*, pp. 221–223.
[76] *Ibid.*, pp. 219–220.

remove this source of conflicting court determinations. The ordinance of Congress passed in 1782, late in the war, is a clear suggestion that American lawyers did look to these British writers and when the sources disagreed, so did the American lawyers and judges who relied on them.

Whereas there hath been great variance in the decisions of several maritime courts within the United States, concerning the pretensions of vessels claiming a share of prizes, as being in sight at the time of capture; some having adjudged that the mere circumstance of being in sight was a sufficient foundation of title, while others have required proof of a more active influence: and whereas this inconvenience hath arisen from the want of an uniform rule of determination in such cases:

Be it therefore ordained by the United States in Congress assembled, that no share of any prize shall be adjudged to a vessel being in sight at the time of capture, unless the said vessel shall have been able at the time when the captured vessel struck, to throw a shot as far as the space between herself and the captured vessel; and that every vessel coming in aid of the captors, which shall have been able at the time when the captured vessel struck, to throw a shot as aforesaid, and shall have been duly authorised to make captures, shall be entitled to share according to the number of her men and the weight of her metal: provided that nothing herein contained shall be construed to effect any agreement which shall have been previously made between vessels cruizing in consort.[77]

Even though the judges of appeals did not state the basis of their determinations, we can now turn to some of the cases they decided and speculate as to what that basis might have been.

Three cases in which joint capture was alleged were finally determined in August, 1780, at the first regular term of the newly established Court of Appeals. The case of the ship *Anna Maria* involved a written agreement between two American privateers to sail together and to share all prizes taken by either privateer. The agreement to keep company was to remain binding even if the privateers had lost sight of each other, unless they had been separated for forty-eight hours. One of the privateers captured the *Anna Maria* after being separated from the other for about twenty-four hou s. A number of old sea captains testified that, during the late

---

[77] Ford, *JCC* **22**: pp. 10–11, and **21**: p. 1172.

French wars, such an agreement of consortship between captains of privateers was always held binding on the owners. One stated that it bound the owners even though the agreement was only verbal. But the Massachusetts maritime court awarded the entire prize to the one privateer which was in sight and actually made the capture, thus ignoring the customary law described in the various depositions. The Court of Appeals affirmed the lower court decree.[78] The trial court and the Court of Appeals most likely accepted arguments based on Lee, who had held that agreements between privateer captains did not bind the owners of the privateers. The prize, therefore, was awarded to the ship which had actually taken the *Anna Maria*.

The British transport vessel *Mermaid* had been wrecked near the shore of New Jersey. Many of the passengers, especially women and children, had lost their lives. Two American privateers approached to assist and also to take possession of the ship. At the same time a boat from shore came out and helped land the men and cargo. When the two privateers libeled the *Mermaid*, the owner of the boat filed a claim as sole captor. In the New Jersey admiralty court the jury awarded the entire prize to the owner and crew of the boat, perhaps because some evidence indicated that the boat had reached the *Mermaid* slightly before the privateers or perhaps because the boat crew were local residents, while the privateers were from other states. The Court of Appeals reversed, ordering that the prize be divided into three equal parts, one for each of the privateers and the other for the claimants.[79] Since all three vessels actually participated in the capture, they were all entitled to a share of the prize according to Lee, as well as the other English writers who required mere presence for a valid claim of joint capture. Lee would have required distribution in proportion to the number of guns and men, which would have led to obviously inequitable results in this case.

Two years later the Court of Appeals finally decided a case

---

[78] *Anna Maria* (*Bucklin v. White*), 18 August, 1780, #21, RCA.

[79] *Mermaid* (*Gleason v. Mapes*), 24 August, 1780, #53, and Miscellaneous Court Records, RCA. The third case of joint capture decided in August, 1780 involved the *Barbary* (*Decatur v. Ridler*), 18 August, 1780, #61 and Miscellaneous Court Records, RCA. There is no evidence in the extant records on which one can even base a speculation as to the reasons why the Court of Appeals rejected the claim of those who purported to be joint captors.

involving the brigantine *Countess of Eglinton* which had been captured seven years earlier in 1776. Two American privateers had been sailing together under an agreement between the captains to share equally in all captures made by either. Both were in sight at the time of the capture, but all the evidence shows that the one privateer, the swift-sailing sloop *America*, actually made the capture and that the *Countess of Eglinton* could easily have escaped the other, the larger, hulking sloop *Retaliation*, which was some five miles away at the time the *Countess of Eglinton* struck. The superior court of Massachusetts awarded six-seventh of the prize to the privateer which effected the capture and one-seventh to the larger privateer which was also in sight at the time of capture. This award must have been based on the jury's opinion of the proportional contribution of each to the capture, and not on the relative size of the two privateers, for the larger received only one-seventh. The Court of Appeals reversed, decreeing that the prize should be shared equally between the two captors, and, surprisingly, that the owners of the *America* should pay the costs of the appeal.[80]

The court's determination in this case at first seems merely to be a rejection of the previously followed position of Lee who thought that prizes should be awarded to the captors who actually engaged in making the seizure, not to those privateers merely in sight at the time of capture. Earlier writers, as we have seen, expressed the view that all privateers present when the prize struck should share equally in the prize. The judges of appeals did award an equal share in the *Countess of Eglinton* to the *Retaliation*, which was five miles astern, but in sight, at the time of capture. The reason for this decree, however, was probably derived not from English writings at all, but from the ordinance of Congress of 1782. We have just seen that Congress, by this act, tried to settle disputes and conflicting court adjudications over joint captures by establishing as a norm that a joint captor had to be within gunshot at the time the prize surrendered. Congress added that nothing in the ordinance should be construed "to effect any agreement which shall have been previously made between vessels cruizing in consort."[81] The

---

[80] *Countess of Eglinton (Jones v. Babcock),* 14 September, 1783, #9, RCA.
[81] Ford, *JCC,* 8 January, 1782, **22:** pp. 10–11, and **21:** p. 1172.

Countess of Eglinton had been captured before this 1782 ordinance and the Court of Appeal's decree was not issued till a year after the ordinance passed. The captains of the two privateer sloops, *America* and *Retaliation*, had agreed to share equally in all captures made by either. Although earlier, in the case of the *Anna Maria*, the judges of appeals had considered just such an agreement as not binding on the owners, probably following Lee's opinion, now they apparently considered the agreement binding on the owners because of the clause in the congressional ordinance purporting not to affect such agreements. If this interpretation of the court's decree is correct, it demonstrates a narrow, confining approach of the judges to the letter of congressional ordinances. Congress probably did not think it was settling the disputed issue about the power of captains to bind the owners of privateers by their agreements, but only intended to leave such agreements as they had been, that is, of no legal force unless approved by the owners. The judges of appeals, however, apparently read the ordinance as retroactively validating such agreements between captains, even without any agreement between the owners.

One final point, the judges of appeals ordered the owners of the small sloop, *America*, the actual captor, to pay all costs of the appeal. Perhaps the judges had concluded that the six-year delay in concluding this appeal had been caused by the owners of the *America*.

The ordinance of Congress of 1782 had set up a single norm for determining joint captures: whether the alleged joint captor was able to throw a shot to the captured vessel. The Court of Appeals heard one case of joint capture made after this ordinance went into effect. The schooner *Squirrel* had been captured by two American privateers. The commander of one of them libeled the schooner as joint captor with the other privateer. But the second privateer filed a separate claim alleging to be the sole captor according to the ordinance of Congress. The claimant had obtained depositions from a mate on the *Squirrel* stating that the shot from the other privateer had fallen some five yards astern, whereas the shot from the claimant's vessel had gone over the *Squirrel*. Therefore the claimant argued that the other privateer should not share in the prize since it was not within gunshot at the time of the capture. But neither the Rhode

Island admiralty court nor the Court of Appeals were swayed
by such a quibble. Both courts decreed that the prize should
be shared between both privateers according to the proportion ordained by Congress.[82]

In these cases of joint capture we get a strong impression
that the judges of appeals listened attentively to arguments
based on the various treatises on prize law, especially Lee, but
that they looked first to any ordinance of Congress that
seemed to apply. As we saw in the last chapter, the judges of
appeals felt constrained by a strict reading of any congressional acts.

The judges of appeals faced no more difficult or complex
type of case than the relatively large number of captures
claimed as neutral or allied property. About fifteen such
cases came before the judges, often with diplomatic interven-
tion to impress upon them the importance of their determinations.

Many principles of the law of nations, as we have already
seen, had been discussed with divergent positions taken by
the different eighteenth-century writers. A few basic norms
regarding neutral rights, however, were widely accepted.
Privateers, for instance, were forbidden to make captures of
enemy vessels within neutral ports.[83] Although neutral vessels had the right of free passage in time of war, they had the
obligation of submitting to visit and search by belligerent
vessels that stopped them at sea trying to find out if they
carried enemy or contraband cargoes.[84] Unless there existed
a treaty altering the law of nations, neutral property captured on board an enemy ship, with the exception of contraband, was not lawful prize. Such neutral cargo was to be
restored to the owner if he could overcome the presumption
that, since found on an enemy ship, it was enemy property.[85]
On the other hand, without a treaty to change the law of
nations, the property of an enemy on board a neutral ship
could be seized and condemned to the captor as lawful prize.

---

[82] *Squirrel (Stoddard v. Read)*, 1 October, 1783, #90, RCA.
[83] Beawes, *Lex Mercatoria*, p. 211; *Laws of the Admiralty* 1: p. 222; Molloy, *De Jure Maritimo*, p. 48.
[84] Beawes, *Lex Mercatoria*, p. 212; *Laws of the Admiralty* 1: p. 223; Molloy, *De Jure Maritimo*, p. 51; Vattel, *Droit des Gens*, Fenwick, tr., 3: p. 272.
[85] Lee, *Treatise of Captures*, pp. 189–197; Vattel, *Droit des Gens*, Fenwick, tr., 3: p. 273; Hugo Grotius, *De Jure Belli ac Pacis, Libri Tres*, Francis W. Kelsey, tr. (2 v., Oxford, 1925) 2: p. 668; Molloy, *De Jure Maritimo*, pp. 13–14.

Only by treaty did free ships make free goods. The neutral vessel carrying enemy property probably would not be liable to confiscation, unless it was carrying contraband or violating a blockade.[86] The brief but authoritative statement of the law of prize in the *Report of the Law Officers of the Crown* summed up many of these widely accepted principles:

> When two powers are at war, they have a right to make prizes of ships, goods, and effects of each other upon the high seas; whatever is the property of the enemy may be acquired by capture at sea; but the property of a friend cannot be taken, provided he observed his neutrality.
>
> Hence the law of nations has established:
>
> That the goods of an enemy on board the ship of a friend may be taken.
>
> That the lawful goods of a friend on board the ship of an enemy ought to be restored.
>
> That contraband goods going to the enemy, though the property of a friend, may be taken as prize, because supplying the enemy with what enables him better to carry on the war is a departure from neutrality.[87]

These norms of international conduct in war could be varied by treaty. The nations agreeing to the treaty then bound themselves to different rules of conduct toward each other concerning, for instance, what would be considered contraband, or what ship papers would be accepted to prove the neutrality of the ship and its cargo. The *Report* continued:

> Though the law of nations be the general rule, yet it may, by mutual agreement between the two powers, be varied or departed from; and where there is an alteration or exception introduced by particular treaties, that is the law between the parties to the treaty; and the law of nations only governs so far as it is not derogated from by the treaty.[88]

During the summer of 1776 the Continental Congress foresaw the need of entering into treaties in order to maintain the recently proclaimed independence. The committee

---

[86] Lee, *Treatise of Captures*, pp. 197–207; Vattel, *Droit des Gens*, Fenwick, tr., **3:** p. 273; Molloy, *De Jure Maritimo*, p. 14. Lee and Molloy would make the neutral vessel liable to condemnation along with the enemy cargo if the master of the vessel knew of the enemy cargo aboard.

[87] In Marsden, *Law of the Sea* **2:** p. 350.

[88] *Ibid.*, pp. 353–354.

appointed to prepare a model treaty, drawing heavily on European practice as reflected in the treaty of Utrecht of 1713, presented to Congress a series of thirty articles which provided the model for most of the American treaties entered into during the next quarter of a century.[89] This plan for treaties was not a treaty and so bound no one. The principles of the plan, however, took on added significance when the Americans and French entered into a treaty of friendship and commerce based principally on this plan. An important aim of American foreign policy in its nascent state was to make trade as free as possible. Since American economic life depended on an uninterrupted flow of commerce even in time of war, Congress realized that neutral rights must be clearly stated and strenuously preserved. Congress looked forward to the day when the American states would be neutral in wars between European nations. The treaty plan of 1776 and the French treaty of 1778, therefore, endorsed the rights of either signatory to engage in neutral trade when the other party was at war. Either party to the treaty could trade with the enemy of the other party and even carry cargo between two enemy ports. Reversing the norm of the customary law of nations, free ships were to give freedom to goods, that is, enemy cargo (except contraband) found on a neutral ship would not be liable to confiscation. Contraband was carefully defined and did not include food or naval stores, the items which Britain had in recent wars added to the contraband list.[90]

Only two cases came before the Court of Appeals based directly on the French treaties. The Americans and French had agreed in the Treaty of Amity and Commerce to protect and defend the vessels and property belonging to each other. Both parties further bound themselves to use all their efforts to recover and restore the vessels and goods belonging to the other. Two French ships had been retaken from the British by American privateers. The trial courts awarded both ships to the recaptors. The judges of appeals, however, adhered to the terms and the spirit of the French treaty by restoring the

---

[89] Samuel F. Bemis, *The Diplomacy of the American Revolution* (reprint, Bloomington, 1959), pp. 45–46; Carlton Savage, *Policy of the United States Toward Maritime Commerce in War* (2 v., Washington, 1934–1936) **1**: pp. 2–4.

[90] G. Chinard, ed., *The Treaties of 1778 and Allied Documents* (Baltimore, 1928), pp. 7–11, 34–43; Felix Gilbert, *To the Farewell Address* (Princeton, 1961), pp. 50–51, 68.

ships to the French claimants and allowing the same proportion of salvage as if they had been American ships recaptured.[91] Perhaps the judges of appeals had heard argument
by counsel for the French owners based on Lee, who held
that goods of a belligerent state recaptured by his ally should
be restored to the original state since "our Allies make as it
were one State with ourselves."[92]

Congress, as we have seen, from the early years of the war
faced serious international embarrassment due to over-
zealous privateers, especially in the capture of the Portuguese vessel *Our Lady of Mount Carmel*.[93] Congress had
issued a proclamation in 1778 ordering all captains and
officers of American vessels to observe strictly the terms of
their commissions and instructions. Neutral rights, the
privateers were told, must be regarded as sacred.[94] Attacks
on Spanish vessels were especially painful to Congress during the early years of the war when Congress still hoped for a
Spanish alliance similar to the French one.

When the Russian Empress Catherine, anxious to protect
neutral rights on the seas, proposed the armed neutrality of
1780, the American Congress quickly recognized an opportunity to reinforce the principles already expressed in the
treaty plan of 1776 and the French treaty of 1778. The
principles which the Empress announced provided that neutral vessels could navigate freely between ports and along the
coast of belligerent nations; except for contraband, the
property of belligerents was not liable to confiscation when
found on neutral vessels (free ships make free goods); contraband did not include naval stores and provisions; a blockaded port existed only where a belligerent had stationed its
vessels near enough to the port to make access clearly
dangerous; and these principles of armed neutrality should
provide the rule of decision in prize cases. As a belligerent, of
course, America could not join the neutral nations who
formed this largely ineffective league. In October, 1780,
however, Congress ordered the board of admiralty to draw
up instructions for the commanders of American armed

---

[91] *Le Vern (de Valnais v. Tucker)*, 25 July, 1780, #56, and *Maria Theresa (Forcan v. Langdon)*, 13 June, 1783, #97, RCA; Ford, *JCC* 11: pp. 425–426.
[92] Lee, *Treatise of Captures*, pp. 210–212.
[93] Chapter II above.
[94] Ford, *JCC* 11: p. 486.

vessels containing the principles of the armed neutrality. The
report of the admiralty board, adopted by Congress on November 27, 1780, instructed the captains of all ships of war
and privateers: to permit all neutral vessels to navigate on the
high seas or coasts of America, unless they carried contraband or soldiers to the British; to capture no property
belonging to the enemy when found on a neutral vessel,
except contraband, and to consider as contraband only those
items expressly enumerated in the French treaty. These instructions, Congress determined, were to serve as the rule of
decision in all prize cases.[95] The treaty plan of 1776 and the
French treaty of 1778 expressed a liberal view of neutral
rights endorsed by Congress, but they had no effect on the
decrees of the judges of appeals dealing with captured neutral property. The new instructions to commanders of armed
vessels, however, clearly expressed the law to govern cases of
capture of neutral ships or cargoes. These instructions of
November, 1780, changed the customary law of neutral
rights as applied by the judges of appeals.

In the early years of the war no cases of capture of neutral
property came before the Commissioners of Appeals. In the
first two weeks of November, 1779, however, the commissioners decided four cases in which ships and cargoes
claimed as neutral property had been captured by American
privateers. The same commissioners in general decided these
four cases and they followed the principles of the customary
law of nations as the basis of their decrees.

The brigantine *Nuestra Señora de Merced* had been seized
and taken into Massachusetts where the captors libeled it as
British property. The brig's commander claimed the ship
and cargo as Spanish property, not liable to forfeiture. The
jury returned a special verdict stating that the brig and part
of the cargo were Spanish property, but that the remainder
of the cargo was British and lawful prize to the captors. The
jury also found that the vessel was entitled to its freight.
After the judge of the trial court drew up his sentence based
on this verdict, both parties appealed to Congress. The
commissioners affirmed the lower court decree touching the
ship and part of the cargo which they restored to the com-

---

[95] *Ibid.* **18:** pp. 864–866, 905–906, 1008, 1097–1098; Hutchinson and Rachal,
Papers of Madison **2:** pp. 165–167; **3:** pp. 43–45; Morris, *Peacemakers*, pp. 164–167;
Bemis, *Diplomacy*, pp. 149–163.

mander as neutral property. But part of the cargo (it is not clear that it was entirely the same part that the lower court condemned) they decreed to be lawful prize. The Commissioners of Appeals, in one of their rare opinions, stated that it appeared to them from the evidence produced that this part of the cargo was British property. They likewise ordered that the captors should pay the claimant the customary freight for the forfeited goods.[96]

This decree followed the generally accepted principles of the law of nations. Lee, for instance, gave the opinions of several authors on the legitimacy of confiscating enemy goods on neutral ships and concluded, with his usual authority, Bynkershoek, that such enemy property was liable to seizure. But Bynkershoek had argued against ordering the captor to pay the captain of the captured vessel freight on the enemy goods. Lee, however, turned to the *Report of the Law Officers* as authority for concluding that, when the goods of an enemy are taken on board the ship of a friend, the captors should pay freight for the enemy goods which were condemned. The judges of appeals could have relied on Vattel who also thought that freight should be paid for enemy goods taken on a neutral ship.[97]

The ship *Valenciano* had likewise been taken and brought into Massachusetts for condemnation. The master of the ship filed a claim to the vessel and cargo as Spanish property not liable to capture. There was strong evidence to show that the ship belonged to Peter White, the captain, who tried to pass himself off as Pedro Blanco, a Spaniard. White, an Englishman, apparently had sold the ship in Spain to get it under Spanish colors. He carried double papers to protect the vessel from capture by the British or the Americans. The jury in the trial court condemned the ship and part of the cargo as British property. It stated that there was strong suspicion that the remainder of the cargo was also British property under false cover. Both parties appealed to the Massachusetts superior court, where the lower court decree was affirmed, except that part of the cargo was released as

---

[96] *Nuestra Señora de Merced (Cabot v. Sagarra)*, 6 November, 1779, #57, RCA. After a careful study of the bills of lading and other ship papers, it remains a mystery how the judges distinguished the Spanish from the British property.

[97] Lee, *Treatise of Captures*, pp. 199–207; *Report of the Law Officers*, in Marsden, *Law of the Sea* 2: p. 356; Vattel, *Droit des Gens*, Fenwick, tr., 3: p. 273.

neutral property. The claimant appealed to Congress and
the Commissioners of Appeals affirmed the lower court decree, except for certain parts of the cargo which they ordered
restored to the claimant.[98] In this case also the decrees in all
three courts follow the widely held principles of the law of
nations as expressed, for example, in Lee or Vattel. Neutral
goods taken on board enemy vessels should be restored to
the neutral owners.[99] In the Massachusetts superior court
this section of Lee had been explicitly referred to in the oral
arguments.[100]

When the Commissioners of Appeals were convinced in
another case that a captured ship and its entire cargo were
neutral property, they reversed the lower court decision and
restored the vessel and cargo to the claimant, ordering the
captors to pay the costs of the trial and appeal.[101] But when
the evidence showed that the property claimed as neutral was
actually British property, the commissioners affirmed the
lower court decree awarding the prize to the captors.[102] Thus

---

[98] *Valenciano (Luca v. Cleveland)*, 1 November, 1779, #58, RCA. In this case also
the present records make it difficult to explain the distinction the commissioners of
appeals made between Spanish and British property.

[99] Lee, *Treatise of Captures*, pp. 189–196; Vattel, *Droit des Gens*, Fenwick, tr., **3:** p.
273.

[100] Jedidiah Foster, Notebook of Appeals to the Superior Court of Massachusetts,
1777–1779 (facsimile, United States Circuit Court of Appeals, library, Boston), pp.
414–417.

[101] *Santander y los Santos Martires (Tracy v. de Llano)*, 6 November, 1779, #60, RCA.

[102] *Good Intent (Ploy v. Gurney)*, 13 November, 1779, #44, RCA. About the same
time the commissioners considered these four cases, they heard two other cases
involving neutral claims. In both cases the neutral ship had been captured by the
British and then recaptured by Americans. The trial court in both cases awarded
one half the value of the prize to the American recaptors as salvage. The commissioners of appeals affirmed both sentences. At first it seems strange to allow salvage
for recapture of neutral property. If the neutral ship had not been liable to
forfeiture to the British captors, the American recaptors should not derive any right
to salvage. In one of these cases, however, the vessel had originally been British
property. After an earlier capture and condemnation by Americans, it was purchased by Spanish subjects. By the British prize acts, British vessels recaptured from
the enemy, even after condemnation, were "in all cases" restored to the original
owner. 22 Geo. II, c. 34, §24 (1756), 16 Geo. III, c. 5, §24 (1776). So in this case the
British admiralty would apparently have restored the vessel to the original British
owner and not allowed the Spanish owners any share in it at all. The American
recaptors, therefore, were entitled to salvage for taking this vessel out of British
hands and saving it from being restored to the original British owner. The vessel
was taken by the Americans just a week before Spain declared war on Britain in
June, 1779, so the fact that Britain and Spain were at war when this case was heard
should not have affected the legal status of the vessel. *Victoria (Ignatio v. Board of War
for Massachusetts)*, 8 November, 1779, #59, RCA. In the other case the claimants
alleged that they were Danish subjects residing on the island of Santa Croix. The

in these four cases which were decided by the Commissioners of Appeals early in November, 1779, it seems clear that the traditional principles of the law of nations, especially as found in Lee and Vattel, provided the rule of decision.

When the Court of Appeals began hearing cases in 1780, the judges continued following the principles of the customary law of nations in cases of neutral captures where the property had been seized before the new instructions of Congress of November, 1780, to captains of armed vessels. The instructions, going along with the principles of armed neutrality and reversing the customary law of nations, declared that free ships should make free goods, that is, enemy cargoes on neutral ships should not be liable to capture. The Courts of Appeals in 1781 heard a case of a Dutch ship carrying a cargo which the trial court had condemned as British property. Since the original capture had taken place before the new congressional instructions to captains went into effect, the Court of Appeals affirmed the lower court decree, which had followed the traditional law of nations in condemning the enemy cargo, releasing the neutral ship and allowing to the owners the payment of freight for the cargo.[103]

Several other cases of allegedly neutral captures came before the Court of Appeals. In all of these, however, either the ship and cargo were considered neutral property and restored to the claimants,[104] or the ship and cargo were adjudged British property and condemned.[105] In these cases the judges did not have a chance to apply the principle that free ships make free goods. As we shall see, the court did write two opinions in which there was some discussion of the relevance of the congressional instructions of November, 1780.

The Court of Appeals also heard three cases of recapture

British had captured their ship, but had been forced by a storm to run it aground. The original owners showed a willingness in the claim to pay any salvage the court might decree. It is not clear whether the salvage was for recapture or for recovering the stranded vessel and towing it ashore. *Jane (Fosset v. Foster)*, 18 January, 1780, #48, RCA.

[103] *Brunette (Williams v. Mackay)*, 4 August, 1781, #75, RCA.

[104] *George (Jennings v. Griffin)*, 23 December, 1780, #40, and *Good Fortune (Allen v. McConnell)*, 14 June, 1783 (*Howell v. McConnell*), 11 May, 1787, #87, RCA. For the subsequent action in the United States Federal Courts in the case of the sloop *George*, see *Jennings v. Carson*, 4 Cranch 2 (1807).

[105] *Nonesuch (Garret v. Fellows)*, 13 May, 1783, #94, RCA.

of neutral vessels which had previously been taken by the British. In all three cases the judges restored the vessel and the entire cargo to the neutral claimants without granting any salvage to the American recaptors. The court applied the principles of the new instructions of November, 1780, which allowed neutral vessels to sail freely along the coast of America and which stated that belligerent goods on a neutral vessel were not subject to seizure.[106] In a case decided by the court before these three cases, the judges, in one of their rare opinions which will be analyzed later in this chapter, had made clear that the ordinance of Congress on recaptures referred to recaptures of American, not of neutral property.[107] Though in these cases the lower courts were not always sensitive to preserve neutral rights, the Court of Appeals restored the three ships and their entire cargoes to the original owners.[108]

The case of the *Minerva* most clearly shows the reliance by the Court of Appeals on the congressional instructions which embodied the principles of armed neutrality. The *Minerva*, a Prussian vessel, had been held by the British for fifteen days before an American privateer recaptured it. The judges of appeals restored the entire property to the Prussian captain, but because of the special circumstances of the relief provided by the American recaptors, the court decreed that the Prussian owner should pay all court costs and also the charges that had arisen from taking care of the ship and its cargo after it had been recaptured. The judges assessed these special costs, which they did not call salvage, at £680 Massachusetts currency.[109] John Lowell, counsel for the owner of the privateer the *Grand Turk*, Elias Hasket Derby of Salem, Massachusetts, wrote to Derby three days before the decree of the Court of Appeals was dated. Apparently the judges had orally expressed this decree along with the reasons for it. This letter gives us a glimpse of the way the court functioned and of the application of the principles of armed neutrality to this capture. Lowell wrote to his client:

---

[106] Ford, *JCC* 18: p. 865.
[107] *Resolution (Miller v. Ingersoll)*, and *(O'Brien v. Miller)*, 15 August, 1781, 2 Dall. 1, RCA.
[108] *Hope (Coakley v. Martin)*, 6 May, 1784, #85, and *Nostra Seigniora da Solidade e St. Miguel e Almas (Randall v. Doo)*, 29 May, 1783, #88, RCA.
[109] *Minerva (Derby v. Koler)*, 27 May, 1783, #96, RCA.

I have the very great Mortification of informing you that the
Minerva & her Cargo are acquitted, after a Trial of five Days.
The Court were informed of the Opinion of the [trial] Judge
but it had not, nor could as they said, have any Weight, they
took it up as if it had never been tried—It seems the late
Judges of this Court had determined a Cause somewhat tho'
not exactly similar to this, & these Gentlemen were of Opinion
that the Resolves of Congress compell'd them to proceed on
the Principles of the armed Neutrality & that the Freedom of
the Vessel which they determined to be Prussian made the
Cargo free. I am still of a different opinion and so I find most
of the Gentlemen to whom I stated the Case here. . . . [A]fter
we had left the Cause with the Court they gave us a second
Hearing on the Point of Law but we could not prevail—they
however declared that they tho't it an hard Case & therefore
instead of ordering you to pay Costs as usual they ordered
them to pay them & we have accordingly got an allowance
from the other Party for Costs & Charges the Sum of £680.[110]

The judges of appeals decided two cases in 1781 and 1782
which demonstrated better than any others their approach in
handling cases of neutral property. In both cases the judges
wrote opinions explaining at length the reasons for their
decisions. The cases of the ship *Resolution* and the brigantine
Eersten involved ships from Amsterdam and Ostend in the
low countries which had been captured by American
privateers for trading with the inhabitants of the island of
Dominica. This island had been British but in September,
1778, had surrendered to the French. The inhabitants had
signed a capitulation in which the French general guaranteed their property and estates from confiscation. By article
seventeen of the capitulation the merchants of Dominica
were allowed to receive vessels from all parts of the world,
English vessels alone excepted, without fear of confiscation.
They were allowed to sell their merchandise and engage in
trade. Confronted in these two cases with subtle nuances of
the law of nations and treaty interpretation, the judges of
appeals, in formulating their opinions, also expressed their
views on some fundamental principles of substantive prize
law which were implicitly operative in the cases of neutral
captures already discussed. These two opinions, therefore,

---

[110] Lowell to Derby, 24 May, 1783, Miscellaneous Bound Collection (MHS). See
also, Lowell to Derby, 9 December, 1782, *ibid.*, explaining Lowell's work on the case
to show the cargo was not Prussian.

make explicit some of the reasoning implied in the cases of neutral property in which no opinion was written. They also tend to confirm some of the hypothetical reconstructions of the sources and mode of argument behind the decrees which have been analyzed throughout this chapter. Since the judges in these opinions listed the arguments of counsel, obviously from the oral arguments, then commented on them, the opinions also demonstrate the type of argument counsel presented to the court.

The ship *Resolution*, owned by merchants of Amsterdam, sailed in March, 1781, from Dominica for Amsterdam with a valuable cargo of sugar and coffee. The cargo belonged to various citizens of Dominica, allegedly capitulants, and it was consigned to the owners of the vessel in Amsterdam. On this voyage the *Resolution* was captured by a British armed vessel, taken to Nevis, and, upon an examination of its papers, released. Again the ship was captured by a British vessel, from which it was recaptured by an American privateer. Another British vessel recaptured the *Resolution* from the American ship, and finally an American privateer, the brig *Ariel*, took the ship and sent it to Philadelphia.

The captors libeled the *Resolution* and its cargo in the Pennsylvania admiralty court. Francis Hopkinson, the admiralty judge, analyzed the arguments of the parties and wrote an opinion expressing his reasons for at least part of the judgment. In the opinion, however, he gave no reasons for acquitting the ship as neutral property. He apparently considered the vessel neutral because of the argument of counsel for the Dutch owners. The British king had by order in council of December, 1780, extended the effect of the capitulation for four months to Dutch vessels carrying the property of capitulants to Holland. Consequently, counsel for the owners contended, notwithstanding the war which had been declared by Britain against the Netherlands in that same month, Dutch ships carrying property from Dominica could not be lawfully seized by British armed vessels. However many British ships might have captured it, the *Resolution* could not have been condemned as lawful prize to the British, so the American recaptors could acquire no legal right to the ship merely by taking it from the British.

But the cargo shipped by the capitulants of Dominica presented a more complex question. Hopkinson declared that allies were not in all cases bound by the agreements one of them entered with a third party. If the French had intended the Americans to be held to the terms of the capitulation, they should have made this explicit in the agreement. Furthermore, the Americans surely had a right to take British property, and a scrutiny of the ship papers gave Hopkinson strong reason to believe that the cargo, though artfully covered, was in fact British property. Therefore he restored the *Resolution* to the Dutch owners, but condemned the cargo as lawful prize to the captors. Both parties appealed: the captors objected to the restoration of the ship to its owners, and the claimants for the shippers of the cargo sought restoration of the cargo.[111]

In August, 1781, judges Griffin and Paca delivered a lengthy and detailed opinion explaining their decree in the case.[112] They began by enunciating the norm which governed all their decrees, that the court must be directed by the resolves and ordinances of Congress, and where Congress was silent, by the laws, usage, and practice of nations. (We have already seen this rule implicitly operative in all the decrees discussed.) The court had heard the alternative legal theories of the captors' case and took up in turn each of the bases for condemnation that the captors had urged. They had argued that both the ship and its cargo were prize, but if not the ship at least the cargo, and if the whole cargo was not lawful prize, at least the principal part of it should be condemned.

Turning first to the legality of the capture of the ship itself, the judges agreed with the trial court and rejected the argument of the captors. The mere fact that the British had held possession of the *Resolution* for more than twenty-four hours did not transfer the property to the British. A capture not authorized by the law of nations could not have that legal effect. Applying a principle we have seen implied in other

---

[111] *Miller v. The Resolution*, 1781, Hopkinson, *Writings* **3**: pp. 70–84. The arguments of counsel are summarized by Hopkinson.

[112] *Resolution*, 2 Dall. 1, RCA. It is important to observe that only the first few pages of this opinion have been preserved in the manuscript case file in the National Archives. For the rest of the opinion one is forced to rely on the report of this case in 2 Dallas 1. Although Dallas was not scrupulously careful as an editor of these opinions, it seems from the part that can be compared with the manuscript and from the other opinion in this case that this opinion was reported by Dallas with substantial accuracy.

decrees, the judges wrote, "[N]ot an Instance had been produced where a Capture not authorized by the Rights of War has been held to change the Property; but many Authorities have been brought to show, that no Change is effected by such a Capture." Unless the property captured belonged to the enemy, there could be no legal prize. There was no evidence that the British privateer had any legal right to make the capture of the *Resolution*. By the proclamation of the British king, a Dutch ship laded with a cargo belonging to the capitulants of Dominica could not be condemned as prize. The British privateer, therefore, acted without authority in making the seizure, so recapture from this British ship gave no more legal right than recapture from a pirate. The libelants had argued before the Court of Appeals that the capture made by the British privateer must be considered legal, for after a capture and occupation for twenty-four hours the legality of the capture was no longer open for question and examination. The judges flatly rejected this line of reasoning. Such an argument would break down the distinction between right and wrong and give sanction to injustice, robbery, and piracy. It had no support in the laws and usage of nations. Turning with a natural ease to British legal precedent, the judges quoted Lord Mansfield to show that the question of the legality of the capture remained open to examination in every libel for condemnation as prize.[113] The judges showed the common law bent of their thinking in refuting the captors' contention that the vessel and cargo were lawful prize because they had been in British possession for more than twenty-four hours.

> Every libel states a title to the thing captured; the title must not only be stated, but it must also be proved. It is stated in the libel, in this case, that the property captured was British property, and the evidence to prove it is, "possession and occupation of it by the British privateer." A title thus traced, is a good one, in a court of common law, except in a single case: it is a good title against all the world, *except the right owner*. This exception is founded on every principle of reason and justice; it ought not only to be adopted in courts of common law, but in every court, where the distinction between right and wrong is

---

[113] The court cited *Goss v. Withers*, 2 Burrow, *Reports*, 683, 693; 97 *English Reports*, 511. The first edition of the first two volumes of Burrow's *Reports* was published in 1766.

preserved, and justice regarded. Possession and occupation ought, upon a question of property, to have the same influence in courts of admiralty, as in courts of common law; it ought to be considered as a good title, and conclusive upon all mankind, except the *right owner*.[114]

The judges next turned to the cargo shipped on the *Resolution* allegedly by the capitulants of Dominica. Two essential issues had to be treated: Was the cargo British property protected by the capitulation against French and British captures, and was America, as the ally of France, bound by the articles of capitulation? Article thirteen of the capitulation bestowed upon the merchants and inhabitants of Dominica who signed them all the privileges of trade of any subject of the French king. The property of the capitulants, therefore, could not be taken as a prize by the French. The owners had produced in court an opinion signed by William Wynne, British advocate general, Alexander Wedderburn, British attorney general, and John Dunning, barrister. In June, 1781, about the time this case came before the trial court in Pennsylvania, these British legal authorities had stated their opinion that British capitulants of Dominica could trade in ships from Ostend without subjecting their property to confiscation in a British admiralty court. (This opinion more properly applied to the case of the brig *Eestern*, which belonged to merchants at Ostend.) The judges of the Court of Appeals accepted this opinion of the British authorities as proof that the cargo of the *Resolution* could not be liable to capture by British ships. The judges concluded that the British king, by his proclamation as interpreted by his legal authorities, had determined that the property of the capitulants of Dominica was not exposed to British capture. Some evidence tended, somewhat obscurely, to suggest that the voyage was really intended for Great Britain, not for Amsterdam. But the judges accepted the evidence of all the ship papers which showed that the vessel had cleared out for Amsterdam. Therefore the whole cargo was not lawful prize.

The judges next considered and rejected various arguments for condemning part of the cargo. Even though some of the owners of the property shipped from Dominica were non-residents and probably lived in England, the judges

---

[114] *Resolution*, 2 Dall. 1, 5. Italics in the original.

thought the terms of the capitulation protected their property as long as they or their lawful attorneys had submitted to the capitulation and maintained neutrality in the war. Evidence in the case showed that the proceeds from the sale of the cargo were to be remitted to some owners resident in Britain. But the judges refused to consider this as a cause for condemning that part of the cargo. When the consignees in Amsterdam sold the cargo, they would become debtors to the owners in Britain. Making remittances in satisfaction of debts, even though to subjects of a nation at war, was not a violation of the law of nations. A letter discovered on board the *Resolution* gave some plausibility to the argument of the captors that part of the cargo belonged to Kender Mason, who was not listed as a capitulant but considered a British subject. (This letter, together with evidence discovered on the *Eersten*, eventually led the Court of Appeals, on rehearing, to condemn part of the cargo.) The judges, however, rejected as too speculative the suggested implications of this letter. They concluded that no part of the cargo of the *Resolution* was lawful prize since the whole cargo was protected by the capitulation.

In the Pennsylvania admiralty court the cargo had been condemned as prize to the captors. This decision had turned on the judge's opinion that America was not bound by the articles of capitulation entered into by its ally, France. The Court of Appeals took up this argument and, with a quote from Vattel, showed that allies, who make war a common cause, act as one body. The French governor of Dominica granted the *Resolution* a passport in which he had ordered all American as well as French and Spanish vessels not to impede the voyage of the ship. From this passport the court could see that the governor thought America was bound by the capitulation. The court stated its opinion that "From the very nature of the connection between allies, their compacts and agreements with the common enemy must bind each other, when they tend to accomplish the objects of the allies. Both nations have one common interest and one common object." So an agreement entered by one party to an alliance bound the other party when it corresponded to the terms of their alliance and was calculated to achieve its purposes. Written at a time when the military and financial situations seemed hopeless for the Americans, when America looked more to France than to itself for salvation, this opinion perhaps reflected the widespread sense of dependence on the French alliance.[115]

Finally, the court turned to an alternative basis for its decision. The claimants had argued that the American Congress's instructions to commanders of armed vessels, issued in response to the armed neutrality, gave a legal basis for acquitting the cargo of the *Resolution*. Congress had ordered captains not to seize enemy property on board neutral vessels, except contraband. Great Britain, before the capture, had begun hostilities with the Dutch. But by a proclamation Britain had exempted from capture for a limited time all Dutch ships carrying the produce or manufactures of Dominica. In this case the judges found that the ship was Dutch property carrying the produce of Dominica according to the capitulation. Even if an American court considered the cargo enemy property, the case came within the congressional instructions to ship captains. The ship, because of the British proclamation, was in the position of neutral property, so enemy property on board should be protected from capture by American privateers. By the congressional instructions free ships would make their cargo free. (In rehearing this case the Court of Appeals completely reversed itself on this point.) The court, therefore, decreed that the sentence below with regard to the ship should be affirmed, but with regard to the cargo should be reversed. The ship and cargo were restored to the claimants upon payment of the stipulated freight.

Just five days after the court issued this decree and opinion, an American privateer captured another allegedly neutral ship, the brigantine *Eersten* which was then sailing with a cargo for the capitulants at Dominica.[116] This capture not only raised new questions of neutral rights, but also provided evidence for reopening the case of the *Resolution*. The brig *Eersten* had been a British ship, the *Favourite*, and in March 1781, was purchased by an Ostend trading firm. Ostend, a neutral port in the Austrian Netherlands, was a favorite port of origin or destination in wartime, since ships ostensibly sailing to or from Ostend could easily slip into French,

---

[115] Stinchcombe, *American Revolution*, pp. 133–135, 153–169.

[116] *Eersten* (*Darby v. Thompson*), 5 February, 1782, 2 Dall. 34, RCA.

Dutch, or English ports. The Ostend firm laded the *Eersten* in London with a cargo of British goods, sailed for Ostend where the cargo was unladed, cleared through customs, and reladed. The owners took out new papers for the cargo, listing it as the property of this Ostend firm. The *Eersten* cleared out for Dominica with a cargo of wine and in August was hailed by a vessel under English colors. The captain of the privateer said he could not release the brig till the captain had signed a statement affirming that the cargo had come from London. The captain, who apparently spoke some English, signed a paper which he later said he could not read, not understanding English. He later discovered that he had been taken by an American privateer and that the paper contained a confession that the ship and cargo were British property. The privateer then took the *Eersten* to Massachusetts and libeled it there as lawful prize. The jury found the claim of the commander of the *Eersten* to be true and the court acquitted the ship and its cargo. Perhaps the state court was influenced by the decision of the Court of Appeals in the *Resolution* case. The captors appealed the decree and the Court of Appeals in February, 1782, reversed and adjudged the ship and cargo to be lawful prize to the captors.

Judges Griffin and Paca wrote an opinion in this case also, considering one by one the arguments of the owners. The judges rejected the argument that the *Eersten* was neutral property protected by the instructions of Congress to the commanders of armed ships, dated November, 1780. They interpreted the ordinance of Congress to mean that neutral ships should be free from capture only as long as they observed neutrality. In cases of flagrant violations of neutrality, however, a vessel could not derive protection from the congressional ordinance. The court stated, "The plain and obvious Construction of the ordinance is that while Neutral vessels observe the rights of Neutrality they shall not be interrupted by American Captures: Congress meant to pay a Regard to *the Rights*, and not to *the Violations* of Neutrality." The court found in this case a clear scheme entered into by British citizens and subjects of Ostend in violation of neutrality. Kender Mason, a British subject, established a plan at Ostend to continue commerce between Great Britain and Dominica by obtaining false and colorable papers from Ostend to cover the cargo from capture. This scheme, to dress up the cargo in the garb of neutrality to screen it from detection and capture, was a glaring violation of neutrality, which placed the ship and cargo beyond the scope of protection afforded by the ordinance of Congress. The judges perceived an offense against neutrality in the fraudulent combination of neutral subjects with British subjects intended to re-establish commerce between Britain and Dominica which had been lost to the British by conquest. Therefore, the court condemned the brig and its cargo as prize to the captors. In spite of strong diplomatic pressure from Luzerne and others on Congress and the court to reopen the case, the court consistently refused to reconsider or revise its decree.[117] Once again it is well to recall that the Court of Appeals did not decide the case till after Yorktown, when America could afford the luxury of disregarding the wishes of the French minister. Finally in 1787, at the court's last session, the judges again refused to grant a rehearing. They based their denial of a rehearing on the fact that the claimants of the *Eersten* had been culpably negligent in not giving proper notice to the interested parties that the court had earlier suspended the execution of its decree. As a result the proceeds from the sale of the prize had long since been distributed beyond recall.[118]

The evidence found on the *Eersten* showing that Kender Mason was involved in a scheme to carry on trade between Britain and Dominica induced the Court of Appeals to grant a stay of execution in the case of the *Resolution* and to rehear the case because of this new evidence.[119] (This is a good example of the willingness of the judges of appeals to admit evidence not found on board the vessel itself to acquit or condemn it. In England it probably would have been more difficult to have such evidence admitted by the Lords Commissioners.) But after a reargument of the case, the Court basically reaffirmed its previous decree acquitting the *Resolu-*

---

[117] Franklin to Vergenes, 18 January, 1782; Luzerne to Livingston, 18 February, 1782; Bouillé to Luzerne, n.d.; Livingston to Luzerne, 20 February, 1782; Livingston to president of Congress, 21 February, 1782; Livingston to Franklin, 23 June, 1782, Wharton, *Correspondence* 5: pp. 118, 176–179, 190–192, 501, and PCC, Item 45, 325; Item 59, IV, 245, 253, 277, 289, and Item 78, X, 467.

[118] *Eersten*, 2 Dall. 34, RCA.

[119] *Resolution*, 25 January, 1782, 2 Dall. 19, RCA. The judges' opinion in the records was published by Dallas, and is substantially accurate, though many minor errors and editorial changes were made in the published version.

tion and its cargo. The judges did, however, condemn to the captors those portions of the cargo thought to belong to Kender Mason, a British citizen and not known to be a capitulant of Dominica. Again they wrote an opinion with a detailed analysis of the arguments raised by counsel in the rehearing. In the prior opinion the judges had acquitted the ship and cargo on the alternative ground of the ordinance of Congress instructing captains not to capture enemy goods on neutral ships. Then the court had considered the *Resolution* a neutral ship which would therefore protect enemy property on board from seizure. But in the second opinion the judges reversed themselves and concluded that a Dutch ship could not be considered neutral. Relying on the "writers upon the law of nations," the judges discussed the distinction, which they probably found in Lee, between perfect and imperfect war.[120] The British had begun a war against the Dutch and thus the Dutch were not any longer common friends to all parties of the war between Britain, America, and France. The British could not by mere proclamation restore to a Dutch ship its status of neutrality. The British proclamation could only operate as a protection from British capture. The *Resolution* therefore, could not be considered as a neutral vessel giving protection from capture to its enemy cargo.

In this opinion the judges made clear that the captors had the burden of proving that a ship was lawful prize. Following the usual practice insisted on by the authorities on the law of nations, they accepted the ship papers as the presumptive evidence of the ownership of the ship and cargo.[121] The judges painstakingly analyzed in turn each argument raised by counsel for the captors during the oral argument. They concluded that the captors had failed to counter the evidence of the ship papers. To have the vessel or cargo condemned the captors had to prove that the ship or the cargo did not belong to the parties indicated in the papers. The court concluded on the basis of these papers that the ship and most of the cargo should be acquitted. Since there was some sug-

---

[120] Lee, *Treatise of Captures*, p. 40. The phrasing by the judges is very close to the phrasing in Lee. Lee perhaps derived the distinction from Grotius, *De Jure Belli ac Pacis*, Kelsey, tr., **2**: pp. 624–625.

[121] The discussion by the judges of the rule of evidence in prize cases might have been an elaboration of Lee, *Treatise of Captures*, pp. 238–240, which in turn was derived from *Report of the Law Officers*, in Marsden, *Law of the Sea* **2**: pp. 350–351.

gestion, in papers from the *Eersten* as well as those of the *Resolution*, that part of the cargo belonged to Kender Mason, a non-capitulant, only that portion of the cargo was condemned to the captors.[122] Subsequent evidence from Dominica that Kender Mason had signed the capitulation did not induce the court to again reopen the case.[123]

In these three opinions concerning the *Resolution* and the *Eersten*, one gets a strong feeling for the close relationship between the arguments presented orally by counsel and the process of decision by the judges. The attorneys (who probably styled themselves advocates for the occasion), rummaged through the books on prize law and the ordinances of Congress to argue for acquittal or condemnation of a prize. They also analyzed the evidence, especially the papers found on the captured vessel, to show that it could be interpreted in a way that would lead to acquittal or condemnation. The judges listened, weighed the arguments, and gave their verbose opinions, based on the same sources and the same type of common-sense reasoning (with occasional common law overtones) that had been presented to them. The writers on the law of nations, especially Lee and Vattel as suggested throughout this chapter, must have been the quarry to which judges and attorneys alike turned to discover materials to build their arguments on the various aspects of prize law.

One final case involving a ship claimed as neutral property, the sloop *Chester*, came before the court in 1787, ten years after the capture and condemnation of the prize in the South Carolina admiralty court. The ship and cargo had been captured in 1777 and the master and crew were removed from the *Chester* and taken to St. Eustatia. The owners asserted that this was done so that no one could file a claim in South Carolina. When the master found his way back to Rotterdam, the Dutch firm which owned the *Chester* attempted through diplomatic channels to obtain the reversal of the admiralty court's sentence. Congress and its secretary for foreign affairs favored a full hearing of the case by the Court of Appeals. Evidence in the records, however, suggested that the ship belonged to British subjects, or at least carried double papers. After years of diplomatic pressure, the Court of

---

[122] *Resolution*, 25 January, 1782, 2 Dall. 19, RCA.
[123] PCC, Item 45, 321; Item 59, 285.

Appeals in 1787 granted a hearing only to determine whether an appeal should be allowed. After hearing the arguments of both parties, the judges refused to allow the appeal. In one of their rare opinions, they decided that appeals should only be admitted where such irregularities had occurred in the proceedings below that substantial justice had been prevented. However blameworthy the captors may have been for not bringing in the master of the *Chester* to allow him a chance to defend the ship in court, or in not producing some of the ship papers, such omissions alone could not justify the court in granting an appeal. Only to assure that substantial justice was achieved would the court grant an appeal. But in this case, the judges wrote, the records showed that the *Chester* would have been condemned even if the irregularities had not occurred in the court below.[124] Although the judges said they were merely denying the petition for an appeal, they appear in fact to have reviewed the record, heard some arguments on the merits, and denied the hearing on the ground of harmless error.

Perhaps this opinion in the case of the *Chester* shows signs of haste as the court was trying to complete, at its last session, all its unfinished business. Between May 3 and May 11, 1787, the judges dismissed five requests for appeals or rehearings and granted none. In one case the judges said that even if the vessel had been illegally condemned by the court below, still, "under all the Circumstances of the present case" justice did not require a hearing on appeal.[125] In these last cases the

---

[124] *Chester (Dubbeldemuts v. Atkinson)*, 3 May, 1787, 2 Dall. 41, RCA, and PCC, Item 45, 95, 97, 101, 149–255; Item 99, 241–254. Goebel, *Law Practice of Hamilton* 2: pp. 892–903.

[125] *Good Fortune*, 11 May, 1787, #87; *Hope (Mead v. Hurlbert)*, 3 May, 1787, #103; *Cumberland (Cruger v. no name)*, 3 May, 1787, #109; *Eersten*, 10 May, 1787, 2 Dall. 34, and *Chester*, 3 May, 1787, 2 Dall. 41, RCA. The great reluctance of the court at this time to review the merits of a case was particularly noticeable in the case of the brigantine *Hope*:

"Congress having established a System of Appeals, and in that System having limited a period, beyond which, Appeals are not to be entered; We think the Resolution of June 1786, could only mean that in Conformity with this prior establishment, the Judges might use a discretionary power where particular Circumstances consistent with Justice and Right may, in their opinion require it—

Whatever decree the Court might have made upon the Merits of the Cause, and although the property may have been illegally condemned in the Maritime Court; yet under all the Circumstances of the present Case, we are unanimously of opinion that Justice and Right do not require, that the Appeal should be now sustained—It is therefore considered that the Petition be dismissed—"

This is rather a harsh notion of "Justice and Right."

judges probably felt a strong reluctance to upset lower court decrees made years before and desired to clear the docket of all cases then pending. So the Court of Appeals in Cases of Capture finished the last of its work in a brief burst of energy only a few months before the completion of the Federal Constitution which would establish the basis for a more adequate system of federal jurisdiction.

An ordinance of the Continental Congress of December, 1781, had declared that the rule of decision in all prize courts should be the resolutions of Congress, public treaties approved by Congress, and the law of nations according to the general usages of Europe.[126] In spite of the fact that the judges of appeals ordinarily did not state the reasons for their determinations, we have been able to reconstruct a fairly accurate view of them at work. The substantive law they applied sometimes seems like a building put together of whatever materials came to hand. Yet we can detect a consistency in their practice and in their decrees in different types of cases. Surely the judges would have been influenced by the decisions of the Lords Commissioners for Prize Appeals, if any had been reported. In at least one case they quoted an opinion of Lord Mansfield in a common law case before King's Bench.[127] Where precise norms had been established by Congress, the judges carefully applied these standards. The main issues in such cases were often factual, and the judges did not hesitate to review, and at times amplify, the facts previously found by a jury. Treaties were seldom applicable, but when they were, the judges followed their terms as the rule of decision. But in a large number of cases concerning the capture of American or neutral property, they often had nowhere to turn for substantive law but the sometimes amorphous rules and principles of the law of nations. Lee and Vattel were probably the authorities most frequently quoted by counsel. The few notes we have of oral arguments, the rare opinions the judges wrote and the pattern of decrees in other cases all suggest a frequent reliance on these two writers. Furthermore (with the exception of Bynkershoek, whose writings were not available in English), Vattel and Lee had written most fully and readably (if not most profoundly

---

[126] Ford, *JCC* **21**: p. 1158.
[127] See note 113 above.

and originally) on the various aspects of prize law and property rights in time of war.

This search in the last two chapters for the procedural and substantive law of the appellate judiciary of the Continental Congress has partially recreated an institution which functioned nearly two hundred years ago. Then it was a functioning court with a developed practice and procedures, with accepted principles and sources of law, and perhaps even with some sense of precedents developing for the judges and attorneys who followed its work closely. Only by such a detailed analysis of the institution, a reassembling of its dry bones, can we now catch some glimpse of it as a living system and appreciate the role and function of the first federal court.

VIII. The Jurisdiction of the Appellate Judiciary of Congress

SINCE THE CONTINENTAL CONGRESS seldom stood on solid, unchallenged ground when it exercised authority over the states, one could hardly expect that any appellate court it created would be fully effective in asserting its jurisdiction over state courts. We have already seen enough examples, especially in the case of the sloop *Active*, where state courts or state governments were able to frustrate the execution of appellate prize decrees.

Congress from the beginning had declared its jurisdiction over all prize appeals. "[I]n all cases an appeal [from state prize courts] shall be allowed to the Congress."[1] Congress reasserted this jurisdiction at the time of the impasse with Pennsylvania over the *Active* case. Prior to the ratification of the Articles of Confederation, there was no clearer basis than this statement for congressional authority over prize appeals. After restating the provision of November, 1775, for appellate jurisdiction, Congress asserted the right of its judiciary to review issues of fact as well as legal issues. Congress then bluntly stated that "no act of any one State can or ought to destroy the right of appeals to Congress."[2] Claiming sovereign power of war and peace, as well as authority to apply the law of nations, Congress told the states it possessed "the authority ultimately [*sic*] and finally to decide on all matters and questions touching the law of nations."[3]

These bold assertions of broad powers to hear appeals in all prize cases raised basic questions as to the scope of the jurisdiction Congress was claiming, the right of a state to limit or restrict this jurisdiction, and ultimately the constitutional basis of this jurisdiction. These questions, though never satisfactorily answered prior to the Constitution, were

---

[1] Ford, *JCC*, 25 November, 1775, **3**: p. 374.
[2] *Ibid.*, 6 March, 1779, **13**: p. 283.
[3] *Ibid.*, p. 284.

raised and discussed in the context of several Revolutionary
War prize cases.

Two cases originally heard in the Pennsylvania admiralty
court sketched the outer limits of the jurisdictional reach of
the congressional Court of Appeals. The court considered
the scope of its jurisdiction in the case of the *Gloucester*, a case
turning on ancillary prize jurisdiction. The captain of the
Philadelphia privateer *Holker* had enlisted a crew who signed
the articles of agreement as the terms of their service. When
the *Holker* had sailed fifteen miles down the Delaware to
Chester, the captain mustered his crew and ordered twenty-five of them ashore. He then forced the remainder of the
crew to sign new articles. On this cruise the *Holker* captured
the brig *Gloucester* and libeled it in the Pennsylvania admiralty court. The twenty-five seamen who had been put ashore
at Chester filed a libel for their share in the prize. The
admiralty court, citing British precedent, held that it could
not only decree a prize lawful or not, but could also determine to whom the prize should be awarded. The court,
therefore, rejected the plea to its jurisdiction by the owners
and captain of the *Holker*, who had contended that only a
common law court could hear a suit for damages. The court
held that this was not a damage suit but a suit for the shares
of a prize legally condemned to the owners, officers, and
crew of the *Holker*. These twenty-five members of the original crew, therefore, were entitled to share in the prize.[4]

The captain and owners of the *Holker* appealed to the
congressional Court of Appeals. The judges in 1783, in one
of their rare opinions, held that the twenty-five crewmen had
a double remedy, an action at common law or the supplemental libel in admiralty they had filed. The supplemental
libel was within the jurisdiction of the prize court since it was
a mere form of proceeding to carry into execution the original prize decree. The Court affirmed the sentence of the
Pennsylvania admiralty court, thereby showing that it considered this case as on the prize side of admiralty, and that
the appeal to the congressional Court of Appeals was therefore proper.[5]

In the case of the *Betsey*, however, which also focused on

[4] *Patrick Mahoon & al. v. The Brig Glocester*, (*sic*) Hopkinson, *Writings* **3**: pp. 55–60.
[5] *Gloucester* (*Keane v. Mahon*), 5 February, 1783, 2 Dall. 36, RCA.

the scope of the jurisdiction of the congressional Court of Appeals, no appeal was carried to that court, so this significant jurisdictional issue was determined by the Pennsylvania High Court of Errors and Appeals just a year after the Court of Appeal's decision in the case of the *Gloucester*.[6]

The Connecticut privateer sloop *Argo* in 1779 had captured a large British privateer, the *Betsey*, which carried a valuable cargo. Three privateer brigs from Philadelphia, sailing under British colors, saw the engagement and surrender. The next day these three American brigs, still under British colors, approached and fired upon the *Betsey*. The British papers aboard the *Betsey*, of course, indicated the British ownership of the vessel. Since the *Argo* had removed eleven men from the *Betsey's* crew and replaced them with an eleven-man prize crew, the size of the crew corresponded to the list of names in the British papers. The three American privateer brigs captured the *Betsey*, removed most of the *Argo's* prize crew, and sent the ship to some American port for condemnation. The *Betsey*, however, was recaptured by a British vessel and restored to its original British owners.

The captain and owners of the *Argo* in 1780 filed a libel for damages in the Pennsylvania admiralty court against the owners and commanders of the three brigs. The owners of the three brigs defended on the ground that this was a case of trespass and should be tried at common law. The Pennsylvania admiralty court dismissed this plea to its jurisdiction and in 1783 decreed some £12,000 damages against the owners and captains of the three brigs. On appeal to the Pennsylvania High Court of Errors and Appeals, the court, speaking by Judge John Dickinson, considered the jurisdiction of the admiralty court and its own jurisdiction the crucial issues.

If this was considered originally a prize case, the appeal should have been carried to the congressional Court of Appeals, not to the Pennsylvania appellate court. The Pennsylvania court cited the standard writers on the law of nations and weighed the authority in America of several British common law cases concerning aspects of prize law. The court concluded that the state admiralty court had properly assumed jurisdiction of the case, but not as prize. It belonged

---

[6] *Talbot qui tam v. The Commanders and Owners of Three Brigs*, 1 Dallas 95 (1784).

on the instance (non-prize) side of admiralty as a maritime trespass. Since the vessel had not been within the jurisdiction of the admiralty court, it was not an *in rem* proceeding which the High Court implied was a necessary characteristic of prize jurisdiction. There were no claimants as in a prize case and the libelants sought damages, not a determination of the legality of a prize. Since this was an instance case, the High Court concluded, appeal to it was appropriate, not to the Court of Appeals set up by Congress. The attitude of the state High Court toward the congressional Court of Appeals was well expressed by Judge Dickinson:

> [A]s far as a Court of Appeals is concerned, [these arguments] can be answered in this Court as fully as in a Court of Appeals to Commissioners there. . . . The [Pennsylvania] Legislature intended to give this Court an authority to receive all Appeals from the Judge of Admiralty, where they were not resigned [by the state] to a Continental Court of Appeals. This [instance case] was not resigned. It therefore belongs to this Court. We will endeavour to promote justice, according to the intentions of the Commonwealth, conveyed in the laws; and not demit any part of her sovereignty, unless we are convinced beyond a doubt, that it is our duty to do so.[7]

The significance of this Pennsylvania case is that a state court took it upon itself to determine finally a significant question as to the scope of the jurisdiction of Congress's Court of Appeals. State sovereignty had to be protected by carefully limiting appeals to the appellate judiciary of Congress. As the Pennsylvania High Court suggested, some British authority might have brought this case within the prize jurisdiction of admiralty. The second captors, after all, could argue that they had taken what they considered a British vessel with a British crew and British papers aboard, or alternatively that they were joint captors because in sight at the time of the original capture. Both theories would be within traditional prize jurisdiction. The congressional Court of Appeals perhaps never had an opportunity to decide whether this type of maritime tort committed in the context of a capture at sea was ancillary to its prize jurisdiction. There is some suggestion that the judges of the Court of Appeals refused to hear the appeal, perhaps out of their

---

[7] *Ibid.*, p. 107.

cautious regard for strictly interpreting their powers, or out
of a realistic appraisal of the confining restrictions the states
placed on Congress' effective authority. No trace of an appeal to Congress in this case can be found in the records.
Perhaps the litigants in Pennsylvania had learned from the
case of the sloop *Active* the futility of carrying their appeal to
Congress.[8]

---

[8] For a British prize appeal in which the prize itself and its cargo was lost in a
storm, and yet the jurisdiction of the admiralty court and of the Lords Commissioners for Prize Appeals was not questioned, see *Christophilus* (Kamp), *Appeal Cases in
Prize Causes* **2**: (LC Law), discussed above in chapter IV. The American Court of
Appeals, in the case of the *Polly* (*Smith v. Wickham*), 26 May, 1784, #100, RCA,
discussed above in chapter V, however, had held that the Rhode Island admiralty
court had never had jurisdiction since the prize was never within its control.

In subsequent litigation in the Pennsylvania admiralty court concerning an aspect
of the case of the *Betsey*, Judge Francis Hopkinson made it clear that he disagreed
with the opinion of the state High Court. Hopkinson also stated that the congressional Court of Appeals had refused to take jurisdiction of the *Talbot* case.
Perhaps he is correct, but there are no hints of such an appeal in the opinion of the
Pennsylvania High Court or in the Records of the Court of Appeals. Hopkinson's
description of the situation in the *Talbot* case is worth quoting:

"It is in obedience to strong conviction, that I thus venture to differ in opinion
from the judgment of the honourable court of errors and appeals—a judgment
which, I am inclined to believe, would not have taken place, but from the peculiar
situation of *Talbot's* cause. The court of appeals for the *United States*, in prize causes,
had rejected the appeal, because the question was not strictly *prize or no prize*, but an
action for damages between citizen and citizen. That court, as I have understood,
looked at that cause in no other point of view, and therefore refused to take
cognizance of it, and soon after adjourned. The appeal was then carried to the high
court of errors and appeals for this commonwealth. The proctors had previously
agreed not to contest the point of jurisdiction, and so the cause came before the
judges on the merits only; and the court proceeded to sentence, without suspecting
their jurisdiction. After sentence, however, some of the judges began to entertain
scruples respecting the jurisdiction of the court, and, upon inquiry, found that the
jurisdiction had only been submitted to by consent. The court well knew, that
consent could not give jurisdiction, and therefore retracted or suspended the
sentence, until an argument should be held on that point; and the question of the
jurisdiction was again agitated. In the meantime, that is, between the rejection of the
cause by the court of appeals for the United States, and its introduction into the
court for the commonwealth, the case of *Le Caux v. Eden* [cited in the opinion of the
Pennsylvania High Court in *Talbot*] as reported by *Douglas*, with lord *Mansfield's*
dissertation on admiralty jurisdiction subjoined, made their first appearance
amongst us, and furnished new ideas respecting the court of admiralty. Then, for
the first time, did the distinction occur, between the *prize* court and the *instance* court
of admiralty. Possessed of this idea, the judges of appeal for the state, looked at the
proceedings which the court of admiralty had adopted in the case before them, and
found they had been *in personam*, by attachment, to answer for damages arising from
a tort committed at sea. This, it was observed, was never the practice in the *prize*
court, which always proceeded *in rem*, by proclamation and monition, whether the
property be, in fact, in the possession of the court or not. . . . And, for this error of
form in the admiralty, *Talbot's* case was considered as belonging to the *instance* court.
The [Pennsylvania] judges of appeal considered themselves as an *instance* court of

The issues in this case differ from those involved in the case of the *Gloucester*, especially since in this case no prize had been brought within the jurisdiction of the admiralty court. In the case of the *Gloucester* the judges of appeals determined the scope of their jurisdiction by hearing and affirming an admiralty court sentence on a supplemental libel. In the case of the *Betsey*, however, either the congressional Court of Appeals refused to assume jurisdiction without a full hearing and articulation of its reasons, or it was never given an opportunity to determine whether its jurisdiction reached a case of trespass committed against a prize vessel. A stronger court, more sure of its authority and whose power was more widely accepted, might well have taken, or been given, the opportunity to determine for itself whether this type of maritime tort was within its appellate prize jurisdiction. Somewhere between the ancillary prize jurisdiction to determine to whom prize shares should be distributed (the *Gloucester*), and ancillary jurisdiction to award damages for a tort committed at sea in the context of a capture as prize (the *Betsey*), lay the line bounding the jurisdictional reach of Congress's appellate prize judiciary. Unfortunately, the Court of Appeals did not itself express the precise boundaries to its jurisdiction.

Several other prize appeals cases involved jurisdictional issues: the authority of a state to restrict the right of appeals to Congress and the constitutional basis of the congressional appellate prize court.

The law of Massachusetts and that of New Hampshire regulating appeals to Congress were practically identical. As we have seen, for the first three years of the war they both allowed appeals from the state courts to Congress only where the vessel making the capture had been fitted out at the charge of the United Colonies.[9]

The case of the ship *Anna Maria*, appealed by petition from Massachusetts, has been discussed in the last chapter. It involved a claim by a privateer to a share in the prize as joint captor. The privateer captains had agreed in writing to share any prizes taken by either one even if the privateer sloops

---

appeals, and so proceeded to the definitive decree." *Dean et al. v. John Angus*, Bee, *Reports*, 369, 372 (1785).

[9] *Acts and Resolves of Massachusetts* 5: p. 477, and Batchellor, *Laws of New Hampshire* 4: p. 31.

were separated and out of each other's sight for forty-eight hours or less. The ship actually making the capture belonged to owners in Massachusetts, while the privateer claiming as joint captor belonged to a citizen of Rhode Island. The jury in Massachusetts, demonstrating the need for special judicial protection for out-of-state litigants, awarded the *Anna Maria* to the Massachusetts owners and crew of the sloop *Revenge*. Bucklin, the alleged joint captor, appealed to the state superior court, only to have the verdict and decree affirmed in February, 1777. When Bucklin requested an appeal to Congress, the superior court refused to grant it.

Bucklin petitioned Congress in June, 1777, for a hearing. He complained that the judges of the superior court, in violation of the resolves of Congress, had refused to admit his appeal. The Committee on Appeals, to whom the petition was referred, reported to Congress that in its opinion Joseph White, commander of the *Revenge*, ought to appear within forty days before the Committee to show cause why the prayer of the petition should not be granted. Congress passed this resolution on August 4, 1777.[10]

In December, 1777, the Committee on Appeals directed that the hearing ordered by Congress be postponed another sixty days, again notifying White that he must appear to show cause. The Committee received a petition from White in February, at the end of the sixty days, in which he complained that he had been notified to appear and did appear, but that Bucklin had not, and so the hearing had been postponed seven days beyond the day assigned. Apparently, there was no hearing in February, but White, by his lawyer William Wetmore, presented Congress with a lengthy answer to Bucklin's petition in which White challenged the authority of Congress to hear this appeal.

White's answer repeated the facts of the capture and the details of the previous court proceedings. He argued that all resolves of Congress respecting maritime matters presumed the legislatures of the several states to be the sole competent authorities to regulate maritime courts. Congress had only recommended that the states set up prize courts and allow

---

[10] *Anna Maria (Bucklin v. White)*, 10 August, 1780, #21, RCA; Court Files Suffolk, #148229 (MSJC), and Ford, *JCC* 8: pp. 493, 602–603. A similar case, also involving an appeal by petition from Massachusetts was the *Countess of Eglinton (Jones v. Babcock)*, 14 September, 1783, #9 & 22, RCA; Ford, *JCC* 8: p. 603.

appeals to Congress. No mandatory words, according to White, could be found in these resolves. Furthermore the Articles of Confederation expressly declared that each state retained its sovereignty, freedom, and independence, and every power, jurisdiction, and right which had not been delegated to Congress. Now, even before the Articles were ratified, Congress appeared to be revising and annulling the laws of a state. Bucklin had not even complied with the resolves of Congress which gave cognizance of prize cases only when the parties proceeded by way of appeal. But in this case appeal was refused. Bucklin had not filed his complaint with Congress after the definitive sentence of the state maritime court but delayed four months after the decree of the state superior court. It would be unjust, therefore, for Congress to compel the respondent to become a party to this appeal. He pointed out the difficulty and confusion which would follow if a party would never know when he might be forced to defend a case on appeal even long after the prize money had been distributed. Consequently, Bucklin should be forever barred from having a decree of the state superior court set aside, especially when he was the one who procured this decree by his own appeal.[11]

The Committee on Appeals, after pondering the challenge raised by this case, postponed it to May, 1778, but whether any further action was taken then cannot be determined. The following October in a report to Congress summarizing the details of the capture, trial, and appeal to the state superior court, the committee concluded that this Massachusetts law limiting appeals to Congress had a dangerous tendency to interrupt the peace, safety, and union of the United States. The report also stated that the committee considered the state law in direct violation of the resolves of Congress which granted an appeal in all cases and that some speedy decision should be given on the validity of that law so far as it contravened those resolves. Furthermore, the report added, the committee had brought the matter to Congress so that a decision on the validity of the state law, when presented to the states, would carry the full weight of congressional authority.[12]

---

[11] *Anna Maria*, #21, RCA; Ford, *JCC* 10: p. 177.
[12] PCC, Item 59, II, 367; Ford, *JCC*, 17 October, 1778, 12: pp. 1022–1023, and

Apparently Congress never seriously considered this report, much less acted upon its daring invitation to invalidate a state law opposed to a resolve of Congress. The further development of this appeal is not recorded, except for the notation that the decree below was affirmed by the Court of Appeals shortly after the court was established, August 10, 1780.[13]

In the spring of 1779, at the same time Congress was discussing the impasse caused by the case of the sloop *Active*, Massachusetts privateers seized two Spanish vessels. The brigantine *Santander y los Santos Martires* (called *Holy Martyrs* in the court records), and the ship *Valenciano* were both tried in the same maritime court in Massachusetts; the former was declared to be neutral property; the latter was condemned as prize. But the cargo of both ships was declared forfeit to the captors as British property. The maritime court at the same time refused appeals to Congress. Within a few weeks, by the end of April, 1779, Congress received a memorial from the French minister, Conrad Alexandre Gerard, complaining of the capture of these Spanish ships. The Committee on Appeals received this petition, as well as memorials from Don Juan de Miralles, who represented Spanish interests, and from the masters of the two Spanish ships. It reported to Congress that by Massachusetts law these two cases could not be appealed to Congress. They were then pending in the superior court of the state. Though the committee knew that a uniform and equal administration of maritime law within the United States was of the utmost importance, it submitted to Congress a resolution which, in effect, admitted that Congress could not cope with such situations. The committee recalled the resolves of Congress passed on March 6 concerning the *Active* case. These resolves had insisted that Congress had the supreme power of war and peace and, implied in that power, it possessed the ultimate authority of executing the law of nations. The authority of Congress over prize cases was clearly provided for in the ninth article of the Articles of Confederation. Since only twelve of the states had ratified the Articles, the provisions of article nine remained without effect. It was absolutely necessary for the tranquillity

---

"Cases Pending in the Committee on Appeals, February–May 1778," *Miscellaneous Court Records*, RCA.

[13] *Anna Maria*, #21, RCA.

of the citizens of the states, as well as for the satisfaction of foreign powers, that these provisions be carried into full effect. The committee, therefore, urged Congress to recommend to the states that they pass laws vesting in Congress the judicial powers specified in article nine. At least the committee hoped this one part of article nine could be approved by all the states, so as to give Congress the essential power needed to satisfy the legitimate complaints of friendly nations.[14] There is no indication that Congress ever acted on this resolution, which would have been an admission that it did not possess the implied powers over questions of war and peace recently claimed in the resolves of March 6.

On May 22, 1779, a special committee appointed to study the complaints in these cases did induce Congress at least to forward to the states the resolutions of March 6, which had asserted Congress's ultimate authority over questions of war and peace, over the law of nations, and hence over all cases of capture. This committee also proposed, and Congress approved, a mild request that Massachusetts take effective measures to facilitate appeals to Congress from its courts in cases of prizes claimed as neutral property.

This same special committee drew up a letter to Gerard, the French minister. Congress deleted the last few paragraphs which tried to explain the inscrutable authority of Congress to preserve inviolate the law of nations without interfering with state judicial proceedings. The rest of the letter was sent to Gerard signed by the president of Congress. Congress assured the French minister that when the matter came before it in due course, it would make sure that the law of nations would be most strictly observed. If it should turn out, after trial, that the owners of the captured vessels had suffered damage from any violation of neutral rights, Congress promised that reparation would be made so as to vindicate the honor of the Spanish flag. Though Congress wanted to cultivate the most friendly relations with Spain, it could not in any case, "consistently with the powers entrusted to [it]," suspend or interrupt the ordinary course of justice.[15] Once again Congress, between the lines of this

---

[14] PCC, Item 29, 371. The resolution of the Committee on Appeals is mistakenly placed on 24 April, 1779 in Ford, *JCC* **14:** pp. 508–510.

[15] PCC, Item 25, I, 111; Item 41, V, 200, 204; Ford, *JCC* **14:** pp. 617, 624, 635–636.

letter full of reassurance, could only convey hollow-sounding promises that it would see to it that justice was done.

The Massachusetts legislature responded to congressional pressure first by granting a continuance before the superior court in the cases of these two Spanish ships, and then on June 30, 1779, by passing an act allowing appeals to Congress in prize cases where a subject of any friendly nation claimed part or all of the vessel or cargo.[16] As a result, the cases of the *Valenciano* and the *Holy Martyrs* were first heard by the Massachusetts superior court which affirmed the lower court sentence for the *Valenciano* and partly modified the decree for the *Holy Martyrs*. Then, following the new state law, the superior court granted appeals to Congress in both cases. The Committee on Appeals, as we saw in the last chapter, decided both cases in November, 1779, restoring the *Holy Martyrs* and cargo and part of the cargo of the *Valenciano* to the Spanish claimants.[17]

These Massachusetts cases demonstrate the difficulty Congress had asserting its jurisdiction over all prize appeals when a state legislature restricted the right of appeal. Congress could reaffirm its own interpretation of the scope of its power, or recommend that the state revise its laws. But when the issue came to a head, especially before the ratification of the Articles of Confederation, Congress simply could not compel the unwilling state to acknowledge its authority. Voluntary compliance by the states was often all Congress could realistically hope for. In the highly sensitive area of neutral rights, this power vacuum in the central government was intolerable.

The case of the brigantine *Lusanna* brings out even more clearly the inherent weakness of Congress's jurisdictional reach. The details of the long voyage of the *Lusanna* and the involved and suspicious explanations of its activities have already been summarized in chapter VII. When the capture of the *Lusanna* was tried in the New Hampshire maritime court, as we have seen, the jury, on December 16, 1777, returned a verdict for the captors. The judge decreed the vessel, its cargo, and appurtenances lawful prize and forfeit

---

[16] *Acts and Resolves of Massachusetts* **5:** pp. 1077–1078; **21:** pp. 60–61.

[17] 31 August, 1779, Minute Book, Appeals from Maritime Court, 1779–1788 (MSJC); *Valenciano* (*Luca v. Cleveland*), 1 November, 1779, #58 and *Santander y los Santos Martires* (*Tracy v. de Llano*), 6 November 1779, #60, RCA.

to the captors. He refused to allow an appeal to Congress because the laws of the state permitted such an appeal only in cases of capture by congressional naval ships. The claimants, therefore, appealed to the superior court of New Hampshire. At the September, 1778, term the superior court affirmed the decree of the maritime court. The claimants requested an appeal to Congress but again were refused.[18]

Immediately after the New Hampshire superior court had denied an appeal to Congress, the owners sent a petition to Congress requesting an opportunity to be heard. The owners of the *Lusanna* briefly described the details of the case and the refusal of the maritime court and the superior court of New Hampshire to grant the appeal to Congress they had requested. They complained of the prejudice they felt had influenced the local juries in favor of the captors, all from New Hampshire, against the owners from Massachusetts. They also asserted the courts had erred in refusing to allow Bourne to testify in the case, because, having divested himself of all interest in the property in issue, he was a competent witness. Congress on October 9, 1778, referred the petition to the Committee on Appeals.[19] The claimants, knowing when they sent their petition that restitution of their property would be difficult, privately accused the New Hampshire parties of despising Congress and of insisting that they would ignore any action Congress might take in the case.[20]

Since the *Lusanna* case came before the Committee on Appeals shortly before the appeal involving the sloop *Active*, the total disruption of the work of the committee caused by the latter case also led to delays in the case of the *Lusanna*. After Congress had confirmed the authority of the Committee on Appeals in the resolves of March 6, 1779, the committee again started hearing appeals. It set June 21 for hearing the *Lusanna* case and ruled that the appellants should give the appellees at least thirty days' notice.

---

[18] *Lusanna* (*Doane v. Penhallow*), 17 September, 1783, #30, RCA. The numerous records and complicated history of the *Lusanna* case are analyzed with precision and detail in Wroth and Zobel, *Legal Papers of Adams* 2: pp. 352–376.

[19] PCC, Item 44, 189. Other papers relative to the *Lusanna* are included in this Item, 191–324; Ford, *JCC* 12: p. 992.

[20] Bourne to Robert Treat Paine, 10 September, 1778, Robert Treat Paine Papers (MHS).

THE APPELLATE JUDICIARY OF CONGRESS

The hearing on June 21 centered mainly on the issue of jurisdiction. Counsel for the captors argued that the law of New Hampshire granted appeals in cases of capture by private armed vessels only to the superior court, not to any court appointed by Congress. Furthermore, Elisha Doane and the other claimants prosecuted an appeal to the state superior court thereby waiving any right they may have had to an appeal to Congress. The appeal to Congress first demanded from the maritime court was not prosecuted for more than forty days after the decree of that court.

In reply Doane and the other claimants asserted that Congress had the power of allowing or disallowing appeals from all verdicts and decrees in any prize case within the United States and that no state law could preclude the court set up by Congress from hearing and determining this case. The claimants also stated that they had demanded an appeal within the time limit set by Congress, but their request had not been allowed so they appealed to the state superior court. From its decree they immediately in open court requested an appeal and offered sufficient bond but again were refused. In no way had they waived their right of appeal to Congress by prosecuting an appeal to the state superior court.

After studying these arguments the Committee on Appeals, on June 26, 1779, gave its opinion on the jurisdictional question. It held that the resolutions of Congress of November 25, 1775, recently explained and confirmed by the resolutions of March 6, 1779, gave it jurisdiction of this case. But since the law of New Hampshire was in conflict with the resolves of Congress and these resolves had just been transmitted to the state, the committee declined any further proceedings in the case till it heard the results of the deliberation of the state concerning the resolves of Congress.[21] The committee obviously did not intend to find itself involved in another head-on collision with a state, like the stalemate in the *Active* case which at that very time was being discussed in Congress.

The following fall Congress debated and in January, 1780, established the Court of Appeals which began its work in May. Nearly another year passed before the Articles of Confederation were finally ratified by all the states in March,

---

[21] *Lusanna*, #30, RCA.

1781. During all this time there was no further action on the
case of the *Lusanna*. New Hampshire had followed the example of Massachusetts and modified the law regulating
appeals in prize cases. On November 18, 1779, the state
legislature expanded the limits of appeals to Congress.
Thereafter appeals would be granted in cases in which any
subject of a friendly nation would claim part or all the vessel
or cargo in dispute. The appeal would have to be requested
within twenty-four hours after judgment in the maritime
court.[22] But this new law in no way touched the jurisdictional
dispute in the case of the brig *Lusanna* since no foreign
parties were involved. The Court of Appeals continued its
policy of waiting, perhaps hoping that eventually the state
would relent and grant appeals to Congress in all cases.

Finally in September, 1783, the Court of Appeals reviewed
the case of the *Lusanna*. After studying the vast quantity of
depositions, ship papers, letters, and lower court records, it
heard oral arguments on jurisdiction and on the merits. The
arguments on the merits, based on some leading authorities
on prize law, have already been analyzed in chapter VII.

After several days for advisement the court published its
definitive decree which reversed the sentence of both lower
courts and ordered restoration of the *Lusanna* and its cargo
to the claimants. Both parties were to pay their own costs.[23]
With this decision, however, the real debate over the court's
jurisdiction only began.

A month after this decree, on October 20, 1783, John
Penhallow, Joshua Wentworth, and the other captors presented a memorial to the New Hampshire legislature. They
complained that the Court of Appeals had assumed jurisdiction in the case in violation of the laws of the state. Their plea
to the jurisdiction of the court had been overruled, their
efforts to win a continuance to get evidence from England
disregarded. They had not even received notice of the final
trial before the Court of Appeals. They turned to the state
legislature to protect them and their property from this
assumed and arbitrary authority by which the previous
judgments had been overturned. The authority claimed by
the Court of Appeals had no justification under the Articles

---

[22] Batchellor, *Laws of New Hampshire* **4**: p. 238; Ford, *JCC* **15**: p. 1413.
[23] *Lusanna*, #30, RCA.

of Confederation, even if they had been ratified at the time of the original trial. The captors urged the legislature to vindicate the laws of the state which were being trampled and to support their cause.[24]

On November 6 the Governor of New Hampshire signed and forwarded to Congress a letter from the state assembly. This strong remonstrance of the state legislature, which transmitted the memorial of the captors, complained that the proceedings and decree of the Court of Appeals had been injurious to the parties concerned and subversive of the sovereignty and independence of the state. By the maritime laws of New Hampshire, the letter reminded Congress, no appeal in the case of the *Lusanna* could have been allowed to Congress or any court appointed by it before the ratification of the Confederation, which took place years after the final sentence of the state superior court. The states had, during the early years of Congress, considered compliance with the resolves of Congress to be optional. No resolve had the force of law till the state legislature sanctioned it. The importunate recommendations of Congress from time to time on the subject of maritime affairs confirmed this impression. After ratification of the Confederation, Congress spoke to the states in a new style. This deepened the conviction that prior to ratification the resolves of Congress had been no more than recommendations. Since the laws of the state forbade appeal to Congress in cases such as the *Lusanna*, no member of Congress from the state had any delegated power to repeal the state laws. Clearly the Court of Appeals had no power to take cognizance of or to reverse the sentences of the courts of New Hampshire. But even conceding that the resolves of Congress could vacate the laws of a state and give its court jurisdiction in all cases brought before it by appeal, yet in this case no appeal was ever granted. The case came before the Court of Appeals by complaint, so the assumption of jurisdiction by the court must have been unwarranted.

Furthermore the legislature maintained that the Articles of Confederation did not give Congress any added power except the final appellate jurisdiction in prize cases in the future. The Articles in no way granted any right to appeals prior to the time they were ratified. Since the Confederation

[24] PCC, Item 44, 197.

guaranteed to the states all the rights of sovereign and independent states not expressly given to Congress, and since the Articles did not give Congress the right of final appellate jurisdiction in this cause, nor warrant the mode of bringing cases by complaint, Congress must conclude that the decree of the Court of Appeals in the case of the *Lusanna* was void. The state legislature promised to take all proper means to prevent the execution of this decree, so derogatory to the dignity of the state and so oppressive to individual rights.[25]

General John Sullivan, agent for the owners of the brig *McClary*, captors of the *Lusanna*, completed the case against the jurisdiction of the Court of Appeals.[26] In a letter to the president of Congress he again reminded Congress that, at the time of the capture, trial and appeal to the state superior court, the law of New Hampshire had allowed appeals to Congress only when the ship making the capture had been fitted out at the congressional expense. More than a year after the original trial, Congress in March, 1779, had requested the legislature of New Hampshire to grant appeals to it in all prize cases as incident to its power of making peace and war. In November, 1779, the state legislature had complied with this request by allowing appeals to Congress in all cases in which the subjects of any foreign power in friendship with the United States were claimants. Clearly this showed that the power of final appellate jurisdiction in all cases had not previously been granted to Congress, unless Congress had been ignorant of the authority with which it had been entrusted. The need Congress felt for the states to grant appellate jurisdiction in all cases involving questions of war and peace did not prove any right in Congress, any more than the need of a national revenue proved the right of Congress to levy an impost without the assent of the states. The powers granted by the Confederation were not vested in Congress prior to the ratification of the Articles.

Sullivan argued that even if one should grant some implied power in Congress resulting from the power of making

---

[25] *Ibid.*, p. 203.

[26] *Ibid.*, p. 207. General John Sullivan was a delegate from New Hampshire to the First and Second Continental Congresses. He served as a brigadier- and later major-general in the army under Washington. After the war he held the offices of attorney general and president in New Hampshire, till he was appointed United States District Judge for New Hampshire. *DAB* 18: pp. 192–193.

war and peace, this power would extend only to cases where the states might violate treaties or neutral rights or involve the United States in hostilities. But the laws of New Hampshire adequately provided for such cases. Appeals to Congress were allowed whenever any friendly foreign nation presented a claim. In disputes between citizens of the various states, on the other hand, no argument could be given for granting Congress final appellate jurisdiction in prize cases which would not also show that Congress should have such jurisdiction over all common law disputes between litigants of diverse states. (Here Sullivan scored, since Congress had repeatedly given as the rationale for its inherent powers over questions of war and peace the danger of hostilities caused by one state's violations of neutral rights. Congress had been more reserved in suggesting that it should have appellate jurisdiction in all prize cases because of the risk of unfairness to out-of-state litigants.)

Any retrospective interpretation of the Articles could put in dispute any prize case long settled by state courts, years after the proceeds had been distributed to the many parties concerned. Moreover, Sullivan continued, civil law courts had always required some power to control them. Prior to the war this control had been exercised by the common law courts. But under the Confederation this control by common law courts was no longer possible. Therefore if Congress could not check an unwarrantable exercise of power in the Court of Appeals, no authority in the country could prevent it from hearing appeals in any matter it wished. General Sullivan concluded with the assurance that it would not be necessary to give notice to the adverse party in this dispute over jurisdiction, since Congress alone could determine what power it had intended to delegate to the Court of Appeals.

Congress received these letters and the memorial of the libelants, read them on January 2, 1784, and referred them to a committee composed of William Ellery, Edward Hand, Richard Dobbs Spaight, Thomas Jefferson, and Arthur Lee. The committee returned on January 13 with a report and a resolution. It had studied the arguments of the New Hampshire parties and had received another letter from Sullivan objecting to any consultation by the committee with the judges of the Court of Appeals. When the opinion of a court was reviewed by a higher court, Sullivan insisted, the judges of the lower court were never called on to account for their conduct.[27]

The resolution, drawn up by Jefferson and brought before Congress on January 13, stated that, in a case where a state before the Confederation had refused to allow appeals to Congress, neither Congress nor any persons deriving authority from it had jurisdiction. Sullivan's states' rights arguments had at least swayed the members of this committee. But since Congress had few members present at this time, the resolution never received enough votes to pass it. Time and again the resolution was brought up for a vote, or some other resolution substituted, but no proposal concerning this case could win the necessary seven states' votes needed to pass. For instance, an effort was made to refer the whole question back to the Court of Appeals and another attempt was made to state as congressional policy that it would be improper in any way to reverse or control the decisions of the Court of Appeals. Neither resolve could pass. But neither could the resolve of Jefferson's committee denying jurisdiction of the court in cases like that of the *Lusanna*. The last recorded attempt to get Congress's approval for this resolution was on March 30. Though Congress had better representation by then, the resolution could win the votes of only six states.[28]

As something of an anticlimax, Shearjashub Bourne returned to the scene. He sent a strong remonstrance to Congress in May, 1784, presenting the constitutional arguments in favor of the jurisdiction of the Court of Appeals in the case of the *Lusanna*.[29] Though Congress, already tired of the case, apparently never read his arguments, they do merit a brief summation as probably the strongest case that could be made for the action by the Court of Appeals.

Bourne reviewed the details of the capture and trial. When

---

[27] Sullivan to Jefferson, 5 January, 1784, PCC, Item 44, 219, 225.

[28] Ford, *JCC* **26:** pp. 3–4, 17–21, 38–41, 53, 151–152, 156, 163, 167, 174–175; Abiel Foster to President of New Hampshire, 8, 17, 24 January and 3 February, 1784; Foster to John Sullivan, 20 January, 1784, Burnett, *Letters* **7:** pp. 408–409, 420, 422, 424–425, 436; and Julian P. Boyd, ed., *The Papers of Thomas Jefferson* (18 v., Princeton, 1950–1971) **6:** pp. 447–455.

[29] PCC, Item 44, 233. Bourne's rhetoric occasionally ran away with him, as when he wrote that the owners would have had no further difficulties, "Except from the feeble Efforts of the turbulent and avaritious men who had preyed upon the Property of the Subjects of a Neighboring State, and might Wish to riot in the Spoils of their Illegal Depredations." Congress merely filed this remonstrance with the other papers in the *Lusanna* case, Ford, *JCC* **26:** p. 363.

the *Lusanna* had been condemned, the owners asked for an appeal to Congress. The maritime court refused this, though the owners were subjects of Massachusetts and could not legally be deprived of the benefits of the resolves of Congress by the laws of another state. (Bourne, of course, failed to mention that the New Hampshire law controlling the case had been modeled on the laws of Massachusetts.) After the decree of the lower court was affirmed by the state superior court, the owners again requested an appeal and offered security. Again this was refused, but nevertheless the appeal and the record of the court proceedings had been lodged with Congress in due time. The Commissioners of Appeals heard a plea to the jurisdiction and decided in favor of their jurisdiction. When the case finally came before the Court of Appeals in 1783, the captors renewed their objection to the jurisdiction. The court reheard the arguments and again determined in favor of its jurisdiction. It then heard the case on the merits and reversed the decree of the lower court. Then, after the owners thought the case settled, the captors had petitioned Congress to have the jurisdiction of the Court of Appeals ousted. Congress had proceeded *ex parte* without any notice to the adverse party.

When Congress was first elected, Bourne contended, it was vested by the united voice of its constituents with all powers of war and peace. This authority was freely resigned by the people to their representatives. By this transfer of power all authority in questions of war and peace was absolutely vested in Congress. This supreme authority in war necessarily embraced the right of authorizing the capture of enemy property. It would be a glaring absurdity, Bourne argued, to suppose that this inherent power of Congress did not imply the right of determining by itself, or by some court set up by Congress, the legality of all captures. From the nature of government, the sovereign who declares war and authorizes captures must have power also to guard against violations of the law of nations which might involve that sovereign in wars with foreign powers. Congress, therefore, could have appointed courts to determine all questions of prize in the first instance. For convenience, however, Congress recommended to the states that they appoint admiralty courts for the trial of prizes. By this recommendation the state legislatures derived from Congress, and subject to the control of

Congress, a power which they otherwise would not have had, since this power had been delegated to Congress by the people at large and by the state legislatures. Congress was not subject to the different legislatures in questions of prize; rather the legislatures had no other power than what Congress was pleased to grant them. By this same resolve Congress had reserved the right of appeals in all prize cases to itself or judges it might appoint.

The fact that the judges in New Hampshire refused to allow an appeal to Congress did not limit Congress's right to take cognizance of the case. It is not the judge *a quo*, Bourne contended, but the judge *ad quem* who has the right to determine whether an appeal lies or not. The consent of the lower court was unnecessary, its refusal immaterial.

Bourne argued that Congress from the beginning, in the resolves of November 25, 1775, had decided in the clearest terms that "in all [prize] cases an appeal shall be allowed to the Congress." In several important cases, such as the *Active*, the *Anna Maria*, the *Countess of Eglinton*, and others, he contended, Congress had decided in favor of the jurisdiction of the Committee on Appeals where various states had limited the right of appeal. (This is the only clear use of precedent from the cases decided by the appellate judiciary of Congress.) On March 6, 1779, Congress had reiterated the authority of the Committee on Appeals to determine finally all cases of capture. All these cases, all these resolves, took place before the Confederation was finally established. The members of Congress and the judges of the Committee on Appeals knew that in matters of peace and war Congress possessed just as much authority before the ratification of the Confederation as it did after.

Therefore, Bourne concluded, the resolution of Jefferson's committee recently proposed in response to the petitions of the captors in the case of the *Lusanna* would be unconstitutional, dangerous in its nature, alarming to former suitors, and unjust in itself. It would be unconstitutional because it was procured *ex parte* and because it would have an *ex post facto* effect. It would be dangerous because it would be an invasion by the legislature into the province of the judiciary. Courts are to determine questions of their own jurisdiction as well as the merits of cases. It would be alarming to former suitors because if the Court of Appeals did not have jurisdiction in the case of the *Lusanna*, it did not have jurisdiction in many other cases it had decided. It would be unjust because the owners in this case, trusting in the faith of Congress to live up to its resolves of November 25, 1775, had at great expense and trouble prosecuted this appeal.

Bourne's argument surpassed anything Congress had been able to say in support of its ultimate power to revise decrees in all prize cases. In other contexts the theory of implied powers of the Continental Congress had been discussed.[30] But Bourne drew together all the arguments and presented them in their most cogent form as applied to the appellate jurisdiction of Congress in questions of captures at sea.

Congress, however, had lost interest in the *Lusanna* case, or perhaps it felt frustrated by its own inability to settle the basic issue of jurisdiction. No further efforts of Congress are recorded to determine the scope of the jurisdiction of the Court of Appeals in this case.

Years later in 1795, however, the United States Supreme Court spoke the last word on the judicial battle between the captors and owners of the brig *Lusanna*.[31] The Court held that the Court of Appeals under the Continental Congress had possessed authority to determine finally this prize appeal, and that its decrees should be enforced as would the decrees of the highest court of a foreign nation. Justice Paterson, in some of his more rhetorical *dicta*, argued that the Continental Congress had possessed sovereignty in questions of war and peace. A careful analysis of the case of the *Lusanna* and several other cases challenging the appellate jurisdiction of Congress, however, gives one grounds to pause before making any sweeping assertions of the authority of the Continental Congress over the states.

The fact of the matter seems clear. Although cogent arguments could be propounded to show that the Continental Congress, especially after the ratification of the Articles of Confederation, had final authority in dealing with questions of prize, the political realities repeatedly frustrated congressional efforts to execute the decrees of its court of prize

---

[30] E.g., James Wilson; see Thomas Burke, Abstract of Debates, 25 February, 1777, Burnett, *Letters* 2: pp. 275–281.

[31] *Penhallow et al. v. Doane's Administrators*, 3 Dallas 53 (1795); Goebel, *Antecedents*, pp. 179–181, 708–710, 766–770.

appeals. If a state government or state court stuck to its determination to negate the effectiveness of these appellate decrees, Congress had no weapons in its scanty arsenal of powers to compel compliance.

The debates over the jurisdiction of the Committee on Appeals and the Court of Appeals demonstrate the ambivalent position of Congress. Because of the uncertainty of its constitutional mandate, Congress could only vacillate, at times assuming the self-assured stance of a strong central government with ultimate power over all questions of war and peace, but at other times resembling a badly fragmented gathering of foreign diplomats from thirteen nations, trying by requests and recommendations to assure some unified action by the states.

One would have to conclude that the jurisdiction of the appellate judiciary of the Continental Congress extended only as far as the states tolerated. In spite of fine-spun arguments as to Congress's inherent powers, at the time it must have been clear to all that the states ultimately could determine how far congressional writs could run. The judges of appeals were hardly bold in extending their jurisdiction. But even the decrees they issued, which were clearly within the scope of authority Congress had granted, could be rendered meaningless by a state's laws or a state's unswerving refusal to respect the decree. Those who knew of the work of Congress's appellate prize judiciary must have realized with greater clarity as the years passed that if the United States was indeed a sovereign nation, it must have an effective central judicial authority.

IX. An End and a Beginning: Transition to the New Judiciary

A CONCLUDING CHAPTER should try to draw together and highlight some of the more significant themes of a historical work and hint at the direction of these themes for the future. But it is all too easy to distort history by isolating such strands and studying their separate influence on subsequent events. As the whole stream is seen out of perspective when one focuses sharply with binoculars on the whirls and eddies of one segment of it, so the larger historical picture can be blurred beyond recognition by singling out one institution and its key themes and attributing to them a special significance in the shaping of the future.

In this work the risk is particularly great. The simple fact is that after 1787 there were few direct references to the appellate prize court of the Continental Congress or its work; explicit evidence of its impact on the formation and early development of the federal judiciary is seldom found. One must work from inference which can devalue certainty to the level of vague probabilities.

The influence of the Committee on Appeal and the Court of Appeals on subsequent judicial institutions can best be appreciated if we view the first federal court as a learning experience for the various participants (parties, attorneys, and judges), a graduate seminar in the problems of a federal appellate court under the Continental Congress. The chief lessons for the participants, as we have seen throughout this book, centered around the problems of federalism (the relationship between the central government and the states), the separation of powers (the relationship between Congress and its appellate prize court), and international relations (the complex interrelationship between the rights of foreign nations and their subjects and the sovereignty and authority inscrutably divided under the Confederation between the states and the central government).

Throughout the history of the United States, the ebb and

319

flow of the federal tide can be marked by key Supreme Court decisions; the court has often been immersed in the turbulent debates that have raged over the extent and the limits of federal power over the states. So also the first federal court, in spite of its inability to cope with many problems presented to it, became the focal point of several of the all-too-frequent tests of strength between the Continental Congress and the states.

This book has repeatedly highlighted various aspects of this problem of federalism. The states, for instance, thought they had the power to define the limits of the right of appeal to Congress in prize cases, even though Congress had resolved that the right of appeal to it should lie in all prize cases. These limitations on the right of appeal led to serious constitutional confrontations in such cases as the sloop *Active*, the ship *Anna Maria*, the brig *Holy Martyrs*, the ship *Valenciano*, and the brig *Lusanna*. If a state court refused to execute the decrees of the court of appeals, the central government had no way to effectuate execution.

The bias of local juries in favor of the hometown litigants occasionally appears beneath the surface of these prize cases. Out-of-state or foreign litigants could be denied justice by state admiralty courts, and their pleas to Congress called forth reassuring promises that justice would be done, but little effective relief. Some of the judges, attorneys, and merchants who were involved in these cases must have readily recognized the desirability of providing national trial courts to better assure justice for out-of-state and foreign litigants.

The problem of federalism appeared in another dimension when some citizens of Connecticut plundered the residents of Long Island who were within the area controlled by the British. Congress finally persuaded the state to stop this practice and the Court of Appeals ultimately decreed the restoration of the captured property to some of the Long Island residents. But the tensions between the states involved were relieved more by voluntary compliance than by any coercive power Congress or its court wielded. The cases of the *Active* and the *Lusanna* led to full airings of the shaky constitutional structure underlying the relations between the states and the Continental Congress.

These were some of the lessons in federalism that the attorneys, judges, and litigants could learn from their experiences with the appellate prize court of Congress. Some must have come to realize the need for an effective federal judicial system if the bond between the states was to last. When we sketch the beginnings of the new federal judicial system later in this chapter, we will be able to suggest a few areas in which the experience from the first federal court had a possible impact on the new system.

The strong centrifugal forces of states' rights at work under the Continental Congress, of course, did not vanish when a federal government based on the new Constitution took power. The familiar incidents of the Kentucky and Virginia Resolutions and the Hartford Convention dispel any doubts as to the vitality of these locally oriented states' rights forces under the Constitution. The Supreme Court in many well-known early decisions, such as *Chisholm v. Georgia*,[1] *Fletcher v. Peck*,[2] *Martin v. Hunter's Lessee*,[3] *McCulloch v. Maryland*,[4] *Cohens v. Virginia*,[5] *Osborn v. Bank of the United States*,[6] exerted its full weight to strengthen and consolidate the forces unifying the nation and to hold in check the asserted sovereignty of the individual states. These Supreme Court decisions demonstrate not only that the centrifugal forces persisted long after the foundation of the new government, but also that the balance of effective power had shifted. No longer did the judiciary of the central government stand impotent when confronted by a state's obstinate refusal to comply with its orders or decrees. Those who had profited from their exposure to the appellate prize court under the Continental Congress helped to construct a new federal judiciary able to assert the nation's authority without having its voice drowned out by the states.

A brief summary of one Supreme Court decision and the reaction of a state to it will suffice to show the intensity of states' rights sentiment under the Constitution. In this case, the epilogue to the case of the sloop *Active*, the Supreme Court finally prevailed where the Committee on Appeals and the Continental Congress had failed.

---

[1] 2 Dallas 419 (1793).
[2] 6 Cranch 87 (1810).
[3] 1 Wheaton 304 (1816).
[4] 4 Wheaton 315 (1819).
[5] 6 Wheaton 264 (1821).
[6] 9 Wheaton 738 (1824).

Gideon Olmsted, surely a persevering litigant, had never given up his efforts to recover from the state of Pennsylvania for himself and his three associates the proceeds from the sale of the sloop *Active* and its cargo. The state had ordered the admiralty court to turn over the proceeds to the state treasurer, David Rittenhouse.[7] Olmsted's first efforts to obtain justice through the state judiciary led nowhere, for the Pennsylvania Supreme Court held the earlier decree of the Committee on Appeals void.[8]

Olmsted turned to the federal courts and in 1803 obtained an order from the Pennsylvania district court that the state treasurer must pay Olmsted and the other first captors of the *Active* the amount of the proceeds held for the state, plus interest.[9] The governor of Pennsylvania, asserting that the state was the real party in interest and had not been heard in the federal court proceedings, sent a message to the state legislature to elicit its reaction to the federal court decree. The legislature, on April 2, 1803, reviewed the long history of the case of the *Active* and declared the jurisdiction of the Committee on Appeals had been illegally usurped and so was void from the beginning.[10] The legislature instructed the governor to protect the state's rights and interests by whatever means might be necessary.

Since the federal district judge took no steps to enforce his decree, fearing another confrontation with the state, Olmsted turned to the United States Supreme Court to obtain a writ of mandamus to compel the district court to secure obedience to its decree (and, thereby, to the long-ignored decree of the Committee on Appeals). Chief Justice Marshall upheld the authority of the Committee on Appeals to decree the whole proceeds of the *Active* to the Olmsted captors in the first place, and the authority of the federal court to enforce this decree even against a recalcitrant state. Marshall held

---

[7] The subsequent history of the case of the *Active* is included in the documents collected in Peters, *Whole Proceedings*, and summarized in Charles G. Haines, *The Role of the Supreme Court in American Government and Politics* (New York, 1944), pp. 270–279. The citations to the various judicial determinations were given in chapter III, note 38.

[8] *Ross v. Rittenhouse*, 2 Dallas 160 (1792).

[9] *Olmsted v. The Active*, 18 Fed. Cases, #10,503a (1803).

[10] James T. Mitchell, Willis Martin and Hampton L. Carson, eds., *Statutes at Large of Pennsylvania* (Harrisburg, 1915) 17: p. 472.

that state legislatures lacked the authority to annul the judgments of federal courts.[11]

When Marshall's decision became public, the governor of Pennsylvania notified the state legislature that he intended to call out the state militia to protect the Rittenhouse residence and prevent the United States marshal from enforcing the decree of the federal district court. The state legislature in its turn appropriated $18,000 to be used by the governor to assure that the good faith of Pennsylvania to its engagements (in opposing the federal court's decree) would be upheld. The governor was to use the funds to carry out the legislature's 1803 instructions.[12]

Ultimately the sovereign Commonwealth of Pennsylvania, whose defiance had been disapproved by the resolutions of eleven states, backed down. The decree of the federal court was not only enforced, but the state militia officers, who in obedience to the governor had forcibly resisted the federal marshal, were tried and convicted in a federal court.[13] Even though the president finally pardoned the defendants, the message had been conveyed in unmistakable terms: The federal courts under the Constitution, unlike the first, pre-constitutional federal court, had the effective authority to enforce their decrees.

Besides this recurring theme of federalism, this book has from time to time mentioned the necessarily close relationship between the Continental Congress and its appellate prize court. Throughout the American states during the Revolution many had come to accept as an immutable principle of good government the proposition that "It is essential to Liberty that the legislative, judicial and executive Powers of Government be, as nearly as possible, independent of and separate from each other."[14] Those who were familiar with the development and work of the congressional appellate prize court could appreciate somewhat more fully the wis-

---

[11] *United States v. Peters*, 5 Cranch 115 (1809).

[12] *Statutes at Large of Pennsylvania* **18:** p. 1163.

[13] *United States v. Bright*, 24 Fed. Cases, #14,647 (1809).

[14] Instructions of the Town of Boston to its Representatives in the General Court, May, 1776, quoted in Wood, *American Republic*, p. 150. On the theme of separation of powers, see *ibid.*, pp. 151–161, 446–453, 549–553, 559–560. On the constitutional dimensions of separation of powers, see Raoul Berger, *Congress v. The Supreme Court* (Cambridge, Mass., 1969).

dom of this doctrine of the separation of powers. They had the occasion to observe Congress, a legislative body, giving birth to a judicial institution from the unlikely womb of a committee of Congress. Soon this committee, staffed with attorneys, appeared in its procedures and style more and more like a court. Congress continued to find itself directly involved in various problems related to captures at sea. After Congress had its fingers burned in the case of the *Active*, it was open to the suggestion of a group of Philadelphia merchants to make its appellate prize judiciary independent of Congress with judges who did not sit in Congress.

Even after the Court of Appeals had been established, Congress hemmed in its powers so narrowly that parties had to seek congressional authorization even for leave to file their appeals late. Congress controlled the choice of places for hearings, the power of appointing judges and determining their salaries, and the authority of the court to grant rehearings. The court had to ask Congress for special authority to discharge a prisoner if it should determine, in a case properly before it, that he was not an enemy. The judges apparently interpreted their grant of authority narrowly, never forgetting that what little power they had came from Congress.

Congress, on the other hand, made clear on several occasions that it would not sit as an appellate judiciary itself to review the strictly judicial determinations of the Committee on Appeals or the Court of Appeals. Perhaps this policy of noninterference in judicial matters was born in part of a desire to avoid involvement in the heated controversies over neutral property or property claimed by parties from different states.

This intimate symbiosis between the legislative and judicial branches of the government reinforced the strongly held conviction of many who accepted as inspired truth Montesquieu's statement that liberty is best preserved where the legislative, executive, and judicial powers of government are separated.[15] Some who, as we shall see, would be influential in writing the new Constitution and in establishing the new government grounded on this principle of the separation of

---

[15] Baron de Montesquieu, *The Spirit of the Laws,* Thomas Nugent, tr. (New York, 1949), pp. 151–152.

powers, must have derived confirmation of their convictions from their experience with the appellate prize judiciary of Congress.

Another theme which has been developed in various ways throughout this work was the difficulties and embarrassments of Congress due to the international disputes caused by privateering and by the inability of the congressional prize court of appeals promptly to satisfy the demands of foreign nationals. Congress had to face more problems in foreign relations than it could readily solve. The capture of neutral vessels created sensitive situations which must have made many Americans aware of the desirability of a central government that could assure justice to aggrieved foreign parties.

Many American lawyers and admiralty judges during the Revolution, as another aspect of their education in international affairs, had to intensify their reading of the leading authors on the law of nations and the practice of prize litigation in European courts. The American bench and bar were open to the incorporation of the law of nations as a part of American substantive prize law. Undoubtedly the inconsistency and abstractness of the principles of the law of nations, as well as the unique circumstances surrounding so many American prize cases, hampered this incorporation.

Under the Constitution the American legal establishment continued to open its arms to welcome imported prize law. During the thirty years after the Constitution, references to British prize decisions far outnumbered the references to the few reported opinions of the congressional court of appeals. The Supreme Court and the early American authors on prize law paid little attention to the work of the Court of Appeals.[16] During these same years the Supreme Court turned continuously to the authority of the reports of the British admiralty cases which had been published starting in 1798.[17] Furthermore, the Supreme Court, between 1789 and

---

[16] 8 Cranch 255, 341; 9 Cranch 249, 276; 1 Wheaton 161; 2 Wheaton 247–248; Henry Wheaton, *A Digest of the Law of Maritime Captures and Prizes* (New York, 1815), pp. 101, 232, 272–273, 274, 281, 284, 287, 299, and Frederic T. Pratt, ed., *Notes and the Principles and Practice of Prize Courts, by the Late Judge Story* (London, 1854), pp. 55, 120, 123.

[17] Christopher Robinson, ed., *Reports of Cases Argued and Determined in the High Court of Admiralty* (6 v., London, 1798–1808). As early as 1800 American attorneys were citing Robinson's Admiralty Reports in argument before the Supreme Court.

1820, repeatedly relied in general on the same writers on the
law of nations to whom the first federal court had turned for
guidance in its prize appeals. Vattel was the writer most
frequently cited in arguments before the early Supreme
Court and in its opinions.[18]

We have now briefly reviewed three of the principal
themes which were intertwined with the study of the first
federal court: federalism, the separation of powers, and an
awareness of the international ramifications of privateering.
We have suggested that each of these undercurrents proved
to be part of the education of some of the lawyers and
merchants who would soon lead the movement for a more
effective central government. We can now look at this first
federal court in the larger context of appellate judicial institutions. The appellate prize court of the Continental Congress, with its narrowly limited jurisdiction, was a significant
link in the chain of institutional continuity between the Privy
Council, which heard and determined the appeals from the
American colonies, and the present Supreme Court. We
must try to assess how much continuity and how much dis-
continuity we can discern as we watch the Revolutionary
appellate prize court grow out of the colonial experience and
in turn contribute to the experience leading to the appellate
judiciary under the Constitution.

It is rare to be able to study a governmental institution with
a clear point of beginning and end, and a brief life span of
some eleven years. But history, as biology, knows no spon-
taneous generation; the appellate prize judiciary which
struggled to its feet in the strange surroundings of a legislative committee, had forebears in the colonial experience and
in turn, when it had matured, left seeds which would grow
and develop under a wholly new Constitution.

We have seen the basic procedural similarities between the
state prize courts set up during the Revolution and the prize
practice in the colonial vice-admiralty courts. We have suggested that even before the Revolution, prize practice in the
colonies had diverged from the practice before the High
Court of Admiralty. The training of an attorney in America

The Eliza, 4 Dallas 36 (1800); The Amelia, 1 Cranch 1 (1801); The Charming Betsy, 2
Cranch 64 (1804); The Blaireau, 2 Cranch 240 (1804).

[18] Edwin D. Dickinson, "Changing Concepts and the Doctrine of Incorporation,"
Amer. Jour. International Law 26 (1932): p. 259 note 132.

at the time rested largely on oral tradition, a "memory jurisprudence."[19] The state prize courts, therefore, followed the familiar patterns of the colonial vice-admiralty courts, with local variations preserved. The vice-admiralty records were close at hand for American lawyers to use as a quarry in their Revolutionary War prize cases, while the intricacies of the distant courts in Great Britain remained largely a mystery. The American prize practitioners, before and during the Revolution, undoubtedly thought of themselves as faithfully carrying on a tradition of prize practice—and so they were, but not as it existed before the High Court of Admiralty. The few published sources that described British prize procedures at all spoke in such vague terms that the Americans probably found reason in them to confirm their conviction that their practice was true to the British usage.

Of course, the esoteric cult practiced before the Lords Commissioners for Prize Appeals was largely unknown even in London, except to the few initiates. The American court of prize appeals bears practically no similarity to the court of the Lords Commissioners. A much closer similarity could be traced to the familiar practices of appeals to the colonial or state common law appellate courts.[20]

The Americans, even when they were at war with the British, were not ashamed of imitating or adapting those British prize forms that were known (such as the instructions to privateers, or various clauses in the British prize acts incorporated in the state prize acts). The American attitude was expressed during the war by the board of admiralty set up by Congress. In July, 1780, the board reported to Congress on an earlier congressional order for the board to revise the regulations concerning the navy and captures at sea. The board reported that it was understaffed and lacked the legal training needed to revise and coordinate the regulations on captures at sea. Regulations for the navy, moreover, would take much time and attention, since the board would have to review existing congressional regulations and study the comparable British regulations. At this point in the report the members inserted an enlightening parenthetical comment: "[F]or the Board do not think it

---

[19] Goebel, *Antecedents*, p. 112.
[20] *Ibid.*, pp. 25–35.

unlawful to be taught by an Enemy, whose naval skill and power, until the reign of the present illustrious King of France, were superior to that of any Kingdom or state on earth."[21] This revealing aside typified the attitude of those connected with the Court of Appeals. With, or more likely without, the touch of guilt expressed by the board of admiralty, the state governments, Congress, and the judges of appeals learned, wherever possible, from the enemy; they did not hesitate to draw upon the experience of the British prize law. The problem was not their reluctance to learn from the British, but rather that so little detailed information was available in the published sources.

Our study of the substantive legal issues has confirmed the conclusion from the analysis of prize procedure. The American attorneys readily turned to the sources that were available on prize law, Lee, Vattel, and others, but in the end they were forced to fashion what they found to the American needs. The legal issues in most prize appeal cases in America differed from the issues most frequently argued before the Lords Commissioners. The American prize cases often turned on issues unique to the type of war being waged. Even if the work of the Lords Commissioners had been reported, it would most frequently have been inapplicable to the American situation. But we have seen the American bench and bar did use the inadequate sources on prize law they could find.

Turning now from the past, from the sources on which American lawyers and judges drew in their Revolutionary War prize practice, we can look to the future, to the influence exerted by the appellate prize court on the origins and birth of the present federal judiciary. Since direct evidence of this impact is rare and inference is shaky, the most we can hope to achieve is some suggestion of possible future influence.

The congressional appellate prize judiciary obviously touched the lives of few individuals, but many of those who had taken part in this learning experience played a significant role in writing and securing ratification of the Constitution and in establishing and making operational the early federal courts under the Constitution.

Twenty-one of the fifty-five members of the Philadelphia convention of 1787 had some direct acquaintance with the

---

[21] Ford, *JCC* **18**: p. 673.

work of the Committee on Appeals or the Court of Appeals, some as lawyers practicing before the court, some as judges of appeals.[22] Most important to the formation of the federal judiciary was the considerable experience of James Wilson and Oliver Ellsworth. Wilson had served as one of the judges of appeals in at least ten cases and had acted as attorney for a party on appeal in six other cases, including the case of the sloop *Active*. Ellsworth, likewise, had been directly involved in at least nine cases as a judge or attorney. He had been one of the judges deciding the *Active* case and had joined in presenting to Congress the report on the refusal of the Pennsylvania admiralty court to execute the decision of the Committee on Appeals in that case. Ellsworth also took part in debating the plan for setting up the Court of Appeals and served on the committee appointed to draw up the compromise proposals for establishing the court which in January, 1780, passed Congress. William Samuel Johnson, Luther Martin, George Read, and Edmund Randolph also had the experience of involvement with a number of cases on appeal. James Madison never acted as judge of appeals, nor did he serve as counsel for parties bringing an appeal, but as a member of Congress he took a leading role in preparing and debating a revised plan to serve as the legislative basis for the Court of Appeals. These men, therefore, knew well of the Court of Appeals and all its limitations. They brought their knowledge of this first federal court to bear as they prepared to establish a national court system in the new Constitution.

Besides the participants in the Federal Convention, most of the political leaders in each state played an active role in the debates over the ratification of the Constitution. A few of

---

[22] The records frequently give no indication of the names of counsel or only an incomplete name, but the following list will indicate the names of those who were listed. The relationship with the congresssional court of prize appeals will be abbreviated: JA = judge of appeals; C = counsel. The number indicates the approximate number of appellate cases with which that individual was connected: Richard Bassett (C, 3); Gunning Bedford (C, 1); George Clymer (JA, 1); Oliver Ellsworth (C, 4, JA, 5); Alexander Hamilton (C, 2); William C. Houston (C, 2); Jared Ingersoll (C, 6); William Samuel Johnson (C, 3); Rufus King (C, 1, JA, 1); Luther Martin (C, 3); Gouverneur Morris (C, 1); Robert Morris (C, 1); William Paterson (C, 1); Charles Pinckney (JA, 1); Charles Cotesworth Pinckney (C, 1); Edmund Randolph (JA, 3); George Read (JA, 28, C, 5); Roger Sherman (JA, 2); James Wilson (JA, 10, C, 6); George Wythe (JA, 5). James Madison, as explained in the text, was the twenty-first member of the Federal Convention with direct knowledge of the congressional court of prize appeals.

the attorneys or judges who had been active in the proceedings before the appellate prize court during the Revolution
opposed the Constitution.[23] In general, however, many of
the attorneys or judges (whether state admiralty judges or
judges of appeals) who had experience with the congressional appellate court actively strove for the ratification
of the Constitution.[24]

After the Constitution was ratified, one of the first tasks
undertaken by the first Congress was to establish a federal
judiciary. The Judiciary Act of 1789 bore the strong imprint
of Oliver Ellsworth, who, as we have seen, had enough experience with the first federal court to appreciate the need
for a federal judiciary able to accomplish its purpose. William
Paterson, who had a minimum contact with the first federal
court, also played a key role in drafting the new Judiciary
Act.[25]

When the Washington administration sought men to sit as
judges of the recently established federal courts, it selected a
large number of men who had practiced before the first
federal court or had sat as judges of that court or of the state
maritime courts. Oliver Ellsworth and James Wilson were
appointed to the Supreme Court. James Iredell, William
Paterson, and Samuel Chase, likewise chosen for the Supreme Court, all had some small amount of experience of
practice before the appellate prize court of Congress. The
United States district courts were also staffed with a number
of judges who had gained experience in federal judicial
problems from their contacts with the first federal court.
William Paca, John Lowell, Henry Marchant, and Cyrus
Griffin had all served as judges of appeals, so their work as

---

[23] For instance, Samuel Chase (JA, 3); Luther Martin (see note 22); William Paca
(JA, 20), all from Maryland.

[24] The participants in the Federal Convention (see note 22), most of whom
supported the Constitution in the ratification debates, will not be relisted here. Some
others who favored ratification were: Nathan Cushing, (Judge, Admiralty Court,
24); Francis Dana (JA, 1, C, 3); Pierpont Edwards (C, 4); William Hooper (JA, 3, C,
1); Francis Hopkinson (Judge, Admiralty Court, 4); Samuel Huntington (JA, 3);
Richard Law (Judge, Admiralty Court, 5); Henry Marchant (JA, 9, C, 1); Thomas
McKean (JA, 17, C, 3); Jesse Root (JA, 13, C, 3); Edward Rutledge (JA, 1, C, 1);
Hugh Rutledge (Judge, Admiralty Court, 3); James Sullivan (C, 5). We have not
been able to discover the position in the ratification debate of many attorneys who
had likewise practiced before the first federal court. (Where judges of state admiralty courts are listed, the number indicates the number of their judgments known
to have been appealed to the congressional court of prize appeals.)

[25] For the extent of the experience of Ellsworth and Paterson, see note 22.

federal court judges was not entirely new. Richard Law and Francis Hopkinson had served in their states as admiralty court judges before being appointed to preside over federal district courts. Gunning Bedford, Robert Morris, and William Lewis had all served as counsel before the first federal court prior to their selection as federal judges.[26]

These were some of the men who had participated in the seminar of the first federal court. Tracing the influence of this one phase of their education is, in general, impossible; rarely do they mention the appellate prize court of the Continental Congress as they debated the Constitution during its drafting or ratification or as they shared in establishing or serving on the new federal judiciary.

A full history of the formation of the new federal court system in the drafting of Article III and in the ratification debates over this judiciary article, or in the congressional debates leading to the Judiciary Act of 1789 would be out of place in this concluding chapter.[27] All we can accomplish here is to suggest a few of the points of contact between the first federal court and the new judicial system established under the Constitution.

The records of the Federal Convention of 1787 give scanty information about the debates over the judiciary in Article III of the Constitution. Perhaps the debates were poorly reported; more likely the delegates exhausted their energy and erudition debating the legislative and executive branches, which seemed to them more important. From the records of the debates, however, it appears that some of the members of the convention had the experience of the first federal court in mind as they were laying the foundations of the new judiciary.

The Virginia plan, which provided the basis for discussion at the convention, included a resolution for a national

---

[26] For a list of the early federal judges, see, "The First Judges of the Federal Courts," *Amer. Jour. Legal History* 1 (1957): pp. 76–78. The extent of the experience of these early federal justices and judges with the first federal court was: Ellsworth (see note 22); Wilson (see note 22); James Iredell (C, 1); Paterson (see note 22); Chase (see note 23); Paca (see note 23); John Lowell (JA, 17, C, 13); Marchant (see note 24); Cyrus Griffin (JA, 48); Law (see note 24); Hopkinson (see note 24); Bedford (see note 22); Morris (see note 22); William Lewis (C, 19).

[27] Especially since just such a history of the formation of the federal judiciary has recently been completed with extraordinary depth of analysis and originality of insights by the late Professor Julius Goebel, Jr. in *History of the Supreme Court* 1: *Antecedents and Beginnings to 1801* (New York, 1971).

judiciary to consist of one or more supreme tribunals and of inferior tribunals, with judges chosen by the national legislature to hold office during good behavior and be paid a fixed compensation (to avoid any undue influence from the legislature which would control their salaries). The jurisdiction of these national courts in the Virginia plan included authority in the inferior courts in the first instance, and in the supreme tribunal as court of last resort, to hear all cases of piracies and felonies on the high seas, all captures from an enemy, as well as cases in which foreigners or citizens of other states had an interest. The federal courts would also have jurisdiction over cases involving collection of the national revenue, impeachments of national officers and cases "which may involve the national peace and harmony."[28] The years of limping along with the congressional appellate prize court had shown that many problems arose if state courts could determine finally cases of captures, cases involving foreign or out-of-state litigants, or cases in which national peace and harmony were at stake. The authority of the central government's judiciary in just such cases would be made secure under the proposed government.

When the members of the convention discussed this article, some opposed establishing inferior national courts since they thought that the state courts could serve the function of a court of first instance in all cases. This would have preserved just the type of judicial structure (state trial courts with one national appellate court to review their judgments) tried and found seriously inadequate under the Continental Congress. John Rutledge argued that the supreme national court would be adequate to secure national rights and uniformity of judgments without the added expense and interference into the states which would result from inferior national courts. James Madison told the convention he strongly disagreed; he insisted that there was a great danger of improper verdicts in the state courts which could not easily be cured by appeals to the supreme national court, for that court could only order a new trial in the same state court. Probably with vivid recollections of the inept efforts of the Continental Congress to exert its authority over the states,

---

[28] Max Farrand, ed., *The Records of the Federal Convention of 1787* (4 v., New Haven, 1911–1937), 29 May, 1787, 1: pp. 21–22.

Madison asserted that a government without a proper executive and judiciary would be the mere trunk of a body without arms or legs to act or move.[29] James Wilson also opposed Rutledge's suggestion. He argued that at least the sphere of admiralty jurisdiction ought to be given wholly to the national government, since admiralty cases were not within the jurisdiction of particular states. Furthermore in these admiralty cases many controversies would involve foreign parties; such cases should be decided entirely by national courts. But upon Rutledge's motion to remove the inferior tribunals from the resolutions before the convention, the states voted to eliminate them.[30]

Wilson and Madison immediately moved to add to the judiciary resolutions the provision "that the National Legislature be empowered to institute inferior tribunals." They argued that, if the convention thought it should not establish such inferior courts, at least it should give the national legislature the discretion of setting them up. This motion carried, and upon this decision after only brief debate the entire federal system of lower courts today depends.[31] Since both Wilson and Madison knew well the efforts and the failures of the first federal court, they had ample grounds for insisting upon the establishment of inferior federal courts. It might well be that in this one brief moment of debate at the Federal Convention, the years of labor of the judges of appeals bore their most important fruit.

The development of the specifics of federal jurisdiction remains obscure. The Convention, while apparently fearful of encroachments on the state judiciaries, approved the broad and undefined proposal of Randolph, seconded by Madison, to grant the federal courts jurisdiction over questions which involved the national peace and harmony.[32] Most of the precise areas of jurisdiction of the federal courts, as now in the Constitution, were worked out by the committee of detail, of which Ellsworth and Wilson were leading members. Apparently the committee intended to keep the jurisdiction broad and inclusive but expressed more accurately than the convention had.[33]

---

[29] *Ibid.*, 5 June, 1787, 1: pp. 115–116, 118, 119–121, 124.
[30] *Ibid.*, 5 June, 1787, 1: pp. 124–125.
[31] *Ibid.* 1: p. 125; see also 2: pp. 45–46.
[32] *Ibid.* 1: pp. 223–224; 2: p. 46.
[33] *Ibid.* 2: pp. 132–133, 136, 144, 146–147, 157, 172–173.

The members of the convention paid very little attention
to the judiciary after they received the report of the committee of detail. But among the few brief debates concerning the
judiciary, two questions were raised which again led some of
the members to draw upon their experience of the first
federal court. First of all, when the convention discussed the
judiciary article, Gouverneur Morris asked whether the appellate jurisdiction of the proposed supreme court extended
to matters of fact as well as law, and to cases of common law
as well as civil law. Wilson, speaking for the committee of
detail, replied that the clause was intended to include review
of the facts as well as appeals of law, and to apply to common
law and civil law appeals. He added that "The jurisdiction of
the federal Court of Appeals [in Cases of Capture] had . . .
been so construed." John Dickinson then moved to add the
words "both as to law and fact" to the clause under discussion, which the convention agreed to without an opposing
voice.[34] Thus with practically no discussion at all, the fram-
ers, justifying their action by the practice of the first federal
court, put into the Constitution a phrase which would prove
explosive in the ratifying conventions. During the debate
over ratification, all the old fears of jury verdicts being undermined would be fanned into flame largely as a result of
this harmless-sounding phrase.

The second question which led some of the members to
recall their experience with the appellate court of Congress
was raised on September 12, just a week before the convention adjourned. For the first time one of the delegates observed that there was as yet no guarantee of jury trial in civil
cases. After a brief exchange, with some strong sentiment
expressed for preparing a bill of rights which would include
a guarantee of trial by jury in civil cases, the states voted
unanimously not to make any such provision. Again on September 15 the question of jury trial in civil cases was raised
and again the proposal was unanimously defeated. The opponents argued that such a provision in the Constitution was
impossible since the various states had different customs with
regard to juries in civil cases.[35] Several months after the

---

[34] *Ibid.*, 27 August, 1787, **2**: p. 431. This is the only explicit mention of the first
federal court in the recorded debates of the Federal Convention. Earlier mention of
review of the facts of a case had occurred, **1**: p. 243; **2**: p. 157.

[35] *Ibid.* **2**: pp. 587–588, 628.

convention, Charles Pinckney at the South Carolina ratifying convention explained why the Constitution did not include a guarantee of jury trial in civil cases. His testimony is especially important since he had been one of the delegates in the Federal Convention in favor of adding a jury trial provision for civil cases. At the South Carolina convention Pinckney stated that the delegates at Philadelphia had been anxious to make some declaration, but "when they reflected that all courts of admiralty and appeals, being governed in their propriety by the civil law and the laws of nations, never had, or ought to have, juries, they found it impossible to make any precise declaration upon the subject."[36]

Throughout the discussions of the judiciary at the Federal Convention runs the underlying premise that the judiciary (and the executive) should be separate and not dependent upon or intermingled with the legislative branch as they had been under the Articles of Confederation. The separation of powers apparently was a universally held conviction of the members of the Philadelphia Convention. This explains in part the disproportionately large amount of debate at the convention over the mode of payment of federal judges' salaries and the method of appointing the federal judges.[37] The convention groped for the best way to assure the choice of highly qualified men for the Supreme Court, men who could carry on their important tasks without interference from the legislature. The experience of many men at the convention with the first federal court must have deepened their appreciation of the wisdom of preserving a healthy distance between the judiciary and the other branches of government. The appellate prize court had achieved a degree of independence of the Continental Congress, perhaps in part due to the many diplomatically sensitive controversies which made the politicians in Congress only too happy to consign all such problems to the exclusive authority of its appellate prize court. In some small way these recollections of the first federal court might have helped sway the Con-

---

[36] Jonathan Elliot, ed., *The Debates in the Several State Conventions on the Adoption of the Federal Constitution* (2d ed., 4 v., Washington, 1854) 4: p. 260.

[37] Farrand, *Records* 1: pp. 22, 116, 119–121, 126–128, 224–226, 230, 232–233, 237, 238, 244, 292; 2: pp. 37–38, 41–45, 71, 72, 80–83, 132, 146, 172, 183, 186, 423, 428–430, 495, 498, 533, 537–540, 574–576, 599–600.

stitutional Convention to build the new judiciary on the cor-
nerstone of the separation of powers.

The debate over the ratification of the new Constitution
focused more on the legislative and executive branches than
on the judiciary. Furthermore, much of the debate over the
judiciary grew out of the deep-seated popular veneration for
the institution of trial by jury. Repeatedly both sides in the
debate (the self-styled federalists who favored the Constitution and the antifederalists who, from many diverse and
conflicting points of view, opposed the Constitution) took up
the antifederalists' objections that the Constitution failed to
guarantee trial by jury in civil cases and undermined the
sacredness of jury verdicts by allowing the Supreme Court to
review the facts as well as the law determined by the lower
court.[38] Considerable attention in the ratification debates was
also given to the jurisdiction of the proposed federal courts
and the need or desirability of creating inferior federal
courts.

Seldom in all these discussions of the new federal judiciary
was there any clear reference to the appellate prize judiciary
of the Continental Congress. In one of these infrequent
explicit references, James Wilson, replying to arguments of
the antifederalist opposition during the Pennsylvania ratifying convention, drew upon the experience of the first federal
court to explain why the Constitution allowed appellate review of the facts of a case. Appellate review of the facts was
essential, Wilson contended, as the experience of the admiralty courts proved. Those who had their vessels captured
knew well what a poor chance of recovery they would have
had if the verdict of state juries had been final. Without the
congressional appellate prize court to reconsider and set
aside state verdicts, these aggrieved parties would never have
gotten their property back. Though some states tried to
destroy this power of the appellate prize court, Congress had
confirmed it in every instance. Many Pennsylvanians listen-

---

[38] Goebel, *Antecedents*, pp. 251–412; Alexander Hamilton, James Madison, and
John Jay, *The Federalist*, Jacob Cooke, ed. (Middletown, Conn., 1961), #81, and 83,
pp. 549–552, 558–574; Paul L. Ford, ed., *Essays on the Constitution of the United States
Published during Its Discussion by the People, 1787–1788* (Brooklyn, 1892), pp. 41, 119,
130–131, 164–165, 184, 241, 308–309, 361, and Cecilia M. Kenyon, *The Antifederalists* (Indianapolis, 1966), pp. 14, 49–51, 101, 157, 164, 182, 195, 211, 231–
232, 363, 398, 413–415, 425–426, 430, 433–434.

ing to Wilson must have recognized his allusion to their state's role in the case of the sloop *Active*.[39]

Madison, in the Virginia ratifying convention, likewise explicitly cited the example of the Court of Appeals in Cases of Capture. He argued that the proposed Supreme Court would undoubtedly hold sessions in different parts of the country for the convenience of litigants, as the court of prize appeals had done under the Continental Congress.[40]

The infrequency of references to the first federal court during the ratification debates undoubtedly reflects the fact that this court touched the lives of few people. Participants in the ratification debates drew more freely upon examples of British or local judicial systems than upon the experience of the Court of Appeals.

In justifying the creation of federal trial courts, the proponents of the new system, like Madison, argued, as they had in the Constitutional Convention, from the need for a system of national courts at least in the area of admiralty jurisdiction, where the rights of foreign nations could be affected.[41]

Proponents of the Constitution also had the Revolutionary War system of prize courts in mind when they contended that trial by jury was not appropriate in all types of civil cases. As Hamilton wrote:

> I feel a deep and deliberate conviction, that there are many cases in which the trial by jury is an ineligible one. I think so particularly in cases which concern the public peace with foreign nations; that is in most cases where the question turns wholly on the laws of nations. Of this nature among others are all prize causes. Juries cannot be supposed competent to investigations, that require a thorough knowledge of the laws and usages of nations, and they will sometimes be under influence of impressions which will not suffer them to pay sufficient regard to those considerations of public policy which ought to guide their enquiries. There would of course be always danger

---

[39] James Wilson and Thomas M'Kean, *Commentaries on the Constitution of the United States of America* (London, 1792), pp. 99–100, 121–122, 124. The opponents of the Constitution had referred explicitly to the case of the *Active*, see Wilson's notes of debates in John B. McMaster and Frederick D. Stone, eds., *Pennsylvania and the Federal Constitution, 1787–1788* (Philadelphia, 1888), p. 779.

[40] Elliot, *Debates* **3**: pp. 535–536. Madison was no more correct in his predictions as to the future than he was accurate in his recollection of the past.

[41] *Ibid.*, pp. 531–532; see also Randolph at the Virginia convention and Virginia's fourteenth proposed amendment, *ibid.*, pp. 571, 660, and a proposed amendment of the New York convention, *ibid.* **2**: p. 408.

that the rights of other nations might be infringed by their decisions [i. e. verdicts], so as to afford occasions of reprisal and war. Though the proper province of juries be to determine matters of fact, yet in most cases legal consequences are complicated with fact in such a manner as to render a separation impracticable.[42]

Thus, although the first federal court was not frequently mentioned during the ratification debates, there were a significant few, who had had the opportunity to view its operation closely, who later drew upon the lessons they learned when they sought to convince their countrymen of the need for a new and more effective federal judicial system. As we shall see, even the antifederalists came to accept the federalists' contention that federal trial courts were appropriate at least for admiralty jurisdiction.

The antifederalists aimed their best ammunition at every section of the proposed Constitution, not just at the judiciary. Some of their shots drew blood, but proved to be nonfatal; others were near misses or completely wide of the mark. In spite of the scattershot objections of the antifederalists, the Constitution was ratified by eleven states and elections were held to select representatives to the new Congress.

When the new-born government struggled shakily to its feet in 1789, Congress realized it must promptly nullify the antifederalists' most telling objection to the Constitution by preparing a bill of rights for eventual state ratification. Similar urgency pressed Congress to complete the constitutionally required form of government by creating the third branch, the judiciary. James Madison shepherded a bill of rights through the House of Representatives, which, among other provisions, guaranteed the right of trial by jury in all suits at common law (therefore not for admiralty cases), and also assured the citizens that the Supreme Court could review facts tried by a jury only according to the rules of the common law. This Seventh Amendment laid to rest the fears of many that the institution of trial by jury would be taken away by the new Constitution. As Madison was drafting a bill of rights, Oliver Ellsworth, William Paterson, and Caleb Strong provided the Senate leadership in preparing a judiciary bill.

---

[42] *Federalist*, Cooke, ed., #83, p. 568; see also Charles Pinckney, Elliot, *Debates* 4: p. 260.

Ellsworth, as we have seen, carried with him to the Senate vivid memories of the congressional appellate prize court. He could not have forgotten how Congress was thwarted by Pennsylvania in the case of the sloop *Active*. Paterson also had a slight acquaintance with the first federal court. One other member of the Senate committee which prepared the judiciary bill, Richard Bassett, also had some experience with the appellate prize court of Congress.[43] Ellsworth was the dominant figure in preparing and assuring passage of the judiciary bill, and to some extent the companion bill to regulate process in the federal courts as well.[44]

There seems to have been surprising unanimity in Congress as to the need for federal trial courts at least for admiralty jurisdiction. Even the antifederalist members, who consistently had argued that state courts could serve as the court of first instance in most cases, agreed that Congress should create inferior federal courts for admiralty cases.[45] Apparently the antifederalists had been won over to the position that federal trial courts were appropriate for all admiralty matters to prevent conflicting state court determinations which could involve the nation as a whole in controversies or even hostilities with foreign nations. This argument had been used by the Continental Congress to support the exclusive jurisdiction of its court of prize appeals, and at the Federal Convention and during the ratification debates, to show the need for inferior federal courts. When the federal district courts were being created, Congress could agree on these courts as the only proper courts to hear and determine in the first instance all cases of admiralty and maritime jurisdiction. This admiralty jurisdiction was the most significant grant of authority to these new federal district courts.[46] Con-

---

[43] See note 23 above.

[44] Goebel, *Antecedents*, pp. 458–460.

[45] *Ibid.*, pp. 439, 442, 461, 470, 473, 474, 494, 510.

[46] "An Act to Establish Judicial Courts of the United States," 1 Stat. 73, §9 (1789): "That the district courts shall have, exclusively of the courts of the several States, cognizance of all crimes and offences that shall be cognizable under the authority of the United States, committed within their respective districts, or upon the high seas; where no other punishment than whipping, not exceeding thirty stripes, a fine not exceeding one hundred dollars, or a term of imprisonment not exceeding six months, is to be inflicted; and shall also have exclusive original cognizance of all civil causes of admiralty and maritime jurisdiction, including all seizures under laws of impost, navigation or trade of the United States, where the seizures are made, on waters which are navigable from the sea by vessels of ten or more tons burthen,

gress was not constitutionally obliged to establish federal trial courts at all. It is hard to escape the conclusion that without the experience of the first federal court impressed upon the memories of a small but influential number of leaders, federal district courts might not have been created in 1789.

We have seen indications of continuity in forms and procedures from the colonial vice-admiralty courts to the state admiralty courts. Each state appears to have preserved the procedures which were familiar to its practitioners at the bar. Similarly we can detect the same tradition-preserving attitude at work in the creation of the federal judiciary. There was a strong sentiment in Congress, as shown in the early process acts, to adopt in the new federal courts the forms and process used in the state in which the district courts sat. This, of course, would be welcome to the attorneys and judges who tended to use the familiar forms for pleadings, writs, and orders.[47]

The Process Act of 1789 did state that equity and admiralty forms and modes of proceedings should be "according to the course of the civil law,"[48] which would hardly have been familiar to most American attorneys. Undoubtedly because this would have caused an unsettling innovation, this provision was apparently ignored in practice and was changed in 1792 to require forms and modes of proceedings in the equity and admiralty jurisdiction of federal courts to be "according to the principles, rules and usages which belong to courts of equity and to courts of admiralty respectively, as contradistinguished from courts of common law,"

---

within their respective districts as well as upon the high seas; saving to suitors, in all cases, the right of a common law remedy, where the common law is competent to give it; and shall also have exclusive original cognizance of all seizures on land, or other waters than as aforesaid, made, and of all suits for penalties and forfeitures incurred, under the laws of the United States. And shall also have cognizance, concurrent with the courts of the several States, or the circuit courts, as the case may be, of all causes where an alien sues for a tort only in violation of the law of nations or a treaty of the United States. And shall also have cognizance, concurrent as last mentioned, of all suits at common law where the United States sue, and the matter in dispute amounts, exclusive of costs, to the sum or value of one hundred dollars. And shall also have jurisdiction exclusively of the courts of the several States, of all suits against consuls or vice-consuls, except for offences above the description aforesaid. And the trial of issues in fact, in the district courts, in all causes except civil causes of admiralty and maritime jurisdiction, shall be by jury." See also, Goebel, *Antecedents*, pp. 473–474.

[47] Goebel, *Antecedents*, pp. 534–535, 537, 540, 543, 545–546, 550–551.

[48] 1 Stat. 93, §2 (1789).

subject to changes in process by the federal courts, or to regulations adopted by the Supreme Court.[49] This made it possible for attorneys and courts to continue to use the familiar forms for admiralty process as they had in their own state admiralty courts during the Revolution. The problem of adopting uniform federal procedures for common law or admiralty was too complex for Congress and too odious to many who still harbored suspicions that the new federal courts would swallow up the state judiciaries. The federal district and circuit courts were given authority to regulate procedures with the possibility of regulations to be adopted by the Supreme Court. This was an obvious attempt to encourage the development of federal court procedures with local eccentricities left intact.

The House in 1793 tried to modify this policy of fostering local procedural differences in federal courts by allowing the Supreme Court to make rules for the federal district and circuit courts. The Senate refused to go along with this attempt at greater national uniformity in procedures. The Act, as passed, continued to allow all the federal courts "to make rules and orders for their respective courts directing the returning of writs and processes, the filing of declarations and other pleadings, the taking of rules, the entering and making up judgments by default, and . . . to regulate the practice of the said courts respectively."[50] Uniformity of procedure, as we have seen, had not been a fact in the colonial vice-admiralty courts or in the state admiralty courts during the Revolution, and would not be a fact even in the new federal judiciary in its common law, equity, or admiralty jurisdiction.

There had been a tendency during the Revolution and before, as we have seen, to use depositions freely in prize cases, regardless of the availability of witnesses for trial, and to include these often voluminous depositions as part of the record sent to the congressional court of prize appeals. Congress in the Judiciary Act of 1789 apparently wanted to preserve this free usage of depositions in admiralty cases. Section 30 of the Act opened with the general policy, "That the mode of proof by oral testimony and examination of

---

[49] 1 Stat. 275, §2 (1792); Goebel, *Antecedents*, p. 599.
[50] 1 Stat. 333, §7 (1793); Goebel, *Antecedents*, pp. 550–551.

witnesses in open court shall be the same in all the courts of the United States, as well in the trial of causes in equity and of admiralty and maritime jurisdiction, as of actions at common law." It further provided, however, that in the trial of an admiralty case in a district court, "if either party shall suggest to and satisfy the court that probably it will not be in his power to produce the witnesses there testifying before the circuit court should an appeal be had," the testimony of such witness would, on motion of the party, be taken down in writing to be used on appeal if the circuit court was satisfied that the witness was unavailable.[51]

Perhaps the lessons learned from close acquaintance with an appellate judiciary unable to assure the execution of its own decrees inclined some in Congress to assure the effectiveness of the decrees and orders of the new federal courts. The federal courts were given authority in the Judiciary Act to issue all customary writs necessary for the exercise of their jurisdiction,[52] to punish by fine or imprisonment all contempts of their authority,[53] and to appoint marshals to execute orders of the courts.[54] We have seen that members of the Continental Congress had realized that the first federal court should have such powers, but could not bring Congress to confer these powers on it. The recollections of the Continental Congress's inability to force or persuade Pennsylvania or New Hampshire to comply with decrees of its appellate prize court in the *Active* and *Lusanna* cases led Congress in the Judiciary Act to give the Supreme Court the unusual power to proceed to a final decision and award execution itself where a case had once before been remanded to a lower court.[55]

The American admiralty courts were returned, by the Judiciary Act, to the mainstream of British admiralty practice by removing jury trials from all admiralty causes.[56] The Revolutionary War prize court experience apparently failed to convince the members of the new Congress that local juries should have a place in determining legal disputes which often involved foreign rights.

---

[51] 1 Stat. 73, §30 (1789); Goebel, *Antecedents*, pp. 486–487, 497–498.
[52] 1 Stat. 73, §14 (1789).
[53] *Ibid.*, §17.
[54] *Ibid.*, §27.
[55] *Ibid.*, §25; Goebel, *Antecedents*, p. 481.
[56] 1 Stat. 73, § 9, 12 (1789).

The lines of influence of the first federal court, already faint, practically vanish with the start of the functioning of the new federal judiciary. New problems, resulting from a European war in which America strove to maintain its neutrality, led to novel legal issues on the admiralty side of the federal courts.[57] New sources of prize law, as we have seen, became available and were immediately used in American admiralty cases. Enough has been said, however, to suggest that, even without explicit references to the Continental Congress's court of prize appeals, the first federal court left its mark on the more solidly based federal judiciary under the Constitution. As a seminar in federal appellate practice, it stimulated the participants to consider the role of a federal judiciary in a loosely knit union of states. When the day came to put the lessons into practice, the experience of the first federal court was not wasted.

[57] Goebel, *Antecedents*, pp. 596–607, 761–778.

Bibliography of Primary Sources

I. NOTE ON THE RECORDS OF THE COURT OF APPEALS IN CASES OF CAPTURE

The Records of the Court of Appeals consist of a series of 114 files, now in the National Archives, with one file generally containing the materials for each case. There are also several miscellaneous files at the end of the series. These records have been microfilmed and are available on National Archives Microcopy Number 162.[1] Citation of these records, however, is unnessarily complex because of the way in which the materials have been assembled, and even more because of the present listing of the materials.

The present records appear to be substantially complete. Some case files contain no records, or only a few papers. This is in part explained by the fact that some appeals which were lodged were never prosecuted, and in part by the loss of records. Although there is no way of proving it, a thorough study of the records suggests that for most cases the present case files contain all the material which was before the judges of appeals.

Unfortunately, the files in several instances do not contain all materials relating to a single case. The records of one case are at times put in different files with headings which conceal the fact that they pertain to the same appeal. For some cases given a number in the National Archives' list, no papers are included in the records. These listings were derived from references to appeals in the *Journals of the Continental Congress*. Furthermore the listing of cases in the pamphlet accompanying Microcopy 162 makes no pretense to a uniform or even to an accurate mode of citing the cases. This pamphlet merely follows, with minor modifications, the list of cases compiled by J. C. Bancroft Davis as it appears in the

---

[1] For a description of the microfilming project, see, John C. Hogan, "The Court of Appeals in Cases of Capture, 1780–1787," *Oregon Law Review* **33** (1954): pp. 95–98. Mr. Hogan was partly responsible for the project of repairing and microfilming the records.

appendix to 131 *U.S. Reports*.[2] This list of the cases sometimes gives the name of one or other party to the appeal, or at times, both or neither. Frequently it includes the name of the ship captured, though occasionally no vessel is mentioned, and there are some instances where it gives the name of the vessel making the capture. The other information given in this list by Davis is sometimes helpful, though not always correct and certainly not uniform.

The mode of footnote citation throughout this book, therefore, attempts a consistent citation of the materials, in the hope of providing a maximum of basic information about each case with a minimum of complexity. In general the cases are captioned as they were in the court's decrees. Since the men who drew up the legal papers in these records had few scruples about correct spelling of the names of the parties or the vessels, it is often impossible to tell which of the several different forms of a name is correct. Unless there is a strong reason in the records for a change, the spelling used in Davis and in the National Archives pamphlet has been followed to make correlation with these earlier lists easier. The first footnote citation in a chapter includes the following information wherever possible, about each case in the records:

(1) The property captured and libeled in the state maritime court. Since prize proceedings are *in rem*, it seems appropriate to use the *res* to identify the case. This will ordinarily mean that the name of the vessel captured will appear first, though there are several appeals from Connecticut in which the *res* was allegedly British goods taken on Long Island. In the cases where the subject of the appeal focused on a captured vessel, the name of the vessel represents all the property in dispute. Usually the libelants requested the condemnation of the vessel with all its tackle, furniture, and apparel, along with all the goods, wares, and merchandise found on board at the time of capture. By the

---

[2] J. C. Bancroft Davis [reporter to the Supreme Court], "Federal Courts Prior to the Adoption of the Constitution," I, "Courts of Appeal in Prize Cases," 131 U.S., xix-xlix (1888). This appendix is a revised and slightly expanded version of a pamphlet by Davis, *The Committees of the Continental Congress Chosen to Hear and Determine Appeals from Courts of Admiralty; and the Court of Appeals in Cases of Capture Established by That Body* (New York, 1888). See also *The Revolutionary War Prize Cases: Records of the Court of Appeals in Cases of Capture*, the National Archives pamphlet accompanying Microcopy 162 (Washington, 1954).

time of the appeal, however, the dispute might be limited to the cargo or part of the cargo, or to part of the value from the sale of the vessel and its cargo, or perhaps one party appealed to gain possession of the ship, while the other party appealed for the cargo. These nuances are omitted from the footnote citations. The name of the prize vessel indicates the focal point of the dispute, though more precisely the appeal might concern only the cargo or some other part of the property captured.

(2) The parties to the appeal. The footnotes give the last name of two of the parties, with the appellant mentioned first. Of course, this is merely a shorthand notation intended to include all the parties involved on each side of the appeal. Though some cases came to the judges of appeals by way of petition, not by appeal, in practically every such case the decree of the judges of appeals refers to the petitioner and respondent as appellant and appellee, so this terminology will be followed. The decrees in the records, besides naming the prize, usually include the names of the parties.

(3) The date of the final disposition of the case by the judges of appeals. Ordinarily this indicates the date of the decree issued by the judges. If a rehearing was requested, the date of the first decree is followed by the date of the disposition of the request for a rehearing. If the case was settled by the parties or dismissed for nonappearance, the date indicates the court's final action in removing the case from the docket. In some cases no date appears in the records, or merely the year or the month of the decision. Whatever information can be discovered has been included in the footnote references.

(4) The number of the case file in the Records of the Court of Appeals in the National Archives, which is also the number in Microcopy 162. Unfortunately this is needlessly complex, for the cases were numbered (apparently by Davis) in a series of files from 1 to 109, and then the last five cases are listed according to the page reference to 2 Dallas in which these five cases were reported. Two of the cases in the numbered series, #90 and 103, were also reported in 2 Dallas, but for some reason were not separated from the rest of the numbered cases and placed with the other five cases reported in 2 Dallas. The footnote citation, therefore, includes either the number of the case or the page reference in 2 Dallas.

This will correspond to the listing of the case in Microcopy 162, as well as the list compiled by Davis for the appendix of 131 *U.S. Reports* (although Davis does not include the last five cases in his list). Besides these two series of records, there are also two files at the end of the records headed "Miscellaneous Case Papers" and "Miscellaneous Court Records." Since these files contain essential information for some of the cases, it often has been necessary to include a citation to these files along with the case number.

Besides the materials pertaining to these 113 appeals found in the Records of the Court of Appeals, much information about them can be found in the Papers of the Continental Congress (National Archives), The *Journals of the Continental Congress*, Worthington C. Ford, ed., (34 v., Washington, 1904–1937), as well as among the records of the state admiralty courts, wherever these have been preserved. Where these supplemental materials were used, they are cited specially in the footnotes. For three cases listed by Davis, however, there are no records at all in the Records of the Court of Appeals. The details concerning these three cases, #12, 26, and 27, are taken from the Papers of the Continental Congress. A reference to this source has been given along with the number which Davis assigned to these cases.

II.   OTHER PRIMARY SOURCES

A. MANUSCRIPT SOURCES

1. PUBLIC RECORDS

a. Court Records

Connecticut. Maritime Court Files. Connecticut State Library.

Continental Congress. Records of the Court of Appeals in Cases of Capture. National Archives.

Great Britain. British Museum Transcripts, Hardwicke Papers. Library of Congress, Manuscript Division.

————. Cases of Appeals in Prize Causes. Library of Congress, Law Division.

————. High Court of Admiralty Papers. Public Record Office, London.

————. Lords Commissioners for Prize Appeals, Cases and Files. Public Record Office, London.

————. Sir George Lee, Admiralty Cases and Admiralty Opinions. Historical Society of Pennsylvania.

————. Sir George Lee, Prize Appeals. New York Public Library, Rare Book Room.
Jamaica. Vice-Admiralty Court Minute Books. Jamaica Archives, Spanish Town.
Maryland. Admiralty Court Papers. Maryland Hall of Records.
————. Admiralty Minute Books. Maryland Hall of Records.
————. Court of Vice-Admiralty Proceedings. Maryland Hall of Records.
Massachusetts. Court Files Suffolk. Supreme Judicial Court of Massachusetts, Office
of the Clerk.
————. Minute Book of Appeals from Maritime Court. Supreme Judicial Court of
Massachusetts, Office of the Clerk.
————. Record Books, Superior Court of Judicature. Supreme Judicial Court of
Massachusetts, Office of the Clerk.
————. Records of the Courts of Admiralty and Vice-Admiralty. Library of Con-
gress, Manuscript Division.
————. Suffolk Minute Books. Supreme Judicial Court of Massachusetts, Office of
the Clerk.
New Hampshire. Admiralty Proceedings relative to the Brig Lusannah. American
Philosophical Society, Philadelphia.
————. Superior Court Minute Books. Rockingham County Court, Office of the
Clerk.
New York. Admiralty Records, Alexander Papers. New York Historical Society.
————. Court of Chancery, Common Pleas, Vice-Admiralty Sessions. New York
Historical Society.
————. Vice-Admiralty Court Minute Book, 1753–1770. New York Public Library,
Manuscript Division.
————. Vice-Admiralty Court Minutes. National Archives.
North Carolina. Records of Vice-Admiralty Court. Library of Congress, Manuscript
Division.
Pennsylvania. Admiralty Court Papers. Historical Society of Pennsylvania.
————. Admiralty Court Records. Historical Society of Pennsylvania.
————. Court of Admiralty Papers, Frederick W. Nicholls Collection. Historical
Society of Pennsylvania.
————. Records of Admiralty Court. Library of Congress, Manuscript Division.
————. Vice-Admiralty Court Records. Library of Congress, Manuscript Division.
Rhode Island. Admiralty Court Minute Book. Rhode Island State House, Archive
Room.
————. Admiralty Papers. Rhode Island State House, Archive Room.
South Carolina. Vice-Admiralty Court Records. Library of Congress, Manuscript
Division.

b. Other Government Records

Papers of the Continental Congress. National Archives.
Records of the States of the United States—A Microfilm Compilation. 1949. Jenkins,
William Sumner, ed. Library of Congress.
Revolutionary War Collection, 1st series. Connecticut State Library.

2. PERSONAL PAPERS

Phineas Bond Papers. Historical Society of Pennsylvania.
Samuel Chase Papers, microfilm. Maryland Historical Society.
Francis Dana Papers. Massachusetts Historical Society.
William Ellery Papers. Rhode Island State House, Archive Room.
Jedidiah Foster. Minutes of Superior Court of Massachusetts, facsimile. United
States Circuit Court of Appeals Library, Boston.
John Foster Papers. Rhode Island Historical Society.

Cyrus Griffin Papers, photostats. New York Historical Society.
Francis Hopkinson Papers. American Philosophical Society, Philadelphia.
Francis Hopkinson Papers. Historical Society of Pennsylvania.
Ezra L'Hommedieu Papers. New York Historical Society.
John Lowell Papers. Historical Society of Pennsylvania.
John Lowell Papers. Massachusetts Historical Society.
Thomas McKean Papers. Historical Society of Pennsylvania.
Abner Nash Papers. Historical Society of Pennsylvania.
Robert Treat Paine Papers. Massachusetts Historical Society.
Timothy Pickering Papers, microfilm. Massachusetts Historical Society.
George Read Papers. Delaware Historical Society.
George Read Papers. Historical Society of Pennsylvania.
Thomas Rodney Papers. Delaware Historical Society.
Thomas Rodney Papers. Historical Society of Pennsylvania.
Thomas Rodney Papers. Library of Congress, Manuscript Division.
James Sullivan Papers. Massachusetts Historical Society.
Jonathan Trumbull Papers. Connecticut State Library.
Nicholas Van Dyke Papers. Historical Society of Pennsylvania.
Nicholas Van Dyke Papers. Library of Congress, Manuscript Division.
James Wilson Papers. Historical Society of Pennsylvania.

B. PUBLISHED SOURCES

1. PUBLIC RECORDS

a. Court Records

BEE, THOMAS, ed.. 1810. *Reports of Cases Adjudged in the District Court of South Carolina* (Philadelphia).

BURROW, JAMES, ed.. 1777–1780. *Reports of Cases Adjudged in the Court of King's Bench* (3d ed., 5 v., London).

CARTHEW, THOMAS, ed.. 1741. *Reports of Cases Adjudged in the Court of King's Bench* (London).

The Case of the Sloop Active, 1779 (Philadelphia).

COKE, EDWARD. 1797. *The Fourth Part of the Institutes of the Laws of England* (London).

DALLAS, A. J., ed.. 1790–1807. *Reports of Cases Ruled and Adjudged in the Several Courts of the United States and of Pennsylvania* (4 v., Philadelphia).

HOUGH, CHARLES M., ed.. 1925. *Reports of Cases in the Vice-Admiralty of the Province of New York and in the Court of Admiralty of the State of New York, 1715–1788* (New Haven).

MARRIOTT, JAMES, and GEORGE HAY, eds. 1801. *Decisions in the High Court of Admiralty . . . 1776 to . . . 1779* (London).

MARSDEN, REGINALD G., ed.. 1885. *Reports of Cases Determined by the High Court of Admiralty and Upon Appeal Therefrom* (London).

———. 1894–1897. *Select Pleas in the Court of Admiralty* (2 v., London).

PETERS, RICHARD, ed.. 1809. *The Whole Proceedings in the Case of Olmsted and Others versus Rittenhouse's Executrices* (Philadelphia).

ROBINSON, CHRISTOPHER, ed.. 1798–1808. *Reports of Cases Argued and Determined in the High Court of Admiralty* (6 v., London).

ROSCOE, E. S., ed.. 1905. *Reports of Prize Cases Determined in the High Court of Admiralty, before the Lords Commissioners of Appeals in Prize Causes, and before the Judicial Committee of the Privy Council, from 1745–1859* (2 v., London).

SCOTT, JAMES B., ed.. 1923. *Prize Cases Decided in the United States Supreme Court,* *1789–1918* (3 v., Oxford).

TOWLE, DOROTHY S., ed.. 1936. *Records of the Vice-Admiralty Court of Rhode Island,* *1716–1752* (Washington).

b. Other Government Records

The Acts and Resolves, Public and Private, of the Province of Massachusetts Bay, 1869– 1922 (21 v., Boston).

ALLEN, GARDNER W., ed.. 1927. *Massachusetts Privateers of the Revolution* (Cambridge, Mass.).

BARTLETT, JOHN R., ed.. 1856–1865. *Records of the Colony of Rhode Island and Provi- dence Plantations in New England* (10 v., Providence).

BATCHELLOR, ALBERT S., *et al.*, eds.. 1904–1922. *Laws of New Hampshire* (10 v., Manchester, N.H.).

BOUTON, NATHANIEL, *et al.*, eds.. 1867–1943. *Documents and Records Relating to the State of New Hampshire* (40 v., Concord, N.H.).

BROWNE, WILLIAM H., *et al.*, eds.. 1883–1964. *Archives of Maryland* (70 v., Baltimore).

CHINARD, G., ed.. 1928. *The Treaties of 1778 and Allied Documents* (Baltimore).

CLARK, WALTER, ed.. 1886–1907. *The State Records of North Carolina* (26 v., Goldsboro, N.C.).

CLARK, WILLIAM B., *et al.*, 1964–   . *Naval Documents of the American Revolution* (7 v., Washington).

A Collection of All Such Statutes, and Parts of Statutes, As Any Way Relate to the Admiralty, Navy and Ships of War . . . down to the 14th Year of King George the Second, 1755 (London).

A Collection of the Statutes Relating to the Admiralty, Navy, Ships of War, and Incidental Matters, to the Eighth Year of King George the Third, 1768 (London).

COOPER, THOMAS, *et al.*, eds. 1836–1841. *The Statutes at Large of South Carolina* (10 v., Columbia, S.C.).

Digest of the Laws of the State of Georgia, 1800 (Philadelphia).

ELLIOT, JONATHAN, ed.. 1827–1830. *The Debates in the Several State Conventions on the Adoption of the Federal Constitution* (5 v., Philadelphia).

Extracts from the Journals of Congress, Relative to the Capture and Condemnation of Prizes, and the Fitting out Privateers, 1776 (Philadelphia).

FARRAND, MAX, ed.. 1911–1937. *The Records of the Federal Convention* (4 v., New Haven).

FORD, WORTHINGTON C., ed.. 1904–1937. *Journals of the Continental Congress* (34 v., Washington).

HAZARD, SAMUEL, ed.. 1852–1855. *Pennsylvania Archives* (1st ser., 12 v., Philadel- phia).

———. 1838–1853. *Pennsylvania, Colonial Records* (16 v., Harrisburg).

HENING, WILLIAM W., ed.. 1809–1823. *The Statutes at Large, Being a Collection of All the Laws of Virginia* (13 v., Richmond).

HOADLY, CHARLES J., *et al.*, eds.. 1894–1953. *The Public Records of the State of Connec- ticut* (9 v., Hartford).

HORNE, THOMAS H., ed.. 1803. *A Compendium of the Statute Laws and Regulations of the Court of Admiralty, Relative to Ships of War, Privateers, Prizes, Re-captures, and Prize Money* (London).

JAMESON, JOHN F., ed.. 1923. *Privateering and Piracy in the Colonial Period, Illustrative Documents* (New York).

Journals of Congress, Containing the Proceedings from Sept. 5, 1774 to Jan. 1, 1776, 1777 (Philadelphia).

Journals of the House of Representatives of the Commonwealth of Pennsylvania, 1776–1781, 1782 (Philadelphia).

Laws of Maryland, Made since M, DCC, LXIII, 1787 (Annapolis).

Laws of the State of Delaware, from . . . [1700] to . . . [1797], 1797 (2 v., New-Castle).

MCILWAINE, H. R., *et al.,* eds.. 1931–1952. *Journals of the Council of the State of Virginia* (3 v., Richmond).

MCMASTER, JOHN B., and FREDERICK D. STONE, eds.. 1888. *Pennsylvania and the Federal Constitution, 1787–1788* (Lancaster).

MARSDEN, REGINALD G., ed.. 1915. *Documents Relating to Law and Custom of the Sea* (2 v., n.p.).

MITCHELL, JAMES T., and HENRY FLANDERS, eds.. 1896–1915. *The Statutes at Large of Pennsylvania from 1682–1801* (18 v., Harrisburg).

PICKERING, DANBY, ed.. 1762–1769. *The Statutes at Large, from Magna Charta to the End of the Eleventh Parliament of Great Britain* (24 v., Cambridge).

ROBINSON, CHRISTOPHER, ed.. 1801. *Collectanea Maritima* (London).

SAVAGE, CARLTON, ed.. 1934–1936. *Policy of the United States Toward Maritime Commerce in War* (2 v., Washington).

Session Laws of Rhode Island, 1747–1800, n.d. [Reprints of originals] (18 v., Providence).

THORPE, FRANCIS N., ed.. 1909. *The Federal and State Constitutions, Colonial Charters, and Other Organic Laws of the States, Territories, and Colonies, Now or heretofore Forming the United States of America* (7 v., Washington).

WHARTON, FRANCIS, ed.. 1889. *The Revolutionary Diplomatic Correspondence of the United States* (6 v., Washington).

WILSON, PETER, ed.. 1784. *Acts of the Council and General Assembly of the State of New Jersey* (Trenton).

2. LEGAL AND POLITICAL TREATISES

BEAWES, WYNDHAM. 1771. *Lex Mercatoria Rediviva, or the Merchant's Directory* (3d ed., London).

BLACKSTONE, WILLIAM. 1765–1769. *Commentaries on the Laws of England* (1st ed., 4 v., Oxford).

BROWNE, ARTHUR. 1802. *A Compendious View of the Civil Law* (2 v., 2nd ed., London).

BURLAMAQUI, J. J.. 1763. *The Principles of Natural and Politic Law.* Nugent, tr. (2nd ed., 2 v., London).

———. 1748. *The Principles of Natural Law.* Nugent, tr. (London).

BYNKERSHOEK, CORNELIUS VAN. 1923. *De dominio maris dissertatio.* Ralph van Deman Magoffin, tr. (New York).

———. 1930. *Quaestionum juris publici libri duo.* Tenney Frank, tr. (2 v., Oxford).

CLERKE, FRANCISCUS. 1743. *Praxis Supremae Curiae Admiralitatis* (rev. ed., London).

C[ONSET]; H.. 1708. *The Practice of the Spiritual or Ecclesiastical Courts* (3d ed., London).

CUNNINGHAM, T.. 1764–1765. *A New and Complete Law Dictionary* (2 v., London).

[GILBERT, GEOFFRY]. 1760. *The Law of Evidence* (London).

GROTIUS, HUGO. 1925. *De Jure Belli ac Pacis, Libri Tres.* Francis W. Kelsey, tr. (2 v., Oxford).

———. 1738. *The Rights of War and Peace* (London).

HALL, JOHN. 1809. *The Practice and Jurisdiction of the Court of Admiralty in Three Parts* (Baltimore).

HAMILTON, ALEXANDER, JAMES MADISON and JOHN JAY. 1961. *The Federalist.* Jacob E. Cooke, ed. (Middletown, Conn.).

The Laws Ordinances, and Institutions of the Admiralty of Great Britain, Civil and Military, 1746 (2 v., London).

LEE, RICHARD. 1759. *A Treatise of Captures in War* (London).

MAGENS, NICOLAS. 1755. *An Essay on Insurances* (2 v., London).

MARRIOTT, JAMES. 1778. *The Case of the Dutch Ships Considered* (4th ed., London).

MOLLOY, CHARLES. 1722. *De jure maritimo et navali, or a Treatise of Affairs Maritime and of Commerce* (7th ed., London).

Observations on the Course of Proceeding in Admiralty Courts in Prize Causes, 1747 (London).

The Practice of the Court of Admiralty in England and Ireland, 1757 (Dublin).

PUFENDORF, SAMUEL. 1934. *De jure naturae et gentium, libri octo.* C. H. Oldfather and W. A. Oldfather, trs. (2 v., Oxford).

————. 1729. *Of the Law of Nature and Nations, Eight Books.* Basil Kennett, tr. (4th ed., London).

[*Report of the Law Officers of the Crown as to the Action of Frederick II in Withholding Payment of Interest on the Silesian Loan in Reprisal for Losses Alleged to Have Been Suffered by His Subjects at the Hands of English Privateers.*] 1753. (London).

ROBINSON, C.. 1801. *Collectanea maritima, Being a Collection of Public Instruments Tending to Illustrate the History and Practice of Prize Law* (London).

RUTHERFORTH, T.. 1754. *Institutes of Natural Law* (2 v., Cambridge).

STOKES, ANTHONY. 1783. *A View of the Constitution of the British Colonies, in North America and the West Indies, At the Time the Civil War Broke Out on the Continent of America* (London).

VATTEL, E. DE.. 1916. *Le Droit des Gens, ou principes de la loi naturelle, appliqués à la conduite et aux affaires des nations et des souverains.* Charles G. Fenwick, tr. (3 v., Washington).

————. 1759–1760. *The Law of Nations or Principles of the Law of Nature Applied to the Conduct and Affairs of Nations and Sovereigns* (2 v. in 1, London).

WHEATON, HENRY. 1815. *A Digest of the Law of Maritime Captures and Prizes* (New York).

WOLFF, CHRISTIAN. 1934. *Jus gentium, methodo scientifica pertractatum.* Joseph H. Drake, tr. (2 v., London).

ZOUCHE, RICHARD. 1911. *Iuris et iudicii fecialis, sive, iuris inter gentes, et quaestionum de eodem explicatio.* J. L. Brierly, tr. (2 v., Washington).

3. COLLECTED PERSONAL PAPERS AND WRITINGS

ADAMS, RANDOLPH G., ed.. 1930. *Selected Political Essays of James Wilson* (New York).

ANDREWS, JAMES D., ed.. 1896. *The Works of James Wilson* (2 v., Chicago).

BAILYN, BERNARD, ed.. 1965. *Pamphlets of the American Revolution, 1750–1776* (Cambridge, Mass.).

BOYD, JULIAN P., ed.. 1950–1965. *The Papers of Thomas Jefferson* (17 v., Princeton).

BURNETT, EDMUND C., ed.. 1921–1936. *Letters of Members of the Continental Congress* (8 v., Washington).

FITZPATRICK, JOHN C., ed.. 1931–1944. *The Writings of George Washington from the Original Manuscript Sources, 1745–1799* (39 v., Washington).

FORD, PAUL L., ed.. 1888. *Pamphlets on the Constitution of the United States Published during Its Discussion by the People, 1787–1788* (Brooklyn).

GOEBEL, JULIUS JR., ed.. 1964–1969. *The Law Practice of Alexander Hamilton, Documents and Commentary* (2 v., New York).

HOPKINSON, FRANCIS. 1792. *Miscellaneous and Occasional Writings* (3 v., Philadelphia).

HUTCHINSON, WILLIAM T., and WILLIAM M. E. RACHAL, eds.. 1962–1967. *The Papers of James Madison* (5 v., Chicago).

KENYON, CECELIA M., ed.. 1966. *The Antifederalists* (Indianapolis).

READ, WILLIAM T. 1870. *Life and Correspondence of George Read* (Philadelphia).

WROTH, L. KINVIN, and HILLER B. ZOBEL, eds.. 1965. *Legal Papers of John Adams* (3 v., Cambridge, Mass.).

WYNNE, WILLIAM, ed.. 1724. *The Life of Sir Leoline Jenkins* (2 v., London).

4. NEWSPAPERS

Boston Evening Post and General Advertiser. 1779.
[Boston] Independent Chronicle and Universal Advertiser. 1779.
[Boston] Independent Ledger and American Advertiser. 1783.
Connecticut Courant. 1775–1783.
Maryland Gazette. 1775–1783.
Pennsylvania Evening Post. 1776, 1778.
Pennsylvania Gazette. 1775–1783.
Pennsylvania Packet. 1777–1780.
[Philadelphia] Independent Gazetteer or Chronicle of Freedom. 1787–1788.

Index